THE HIGHWAY ANGLER 5

Fishing Alaska's Road System

Best-Seller!

BY GUNNAR PEDERSEN

CW00822272

FISHING ALASKA PUBLICATIONS

THE HIGHWAY ANGLER 5: Fishing Alaska's Road System

Copyright © 2007 by Fishing Alaska Publications. All rights reserved.

ISBN 1-57833-366-0

Printed in the USA.

Second Printing April, 2008

No part of this work may be reproduced or transmitted in any form or by any means, electronic or mechanical, including photocopying and recording, or by any information storage or retrieval system, except as may be expressly permitted by the 1976 Copyright Act or in writing from the publisher. Requests for permission should be addressed in writing to the publisher.

Fishing Alaska Publications
P.O. Box 90557
Anchorage, AK 99509

Photo Descriptions/Credits

Front Cover: Author poses with Glacier Creek silver salmon.

Back Cover
A. Roy Bailey with Resurrection Bay silver salmon, caught at Lowell Point.
B. Slightly blushed silver salmon about to be released.
C. Autumn view of Long Lake along the Glenn Highway near Chickaloon.
D. Late summer fly-fishing for salmon and char on a roadside stream.

Section One, Introduction
Page 1: Lone angler working a hole for salmon on a Turnagain Arm stream.

Section Two, Alaska's Sport Fish
Page 7: Angler Roy Bailey brings in a large Upper Kenai River rainbow trout.
Page 9: Shayla Pedersen holds up a chrome Turnagain Arm silver salmon.
Page 33: Anglers line the banks of Bird Creek along the Seward Highway.

Section Three, Roadside Locations
page 41: Angling scene from the mouth of Russian River at Cooper Landing.

Fish Mounts between page 16 & 17 courtesy of Ken and Carol Guffey of Ken's Taxidermy.

SPECIAL THANKS

To my family and friends, without whom this book would not have been possible; with special mention my wife Shayla, parents Ingrid and Einar Pedersen, brothers Einar and Sverre – all contributing unrelenting support for this project and in life. And, of course, remembering the great times on Alaska's many watersheds.

Table of Contents

page

Section One .... *Introduction*

Words From The Author

Welcome to the fifth edition of The Highway Angler. It is based on nearly thirty years worth of information gathered from personal observations and first-hand experiences living in Alaska and fishing along the state's road system all year long. Additionally, included in the book is general and more specific information as put forth by the Alaska Department of Fish & Game as well as numerous other sources, such as knowledgeable local anglers and sport fishing guides. Even though many facets are discussed in various chapters throughout, the strong point of The Highway Angler remains the multitude of fishing locations – all of them within reasonable driving and hiking distance from the road – and the necessary details to fish them properly.

There are several important changes in this new edition compared to the previous one, all of which serve to provide the reader with better and more accurate information pertaining to places to fish and the species available. These changes include updates regarding stocked lakes and access points, new hatchery enhanced salmon runs, and brief summary information of angling opportunities in all of the listed fishing locations. A few old locations have been deleted due to access issues (resulting from private property) or no longer supporting viable fish populations. But there are also several new locations that have been added, giving anglers increased opportunities.

A new companion volume is The Alaska Roadside Angler's Guide, a full-color publication that is designed to work hand-in-hand with The Highway Angler. Whereas the latter book deals with most all of the fishing locations on the continuous road system in Alaska (over 750 of them), the new publication focuses only on a selected few popular fisheries and covers them in utmost detail. For more information about this title, as well as other fishing books, refer to the appendix on page 321 at the end of the book.

Finally, please help keep Alaska clean and pure. Pack in what you pack out and practice conservation. Kill and keep only what is needed, releasing other fish with care. Stay safe and enjoy the Alaska so many of us have come to cherish.

Good luck and good fishing!

Gunnar Pedersen

Fishing The Road System

Alaska has a quite vast road network, which one way or another connects to the Lower 48 states through Canada. Most routes tie together larger cities with towns or communities by paved highways and grated gravel roads that offer anglers ample opportunities to sample some truly great fishing. Many roadside waters produce catches comparable to the remotest rivers and streams. Even along the busiest highways, it is possible to find excellent action for all five species of salmon, trout, char, grayling, and other game species. However, Alaskan waters, remote or roadside, are not always packed with fish just waiting to assault anglers' lures. As a matter of fact, it's just as easy to get skunked in Alaska as anywhere else in the world.

The key is timing. Most species in the state, particularly in flowing water, have very specific periods of the year when they congregate in numbers. Timing is especially crucial in salmon fishing, as just a week or two can mean the difference between a successful fishing trip and a disappointing one. And to complicate matters even further, various species and watersheds have their own unique timing. This book focuses heavily on the issue of timing for various species and drainages.

The most significant difference between roadside and remote fishing locations is certainly not a lack of scenery, but rather the fact that one must almost always expect to share a stretch of water with other anglers. After all, sport fishing is the number one recreational activity in the state and nowhere is this as evident as it is along our road-accessible waters.

However, keep in mind that, though large crowds of anglers are often found at the more popular salmon fisheries, there are many locations that receive relatively little angling pressure. Particularly under crowded conditions does tolerance, courtesy, and respect become a must. One way to counter the presence of other anglers is to hike up- or downstream a few hundred yards. Often, just a little distance from the highway makes a tremendous difference in the rewards you will reap – usually less company and more fish. But the main point is, of course, to treat everyone around you as you would like to be treated yourself.

How To Use This Book

This part of the introduction section intends to shed some light on how various chapters of The Highway Angler are presented. Read it carefully to become more familiar with the structure used and to better apply the material for your angling needs. The Highway Angler was designed specifically for ease of use through charts, tables, summaries, and cross-references, thus packing as much information into each page as possible.

Alaska Sport Fish Chapter

Presented here are the more common sport fish species available along Alaska's road system, including general descriptions on biological information (identification and life history/habits) and sport fishing facts (terminal gear, best lures, areas, timing, etc). Some fish species may be introduced in less detail than others because they are either uncommon catches in the roadside fisheries or are not recognized as "sporting" species. All information is based on knowledge and conditions associated with the road system, except for a few minor details regarding species biology which may or may not apply.

Location Chapters

These chapters, representing the core of this book, systematically deal with the multitude of waters found along Alaska's road and highways. First, a brief summary is given in terms of what to expect in terms of angling opportunities, followed by a "Quick Reference" section of all locations and accompanying area maps. Then, each location is broken down in more detail in regards to access and pertinent fishing information. At the end of each chapter a listing of less productive waters are described, in addition to a location/species appendix.

Quick Reference. Found in the beginning of the location chapters, this section was designed to provide a quick overview of the fishing spots along Alaska's roads and highways, including map locations and mileposts, facility information, the page number on which to find detailed access and fishing information for any one watershed, and several other descriptive features.

The key to symbols used are listed on page 6.

Units. Major drainages, sub-regions, primary and important secondary roads are divided into individual sections, or units, in order to separate area-sensitive fishing opportunities and regulations. Each unit has a general species timing chart and a short summary of unit-wide angling restrictions to alleviate redundancy throughout the listing of locations.

Locations. All road-accessible locations are grouped into units as described above and contain the following information: a) Access based on common/public routes of access from official Mileposts (MP) (If access is across private property, a contact number is given to seek trespass permission); b) Fishing information listing types of fish available, quality of fishing to expect in an average year (poor, fair, good, excellent), peak seasonal timing, size range (maximum size shown in parenthesis), and some of the top lures of choice for each individual species. Major or important locations are slightly more detailed than other locations and also display a species timing chart.

Timing Charts. These charts graphically outline what time of year indicated species are present and/or available on a week-to-week, year-round basis and correlate to when fish are in their prime for both angling sport and consumption, unless otherwise noted. The key to color shades is given below.

(Gray Area) Indicates species are present in small numbers and/or are inactive.

(Dark Area) Indicates species are present in peak numbers and/or are very active. If the sport fishing regulations allow it, this would be the prime time to fish

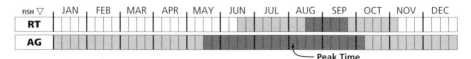

Note: The quality of fishing may vary according to weather and water conditions, angler experience, number of fish present, and other factors determining success.

Other Locations. This segment at the end of each location chapter lists less productive waters followed by a short note on access and the species that may be present. Species shown within parenthesis are either closed to fishing and/or are very rarely encountered. Angling in these locations is typically limited due to several factors (usually biological and/or environmental).

Location/Species Appendix. These charts at the end of every location chapter shows all species present in varying degrees of abundance or availability for each river, stream, lake or bay. In addition, the charts mark which waters are stocked with hatchery fish and which have wild populations.

The key to abbreviations and symbols used are listed on page 6.

Important: As always, check the official sport fishing regulations or contact the nearest Alaska Department of Fish & Game office for exact information on seasons, open areas, legal gear and methods, and bag/possession limits before trying any of the locations listed.

Sport Fishing Regulations

The Alaska Department of Fish & Game (ADF&G), through laws enacted by the Board of Fisheries, publishes several booklets annually, each according to designated state-wide regions, describing open or closed seasons and areas, gear restrictions, bag and possession limits, and many other points to follow in order to protect fish populations from potential over-exploitation.

Due to the ever-changing and near unpredictable nature of fishing rules and regulations, they have been practically omitted from this book to prevent the content of becoming out of date too soon. Besides, certain locations have very specific and lengthy restrictions that would almost require a book in itself to list and explain. The information contained within all chapters adhere as much as possible to current laws. However, any set rule and regulation is, of course, subject to change as through "emergency orders" posted by ADF&G and the Board of Fisheries. Emergency orders generally function to either liberalize or restrict a fishery according to a situation of biological concern and are usually broadcast in the news media days in advance of taking effect.

Also, it's entirely the responsibility of the individual angler to have knowledge and be in complete compliance of existing rules and regulations for the water he or she intends to fish. In other words, always consult a current and official copy of the sport fishing regulations before making that first cast. If in doubt or have any questions, contact the nearest ADF&G office.

Wildlife

Now for some words about Alaska's wildlife. Avoid close encounters, especially with moose and bear, which could promote a life-threatening situation. These large animals may be encountered most anywhere in the state, in remote as well as urban areas.

Bears are of utmost concern. They are especially numerous along clearwater streams in late summer and fall, scouting for salmon in the shallows, and are often sighted by anglers. The bears will forage on fish to fatten up for the long, cold winter ahead. Bears are, for the most part, very shy creatures and will avoid confrontation with humans as much as possible. But just because one isn't able to spot any bears doesn't mean that none are present. With a very keen sense of smell and hearing, a bear can pick up the scent or sound of a person approaching from a long distance away. At such time, the bears usually leave the area and hurry off into thick brush. But don't count on it.

The best precautions to employ when hiking along trails away from the road is to make a lot of noise. Clap hands, sing, shout, talk loudly, wear a bell, blow a horn or whistle, shake a can of rocks, or bring a boom box. Also, keep all foods away from the tent and sleeping area to prevent a potentially dangerous situation.

Key To Abbreviations And Symbols

Facility/Services Abbreviations:ns:

 Road Condition   Parking Area   Camp Sites   Hiking Trails   Boat Launch   Handicap Access   Fishing Pressure

Symbols Used for Facility/Services Charts:

- ■ - Good to Highly developed/conditions, intense pressure
- ● - Fair to Moderately developed/conditions, moderate pressure
- ◆ - Poor to marginally developed/conditions, limited pressure
- × - Prohibited

Symbols Used For Location/Species Appendix Charts:

- ● - Wild/Native fish, fishable numbers.
- ◆ - Present in small numbers and/or only occasionally caught.
- ▲ - Stocked/Hatchery fish, fishable numbers.
- ■ - Mix of Wild and Hatchery fish, fishable numbers.
- × - Indicated species present but currently protected by law (PROHIBITED).

Species Abbreviations:

KS - King Salmon **RS** - Red Salmon **PS** - Pink Salmon **CS** - Chum Salmon

SS - Silver Salmon **KO** - Kokanee **LS** - Landlocked Salmon **ST** - Steelhead Trout

RT - Rainbow Trout **LT** - Lake Trout **DV** - Dolly Varden **AC** - Arctic Char

SF - Sheefish **AG** - Arctic Grayling **WF** - Whitefish **NP** - Northern Pike

BB - Burbot **PH** - Pacific Halibut **LC** - Ling Cod **RF** - Rockfish

Section Two.........................*Alaska's Sport Fish*

Trophy & Record Fish Chart

Trophy And Alaska State Record Sport Fish Catches

The list on the following page shows the current record game fish taken on sport gear for each species, including location and region caught, and the minimum trophy weight required to qualify as a state trophy.

Species	Lbs.-Oz.	Location/Region	Trophy Weight
Arctic Char/Dolly Varden	27-6	Wulik River (NW)	10 Lbs.
Arctic Grayling	4-13	Ugashik Narrows (SW)	3 Lbs.
Burbot	24-12	Lake Louise (SC)	8 Lbs.
Chum Salmon	32-0	Caamano Point (SE)	15 Lbs.
Cutthroat Trout	8-6	Wilson Lake (SE)	3 Lbs.
King Salmon	97-4	Kenai River (SC)	75/50 Lbs.*
Lake Trout	47-0	Clarence Lake (SC)	20 Lbs.
Ling Cod	81-6	Monty Island (SC)	45 Lbs.
Northern Pike	38-0	Innoko River (IN)	15 Lbs.
Pacific Halibut	459-0	Unalaska Bay (SW)	250 Lbs.
Pink Salmon	12-9	Moose River (SC)	8 Lbs.
Rainbow/Steelhead Trout	42-3	Bell Island (SE)	15 Lbs.
Red Salmon	16-0	Kenai River (SC)	12 Lbs.
Rockfish	38-11	Prince William Sound (SC)	18 Lbs.
Sheefish	53-0	Pah River (NW)	30 Lbs.
Silver Salmon	26-0	Icy Strait (SE)	20 Lbs.
Whitefish	9-0	Tozitna River (IN)	4 Lbs.

Abbreviations:
SC = Southcentral   IN = Interior   NW = Northwest
SW = Southwest   SE = Southeast

Anyone who has caught a fish equal to or greater than the specified trophy weight may earn a trophy certificate from the ADF&G. Contact one of the department's offices for information on how to participate.

Trophy weight for king salmon in the Kenai River is 75 pounds, and the rest of the state 50 pounds.

The Fish

There are nine general groups or families of sport fish in Alaska's roadside waters. These consists of salmon, trout, char, grayling, whitefish, pike, cod, halibut, and rockfish. All occur in varying degrees of abundance according to season and location.

Some families have from only one or two member species present in Alaska, like grayling and halibut, or up to several dozen, such as rockfish. Additionally, there are also sub-species that display near identical appearance as main derived species but may have certain habits setting them apart. Many species, like those in fresh water (salmon in particular), exhibit obvious physical changes in appearance between the life stages of feeding and spawning, with color and shape typically alternating drastically.

Seasonal movement is clearly defined in all types of fish, both in salt- and freshwater, and usually relates to defined migrations between feeding and spawning areas. But other reasons, such as temperature changes and age, also play a large role in some instances. In fresh water, these migrations are often referred to as "runs" and determined by various biological factors. Each run is precisely timed to provide the adult fish the safest passage possible, and to give the eggs and juvenile fish the greatest chances of survival. It is not unusual for extensive watersheds with a multitude of tributaries, each with its own unique characteristics, to experience two or more distinct runs of one kind of fish, and some may even have multiple runs of several fish species.

This chapter deals with all of the fish species present in roadside fisheries with varying degrees of detail (depending on availability and abundance), with particular emphasis on the sporting kind.

Content
Pages

King Salmon

King Salmon, spawning color phase

Red Salmon

Red Salmon, spawning color phase

Pink Salmon

Pink Salmon, spawning color phase

Chum Salmon

Chum Salmon, spawning color phase

Silver Salmon

Silver Salmon, spawning color phase

Rainbow Trout

Rainbow Trout, spawning color phase

Steelhead Trout

Lake Trout

Dolly Varden / Arctic Char

Arctic Char, spawning phase

Dolly Varden, spawning phase

Sheefish

Arctic Grayling

Whitefish (Round)

Northern Pike

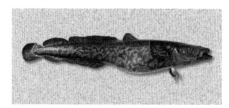

Burbot

Pacific Halibut

Rockfish

The following introduces more facts on each species of sport fish found in Alaska's roadside waters, such as identification, size, habitat and abundance, life cycle, and some basic sport fishing information.

FRESHWATER SPECIES

Salmon

Alaska enjoys an abundance of five species of Pacific salmon – king, red, pink, chum, and silver salmon. All of them are readily available along the road system with pink and red salmon being the most numerous, followed in order by chum and silver salmon, and last but not least, king salmon.

Salmon are for the most part anadromous, but strictly fresh water populations are also common. The anadromous, or sea-run, variety are born in fresh water, migrate to salt water to feed and grow for a year or more, and eventually return to the river, stream, or lake of birth to spawn and die. Generally, the mighty king salmon is the first species to enter fresh water, closely followed by the red, then the pink and chum, and finally the silver.

Non-anadromous, or land-locked, salmon occur either as a result of artificial stocking (pink/king hybrid, king and silver) or natural occurrence (red or Kokanee). All share the distinction of being significantly smaller in size (usually less than 20 inches) than anadromous fish and spend their entire lives in lakes.

KING SALMON

Scientific Name: *Oncorhynchus tshawytscha.*
Other Common Names: Chinook, Spring, Blackmouth, Tyee, Quinnat, and Tule.

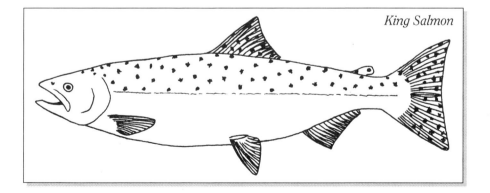

King Salmon

BIOLOGY

Identification: Black irregular cross-markings on back and upper sides. Both lobes of tail fin and top of head are covered with black spots, tongue and gum line on lower jaw is black. *Ocean phase:* Greenish blue-black on back; silvery to white on lower sides and belly. Flesh color is orange-red. *Spawning phase:* Dark red to copper, brown, even almost black. Males develop a kype, large teeth protrude from their jaw, spine takes on a ridgeback condition. Flesh color is white.

Size: 18 to 35 pounds; maximum 50 to 75 pounds, up to 135 pounds. *Land-locked:* 7 to 15 inches; up to 20 inches and 5 pounds.

Habitat/Abundance: Clear to semi-glacial coastal, inland and interior drainages. Large or important populations are found in tributaries of the Susitna, Talkeetna, Chulitna, Copper, Yukon, and Tanana rivers, and in drainages of Knik Arm, Turnagain Arm, and the Kenai Peninsula.

Life Cycle: Anadromous/non-anadromous. *Diet:* Young eat insects and zooplankton, adults primarily fishes and crustaceans. *Presence:* Year-round offshore, peaking May and June. Fish enter fresh water from late April to early October, peaking late May to mid-July. *Spawning:* Rivers and streams from mid-June to late October, most July and August. Females deposit 2,000-14,000 eggs, hatching in late winter or early spring. *Life Span:* 1 to 2 years in fresh water, 1 to 6 years at sea; up to 8 years of age. *Land-locked:* Year-round in lakes; reach 3 years of age; not capable of reproduction.

SPORT FISHING

Terminal Gear: Medium to heavy action rod/reel; 20- to 30-lb. test line/tippet; medium- to large-sized lures.

Saltwater: *Lures:* Spinners, attractors, and bait. *Areas:* Tidal rips and stream mouths. *Timing:* Mid-May to mid-August.

Freshwater: *Lures:* Spoons, spinners, plugs, attractors, flies, and bait. *Areas:* Semi-glacial, murky, and clear rivers and streams; deep holes, runs, and pools with moderate to slow current; tributary confluences and tidal areas. *Timing:* Late May to mid-August (sea-run); late October to mid-April (land-locked).

Hot Spots: *Kenai Peninsula* - Anchor, Kasilof, Kenai, Ninilchik rivers; Deep Creek; Cook Inlet; Dudiak Lagoon; Resurrection Bay. *Knik Arm* - Eklutna Tailrace, Little Susitna River; Ship Creek. *Susitna Valley* - Caswell, Goose, Montana, Little Willow, Sheep, Willow creeks. *Copper Valley* - Gulkana, Klutina rivers. *Tanana Valley* - Chatanika, Chena, Salcha rivers.

RED SALMON

Scientific Name: *Oncorhynchus nerka.*
Other Common Names: Sockeye, Blueback, and Kokanee (land-locked).

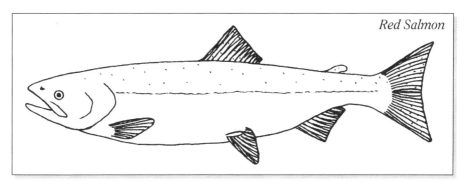

Red Salmon

BIOLOGY

Identification: Very minute black freckles may occasionally be seen on back, usually none at all. *Ocean phase:* Dark steel-blue to greenish blue on back; sides are silvery, fading to silvery white on belly. Flesh color is ruby red. *Spawning phase:* Brilliant red, also dirty brown, pale red, dark purplish to almost black. Distinct olive green head. Males develop a slight humped back and tooth-filled kype. Flesh color is white.

Size: 3 to 8 pounds; maximum 10 to 14 pounds, up to 16 lbs. *Land-locked:* 7 to 14 inches; up to 16 inches and 2 pounds.

Habitat/Abundance: Clear to semi-glacial coastal and inland drainages associated with lakes. Large or important populations are found in tributaries of the Susitna, Talkeetna, Copper, and Kenai rivers, and in drainages of Knik Arm and Turnagain Arm.

Life Cycle: Anadromous/non-anadromous. *Diet:* Young eat insects and zooplankton, adults primarily crustaceans. *Presence:* April to October offshore, peaking May to August. Fish enter fresh water from early May to late October, peaking early June to mid-August. *Spawning:* Lakes, rivers, streams, and springs from mid-June to mid-March, most July to October. Females deposit 2,000-4,500 eggs, hatching in late winter or early spring. *Life Span:* 1 to 3 years in fresh water, 1 to 4 years at sea; up to 5 years of age. *Land-locked:* Year-round in lakes; reach 3 years of age; capable of reproduction.

SPORT FISHING

Terminal Gear: Light to medium action rod/reel; 8- to 15-lb. test line/tippet; small- to medium-sized lures.

Saltwater: *Lures:* Spoons and spinners; snag hooks. *Areas:* Stream mouths. *Timing:* Late May to mid-August.

Freshwater: *Lures:* Spinners, flies, bait. *Areas:* Semi-glacial and clear rivers and streams; holes and runs with moderate to fast current; tributary confluences and tidal areas. *Timing:* Mid-June to late August (sea-run); mid-May to late June (land-locked).

Hot Spots: *Kenai Peninsula* - Kenai, Moose, Russian rivers. *Knik Arm* - Cottonwood, Jim creeks. *Copper Valley* - Gulkana, Klutina rivers.

PINK SALMON

Scientific Name: *Oncorhynchus gorbuscha.*
Other Common Names: Humpy and Humpback.

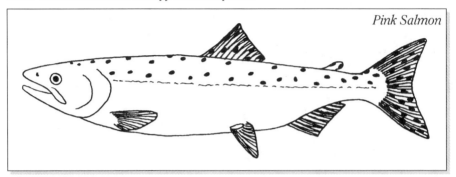

Pink Salmon

BIOLOGY:

Identification: Faint oval-shaped black spots cover back and both lobes of tail fin. *Ocean phase:* Steel blue to blue green on back; silver on sides fading to white on belly. Flesh color is light orange. *Spawning phase:* Dirty brown on back; sides are yellowish green; belly creamy white. Males develop very distinct humped back and elongated, hooked snout. Large, black oval spots are visible on back, dorsal fin, both lobes of tail fin. Flesh color is white.

Size: 2 to 5 pounds; maximum 7 to 10 pounds, up to 14 pounds.

Habitat/Abundance: Clear to semi-glacial coastal and inland drainages. Large or important populations are found in tributaries of the Susitna and Talkeetna rivers, and in Kenai Peninsula, Prince William Sound, and Turnagain Arm drainages.

Life Cycle: Anadromous. *Diet:* Young eat insects and zooplankton, adults primarily fish and crustaceans. *Presence:* May to October offshore, peaking July and August. Fish enter fresh water from mid-June to early October, peaking mid-July to mid-August. *Spawning:* Rivers, streams, and estuaries from early July to late October, most August and September. Females deposit 800-2,000 eggs, hatching in winter. *Life Span:* A few weeks in fresh water, 2 years at sea.

SPORT FISHING

Terminal Gear: Ultra light to light action rod/reel; 4- to 8-lb. test line/tippet; small- to medium-sized lures.

Saltwater: *Lures:* Spoons, spinners, flies, and bait. *Areas:* Tidal rips, coves, and stream mouths. *Timing:* Early July to mid-August.

Freshwater: *Lures:* Spoons, spinners, plugs, attractors, and flies. *Areas:* Semi-glacial, murky, and clear rivers and streams; holes and runs with moderate current; tributary confluences and tidal areas. *Timing:* Mid-July to late August.

Hot Spots: *Kenai Peninsula* - Anchor, Kenai, Moose, Ninilchik rivers; Deep, Stariski creeks; Cook Inlet; Homer Spit; Resurrection Bay. *Turnagain Arm* - Bird, California, Ingram, Resurrection, Sixmile creeks. *Knik Arm* - Little Susitna River. *Susitna Valley* - Caswell, Goose, Montana, Little Willow, Sheep, Sunshine, Willow creeks. *Valdez Arm* - Allison Point; Port Valdez, Solomon Gulch Creek

CHUM SALMON

Scientific Name: *Oncorhynchus keta.*
Other Common Names: Calico, Dog, Keta, Silver, and Silver Bright.

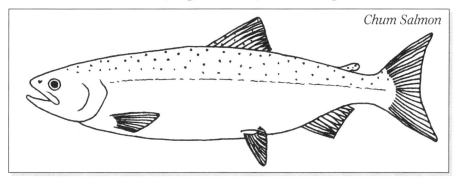

Chum Salmon

BIOLOGY

Identification: Iris of eye is large, base of tail thin. Fine dusting of small specks are visible on back and top of head. Fins have distinctive white tips. *Ocean phase:* Dark metallic blue on back; silvery on sides; silver white on belly. Flesh color is light orange. *Spawning phase:* Crimson markings cover sides in bright red, black, and dirty yellow. Back is olive green, black, or brown. Pectoral, anal, and pelvic fins have white tips. Males develop a hooked jaw with protruding canine-like teeth, females a dark horizontal band across sides. Flesh color is white.

Size: 6 to 12 pounds; maximum 15 to 20 pounds, up to 35 pounds.

Habitat/Abundance: Clear to semi-glacial coastal, inland, and interior drainages. Large or important populations are found in tributaries of the Susitna, Talkeetna, Chulitna, Nenana, Yukon, and Tanana rivers, and in drainages of Knik Arm, Turnagain Arm, Prince William Sound, and Resurrection Bay.

Life Cycle: Anadromous. *Diet:* Young eat insects, adults primarily fish and crustaceans. *Presence:* May to October offshore, peaking July and August. Fish enter fresh water from mid-May to early October, peaking early July to mid-August. *Spawning:* Rivers, streams, springs, and estuaries from late June to early February, most July to November. Females deposit 2,000-4,000 eggs, hatching in late winter or spring. *Life Span:* A few months in fresh water, 2 to 5 years at sea; up to 6 years of age.

SPORT FISHING

Terminal Gear: Light to medium action rod/reel; 8- to 15-lb. test line/tippet; medium-sized lures.

Saltwater: *Lures:* Spoons, spinners, and bait. *Areas:* Coves and stream mouths. *Timing:* Late June to mid-September.

Freshwater: *Lures:* Spoons, spinners, attractors, flies, and bait. *Areas:* Clear rivers and streams; holes and runs with moderate current; tributary confluences and tidal areas. *Timing:* Early July to early October.

Hot Spots: *Kenai Peninsula* - Resurrection Bay. *Turnagain Arm* - Bird, Resurrection, Sixmile creeks. *Knik Arm* - Little Susitna River; Jim Creek; Eklutna Tailrace. *Susitna Valley* - Goose, Montana, Sheep, Willow creeks. *Tanana Valley* - Chena, Salcha rivers.

SILVER SALMON

Scientific Name: *Oncorhynchus kisutch.*
Other Common Names: Coho, Silverside, and Blueback.

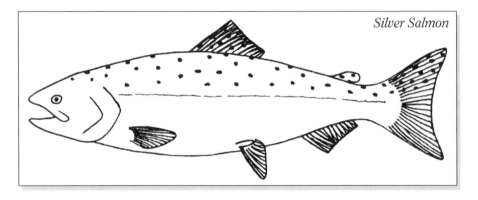

Silver Salmon

BIOLOGY

Identification: Gum line is white. Moderately small black spots cover top of head, back, and upper lobe of caudal fin. Tail base is thick. *Ocean phase:* Metallic blue on back; silvery on sides; white on belly. Flesh color is orange red. *Spawning phase:* Brilliant red, also bronze, greenish brown, even almost black. Back is dark olive green to a faded red or copper. Males develop a very distinct hooked snout, prolonged teeth, and a slightly humped back. Flesh color is white.

Size: 5 to 12 pounds; maximum 15 to 22 pounds, up to 30 pounds. *Land-locked:* 7 to 15 inches; up to 20 inches and 5 pounds.

Habitat/Abundance: Clear to semi-glacial coastal, inland, and interior drainages. Large or important populations are found in tributaries of Susitna, Talkeetna, Chulitna, Copper, Nenana, and Tanana rivers, and drainages of Knik Arm, Turnagain Arm, Kenai Peninsula, and Prince William Sound.

Life Cycle: Anadromous/non-anadromous. *Diet:* Young eat insects and salmon fry, adults primarily fish and crustaceans. *Presence:* May to December offshore, peaking July to October. Fish enter fresh water from mid-June to early January, peaking late July to early

October. *Spawning:* Rivers, streams, and springs from early August to late April, most September to December. Females deposit 1,400-5,700 eggs, hatching in winter or spring. *Life Span:* 1 to 3 years in fresh water, 1 to 3 years at sea; up to 5 years of age. *Land-locked:* Year-round in lakes; reach 3 years of age; not capable of reproduction.

SPORT FISHING

Terminal Gear: Light to medium action rod/reel; 8- to 15-lb. test line/tippet; medium-sized lures.

Saltwater: *Lures:* Spinners, attractors, flies, and bait. *Areas:* Tidal rips, coves, and stream mouths. *Timing:* Mid-July to early October.

Freshwater: *Lures:* Spoons, spinners, plugs, attractors, flies, and bait. *Areas:* Semi-glacial, murky, and clear rivers and streams; deep holes, runs, and pools with moderate to slow current; tributary confluences and tidal areas. *Timing:* Late July to late October (sea-run); late October to mid-April (land-locked).

Hot Spots: *Kenai Peninsula* - Anchor, Kasilof, Kenai, Moose, Ninilchik, Russian, Swanson rivers; Deep Creek; Cook Inlet; Dudiak Lagoon; Resurrection Bay. *Turnagain Arm* - Bird, Resurrection, Sixmile creeks. *Knik Arm* - Little Susitna River; Cottonwood, Fish, Jim creeks; Eklutna Tailrace. *Susitna Valley* - Caswell, Goose, Little Willow, Montana, Peters, Rabideux, Sheep, Sunshine, Willow creeks; *Copper Valley* - Little Tonsina River. *Valdez Arm* - Robe River; Allison Point; Port Valdez . *Tanana Valley* - Delta Clearwater River.

Trout

Trout are widespread in the Southcentral and Interior regions of Alaska, but are absent from the Arctic. They thrive well in both saltwater and fresh water environments, and occupy a variety of waters from the tidal areas of large glacial rivers to mere trickles of creeks in the high mountains.

The trout family are represented in Alaska by the rainbow and the cutthroat. The latter species is not found along the road system in Southcentral or Interior Alaska and therefore excluded from this book. The rainbow trout, on the other hand, is a very common species that is present in two distinct varieties. One is the strictly fresh water form, and the other is sea-run rainbow trout, popularly called steelhead.

STEELHEAD TROUT

Scientific Name: *Oncorhynchus mykiss.*
Other Common Names: Steelie, Metalhead, Kelt, and Rainbow.

(Drawing on next page)
BIOLOGY

Identification: Small black spots present on back, upper sides, and both lobes of caudal fin. *Ocean phase:* Back is almost black; sides are silvery; belly is white. A very distinct horizontal pinkish band appear on sides after a few days of fresh water residence. Flesh color is orange. *Spawning phase:* Black spots are more pronounced. Sides and cheeks are

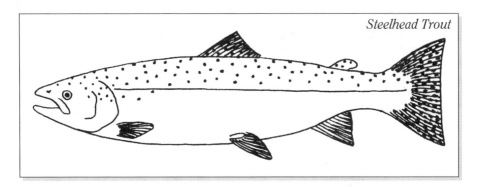

Steelhead Trout

dirty red; back is greenish yellow or grey. Post-spawn fish often return to a silvery shine on the sides, belly turning white and back dark. Flesh color is white.

Size: 5 to 12 pounds; maximum 15 to 20 pounds, up to 45 pounds.

Habitat/Abundance: Clear coastal and inland drainages. Important populations are found in drainages on the Kenai Peninsula and tributaries of Copper River.

Life Cycle: Anadromous. *Diet:* Young eat fish, fish eggs, and insects, adults primarily fish and crustaceans. *Presence:* April to November offshore, peaking in September. Fish enter streams from late March to early June and early August to mid-December, peaking in mid- to late September. *Spawning:* Rivers and streams from mid-March to mid-July, most May. Females deposit 100-12,000 eggs, hatching in summer or early fall. May reproduce more than once, up to four times. *Life Span:* 1 to 4 years in fresh water, 2 to 5 years at sea; up to 7 years of age.

SPORT FISHING

Terminal Gear: Light to medium action rod/reel; 8- to 15-lb. test line/tippet; small- to medium-sized lures.

Saltwater: No consistent opportunities exist at this time.

Freshwater: *Lures:* Spinners, plugs, attractors, flies, bait. *Areas:* Semi-glacial, murky, and clear rivers and streams; holes and runs with moderate current; tributary confluences and tidal areas. *Timing:* Late April to late May, mid-September to late October.

Hot Spots: *Kenai Peninsula* - Anchor, Ninilchik rivers; Deep Creek.

RAINBOW TROUT

Scientific Name: *Oncorhynchus mykiss.*
Other Common Names: 'Bow.

(Drawing on next page)
BIOLOGY

Identification: Numerous black spots present on sides, back, top of head, and both lobes of caudal fin. *Feeding phase:* Coloration may vary greatly from watershed to watershed.

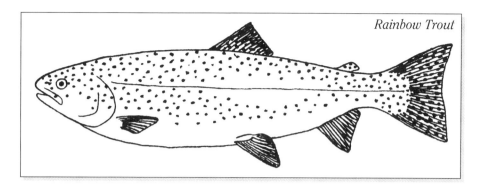

Rainbow Trout

Sides are silvery to copper, light brown, or olive with a light red stripe of varying width and pronunciation. Back is black or dark green. Flesh color is orange. *Spawning phase:* Reddish pink on sides and cheeks. Belly is grayish or brown; back black or dirty dark green. Black spots are enlarged and more pronounced. Flesh color is white.

Size: 8 to 20 inches; maximum 5 to 10 pounds, up to 28 pounds.

Habitat/Abundance: Clear to semi-glacial coastal and inland drainages. Large or important populations are found in lakes and streams on the Kenai Peninsula and in Matanuska, Susitna, and Copper valleys, and stocked lakes around Tanana Valley.

Life Cycle: Non-anadromous. *Diet:* Primarily fish, fish eggs, and insects. *Presence:* Year-round in lakes and large rivers; April to December in smaller streams, peaking mid-May to mid-October. *Spawning:* Rivers and streams from mid-March to early July, most May and June. Females deposit 200-12,700 eggs, hatching in late spring and summer. May reproduce several times. *Life Span:* Up to 11 years of age.

SPORT FISHING

Terminal Gear: Ultra light or light action rod/reel; 4- to 10-lb. test line/tippet; small-sized lures.

Freshwater: *Lures:* Spoons, spinners, plugs, attractors, flies, and bait. *Areas:* Semi-glacial, murky, and clear rivers, streams, lakes, and ponds; holes, runs, and pools with moderate current; tributary confluences, around island, steep drop-offs, and lake inlets/outlets. *Timing:* Mid-May to mid-June, late August to late December (lakes); mid-May to late June, mid-August to mid-October (streams).

Hot Spots: *Kenai Peninsula* - Kenai, Moose, Russian, Swanson rivers; Ptarmigan Creek; Kenai Spur Highway, Swanson River Road lakes. *Turnagain Arm* - Portage area lakes. *Knik Arm* - Anchorage area, Palmer-Wasilla area, Big Lake area, Point McKenzie area lakes. *Susitna Valley* - Kashwitna, Middle Fork Chulitna, Talkeetna rivers; Byers, Montana, Little Willow, Sheep, Willow creeks; Nancy Lake area lakes. *Copper Valley* - Gulkana River; McCarthy Road lakes. *Tanana Valley* - Steese Highway, Chena Hot Springs, Fairbanks area lakes/ponds; Piledriver Slough.

Char

The char family consists of two distinct species, the Arctic char/Dolly Varden and the lake trout. Arctic char and Dolly Varden are considered to be two slightly different variations of one species and are often grouped under the generic term "char" as there are only a few very minor differences between them, none of which are really apparent to the untrained eye. Another char species, labeled erroneously as a trout, is the lake trout. This species is very common in certain areas of Southcentral, but does not appear in the numbers of the other char species, nor does it thrive in the same wide range of environments.

LAKE TROUT

Scientific Name: *Salvelinus namaycush.*
Other Common Names: Mackinaw, Grey Trout, and Laker.

Lake Trout

BIOLOGY

Identification: Tail is distinctly forked. Mouth extends well beyond eye. Scales are small. *Feeding phase:* Color may vary from watershed to watershed. Sides and back are dark green, grayish, brown, or even almost black; belly is white. Whitish or yellowish markings are scattered throughout body, including head and some fins. Flesh color is white or light pink. *Spawning phase:* Dark lateral band cover sides of males. Back becomes a lighter shade. Pectoral, pelvic, and anal fins may take on a slight orange or reddish hue. Flesh is white.

Size: 3 to 12 pounds; maximum 15 to 30 pounds, up to 50 pounds.

Habitat/Abundance: Clear to semi-glacial inland and interior lakes. Large or important populations are found in Susitna, Copper, and Tanana valleys, central Kenai Peninsula, and Brooks Range.

Life Cycle: Non-anadromous. *Diet:* Young eat insects and plankton, adult primarily fish and insects. *Presence:* Year-round in lakes; June to October in larger rivers. *Spawning:* Lakes from early September to late November, most in October. Females deposit 200-17,000 eggs, hatching in winter and early spring. May reproduce several times. *Life Span:* Up to 50 years of age.

SPORT FISHING

Terminal Gear: Light to medium action rod/reel; 10- to 20-lb. test line/tippet; medium- to large-sized lures.

Freshwater: *Lures:* Spoons, spinners, plugs, flies, and bait. *Areas:* Semi-glacial to clear lakes; fairly shallow water in spring and fall, deep in summer and winter; lake inlets and outlets, around islands, and the edge of steep drop-offs. *Timing:* Mid-May to early July, late August to late November.

Hot Spots: *Kenai Peninsula* - Hidden, Kenai, Skilak lakes. *Knik Arm* - Long Lake. *Copper Valley* - Louise, Paxson, Summit lakes. *Tanana Valley* - Fielding, Harding lakes. *North Slope* - Island, Galbraith, Toolik lakes.

DOLLY VARDEN

Scientific Name: *Salvelinus malma.*
Other Common Names: Dolly, Goldenfin, Golden Trout, and Char.

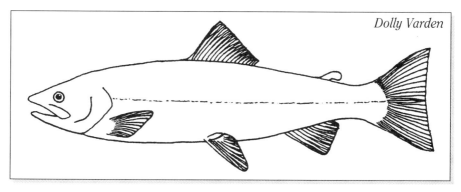

Dolly Varden

BIOLOGY

Identification: Spots in varying degrees of color decorate sides only. Scales small. *Ocean phase:* Black or dark greenish to blue on back; sides silvery with faint white spots; belly is white. Flesh color is light orange to white. *Lake/Stream Phase:* Back is dark brown, green, or black; sides yellowish brown with pink spots. Flesh color is light orange. *Spawning phase:* Dirty-green or dark on back and upper sides; lower sides and belly bright orange or reddish. Large pink or red spots accent dark sides. Males develop a kype on lower jaw. Pectoral, pelvic, anal, and lower caudal fins have clear white edges. Flesh color is yellowish white.

Size: 10 inches to 6 pounds; maximum 5 to 15 pounds, up to 30 pounds. *Land-locked:* 7 to 12 inches; up to 20 inches.

Habitat/Abundance: Saltwater and clear to semi-glacial coastal and inland drainages. Large or important populations are found on the Kenai Peninsula and North Slope, in drainages of Turnagain Arm and Prince William Sound, and tributaries of Talkeetna and Copper rivers.

Life Cycle: Anadromous/non-anadromous. *Diet:* Young and adults primarily eat fish, insects, crustaceans, plankton, and salmon eggs. *Presence:* Year-round in lakes and large rivers; March to January, peaking May to October in smaller streams; February to October, peaking May and June in salt water. *Spawning:* Rivers, streams, and springs from mid-August to late November, most September and October. Females deposit 350-10,000 eggs, hatching in spring. May reproduce several times. *Life Span:* Up to 18 years of age.

SPORT FISHING

Terminal Gear: Ultra light to light action rod/reel; 4- to 10-lb. test line/tippet; small- to medium-sized lures.

Saltwater: *Lures:* Spoons, plugs, flies, and bait. *Areas:* Tidal rips, exposed beaches, and stream mouths. *Timing:* Mid-May to mid-July.

Freshwater: *Lures:* Spoons, spinners, plugs, attractors, flies, and bait. *Areas:* Semi-glacial, murky, and clear systems; moderate to deep holes, runs, and pools; tributary confluences and tidal areas; lake inlets and outlets; submerged structures. *Timing:* Mid-May to late June, late August to late December (lakes); mid-May to early June, mid-July to late October (rivers); early May to early June, mid-July to mid-October (streams).

Hot Spots: *Kenai Peninsula* - Anchor, Kenai, Kasilof, Ninilchik, Swanson rivers; Crooked, Deep, Quartz, Stariski, Ptarmigan creeks; Grouse, Lower Summit, Upper Summit lakes; Preacher Pond; Homer Spit; Resurrection Bay. *Turnagain Arm* - Bird, California, Campbell, Portage, Sixmile creeks. *Susitna Valley* - Talkeetna River. *Copper Valley* - Little Tonsina, Klutina rivers. *Valdez Arm* - Lowe, Robe rivers. *Tanana Valley* - Baker Creek. *North Slope* - Sagavanirktok River.

ARCTIC CHAR

Scientific Name: *Salvelinus alpinus.*
Other Common Names: Blueback Char, Blueback Trout, and Char.

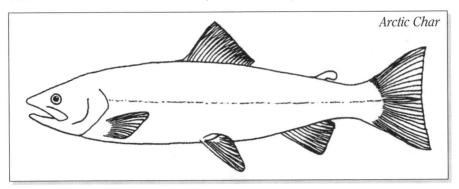

Arctic Char

BIOLOGY

Identification: Spots in varying degrees of color decorate sides, but not head, back, or any fins. Scales small. *Feeding phase:* Dark green, blue, or brownish green back; upper sides are tan or yellowish brown; lower sides and belly white. Spots are light pink. Flesh color is light orange. *Spawning phase:* Orange red to bright red lower sides and belly. Pectoral, pelvic, and anal fins have creamy white leading edges. Spots are pink or red, the ones along the lateral line often larger than pupil of eye. Tip of lower jaw on males may turn orange or reddish brown. Flesh color is yellowish white.

Size: 2 to 4 pounds; maximum 6 to 12 pounds, up to 16 pounds.

Habitat/Abundance: Clear to semi-glacial coastal and inland lakes. Large or important populations are found in lakes on the Kenai Peninsula, in Brooks Range, and the Matanuska and Copper valleys.

Life Cycle: Non-anadromous. *Diet:* Young and adult eat primarily fish, insects, worms, and salmon eggs. *Presence:* Year-round in lakes; June to November in streams. *Spawning:* Lakes from early September to late December, most October and November. Females deposit 200-6,000 eggs, hatching in spring. May reproduce several times – annually in the south, alternate years in the north. *Life Span:* Up to 24 years of age.

SPORT FISHING

Terminal Gear: Ultra light to light action rod/reel; 4- to 6-lb. test line/tippet; small- to medium-sized lures.

Freshwater: *Lures:* Spoons, spinners, plugs, flies, bait. *Areas:* Semi-glacial, murky, and clear systems; moderate to deep holes, runs, and pools; lake inlets and outlets, submerged structures, and edges of steep drop-offs. *Timing:* Mid-May to mid-June, mid-August to late January (lakes); late June to late October (streams).

Hot Spots: *Kenai Peninsula* - Dabbler, Finger, Silver, Skookum, Stormy lakes. *Knik Arm* - Big, Clunie, Finger, Irene, Marion, Matanuska lakes. *Turnagain Arm* - Campbell Point Lake. *Susitna Valley* - Benka and Lynne lakes. *Tanana Valley* - Birch, Chena, Harding, Quartz lakes; Coal Mine Road, Meadows Road, Ridge Road lakes. *North Slope* - Island, Galbraith, Toolik lakes.

Grayling

The Arctic grayling is the only member of its family represented in Alaska and is believed to be an intermediate species between the trouts and whitefishes. It is typically found in clear and clean waters and has earned a solid reputation among anglers as being a superb sport fish due to its aerial antics and aggressiveness towards artificial lures.

ARCTIC GRAYLING

Scientific Name: *Thymallus arcticus.*
Other Common Names: Grayling and Sailfin.

(Drawing on next page)
BIOLOGY

Identification: Exceptionally large dorsal fin. Black or dark brown spots from gills to almost

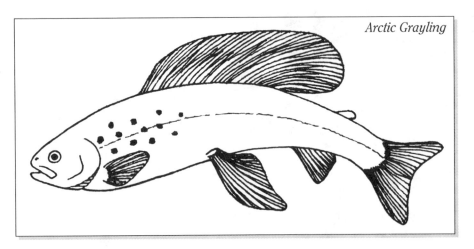

Arctic Grayling

midway down the fish. Large scales; small mouth. Tail is forked.

Feeding phase: Silvery grey, light brown, or copper on sides; back is dark or brown; belly is white. Dorsal and pelvic fins have vague spots or stripes. Flesh color is white. *Spawning phase:* Dark brown to deep purple on back and sides. Red and pink spots and stripes decorate fins. Belly is bluish white. Flesh color is white.

Size: 7 to 14 inches; maximum 18 to 20 inches, up to 5 pounds and 23 inches.

Habitat/Abundance: Clear and murky inland and interior drainages. Large or important populations are found in lakes and streams of the Matanuska, Susitna, Copper, Nenana, Tanana, Yukon, and Koyukuk valleys, Brooks Range, and on the North Slope.

Life Cycle: Non-anadromous. *Diet:* Young and adults primarily eat fish, insects, insect larvae, and fish eggs. *Presence:* Year-round in lakes and large rivers; early April to early November in smaller streams, peaking May to October. *Spawning:* Rivers and streams from mid-April to late June, most May. Females deposit 1,700-14,000 eggs, hatching after three weeks. May reproduce several times. *Life Span:* Up to 22 years of age.

SPORT FISHING

Terminal Gear: Ultra-light action rod/reel; 2- to 4-lb. test line/tippet; small-sized lures.

Freshwater: *Lures:* Spinners, attractors, and flies. *Areas:* Clear or muskeg-stained rivers, streams, and lakes; moderate to fast current over shallow runs in spring and summer, deep holes and pools in fall. *Timing:* Mid-May to mid-October (lakes); late April to early June, mid-August to mid-October (rivers); early May to early October (streams).

Hot Spots: *Kenai Peninsula* - Crescent, Grayling, Lower Fuller lakes. *Knik Arm* - Beach, Canoe, Finger, Kepler/Bradley, Lorraine, Meirs, Reed. *Susitna Valley* - East Fork Chulitna, Kashwitna, Talkeetna rivers; Goose, Little Willow, Montana, Sheep, Willow creeks. *Copper Valley* - Gulkana, Little Tonsina rivers; Gunn, Mendeltna, Moose, Sourdough, Tulsona, Tolsona creeks; Louise, Paxson, Summit lakes; Lake Louise Road, McCarthy road lakes. *Tanana Valley* - Chatanika, Chena, Delta Clearwater rivers; Mineral lakes. *North Slope* - Sagavanirktok River; Dalton Highway lakes/streams.

Whitefish

The whitefish family covers three major kinds – the ciscos, the whitefishes, and the sheefish. All of these are closely related and share much the same habits and appearance. When grouping the cisco and whitefish together, there are 8 species present in Alaska of which 4 are regularly encountered by anglers along the road system. While most of these species are strictly of the fresh water kind, some are anadromous and commit seasonal migrations much like sea-run char.

Sheefish is by far the largest member species of the whitefishes, but do not appear in the numbers which is characteristic for this family. Although both sea-run and resident varieties are known, only the latter kind is present in the state's roadside waters.

SHEEFISH

Scientific Name: *Stenodus leucichthys nelma*
Other Common Names: Inconnu, Shee, Cony, Arctic Tarpon, and Eskimo Tarpon.

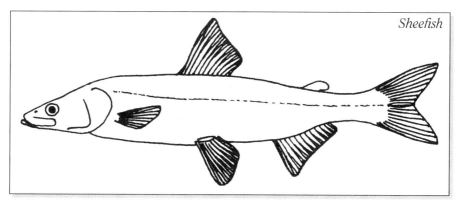

Sheefish

BIOLOGY

Identification: Large scales. Mouth is large and contain a multitude of very small teeth above a protruding jaw. *Feeding phase:* Sides generally silver; back is dark green or blue; belly is silvery white. *Spawning phase:* Back and sides may turn a very light shade of metallic yellowish brown or tan, but often no apparent change from feeding phase.

Size: 5 to 10 pounds; maximum 15 pounds, up to 25 pounds. *Sea-run:* 10 to 20 pounds; up to 60 pounds.

Habitat/Abundance: Clear and murky coastal, inland, and interior drainages. Large or important populations are found in drainages of the Yukon, Koyukuk, and Tanana rivers.

Life Cycle: Anadromous/non-anadromous. *Diet:* Young eat insects and plankton, adults primarily fish. *Presence:* Year-round in lakes and large rivers; mid-May to early November, peaking July to October in streams. Sea-run fish overwinter in river estuaries, resident fish in lakes and rivers. *Spawning:* Rivers and streams in late September and early October. Females deposit 100,000-400,000 eggs, hatching in late winter and early spring. May reproduce several times, most in alternate years. *Life Span:* Up to 21 years of age.

SPORT FISHING

Terminal Gear: Light to medium action rod/reel; 8- to 15-pound test line/tippet; medium-sized lures.

Freshwater: *Lures:* Spoons, spinners, plugs, flies, and bait. *Areas:* Murky and clear lakes, rivers, and streams; holes and runs with moderate current; lake inlets and outlets and submerged structures. *Timing:* Early June to mid-August (lakes); mid-July to late October (rivers); late September and early October (streams).

Hot Spots: *Tanana Valley* - Chatanika River.

WHITEFISH

Species: Round (*Prosopium cylindraceum*), Pygmy (*Proposium coulteri*), Broad (*Coregonus nasus*), Humpback (*Coregonus oidschian*), Least Cisco (*Coregonus sardinaella*), Arctic Cisco (*Coregonus autumnalis*), Bering Cisco (*Coregonus laurettae*).
Note: Only the more commonly caught species - round, humpback, and least cisco - will be discussed in this section, except as noted.

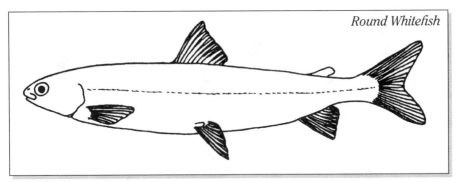

Round Whitefish

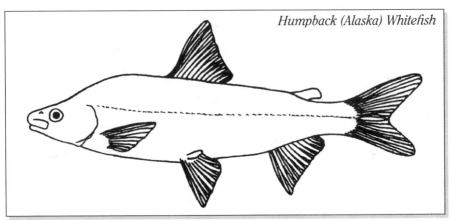

Humpback (Alaska) Whitefish

BIOLOGY

Identification: Body shape varies with species from tubular to compact. Scales are large;

Least Cisco

mouth small with very tiny or no teeth. *Feeding phase:* Sides are silvery; back is dark grey or green; silvery white on belly. *Spawning phase:* Sides are grayish silvery, light brown, yellowish, or bronze; back is dirty brown; fins may take on a slight orange coloration.

Size: Varies according to species, but generally 10 to 20 inches; maximum 3 to 5 pounds, up to 15 pounds (broad whitefish).

Habitat/Abundance: Clear to semi-glacial coastal, inland, and interior drainages. Large or important populations are found in drainages of the Susitna, Talkeetna, Copper, Nenana, Tanana, Koyukuk, and Yukon rivers, central Kenai Peninsula, and the North Slope.

Life Cycle: Anadromous/non-anadromous. *Diet:* Young eat insect larvae and zooplankton, adults primarily insects and fish eggs. *Presence:* Year-round in lakes and large rivers; May to September in salt water; late May to early January, peaking July to November in streams. Sea-run fish overwinter in river estuaries, resident fish in lakes and rivers. *Spawning:* Lakes, rivers, and streams from mid-September to mid-December, most October and November. Females deposit 1,000-150,000 eggs, hatching in spring. May reproduce several times. *Life Span:* Up to 16 years of age.

SPORT FISHING

Terminal Gear: Ultra-light or light action rod/reel; 2- to 6-lb. test line/tippet; small-sized lures.

Saltwater: No consistent opportunities exist at this time.

Freshwater: *Lures:* Flies and bait. *Areas:* Clear, murky, and semi-glacial rivers and streams; holes, pools, and runs in summer; fairly shallow in fall; moderate to fast current. *Timing:* Early July to mid-September (lakes); early July to mid-November (rivers/streams).

Hot Spots: *Kenai Peninsula* - Kenai River. *Knik Arm* - Little Susitna River; Fish Creek. *Susitna Valley* - Little Willow, Sheep creeks. *Copper Valley* - Gulkana, Slana rivers. *Tanana Valley* - Chatanika River. *North Slope* - Sagavanirktok River.

Pike

Pike in Alaska are represented by the northern pike, a species with a reputation for being exceptionally aggressive both in territorial expansion and appetite. It is considered a very serious predator of other game fish, hence the nicknames "waterwolf" and "devil fish." Pike often use ambush tactics in catching its prey and are capable of out-speeding a salmon over shorter distances. Illegal introductions of this species has been made to small lakes with previous populations of only trout and char with the ending result being the pike literally decimating entire native fish populations. However, larger lakes and rivers are better suited to absorb the predatory habits of these fish.

NORTHERN PIKE

Scientific Name: *Esox lucius.*
Other Common Names: Pike, Jackfish, and Pickerel.

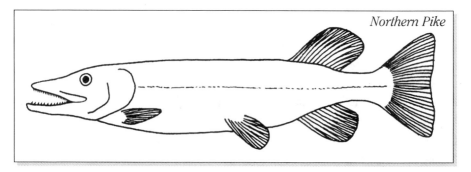

Northern Pike

BIOLOGY

Identification: Dorsal fin is placed far back on body. Long, flat duck-bill snout. Scales are moderately small; mouth is large and equipped with long, sharp teeth. Feeding/*Spawning phase:* Dark grayish green, green, or dark brownish on back and sides; creamy white or yellowish on belly. Numerous yellow spots in irregular longitudinal rows decorate sides. Fins are green, yellowish, or even orange and marked with dark blotches. Flesh color is white.

Size: 3 to 10 pounds; maximum 15 to 25 pounds, up to 45 pounds.

Habitat/Abundance: Clear to semi-glacial inland and interior drainages. Large or important populations are found in drainages of the Susitna, Tanana, Koyukuk, and Yukon rivers.

Life Cycle: Non-anadromous. *Diet:* Young eat insects and plankton, adults primarily fish, insects, and young aquatic birds. *Presence:* Year-round in lakes and large rivers; early May to mid-November, peaking June to September in streams. *Spawning:* Lakes, rivers, streams, and sloughs from mid-May to late July, most June. Females deposit 2,000-600,000 eggs, hatching a few weeks later. May reproduce several times. *Life Span:* Up to 25 years of age.

SPORT FISHING

Terminal Gear: Light or medium action rod/reel; 6- to 15-lb. test line/tippet; medium- to large-sized lures; wire leader is required due to pike's sharp teeth.

Freshwater: *Lures:* Spoons, plugs, flies, bait. *Areas:* Clear, murky, and semi-glacial lakes, rivers, streams, and sloughs; deep, quiet holes and pools; confluence of glacial rivers and clearwater tributaries; areas with slow or still water on edge of faster current; shallow, vegetated lake shores. *Timing:* Early May to early July, early September to late November (lakes); mid-June to mid-September (rivers/streams).

Hot Spots: *Kenai Peninsula* - Union Lake, Stormy Lake. *Knik Arm* - Prator Lake. *Susitna Valley* - Rainbow, Shirley, Rhein, Tanaina, Red Shirt lakes. *Tanana Valley* - Island, Deadman, Yarger, Eliza, Mineral lakes; Minto Flats. *Yukon River* - Ray, Jim rivers; Medicine Lake.

Cod

Burbot are the only member of the codfish family strictly found in fresh water and are the only species accounted as a sport fish as well. It is primarily a bottom dweller and usually encountered by anglers in late fall, winter, and early spring. Despite its somewhat less appealing appearance, it is a popular quarry among many fishers who have labeled the fish "poor man's lobster."

BURBOT

Scientific Name: *Lota lota.*
Other Common Names: Ling, Lush, Freshwater Lush, Kusk, Eelpout, Maria, Lawyer, Loache, Methy, Mud Shark, Metling, and Ling Cod.

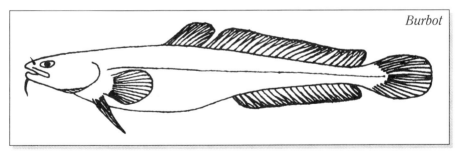

Burbot

BIOLOGY

Identification: Long and slender. Head is wide and broad. Mouth is large. Characteristic barbel adorns tip of lower jaw. Dorsal and anal fins extend from middle of body almost to caudal fin. Caudal fin is rounded rather than square or forked. Scales are very small, almost microscopic. *Feeding/Spawning phase:* Mottled brown, olive-black, or dark green on back and sides; belly a lighter hue. Numerous dirty yellow patches or markings cover back, sides, and belly in dirty yellow. Flesh color is white.

Size: 2 to 6 pounds; maximum 8 to 15 pounds, up to 75 pounds.

Habitat/Abundance: Clear to glacial inland and interior drainages. Large or important populations are found in the Susitna, Talkeetna, Chulitna, Copper, Nenana, Tanana, Yukon, Koyukuk, and Sagavanirktok rivers.

Life Cycle: Non-anadromous. *Diet:* Young eat insect larvae and plant material, adults primarily fish, insects, mollusks, snails, and fish eggs. *Presence:* Year-round in lakes, large rivers, and stream mouths; May to October in smaller streams. *Spawning:* Lakes, rivers, and streams from mid-December to early April, most February and March. Females deposit 600,000-3,000,000 eggs, hatching in late winter and spring. May reproduce several times. *Life Span:* Up to 25 years of age.

SPORT FISHING

Terminal Gear: Medium action rod/reel; 12- to 15-lb. test line/leader; set lines with multiple hooks require heavier pound test.

Freshwater: *Lures:* Bait. *Areas:* Semi-glacial, murky, and clear lakes, rivers, and stream mouths; deep, quiet holes and pools; confluence of glacial rivers and clearwater tributaries; areas with slow or still water on edge of faster current. *Timing:* Mid-March to mid-May, mid-September to late December (lakes); mid-March to mid-May, mid-October to late December (rivers/streams).

Hot Spots: *Matanuska Valley* - Long Lake. *Susitna Valley* - Susitna River stream mouths (Willow, Sheep, Caswell, Montana, Rabideux, Sunshine creeks). *Copper Valley* - Paxson, Summit lakes. *Tanana Valley* - Tanana River stream mouths (Chena, Salcha rivers; Shaw, Moose creeks). *Middle Yukon* - Ray River. *Koyukuk Valley* - Jim River. *North Slope* - Sagavanirktok River.

SALTWATER SPECIES

Bottomfish

Even though halibut, ling cod, and rockfish are abundant in coastal waters, they are much less common to roadside anglers trying their luck casting from beaches, docks, and cliffs due to the fact that the fish are usually found too deep and just out of range. With the exception of a few species of rockfish, a boat is the way to go to truly experience the best these fish have to offer. However, with some patience, knowledge of bottom structure, and a little luck, they can be caught from shore.

PACIFIC HALIBUT

Scientific Name: *Hippoglossus stenolepis*
Other Common Names: Halibut, Northern Halibut, Right Halibut, and Albato.

BIOLOGY
Description: Body is somewhat elongated in shape in contrast to other species of flounder.

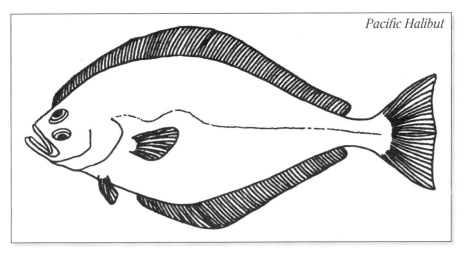

Pacific Halibut

Top side is dark brown or dirty brown with irregular blotches, bottom side being bright or dirty white. Flesh is white and firm.

Size: *Average:* 20 to 60 lbs. *Maximum:* 550 lbs. and 9.5 ft. Halibut caught from shore are typically small (less than 10 lbs.) but may on occasion reach 80 lbs. or more.

Abundance: Large or important populations are found along coastal Kenai Peninsula and in Prince William Sound.

Habits: Shallow from spring to fall (20-100 ft.), deep in winter (down to 3,600 ft.). Spawning occurs in deep water from November through March.

Timing: Year-round offshore, spring through fall inshore. Occasionally encountered by anglers fishing from deep-water docks during June, July, and August.

Structure: Sand, mud, or gravel bottom; good current flow.

SPORT FISHING

Terminal Gear: Heavy action rod/reel; 30 to 80 lb. test line/tippet; medium- to large-sized lures.

Lures: Jigs and bait.

ROCKFISH

Number of Species: Over 60 kinds in Alaska.

Common Species: Yelloweye and Black most dominant, but also Rougheye, Dusky, Quillback, China, Tiger, Bocaccio, and Pacific Ocean Perch.

(Drawing on next page)

BIOLOGY

Description: Broad body; large eyes and mouth; varying shades of color according to

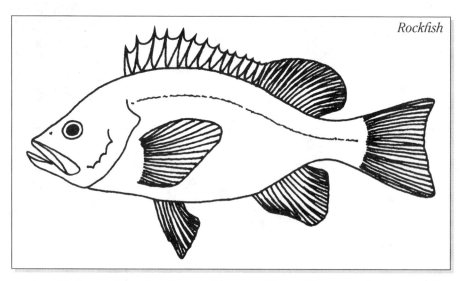

Rockfish

species - black, carmine-red, yellow, and brown with possibly orange, brown, or yellow spotting or stripes; flesh is white and firm.

Size: 2 to 4 lbs. average, especially specimens taken by shore anglers. Yelloweye rockfish may reach up to 40 lbs. in coastal, offshore waters.

Abundance: Large or important populations are found along coastal Kenai Peninsula and in Prince William Sound.

Habits: Fairly shallow (20-200 ft.) in summer and fall, deep (down to 2,000 ft.) in winter and spring. Spawning occurs from March to June. May reach 100 years of age.

Timing: Year-round offshore, summer and fall inshore. Sometimes taken in roadside fisheries from June to September.

Structure: Coastal, hard bottom areas; kelp beds, steep drop-offs.

SPORT FISHING

Terminal Gear: Medium to heavy action rod/reel; 12 to 20 lb. test line/tippet; medium- to large-sized lures.

Lures: Jigs and bait.

OTHER SPECIES

Various "non-sporting," yet highly edible, kinds of bottomfish frequently encountered by both boat and shore anglers include cod, pollock, sablefish, greenling, and flounder. These fish are abundant year-round in deeper, off-shore areas and from spring into fall in shallow, near-shore waters. They are often taken incidentally to fishing for other more popular quarries, such as salmon and char, but can yield excellent action for anglers targeting them intentionally using jigs or cut bait.

Fishing Tips

This chapter was written with the novice angler in mind but may also prove helpful with anyone not familiar with fishing Alaskan waters. It briefly touches on some of the general aspects of angling and include topics such as where to locate fish in certain types of water and conditions, fighting skills in hooking, playing, and landing fish, a few points to consider in proper techniques of catch and release, a list of the most popular lures available on the market, the types of fish they are known to attract, and tips on lure selection. If the basics described here are applied correctly, chances for success are much improved.

Locating the Fish

It is well known that fish do have special preferences for the environment they choose to rest and feed in, and migrate through. Knowing where and at what time in a stream, lake, or bay to look for fish is at least as important - if not more so - as having the right gear and skill. Although angling for most species of fish can be productive at any time or place of the day or year, there are definitely times and locations when the action is better and more predictable. The most common factors to consider are lighting conditions, available structure, current flow, depth, seasonal behavior, and water temperature. Being able to "read" the water, or in other words, having sufficient information on fish habits to know exactly where a fish is most likely to be found is the key and, if mastered, can bring much success.

The following points illustrate the very basics in locating fish in various types of water conditions and the factors involved.

RIVERS AND STREAMS

1. Locate deep holes, pools, and eddies. Many species have a tendency to congregate in such areas as they find security there while either feeding or migrating to or from spawning grounds.

2. Try moderate- to slow-flowing water. This attracts fish since they do not have to fight strong current. Avoid very fast-flowing, white-water stretches of rivers and streams.

3. Concentrate on river and stream confluences. The mixing area of larger rivers and smaller streams is a superb location to find all species of fish and serves as a resting and feeding area.

4. Fish the tides. In coastal rivers and streams the fishing can vary greatly according to tidal movements. Work the mouth of these waters on an incoming tide as salmon and other sea-run species migrate into fresh water. Also try deep holes and runs as the tide recedes or upstream areas during or after mean high tide.

5. Locate spawning salmon. Resident species such as trout, char, grayling and others depend largely on salmon eggs to supplement their diet and are often found within a few feet of spawning fish.

6. Fish the low light hours. The best action is generally experienced in early morning and evening and on cloudy days. Trout, char, grayling, and other species feed most heavily then, and salmon and steelhead trout respond with more enthusiasm to anglers' offerings. Avoid bright sunshine.

LAKES AND PONDS

1. Fish according to the seasons. Late spring, fall, and early winter are probably the best times to fish lakes and ponds because of ideal water temperatures and high oxygen levels. Fish are often lethargic in mid-summer and late winter due to low oxygen levels and too warm or cold water temperatures.

2. Fish after break-up. Trout, char, grayling, and pike are often concentrated fairly close to shore in shallow water as they prepare to spawn, engage in a feeding frenzy, or migrate to summer feeding areas.

3. Try before and after freeze-up. All resident species are very active at this time, feeding heavily near shore in shallow water.

4. Concentrate on feeding areas. Fish thrive best in areas of the lake where there is an abundance of feed. Inlets and outlets, vegetated shorelines, and submerged structures are very productive places. During windy conditions, avoid protected areas and focus effort where wave activity is greatest.

5. Fish the low light hours. All species are most active during early morning and evening or on cloudy days, especially in summer. Avoid bright, mid-day sunshine as fish become shy and move into deep water or shaded areas.

SALT WATER

1. Fish the tides. Salmon and bottomfish tend to move close to shore or into shallow water on incoming and high tides. As the tide recedes, the fish move offshore into deeper or more open water. Boaters fishing for halibut, ling cod, rockfish, and other species do best right on the high or low (slack) tides.

2. Concentrate on feeding areas. Salmon, char, and bottomfish all seek out locations that attract baitfish, such as reefs, points, shoals, docks, and the like, including the mouths of rivers and streams.

3. Fish the low light hours. Salmon and char are most active in the early morning and evening, but all fish respond better to anglers' lures during cloudy or rainy weather. Bright sunshine tend to drive salmon deep and slows the bite.

4. Try stream mouths. The mix of salt and fresh water attracts a number of species, most notably salmon and char. Salmon often congregate here prior to moving upstream and char use the area as a feeding ground.

Additional Tips

1. Many of the lakes along the highways in Alaska offer good fishing but may be somewhat tricky to fish from shore due to very shallow, weedy shorelines. Such areas are best tackled by boat, canoe, inflatable raft, or float tube. This is also true of certain sloughs and large, calm rivers.

2. If you are serious about catching fish, it is a good idea to invest in some hip boots or chest waders. The boots or waders will allow you to move freely around the fishing area, through shallow channels or into deeper waters of a lake or river.

3. Polarized glasses are ideal when sight fishing for individual fish or schools of fish in clearwater streams. They also protect your eyes from the intense glare from the sun's rays reflecting off the surface of the water. And they serve as effective shields from flying lures with sharp hooks.

4. Some roadside waters attract considerable crowds. One way to counter the presence of other anglers is to hike up- or downstream a few hundred yards. Often, just a little distance from the highway or an access point makes a tremendous difference in the rewards you will reap - usually less company and more fish.

Hook-Up/Fighting Skills

The following is a short summary on the skill of hooking, playing, and landing fish. These points certainly apply to nearly any fish, but are particularly useful in battling salmon and large trout, char, and pike.

1. Keep hooks sharp. Dull hooks lose fish. Some fish, like king salmon, have very hard mouths and hooks must be sticky-sharp to penetrate and hold. Check the points after each hook-up or snag in the bottom to make sure they have not broken off or become dull in any way. Sharpen or change hooks as needed.

2. Keep the line tight. Avoid slack line. Sensitivity, is the key to making a successful hook-set. Oftentimes, fish will bite or "tug" very gently. If line is not tight, the strike will be missed and fish lost.

3. Set the hook hard. It does not matter how sharp a hook is if one does not set it properly - hard! If the lure stops or hesitates for a moment, set the hook by jerking the rod upwards. This will make sure the needle-sharp point penetrates and holds. Do not wait to set the hook until the fish takes out line or thrashes at the surface. By then it could be too late.

4. Play the fish carefully. After a solid hook-up, let the fish tire itself out before trying to bring it to shore. Let the rod and reel do most of the work. Keep the rod high so it can absorb the sharp and unpredictable movements of the fish. When the fish panics and runs, the drag of the reel should be loose enough to give out line, yet firm enough to provide resistance to the rampaging fish. Pump the rod with slow, even movements. Take in line with the reel when the fish begins to show signs of exhaustion, and let it take line back out when it wants to. Sooner or later the fish will give up and come to shore.

5. Let the fish come to the net. Do not thrash around in the water chasing the fish with the net. This will cause the fish to panic, and many times it will escape. The angler battling the fish must tire it out properly so it can be led to the net. Make sure the fish is netted head first. This will lessen the chances of the fish escaping the net, which is commonly the case when trying to net a fish from the side or tail first.

Catch And Release Techniques

The following steps should be heeded in releasing a fish unharmed back into the water.

Step 1. Get the fish within reach to provide easy access to the point where it is hooked or snagged. Do not drag the fish up on shore through harsh sand or mud. The skin of the fish is a vital and sensitive organ - try not to damage it, causing an infection.

Step 2. Hold the fish gently under the belly in shallow water if possible. If the fish struggles intensely to free itself, grasp it firmly around the base of the tail with one hand. It may at times be necessary to remove the fish from the water (if legal) in order to gain control of the situation. Never insert foreign objects into the gills of the fish, including fingers, sticks, etc. The gills are the breathing organ of the fish, and are extremely sensitive. The slightest touch can cause the gills to begin bleeding, which often results in death of the fish.

Step 3. Holding the fish steadily, grasp the shank of the hook(s) with a long-nosed plier or similar tool and remove the lure. Try to avoid using unnecessary force. If the fish is hooked deep in the throat (as is common when fishing with bait), avoid making an attempt to remove the lure. Cut the line or leader instead. Leaving the hook in the fish is actually safer than trying to remove it.

Step 4. Once the hook has been removed, or the line cut, transfer the fish into water that is deep enough for it to move freely. With one hand clasping the base of the tail and the other supporting the fish under the belly, move the fish gently back and forth repeatedly until its strength returns. Make sure the head of the fish is facing into the current, so that fresh water can circulate through the mouth and gills. Never toss or kick a fish back into the water. Such actions will only cause further shock and almost certain internal injuries, which in turn means a slow death for the fish.

Step 5. When the fish starts struggling to get free, carefully let go and watch it swim off. But make sure the fish really does have the strength to continue once on its own. A fish that turns belly-up will almost certainly die.

Other points to consider: Do not play fish to the point of complete exhaustion. Avoid bait if possible. Use single hooks, not treble. Bend down barb on hook or use barb-less hooks for easy release.

Top Lures

Although there are times when fish may strike at virtually any type of lure, it is recognized that some lures work consistently better than others. Most effective lure type for a particular species of fish is usually determined by predatory behavior of the fish. In other terms, a fish will respond better to something that seems to imitate its major food source. Additionally, fish also attack lures out of irritation or perhaps even sheer boredom.

The list below illustrates the more popular name brand lures on the market and the general category they fall under: Spoons, spinners, plugs, attractors, jigs, flies, and bait.

Hence, this information can be easily cross-referenced with that presented in the location chapters. However, keep in mind that this list is by no means complete and only meant as a simple guideline. Specific lure type and color may vary from watershed to watershed, time of day and season, and size of fish among other factors.

LURE / FLY / BAIT	King Salmon	Red Salmon	Pink Salmon	Chum Salmon	Silver Salmon	Landlocked Salmon	Steelhead Trout	Rainbow Trout	Lake Trout	Arctic Char	Dolly Varden	Sheefish	Arctic Grayling	Whitefish	Northern Pike	Burbot	Pacific Halibut	Rockfish
Spoons																		
Pixee	●		●	●	●			●	●	●	●	●			●			
Krocodile	●		●	●	●	●	●	●	●	●	●	●			●		●	●
Daredevle	●		●	●	●			●	●	●	●	●			●			
HotRod	●		●	●	●			●	●	●	●	●			●		●	●
Syclops	●		●	●	●		●	●	●	●	●	●			●		●	●
Trixee	●		●	●				●			●				●			
Tor-P-Do	●		●	●	●			●	●	●	●				●			
Super Duper	●		●	●	●	●	●	●	●	●	●	●			●	●		
Little Cleo	●		●	●	●	●	●	●	●	●	●	●			●	●		
Fiord Spoon	●		●	●	●	●	●	●	●	●	●	●			●	●	●	●
Spinners																		
Vibrax	●		●	●	●	●	●	●	●	●	●	●			●	●		
Aglia	●		●	●	●		●	●	●	●	●	●		●				
Black Fury	●	●	●	●	●	●	●	●			●	●			●	●		
Giant Killer	●																	
Panther Martin	●		●	●	●	●	●	●	●	●	●	●			●	●		
Bolo	●		●	●	●			●	●	●	●	●			●	●		
Rooster Tail	●	●	●	●	●	●	●	●		●	●	●			●	●		
Bang Tail	●	●	●	●	●			●	●	●	●	●			●	●		
Skagit Special	●																	
Tee Spoon	●		●	●							●			●				
Monti	●		●	●	●		●	●	●	●	●	●			●	●		
Plugs																		
Kwikfish	●		●	●	●	●	●	●	●	●	●	●			●			
Tadpolly	●		●	●	●			●	●	●	●	●			●			
Rapala	●		●	●	●	●	●	●	●	●	●	●			●	●		
Flatfish	●		●	●	●	●	●	●	●	●	●	●			●	●		
Wiggle Wart	●		●	●	●			●	●	●	●	●	●		●	●		
Hot Shot	●		●	●	●			●	●	●	●	●			●	●		
J-Plug	●										●					●		
Attractors																		
Spin-N-Glo	●		●	●	●			●	●			●	●		●	●		
Okie Drifter	●				●			●	●			●	●		●			
Lil' Corkie	●				●			●	●			●	●		●	●		
Cheater	●		●	●	●			●	●			●	●		●			
Jigs																		
Krocodile	●				●	●		●	●	●	●					●	●	●
Diamond Jig																	●	●
Yo-Ho-Ho																	●	●
Buzz Bomb	●		●		●			●	●	●	●						●	●
Kastmaster	●		●	●	●		●	●	●	●	●	●	●		●	●	●	●
Swedish Pimple	●		●	●	●	●	●	●	●	●	●	●	●		●	●	●	●
Sebastes Jig																	●	●

LURE / FLY / BAIT	KING SALMON	RED SALMON	PINK SALMON	CHUM SALMON	SILVER SALMON	LANDLOCKED SALMON	STEELHEAD TROUT	RAINBOW TROUT	LAKE TROUT	ARCTIC CHAR	DOLLY VARDEN	SHEEFISH	WHITEFISH	ARCTIC GRAYLING	NORTHERN PIKE	BURBOT	PACIFIC HALIBUT	ROCKFISH
Vi-Ki																	•	•
NeedleFish							•	•	•	•	•	•			•	•		
Nordic	•		•		•			•	•	•	•					•	•	•
Flies																		
Coho (Russian River Fly)	•	•	•	•	•					•	•	•			•			
Sockeye Willie		•	•	•	•			•		•	•							
Outrageous	•		•	•	•			•		•	•	•			•			
Maker's Rogue	•			•	•			•		•	•							
Herring Fly	•		•	•	•			•	•	•	•	•			•			
Comet	•	•	•	•	•			•		•	•	•						
Flash Fly	•	•	•	•	•		•	•	•	•	•	•			•			•
Muddler Minnow	•			•	•			•	•	•	•	•		•	•			
Black Fury								•		•	•				•			
Green Butt Skunk							•	•		•	•	•						
Woolly Bugger	•		•		•			•	•	•	•	•			•			•
Egg Sucking Leech	•		•	•	•		•	•	•	•	•	•		•	•			
Polar Shrimp	•	•	•	•	•		•	•	•	•	•	•						
Two-Egg Sperm Fly	•	•		•	•		•	•		•	•	•			•			
Bunny Fly	•			•	•		•	•	•	•	•	•				•		
Alaskabou	•			•	•			•	•	•	•	•			•			
Fat Freddy	•	•		•	•			•		•	•	•						
Glo Bug	•	•			•		•	•		•	•	•			•			
Iliamna Pinkie							•	•		•	•			•	•			
Mouse					•			•	•	•	•	•				•		
Elk Hair Caddis					•			•		•	•				•			
Black Gnat								•						•	•			
Adams								•		•	•			•	•			
Midge						•		•		•	•			•	•			
Gold Ribbed Hare's Ear							•	•		•	•			•	•			
Lake Leech								•		•	•	•			•			
Bait																		
Salmon Roe Cluster	•	•		•	•			•		•	•			•	•			
Single Salmon Egg						•		•		•	•			•	•			
Herring	•		•	•	•			•	•	•	•	•				•	•	•
Shrimp	•							•		•	•			•	•	•	•	•
Smelt									•				•				•	•
Whitefish									•				•				•	•
Worm								•			•	•		•	•			•
Squid	•				•												•	•
Octopus	•																•	•

Lure Tips

1. Keep lure close to or near the bottom. Species such as salmon and large trout and char, whitefish, burbot, and others commonly "hug" the bottom and will seldom move much of a distance to intercept a lure floating on or near the surface.

2. Try high-visibility lures in glacially-fed waters. Lures in fluorescent red, orange, and chartreuse work best. Sometimes a touch of silver combination works well. Water color such as greenish-grey or greenish-blue produce fish. Avoid dark brown or gray (milky) waters. Use bait or bait-scented lures if legal and fish lures slowly or stationary.

3. Use flashy or colorful lures in murky conditions. Visibility is important and even more so in glacial waters or during low light conditions such as rain, heavy clouds, and between dusk and dawn. Deep drainages often command bright lures. Main colors: Red, orange, chartreuse, pink, yellow, silver.

4. Use dark or neutral lures in bright conditions. Too much flash can spook fish, especially in bright sunshine and in crystal clear water. Also, fish respond better to less colorful lures in shallow drainages and when angler pressure is high. Main colors: Green, brown, black, copper, purple, blue, silver.

5. Match lure size and color with mood of fish. If fish appear spooked, try small and/or neutral-colored lures; if aggressive, use something larger and more colorful.

6. Match lure selection with conditions. When salmon smolt migrate towards the sea, try small, shiny lures in blue or green mixed with silver to catch trout, char, grayling, and other predatory species. Select flies to imitate type of insects in the area. Try flesh- and egg-imitation lures around spawning salmon to attract opportunistic fish.

Section Three .... *Roadside Locations*

Alaska Highway

CHAPTER
3

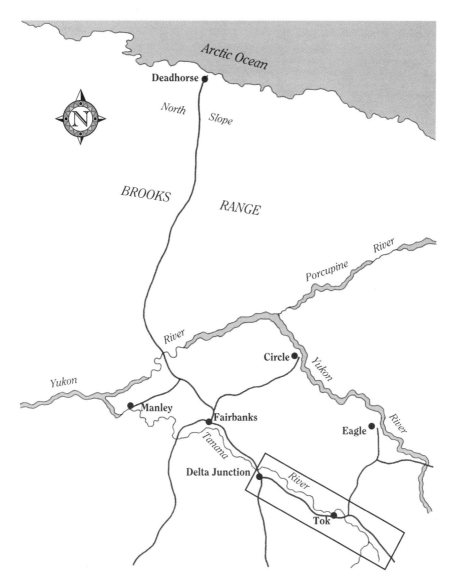

Area Covered: U.S./Canada Border to Delta Junction; 200 miles
Regulatory Units: (A) Chisana River Drainage; (B) Tanana River Drainage
Number of Locations: 25

Fishing the Alaska Highway

The Alaska Highway more or less parallels two major glacial rivers, the Chisana and Tanana, and provides good access to several lakes and streams in the region. The more common types of sport fish in these waters include trout, grayling, pike, and burbot, as well as a smaller population of stunted char. Lake fishing is considered more productive as large numbers of rainbow trout are stocked in early summer, but the annual spring spawning runs of grayling into area streams are certainly also worth a try. Salmon, although present in the mainstem of Chisana and Tanana rivers, are scarce or absent in most roadside streams, except in the Delta Clearwater River where heavy runs of silver salmon occur. Angler success is fair to good in both lakes and streams.

Angling pressure is typically very light throughout the region, yet the Delta Clearwater River does receive a fair amount of attention during the fall salmon runs.

Recommended Hot Spots: Delta Clearwater River; Island, Hidden, Robertson #2, Jan, Lisa, Craig, Big Donna, and Little Donna lakes.

Content

QUICK REFERENCE

 Road Condition   **P** Parking Area   Camp Sites   Hiking Trails   Boat Launch   Handicap Access   Fishing Pressure

- ■ - Good to Highly developed/conditions, intense pressure
- ● - Fair to Moderately developed/conditions, moderate pressure
- ◆ - Poor to marginally developed/conditions, limited pressure
- ✕ - Prohibited

#	LOCATION	MILE POST	🚗	**P**	⛰	🚶	🛥	♿	🎣	PAGE
1.	Scottie Creek	1223.4	■	◆					◆	46
2.	Desper Creek	1225.7	■	●					◆	46
3.	Island Lake	1230.2	■	◆		●			◆	46
4.	Hidden Lake	1237.0	■	●		●			◆	47
5.	Gardiner Creek	1246.6	■	●					◆	47
6.	Deadman Lake	1249.4	●	●	■		●	●	◆	47
7.	Yarger Lake	1256.7	●	●	●			●	◆	47
8.	Eliza Lake									
	Access A	1258.0	■	◆		●			◆	47
	Access B	1258.8	●	◆		◆			◆	47
9.	Moose Creek									
	Access A	1264.0	●	◆			◆		◆	47
	Access B	1264.0	●	◆			◆		◆	47

Map: Unit A: Chisana River Drainage
Unit B: Tanana River Drainage

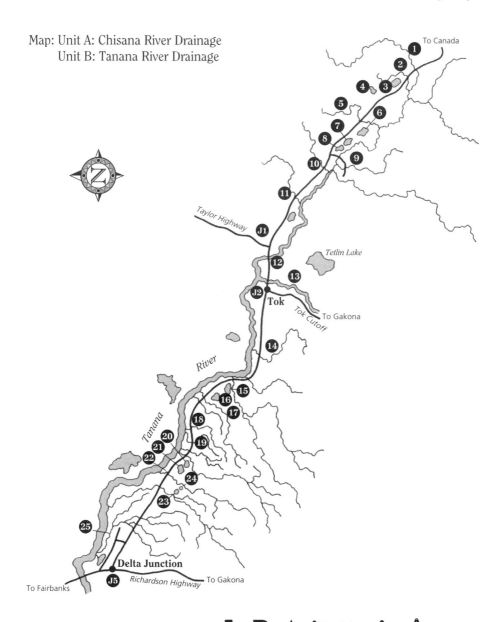

#	LOCATION	MILE POST	🚐	**P**	Λ	🏃	🛶	♿	ᛢ	PAGE
10.	Beaver Creek	1268.1	■	◆					◆	47
11.	Bitters Creek	1280.3	■	◆					◆	48
J1.	Taylor Hwy.	1301.7								
12.	Tanana River (Upper)	1303.4	■	●			●		◆	48
13.	Tok River (Lower)	1309.4	■	●	■				◆	48
J2.	Tok Cutoff	1314.2								
14.	Yerrick Creek	1333.6	■	●					◆	48
15.	Robertson #2 Lake	1348.1	●	●		●			◆	48

#	LOCATION	MILE POST	🚗	P	⛺	🥾	🛶	♿	🚰	PAGE
16.	Jan Lake	1353.6	●	●				●	◆	48
17.	Bear Creek	1357.3	■	●					◆	48
18.	Berry Creek	1371.4	■	■					◆	49
19.	Sears Creek	1374.5	■	●					◆	49
20.	Lisa Lake	1381.0	●	●		●			◆	49
21.	Craig Lake	1383.7	●	◆		●			◆	49
22.	Little Gerstle River	1388.4	■	◆					◆	49
23.	Big Donna Lake	1391.9	■	●		●			◆	49
24.	Little Donna Lake	1391.9	■	●		●			◆	49
25.	Delta Clearwater River	1414.9	■	●	■		●		●	49
J3.	Richardson Hwy.	1422.0								

ALASKA HIGHWAY LOCATIONS

Unit A: Chisana River Drainage

Includes all roadside waters flowing into and surrounding Chisana River.

UNIT REGULATIONS:

* Northern pike fishing prohibited: All waters, April 1 – May 31.

UNIT TIMING:

FISH ▽	JAN	FEB	MAR	APR	MAY	JUN	JUL	AUG	SEP	OCT	NOV	DEC
CS*												
RT												
AG												
WF												
NP												
BB												

Note: Timing shown for salmon indicates fish in all stages of maturity.

1. Scottie Creek

Access: MP 1223.4; highway crosses stream.
Fishing: Good runs of grayling and burbot early and late in the season.
Arctic Grayling / good / May, mid-September – mid-October / 7-12 in. / spinners, flies.
Northern Pike / poor-fair / mid-June – late August / 2-4 lbs. / spoons, plugs, bait.
Burbot / fair-good / April, mid-September – mid-November / 2-4 lbs. / bait.

2. Desper Creek

Access: MP 1225.7; highway crosses stream.
Fishing: Limited opportunities for mainly small pike in summer.
Northern Pike / poor-fair / mid-June – late August / 2-4 lbs. / spoons, plugs, bait.

3. Island Lake

Access: MP 1230.2; cat trail leads 0.5 mile NE to lake.
Fishing: Lake supports a decent population of pike. Use canoe/float tube.
Northern Pike / good / June, August – September / 2-5 lbs. / spoons, plugs, bait.

4. Hidden Lake

Access: MP 1237.0; trail leads 0.8 mile S to lake.
Fishing: Lake is stocked with trout. Use canoe/float tube.
Rainbow Trout / good / June, September – December / 7-16 in. / spoons, flies, bait.

5. Gardiner Creek

Access: MP 1246.6; highway crosses stream.
Fishing: Seasonal runs of grayling, opportunity for a few pike.
Arctic Grayling / fair-good / May, September / 7-12 in. / spinners, flies.
Northern Pike / poor-fair / mid-June – late August / 2-4 lbs. / spoons, plugs, bait.

6. Deadman Lake

Access: MP 1249.4; S on gravel road 1.2 mile to lake.
Fishing: Lake supports a decent population of pike and burbot. Use canoe/float tube.
Northern Pike / fair-good / June, August – September / 2-5 lbs. / spoons, plugs, bait.
Burbot / fair / March – April, September – December / 2-4 lbs. / bait.

7. Yarger Lake

Access: MP 1256.7; SW on gravel road 0.2 mile to lake.
Fishing: Lake supports a decent population of pike. Use canoe/float tube.
Nortern Pike / fair - good / June, August – September / 2-5 lbs. / spoons, plugs, bait.

8. Eliza Lake

Access A: MP 1258.0; trail leads 0.25 mile W to lake.
Access B: MP 1258.8; W on rough dirt road 0.2 mile, park and hike 100 yards to lake.
Fishing: Lake supports a decent population of pike. Use canoe/float tube.
Northern Pike / fair - good / June, August – September / 2-5 lbs. / spoons, plugs, bait.

9. Moose Creek

Access A: MP 1264.0; SW on gravel road towards town of Northway, 2.8 miles to confluence of Moose Creek and Fish Camp Creek on right.
Access B: MP 1264.0; SW on gravel road towards town of Northway, 5.3 miles to stream crossing.
Fishing: Slow-flowing tannic stream containing moderate numbers of pike and burbot.
Northern Pike / fair / mid-June – late August / 2-5 lbs. / spoons, plugs, bait.
Burbot / fair / May, mid-September – mid-October / 2-4 lbs. / bait.

10. Beaver Creek

Access: MP 1268.1; highway crosses stream.
Fishing: Small clearwater stream containing moderate numbers of pike and burbot.
Arctic Grayling / fair-good / mid-May – mid-September / 7-12 in. / spinners, flies.

Unit B: Tanana River Drainage

Includes all roadside waters flowing into and surrounding Tanana River.

UNIT REGULATIONS:

* Northern pike fishing prohibited: All waters, April 1 – May 31.

UNIT TIMING:

FISH ▽	JAN	FEB	MAR	APR	MAY	JUN	JUL	AUG	SEP	OCT	NOV	DEC
KS*												
CS*												
SS*												
RT												
DV												
AG												
WF												
NP												
BB												

Note: Timing shown for salmon indicates fish in all stages of maturity.

11. Bitters Creek

Access: MP 1280.3; highway crosses stream.
Fishing: Small clearwater stream containing population of grayling. Bigger fish in spring.
Arctic Grayling / fair-good / mid-May – mid-September / 7-12 in. / spinners, flies.

12. Tanana River (Upper)

Access: MP 1303.4; highway crosses river.
Fishing: Primarily a late winter/early spring fishery for migrating grayling and burbot.
Arctic Grayling / fair / March – April, November / 7-14 in. / spinners.
Burbot / fair-good / March – April, November – December / 3-10 lbs. / bait.

13. Tok River (Lower)

Access: MP 1309.4; highway crosses river.
Fishing: Late season opportunity for out-migrating grayling when water clears.
Arctic Grayling / fair / mid-September – late October / 7-14 in. / spinners, flies.

14. Yerrick Creek

Access: MP 1333.6; highway crosses stream.
Fishing: Small clearwater stream containing grayling and a few smal char.
Dolly Varden / poor-fair / mid-July – mid-September / 7-12 in. / flies, bait.
Arctic Grayling / fair-good / early June – mid-September / 7-12 in. / spinners, flies.

15. Robertson #2 Lake

Access: MP 1348.1; W on Jan Lake Rd. 0.2 mile to parking area. Trail leads 0.25 mile to lake.
Fishing: Lake is stocked with trout. Use canoe/float tube.
Rainbow Trout / good / June, September – December / 7-16 in. / spoons, flies, bait.

16. Jan Lake

Access: MP 1353.6; W on Jan Lake Rd. 0.5 mile to lake.
Fishing: Lake is stocked with trout. Popular ice fishing lake. Use canoe/float tube.
Rainbow Trout / good / June, September – December / 7-18 in. / spoons, flies, bait.

17. Bear Creek

Access: MP 1357.3; highway crosses stream.
Fishing: Small clearwater stream containing grayling and a few small char.

Dolly Varden / poor-fair / mid-July – mid-September / 7-12 in. / flies, bait.
Arctic Grayling / fair-good / mid-May – mid-September / 7-12 in. / spinners, flies.

18. Berry Creek
Access: MP 1371.4; highway crosses stream.
Fishing: Small clearwater stream containing grayling and a few small char.
Dolly Varden / poor-fair / mid-July – mid-September / 7-12 in. / flies, bait.
Arctic Grayling / fair-good / mid-May – mid-September / 7-12 in. / spinners, flies.

19. Sears Creek
Access: MP 1374.5; highway crosses stream.
Fishing: Small clearwater stream containing population of grayling. Bigger fish in spring.
Arctic Grayling / fair-good / mid-May – mid-September / 7-12 in. / spinners, flies.

20. Lisa Lake
Access: MP 1381.0; turnout. Trail leads 0.7 mile SW to lake.
Fishing: Lake is stocked with trout. Popular ice fishing lake. Use canoe/float tube.
Rainbow Trout / good / June, September – December / 7-18 in. / spoons, flies, bait.

21. Craig Lake
Access: MP 1383.7; SW on Craig Lake Rd. 1.1 mile to sign on right. Trail leads 0.25 mile to lake.
Fishing: Lake is stocked with trout. Popular ice fishing lake. Use canoe/float tube.
Rainbow Trout / good / June, September / 7-18 in. / spoons, spinners, flies.

22. Little Gerstle River
Access: MP 1388.4; highway crosses river.
Fishing: Glacial stream; limited grayling opportunities in fall when water clears.
Arctic Grayling / poor-fair / early September – mid-October / 7-12 in. / spinners, flies.

23. Big Donna Lake
Access: MP 1391.8; trail leads 3.5 miles S to lake.
Fishing: Lake is stocked with trout. Some big fish present. Use canoe/float tube.
Rainbow Trout / good / June, September – December / 7-18 in. / spoons, flies, bait.

24. Little Donna Lake
Access: MP 1391.8; trail leads 4.5 miles S to lake (1 mile beyond Donna Lake).
Fishing: Lake is stocked with trout. Popular ice fishing lake. Use canoe/float tube.
Ranbow Trout / good / June, September – December / 7-18 in. / spoons, flies, bait.

25. Delta Clearwater River (Middle)
Access: MP 1414.9; NE on Clearwater Rd. 5.3 miles to a "T," right on Remington Rd. 2.8 miles to gravel road on left next to a sign, short distance to river.
Fishing: This spring-fed river enjoys the largest run of silver salmon in the Interior, as well as a healthy population of grayling, some which may reach trophy proportions. Good action from shore, but a boat is necessary to reach river mouth or headwaters.
Silver Salmon / excellent / 6-10 lbs. (15 lbs.) / spoons, spinners, flies.
Arctic Grayling / good / 8-14 in. (20 in.) / spinners, flies.
(continues on next page)

N0. 25 - Delta Clearwater River continued.

FISH ▽	JAN	FEB	MAR	APR	MAY	JUN	JUL	AUG	SEP	OCT	NOV	DEC
SS*												
AG												

*Note: Timing shown for salmon indicates fish in all stages of maturity.

Other Locations

Unit B: Tanana River Drainage:

Moon Lake - MP 1331.9; NP,(AG) Robertson River - MP 1347.5; AG,(WF) Chief Creek - MP 1358.7; DV,AG Dry Creek - MP 1378.0; DV,AG Johnson River - MP 1380.5; DV,AG,(WF) Gerstle River - MP 1392.7; AG,(WF)

LOCATION & SPECIES APPENDIX

- ● - Wild/Native fish, fishable numbers.
- ◆ - Present in small numbers and/or only occasionally caught.
- ▲ - Stocked/Hatchery fish, fishable numbers.
- ■ - Mix of Wild and Hatchery fish, fishable numbers.
- ✕ - Indicated species present but currently protected by law (PROHIBITED).

#	LOCATION	KING SALMON	RED SALMON	PINK SALMON	CHUM SALMON	SILVER SALMON	LANDLOCKED SALMON	KOKANEE	STEELHEAD TROUT	RAINBOW TROUT	LAKE TROUT	ARCTIC CHAR	DOLLY VARDEN	SHEEFISH	ARCTIC GRAYLING	WHITEFISH	NORTHERN PIKE	BURBOT	PACIFIC HALIBUT	LING COD	ROCKFISH
1.	Scottie Creek														●	◆	●	●			
2.	Desper Creek														◆	◆	●				
3.	Island Lake																●				
4.	Hidden Lake									▲											
5.	Gardiner Creek														●	◆	●				
6.	Deadman Lake																●	●			
7.	Yarger Lake															◆	●	◆			
8.	Eliza Lake															◆	●	◆			
9.	Moose Creek														◆	◆	●	●			
10.	Beaver Creek														●	◆					
11.	Bitters Creek														●	◆	◆				
12.	Tanana River (upper)				◆	◆							◆	◆	●	◆	◆	●			
13.	Tok River (lower)												◆		●	◆	◆	◆			
14.	Yerrick Creek												●		●	◆	◆				
15.	Robertson #2 Lake									▲											
16.	Jan Lake							▲		▲											
17.	Bear Creek												●		●						
18.	Berry Creek												●		●	◆					
19.	Sears Creek												◆		●						
20.	Lisa Lake									▲											
21.	Craig Lake									▲											
22.	Little Gerstle River														●	◆					
23.	Big Donna Lake									▲											
24.	Little Donna Lake									▲											
25.	Delta Clearwater River	◆			◆	●									●	◆	◆	◆			

Anchorage Area

CHAPTER 4

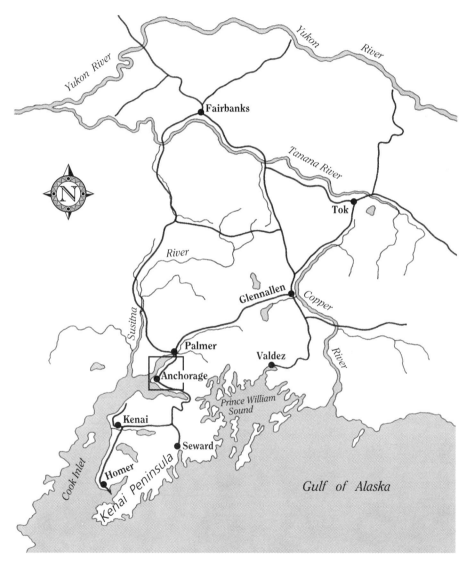

Area Covered: Greater Anchorage area roads and highways, including military bases, Eagle River, and Chugiak
Regulatory Units: (A) Knik Arm Drainages; (B) Anchorage City Drainages
Number of Locations: 36

FISHING THE ANCHORAGE AREA

The Anchorage Area roads and highways provide excellent access to lakes and streams within the city of Anchorage, the communities of Eagle River and Birchwood, and on the military installations of Elmendorf Air Force Base and Fort Richardson. Although permits are required to access the bases, it is a simple process which puts anglers within reach of lakes and ponds stocked with land-locked salmon, trout, char, and grayling. These are also the kinds of fish stocked in Anchorage and the communities north of the city. Runs of salmon and native char are available in rivers and streams, Campbell and Ship creeks being the most productive locations. Campbell supports a good return of mixed wild and hatchery silver salmon, while Ship has runs of primarily stocked king and silver salmon. Angler success is good to excellent in both lakes and streams.

Angling pressure is light to moderate in most locations, but can be heavy in the summer salmon fisheries of Campbell and Ship creeks. Some increased effort is also given on a few of the more popular stocked lakes after break-up and before and after freeze-up.

Recommended Hot Spots: Ship and Campbell creeks; Jewel, Sand, DeLong, Campbell Point, Upper Sixmile, Cheney, Otter, Clunie, Beach, and Mirror lakes.

Content   Pages

QUICK REFERENCE

🚗 Road Condition   **P** Parking Area   **A** Camp Sites   🚶 Hiking Trails   🛶 Boat Launch   ♿ Handicap Access   🎣 Fishing Pressure

■ - Good to Highly developed/conditions, intense pressure
● - Fair to Moderately developed/conditions, moderate pressure
◆ - Poor to marginally developed/conditions, limited pressure
✕ - Prohibited

#	LOCATION	MILE POST	🚗	P	A	🚶	🛶	♿	🎣	PAGE
	Elmendorf AFB									
1.	Upper Sixmile Lake	(Base)	●	◆				■	●	56
2.	Sixmile Creek / Knik Arm	(Base)	◆	●				■		56
3.	Fish Lake	(Base)	●	◆				◆	◆	57

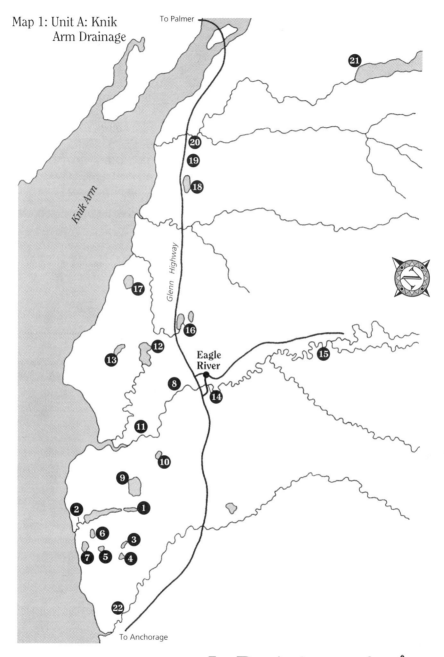

Map 1: Unit A: Knik Arm Drainage

#	LOCATION	MILE POST	🚕	**P**	⛺	🥾	🛶	♿	🎣	PAGE
4.	Triangle Lake	(Base)	●	●				●	◆	57
5.	Hillberg Lake	(Base)	●	●	◆			◆	◆	57
6.	Green Lake	(Base)	●	●	◆			●	◆	57
7.	Spring Lake	(Base)	●	●		●			◆	57
8.	Eagle River (Lower)	(Base)	●	●				●	◆	57

Map 2: Unit B: Anchorage City Drainages

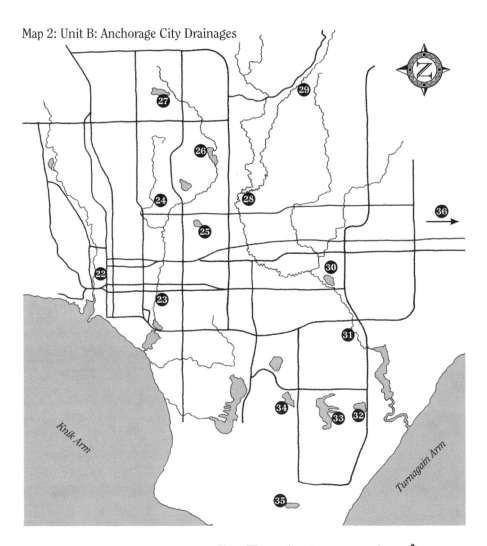

#	LOCATION	MILE POST	🚐	P	⛺	🥾	⛵	♿	⚓	PAGE
	Fort Richardson									
9.	Otter Lake	(Base)								
	Access A		●	●	◆			●	●	58
	Access B		●	■	●			■	●	58
10.	Gwen Lake	(Base)								
	Access A		●	●				■	◆	58
	Access B		●	●	●			●	◆	58
11.	Eagle River (Lower)	(Base)								
	Access A		●	●			●	●	◆	58
	Access B		●	●					◆	58
12.	Clunie Lake	(Base)	●	●	◆			■	●	58
13.	Waldon Lake	(Base)	●	●	◆			■	◆	58

#	LOCATION	MILE POST	🚗	P	⛺	🚶	🛥	♿	⚓	PAGE
	Eagle River-Chugiak									
14.	Eagle River (Middle)									
	Access A	11.6	●	●		●			◆	59
	Access B	11.6	●	■	■		●	●	◆	59
15.	North Fork Eagle River	15.3	■	■	◆	■		◆	◆	59
16.	Lower Fire Lake	15.3	●	◆				●	●	59
17.	Beach Lake	20.9	●	■	◆		●	●	◆	59
18.	Mirror (Bear) Lake	23.6	■	■	◆		◆	●	●	59
19.	Edmonds Lake	23.6	●	◆				◆	◆	60
20.	Eklutna River									
	Access A	25.7	■	◆					◆	60
	Access B	26.3	■	■					◆	60
21.	Eklutna Lake	26.3	●	■	■			◆	◆	60
	Anchorage City									
22.	Ship Creek (Lower)	(Downtown)	■	■	◆		■	●	■	61
23.	Chester Creek (Lower)	(NW Anch.)								
	Access A		■	■	✕			●	◆	61
	Access B		■	■	✕			●	◆	61
	Access C		■	■	✕			◆	◆	61
24.	Chester Creek (Upper)	(NE Anch.)	●	●		■			◆	62
25.	Otis Lake	(NE Anch.)	■	◆	✕	●		◆	◆	62
26.	University (APU) Lake	(NE Anch.)	■	■	✕	●			◆	62
27.	Cheney Lake	(NE Anch.)	■	■	✕			■	●	62
28.	Campbell Creek (Middle)	(E Anch.)								
	Access A		■	■	✕			■	◆	62
	Access B		■	●	✕			■	●	62
29.	South Fork Campbell Creek	(E Anch.)								
	Access A		●	●	◆	●			◆	63
	Access B		●	●	◆	●			◆	63
30.	Taku-Campbell Lake	(W Anch.)	■	■	✕			●	◆	63
31.	Campbell Creek (Lower)	(W Anch.)								
	Access A		●	■	✕	■			◆	63
	Access B		■	◆					◆	63
	Access C		■	◆					◆	63
	Access D		■	●		■		●	◆	63
	Access E		■	■	◆			■	●	63
32.	Jewel Lake	(W Anch.)								
	Access A		●	■	✕			■	◆	64
	Access B		■	■	✕			■	●	64
33.	Sand Lake	(W Anch.)								
	Access A		●	◆		■			◆	64
	Access B		●	●					●	64
34.	DeLong Lake	(W Anch.)	■	■	✕			■	●	64
35.	Campbell Point Lake	(W Anch.)	●	■	✕			■	●	64
36.	North Fork Rabbit Creek	(S Anch.)	■	●	✕				◆	65

ANCHORAGE AREA LOCATIONS

Unit A: Knik Arm Drainages

Includes all roadside waters in the greater Anchorage area north of town draining into and surrounding Knik Arm.

UNIT REGULATIONS:

King salmon fishing prohibited: All waters (except Eagle River), year-round.

UNIT TIMING:

FISH ▽	JAN	FEB	MAR	APR	MAY	JUN	JUL	AUG	SEP	OCT	NOV	DEC
KS												
RS												
PS												
CS												
SS												
KO												
LS												
RT												
AC												
DV												
AG												
NP												

Elmendorf AFB

Area locations on military base. Directions originate from main gate at the west end of Boniface Parkway/beginning of Davis Highway, MP 3.0 Glenn Highway. **Note:** A permit is required to fish on base. Public must check in at Elmendorf AFB main gate prior to entering area. Call 552-2436 for information.

1. Upper Sixmile Lake

Access: Mile 1.5 Davis Hwy., left at "Y" short distance to another "Y," right on Spur Rd. 1.1 mile, right on Burns Rd. 0.3 mile, right on Hubble Rd. 0.8 mile to lake on right.
Fishing: Lake is stocked with trout. Use canoe/float tube, cast from shore.
Rainbow Trout / good / May, September – December / 7-16 in. / spinners, flies, bait.
Dolly Varden / poor / August – October / 7-12 in. / spinners, flies, bait.

2. Sixmile Creek / Knik Arm Confluence

Access: Mile 1.5 Davis Hwy., left at "Y" short distance to another "Y," right on Spur Rd. 1.1 mile, right on Burns Rd. 0.3 mile, right on Hubble Rd. 2.1 miles, left on Loop Rd. 1.4 mile, right short distance to rough dirt access road 0.5 mile to stream mouth.
Fishing: Limited salmon and sea-run char opportunities in summer off mouth of creek. Closed to fishing in stream proper — look for marked boundary.
Red Salmon / fair / mid-, late July / 4-7 lbs. / spoons, spinners, bait.
Pink Salmon / poor-fair / late July / 2-4 lbs. / spoons, spinners.
Silver Salmon / poor / mid-, late August / 5-10 lbs. / spoons, spinners, bait.
Dolly Varden / fair / early June – mid-July / 7-15 in. / spoons, spinners, bait.

3. Fish Lake

Access: Mile 1.5 Davis Hwy., left at "Y" short distance to another "Y," right on Spur Rd. 1.1 mile, right on Burns Rd. 0.3 mile, left on Ridge Rd. 0.3 mile, right on gravel road 0.7 mile, left on access road 0.1 mile to parking area and lake.

Fishing: Lake is stocked with trout. Use canoe/float tube, cast from shore.

Rainbow Trout / good / May, September – December / 7-16 in. / spinners, flies, bait.

4. Triangle Lake

Access: Mile 1.5 Davis Hwy., left at "Y" short distance to another "Y," right on Spur Rd. 1.1 mile, right on Burns Rd. 0.3 mile, left on Ridge Rd. 0.9 mile, right on access road short distance to lake.

Fishing: Lake is stocked with trout. Use canoe/float tube, cast from shore.

Rainbow Trout / good / May, September – December / 7-16 in. / spinners, flies, bait.

5. Hillberg Lake

Access: Mile 0.8 Davis Hwy., left on 2nd St. 2.4 miles, right on Plum St. 1.8 mile, left on Loop Rd. 1.8 mile, right on access road 0.4 mile to lake.

Fishing: Lake is stocked with salmon and trout. Use canoe/float tube, cast from shore.

Landlocked Salmon / excellent / June – March / 7-12 in. / spinners, jigs, flies, bait.

Rainbow Trout / good / May, September – December / 7-16 in. / spoons, flies, bait.

6. Green Lake

Access: Mile 0.8 Davis Hwy., left on 2nd St. 2.4 miles, right on Plum St. 1.8 mile, left on Loop Rd. 2.1 miles, left on access road 0.1 mile to lake.

Fishing: Lake is stocked with salmon and trout. Use canoe/float tube, cast from shore.

Landlocked Salmon / excellent / June – March / 7-12 in. / jigs, bait.

Rainbow Trout / good / May, September – December / 7-16 in. / spinners, flies, bait.

7. Spring Lake

Access: Mile 0.8 Davis Hwy., left on 2nd St. 2.4 miles, right on Plum St. 1.8 mile, left on Loop Rd. 2.4 miles, left on access road 0.4 mile to parking area on right. Trail leads NE 150 yards to lake.

Fishing: Lake is stocked with trout. Use canoe/float tube, cast from shore.

Rainbow Trout / good / May, September – December / 7-16 in. / spinners, flies, bait.

Fort Richardson

Area locations on military base west and east of Glenn Highway. Mileposts indicated are for Glenn Highway. **Note:** A permit is required to fish on base. Public must check in at Ft. Richardson main gate at MP 7.5 prior to entering area. Call 384-0431 for information.

8. Eagle River (Lower)

Access: MP 7.5; W on D st. from main gate 0.7 mile, right on 6th Ave. 0.5 mile, right on Davis Hwy. 1.8 mile, left on dirt road 3.6 miles to river crossing.

Fishing: Glacial drainage with limited opportunities for salmon and char. Use bait.

King Salmon / poor / mid-June / 15-30 lbs. / spinners, attractors, bait.

(continues on next page)

N0. 8- Eagle River continued.

Silver Salmon / poor-fair / mid-, late August / 5-10 lbs. / attractors, bait.
Dolly Varden / fair / mid-July – late August / 7-15 in. / attractors, bait.

9. Otter Lake
Access A: MP 7.5; W on D St. from main gate 1.9 mile to a "Y," right on Loop Rd. 2.0 miles to a "Y," left fork 0.3 mile, left on Otter Lake Rd. 0.8 mile, left on dirt road short distance to lake.
Access B: From access point above, continue on Otter Lake Rd. 0.2 mile, road parallels lake next 0.3 mile.
Fishing: Lake is stocked with trout. Fish to eight pounds present. Popular location.
Rainbow Trout / good / May, September – December / 8-18 in. / spinners, flies, bait.

10. Gwen Lake
Access A: MP 7.5; W on D St. from main gate 1.9 mile to a "Y," right on Loop Rd. 2.0 miles to a "Y," left fork 0.3 mile, straight on Route Bravo 1.3 mile, right on gravel road short distance to access road on right leading to lake.
Access B: From access point above, continue 0.1 mile, right on dirt road 0.1 mile to lake.
Fishing: Lake is stocked with trout but suffers winterkill in some years.
Rainbow Trout / good / May, Sept. – Dec. / 7-16 in. / spinners, flies, bait.

11. Eagle River (Lower)
Access A: MP 7.5; W on D st. from main gate 1.9 mile to a "Y," right on Loop Rd. 2.0 miles to a "Y," left fork 0.3 mile, straight on Route Bravo 1.7 mile, right on access road 0.3 mile to river.
Access B: From above access point, continue on Route Bravo 0.2 mile to river crossing.
Fishing: Glacial drainage with limited opportunities for salmon and char. Use bait.
Silver Salmon / poor / mid-, late August / 5-10 lbs. / attractors, bait.
Dolly Varden / fair / early July – early August / 7-15 in. / bait.

12. Clunie Lake
Access: MP 7.5; W on D st. from main gate 1.9 mile to a "Y," right on Loop Rd. 2.0 miles to a "Y," left fork 0.3 mile, straight on Route Bravo 4.8 miles, right 3.8 miles, right on access road 0.1 mile to lake.
Fishing: Lake is stocked with landlocked salmon and trout. Big rainbows possible. Great spot for ice fishing and one of the more productive lakes in the area.
Landlocked Salmon / excellent / June – March / 7-12 in. / spinners, jigs, flies, bait.
Rainbow Trout / good / May, September – December / 7-16 in. / spinnerss, flies, bait.
Lake Trout / poor / May, September – October / 2-5 lbs. / spoons, jigs, bait.
Arctic Char / poor / May, September – January / 18-24 in. / spoons, jigs, bait.

13. Waldon Lake
Access: MP 7.5; W on D st. from main gate 1.9 mile to a "Y," right on Loop Rd. 2.0 miles to a "Y," left fork 0.3 mile, straight on Route Bravo 4.8 miles, right 4.4 miles, left on access road short distance to lake.
Fishing: Lake is stocked with trout. Use canoe/float tube, cast from shore.
Rainbow Trout / good / May, September – December / 7-16 in. / spoons, flies, bait.

Eagle River-Chugiak

Area locations in and around the communities of Eagle River, Peters Creek, Birchwood, and Eklutna along the stretch of Glenn Highway from MP 10.0 to MP 27.0.

14. Eagle River (Middle)

Access A: MP 11.6 - Eagle River Campground; Northbound - straight across Hiland Rd. from exit ramp by sign 1.3 mile to end of road and river. Southbound - E on Hiland Rd. 0.1 mile (east end of Glenn Hwy. bridge), left on access road 1.3 mile to river.

Access B: MP 11.6; E on Hiland Rd. 1.6 mile, right on access road 0.1 mile to parking area on left. Trail leads 100 yards to river.

Fishing: Glacial drainage with limited opportunities for char. Use bait.

King Salmon / poor / mid-June / 15-30 lbs. / attractors, bait.

Silver Salmon / poor / mid-, late August / 5-10 lbs. / attractors, bait.

Dolly Varden / fair / mid-July – late August / 7-15 in. / bait.

15. North Fork Eagle River

Access: MP 15.3; E on Eagle River access road short distance to intersection, SE on Eagle River Road to MP 7.4, S on access road 0.1 mile to parking area. Trail leads short distance to river.

Fishing: Glacial stream with limited opportunities for char in fall when water clears.

Dolly Varden / fair / mid-July – late August / 7-15 in. / bait.

16. Lower Fire Lake

Access: MP 15.3; SE on N Eagle River exit 0.1 mile, left on Old Glenn Hwy. 0.5 mile, left on West Lake Ridge Dr. short distance to lake on right.

Fishing: Lake is stocked with trout. Small number of pike present. Use canoe/float tube.

Ranbow Trout / good / May, September – December / 7-16 in. / spoons, flies, bait.

Dolly Varden / poor-fair / May, September – January / 7-15 in. / spoons, flies, bait.

Northern Pike / poor-fair / May, September – October / 2-5 lbs. / spoons, plugs, bait.

17. Beach Lake

Access: MP 20.9; W on S. Birchwood (Loop) Rd. 0.9 mile, left on Beach Lake Rd. 2.0 miles to parking area and lake.

Fishing: Lake is stocked with fish. One of the more popular locations in the area.

Landlocked Salmon / excellent / June – March / 7-12 in. /spinners, jigs, flies, bait.

Rainbow Trout / good / May, September – December / 7-16 in. / spinners, flies, bait.

Arctic Grayling / excellent / June – September / 7-14 in. / spinners, flies.

18. Mirror (Bear) Lake

Access: MP 23.6; Northbound - SE at posted exit short distance to a "T," right at sign short distance to lake on left. Southbound - SW at posted exit to stop sign, left 0.1 mile to a "T," right at sign short distance to lake on left. Additional access continue 0.2 mile to lake on left.

(continues on next page)

NO. 18 - Mirror (Bear) Lake continued.

Fishing: Lake is stocked with landlocked salmon and trout.
Landlocked Salmon / excellent / June – March / 7-12 in. / spinners, jigs, flies, bait.
Rainbow Trout / good / May, September – December / 7-16 in. / spinners, flies, bait.
Arctic Char / poor / May, September – January / 18-24 in. / spoons, jigs, bait.

19. Edmonds Lake
Access: MP 23.6; Northbound - SE at posted exit short distance to a "T," left 1.3 mile to Paradise Ln., right 0.5 mile to South Hill, right short distance to lake. Southbound - SW at posted exit short distance to intersection, left 0.1 mile to a "T." Follow directions as given above from "T."
Fishing: Lake is stocked with trout. Use canoe/float tube, cast from shore.
Rainbow Trout / good / May, September – December / 7-15 in. / spinners, flies, bait.

20. Eklutna River
Access A: MP 25.7; highway crosses stream.
Access B: MP 26.3; E at Eklutna exit, short distance, right on Old Glenn Hwy., 0.6 mile to stream crossing.
Fishing: Semi-glacial streem containing a population of small char. Few salmon present.
Chum Salmon / poor / late July / 6-10 lbs. / spoons, spinners, flies.
Silver Salmon / poor / mid-August / 5-10 lbs. / spinners, flies, bait.
Dolly Varden / fair / mid-July – mid-September / 7-10 in. / spinners, flies, bait.

21. Eklutna Lake
Access: MP 26.3; E at Eklutna exit, short distance, right on Old Glenn Hwy. 0.4 mile to paved road on left, 9.8 miles to campground and lake.
Fishing: Angling can be difficult in this glacial lake. Best at mouth of clearwater streams.
Kokanee / poor-fair / June – September / 6-9 in. / spinners, bait.
Rainbow Trout / fair-good / June, September – October / 8-18 in. / spinners, bait.
Dolly Varden / fair / June, September – October / 8-18 in. / spinners, bait.

Unit B: Anchorage City Drainages
Includes all roadside waters in the Anchorage area draining into and surrounding Knik Arm and Turnagain Arm.

UNIT REGULATIONS:
* King salmon fishing prohibited: All waters (except Ship Creek), year-round.

UNIT TIMING:

FISH ▽	JAN	FEB	MAR	APR	MAY	JUN	JUL	AUG	SEP	OCT	NOV	DEC
KS*					▒▒	▓▓	▓▓	▓▒				
RS*					▒	▓▓	▓▓	▒▒	▒			
PS*							▒▓	▓▒				
CS*						▒	▓▓	▓▒				

FISH ▽	JAN	FEB	MAR	APR	MAY	JUN	JUL	AUG	SEP	OCT	NOV	DEC
SS*												
LS												
RT												
AC												
DV												
NP												

Note: Timing shown for salmon indicates fish in all stages of maturity .

22. Ship Creek

Access: MP 0 Glenn Highway; continue W on E 5th Ave. 2.2 miles, right on E St. MP 127.0 Seward Highway; continue N on Ingra St. 0.3 mile, left on E 5th Ave. Both access options N on E 5th Ave. 0.1 mile, right on N C St. 0.3 mile to junctions of Ship Creek Ave. and 0.4 mile to Whitney Rd., right on Ship Creek Ave. to access south bank of stream, right again on Whitney Rd. to access north bank. A multitude of access points available along both roads.

Fishing: One of the most popular salmon fisheries in all of Southcentral. Stream is stocked with early-run king and silver salmon. Smaller native runs of pink, chum and late-run silvers present. Trout fishing is best in holes upstream of lower dam.

King Salmon / good-excellent / 15-30 lbs. (65 lbs.) / attractors, flies, bait.

Pink Salmon / fair / 2-4 lbs. (6 lbs.) / spoons, spinners, flies.

Chum Salmon / poor-fair / 6-10 lbs. (16 lbs.) / spoons, spinners, flies.

Silver Salmon / good-excellent / 5-10 lbs. (18 lbs.) / spinners, flies, bait.

Rainbow Trout / fair / 7-16 in. (10 lbs.) / spinners, flies.

Dolly Varden / poor-fair / 7-15 in. (5 lb.) / spoons, spinners, bait.

FISH ▽	JAN	FEB	MAR	APR	MAY	JUN	JUL	AUG	SEP	OCT	NOV	DEC
KS												
PS												
CS												
SS												
RT												
DV												

23. Chester Creek (Lower)

Access A: MP 126.7 New Seward Highway - Community Gardens; W on 15th Ave. 0.6 mile, left on C St. 0.3 mile to access site on right and stream.

Access B: MP 125.8 New Seward Highway -Valley of the Moon Park; W on Northern Lights Blvd. 1.0 mile, right on Arctic Blvd. 0.6 mile to stream crossing. Main access to park, right on W 17th Ave. 0.1 mile to access site on right. Short hike across open field to stream.

Access C: MP 125.8 New Seward Highway; W on Northern Lights Blvd. 1.3 mile, right on Spenard Rd. 0.7 mile to stream crossing.

(continues on next page)

N0. 23 - Chester Creek (Lower) continued.

Fishing: Mainly a summer and fall fishery for trout and char. Big fish possible in spring.
Rainbow Trout / poor-fair / mid-July – mid-September / 7-12 in. / flies, bait.
Dolly Varden / poor-fair / mid-July – mid-September / 7-12 in. / flies, bait.

24. Chester Creek (Upper)

Access: MP 125.7 New Seward Highway - East Chester Park; E on Benson Blvd. 1.0 mile,
left on Lake Otis Pkwy. 0.3 mile, left on E 24th Ave. Road parallels stream.
Fishing: Mainly a summer and fall fishery for trout and char. Big fish possible in spring.
Rainbow Trout / poor-fair / mid-July – mid-September / 7-12 in. / flies, bait.
Dolly Varden / poor-fair / mid-July – mid-September / 7-12 in. / flies, bait.

25. Otis Lake

Access: MP 125.3 New Seward Highway - Carlson Park; E on 36th Ave. 0.8 mile, left on
Lake Otis Pkwy. 0.2 mile, left on Cornell Ct. 0.1 mile to sign with street parking. Trail leads
100 yards to lake.
Fishing: Lake is stocked with trout. Use canoe/float tube, cast from shore.
Rainbow Trout / good / May, September – December / 7-15 in. / spinners, flies, bait.

26. University (APU/Behm) Lake

Access: MP 124.7 New Seward Highway; E on Tudor Rd. 1.6 mile, left on Bragaw St. 0.5
mile, right on University Lake Dr. 0.2 mile to parking behind University Lake Bldg. Short
hike to lake on right.
Fishing: Lake is stocked with trout. A few large fish present. Salmon spawn at outlet.
Rainbow Trout / fair / May, September – December / 7-15 in. / spinners, flies, bait.
Dolly Varden / poor / August – October / 7-12 in. / spinners, flies, bait.

27. Cheney Lake

Access: MP 4.4 Glenn Highway; E on Muldoon Rd. 1.1 mile, right on Debarr Rd. 0.9 mile,
left on Beaver Pl. 0.6 mile to access site on left. Lake is adjacent to road.
Alternate Access: MP 124.7 New Seward Highway; E on Tudor Rd. 2.7 miles, left on
Boniface Pkwy. 1.0 mile, right on E Northern Lights Blvd. 0.5 mile, left on Baxter Rd. 0.5
mile to access site on right. Lake is adjacent to road.
Fishing: Lake is stocked with landlocked salmon and trout.
Landlocked Salmon / excellent / June – March / 7-12 in. / spinners, jigs, flies, bait.
Rainbow Trout / good / May, September – December / 7-16 in. / spinners, flies, bait.

28. Campbell Creek (Middle)

Note: Access points originate from MP 124.7 New Seward Highway.

Access A: Campbell Creek Park (W); E on Tudor Rd. 0.7 mile, right on Lake Otis Pkwy.
0.2 mile, left on E 48th Ave. short distance to access site on left and stream.
Access B: Campbell Creek Park (E); E on Tudor Rd. 0.9 mile, right on Folker St. 0.1 mile
to parking area and stream.

Fishing: Clearwater stream open to fishing for silver salmon and resident species. Bright silvers available early in season. Trout and char best upstream of the forks.

Silver Salmon / fair-good / 5-10 lbs. (15 lbs.) / spinners, flies, bait.
Rainbow Trout / good / 7-16 in. (5 lbs.) / spinners, flies, bait.
Dolly Varden / good / 7-15in. (4 lbs.) / spinners, flies, bait.

FISH ▽	JAN	FEB	MAR	APR	MAY	JUN	JUL	AUG	SEP	OCT	NOV	DEC
SS												
RT												
DV												

29. South Fork Campbell Creek

Note: Access points originate from MP 124.7 New Seward Highway.

Access A: E on Tudor Rd. 3.2 miles, right on Campbell Airstrip Rd. 1.1 mile, right on access road short distance to parking area. Trail leads 75 yards to stream.
Access B: E on Tudor Rd. 3.2 miles, right on Campbell Airstrip Rd. 2.0 miles, right short distance to parking area. Trail leads 50 yards to a "Y," right fork leads 0.25 mile to stream.
Alternate Access: MP 4.4 Glenn Highway; S on Muldoon Rd. 4.0 miles, left on Campbell Airstrip Rd. Follow above directions from this point on to access sites A and B.
Fishing: Small stream with opportunities for trout and char. Salmon spawning area.
Rainbow Trout / good / mid-August – early October / 7-16 in. / spinners, flies.
Dolly Varden / good / mid-August – early October / 7-15 in. / spinners, flies.

30. Taku-Campbell Lake

Access: MP 122.2 New Seward Highway - Taku/Campbell Park; W on Dimond Blvd. 0.7 mile, right on King St. 0.5 mile, left on 76th Ave. short distance to access site and lake.
Fishing: Lake is stocked with landlocked salmon and trout.
Landlocked Salmon / excellent / June – march / 7-12 in. / spinners, jigs, flies, bait.
Rainbow Trout / good / May, September – December / 7-16 in. / spinners, flies, bait.

31. Campbell Creek (Lower)

Note: Access points originate from MP 122.2 New Seward Highway.

Access A: Taku/Campbell Park - W on Dimond Blvd. 2.0 miles, right on Stormy Pl. 0.1 mile to parking area. Trail leads to and along stream.
Access B: W on Dimond Blvd. 0.9 mile, right on C St. 0.3 mile to stream crossing.
Access C: W on Dimond Blvd. 1.1 mile, right on Arctic Blvd. 0.2 mile to stream crossing.
Access D: W on Dimond Blvd. 2.3 miles, right on Northwood Dr. short distance to end of road. Trail leads to and along stream.
Access E: W on Dimond Blvd. 2.4 miles to stream crossing.
Fishing: Small clearwater stream open to fishing for silver salmon, trout, and char. Look for fresh silvers after a good rain. Hike along stream to find best holes.
Silver Salmon / good / 5-10 lbs. (15 lbs.) / spinners, flies, bait.
Rainbow Ttrout / fair / 7-16 in. (5 lbs.) / spinners, flies, bait.
Dolly Varden / fair / 715 in. (4 lbs.) / spinners, flies, bait.

FISH ▽	JAN	FEB	MAR	APR	MAY	JUN	JUL	AUG	SEP	OCT	NOV	DEC
SS												
RT												
DV												

32. Jewel Lake

Note: Access points originate from MP 122.2 New Seward Highway.

Access A: Jewel Lake Park (E); W on Dimond Blvd. 3.2 miles, right on Jewel Lake Rd. 0.2 mile, left on 88th Ave. 0.2 mile to parking area and lake.

Access B: Jewel Lake Park (W); W on Dimond Blvd. 3.7 miles to access site on right. Lake is adjacent to road.

Fishing: Lake is stocked with landlocked salmon and trout. Very productive ice fishing and one of the most popular spots in the Anchorage area.

Landlocked Salmon / excellent / June – March / 7-12 in. / spinners, jigs, flies, bait.
Rainbow Trout / good / May, September – December / 7-16 in. / spinners, flies, bait.
Arctic Char / poor / May, September – January / 18-24 in. / spoons, jigs, bait.

33. Sand Lake

Note: Access points originate from MP 122.2 New Seward Highway.

Access A: W on Dimond Blvd. 3.7 miles, right on Jewel Lake Rd. 1.1 mile, left on Caravelle Dr. 0.1 mile. Trail on left leads 100 yards to lake.

Access B: W on Dimond Blvd. 4.2 miles, right on Sand Lake Rd. 0.7 mile, right on 80th Ave. 0.5 mile to cul-de-sac. Straight to canal access to lake.

Fishing: Lake is stocked with landlocked salmon, trout, and char. A few pike also available. Char up to 10 pounds or more possible. Popular location for ice fishing.

Landlocked Salmon / excellent / June – March / 7-12 in. / spinners, jigs, flies, bait.
Rainbow Trout / good / May, September – December / 7-16 in. / spinners, flies, bait.
Lake Trout / poor / May, September – October / 2-4 lbs. / spoons, jigs, bait.
Arctic Char / fair-good / May, September – January / 8-24 in. / spoons, jigs, bait.
Northern Pike / poor / May, September – October / 2-4 lbs. / spoons, plugs, bait.

34. DeLong Lake

Access: MP 122.2 New Seward Highway - DeLong Lake Park; W on Dimond Blvd. 3.2 miles, right on Jewel Lake Rd. 1.7 mile, left on 63rd Ave. short distance to parking area and lake.

Fishing: Lake is stocked with landlocked salmon, trout. One of the best spots in town.

Landlocked Salmon / excellent / June – March / 7-12 in. / spinners, jigs, flies, bait.
Rainbow Trout / good / May, September – December / 7-15 in. / spinners, flies, bait.
Arctic Char / good / May, September – January / 8-24 in. / spoons, jigs, bait.

35. Campbell Point (Little Campbell) Lake

Access: MP 122.2 New Seward Highway - Kincaid/Pt. Campbell Park; W on Dimond Blvd. 3.2 miles, right on Jewel Lake Rd. 1.3 mile, left on Raspberry Rd. 2.0 miles, right on access road at park entrance 0.6 mile to parking area and lake.

Fishing: Lake is stocked with landlocked salmon, trout, and char. Productive ice fishing.

Landlocked Salmon / excellent / June – March / 7-12 in. / spinners, jigs, flies, bait.
Rainbow Trout / good / May, September – December / 7-16 in. / spinners, flies, bait.
Arctic Char / fair-good / May, September – January / 8-24 in. / spoons, jigs, bait.

36. North Fork Rabbit Creek

Access: MP 117.8 New Seward Hightway; E. Rabbit Creek Rd. 0.6 mile, right on Old Seward Hwy. short distance to small parking area on left. Trail leads 100 yards to stream.
Fishing: Small stream with limited opportunities for char. Salmon spawning area.
Dolly Varden / fair / early July – late September / 7-12 in. / spinners, flies, bait.

Other Locations

Unit A: Knik Arm Drainages:
Glenn Highway: Ship Creek - MP 6.2; RT,DV Peters Creek - MP 21.5; DV,(KS,PS,SS,RT)
Unit B: Anchorage City Drainages:
City Drainages: N. Fork Campbell Creek - (Campbell Airstrip Rd.); RT,DV,(KS,PS,SS)
Rabbit Creek - (New Seward Hwy.) *** Closed to Fishing ***
Potter Creek - (New Seward Hwy.) *** Closed to Fishing ***

LOCATION & SPECIES APPENDIX

● - Wild/Native fish, fishable numbers.
♦ - Present in small numbers and/or only occasionally caught.
▲ - Stocked/Hatchery fish, fishable numbers.
■ - Mix of Wild and Hatchery fish, fishable numbers.
✕ - Indicated species present but currently protected by law (PROHIBITED).

(Chart on next page)

#	LOCATION	King Salmon	Red Salmon	Pink Salmon	Chum Salmon	Silver Salmon	Landlocked Salmon	Kokanee	Steelhead Trout	Rainbow Trout	Lake Trout	Arctic Char	Dolly Varden	Arctic Grayling	Sheefish	Whitefish	Northern Pike	Burbot	Pacific Halibut	Ling Cod	Rockfish
	Elmendorf AFB																				
1.	Upper Sixmile Lake		×	×		×							■				●				
2.	Sixmile Creek / Knik Arm	×	●	●	◆	●							◆				●				
3.	Fish Lake												▲					◆			
4.	Triangle Lake												▲								
5.	Hillberg Lake						▲						▲								
6.	Green Lake						▲						▲								
7.	Spring Lake												▲								
	Fort Richardson																				
8.	Eagle River (Lower)	●	◆	◆	◆	●							◆				●	◆			
9.	Otter Lake												■					◆			
10.	Gwen Lake												▲					◆			
11.	Eagle River (Lower)	×	◆	◆	◆	●							◆				●				
12.	Clunie Lake									▲			■	▲	▲						
13.	Waldon Lake												▲								
	Eagle River-Chugiak																				
14.	Eagle River (Middle)	●	◆	◆	◆	●							◆				●	◆			
15.	North Fork Eagle River	×	×	×	×	×							◆				●	◆			
16.	Lower Fire Lake												●				●	◆	●		
17.	Beach Lake									▲			▲				▲				
18.	Mirror (Bear) Lake									▲			▲	▲				◆			
19.	Edmonds Lake												▲								
20.	Eklutna River	×	◆	◆	●	●											●				
21.	Eklutna Lake										●		■				■				
	Anchorage City																				
22.	Ship Creek	■	◆	●	●	■							●				●				
23.	Chester Creek (Lower)			×	×	×							■				●				
24.	Chester Creek (Upper)				×	×							■				●				
25.	Otis Lake												▲				◆				
26.	University (APU) Lake					◆	◆						■			◆	●				
27.	Cheney Lake									▲			▲								
28.	Campbell Creek (Middle)	×	×	×	×	■							■				●	◆			
29.	South Fork Campbell Creek	×		×		×							■				●				
30.	Taku-Campbell Lake									▲			▲					◆			
31.	Campbell Creek (Lower)	×	×	×	×	■							■				●	◆			
32.	Jewel Lake									▲			▲	▲				◆			
33.	Sand Lake									▲		▲	▲	▲				●			
34.	DeLong Lake									▲			▲	▲				◆			
35.	Campbell Point Lake									▲			▲	▲							
36.	North Fork Rabbit Creek	×	×	×	×								◆				●				

Dalton Highway

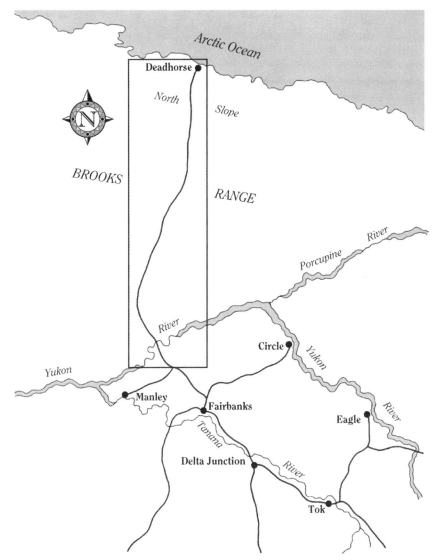

## CHAPTER 5

Area Covered: Elliott Highway Junction to Deadhorse; 414 miles
Regulatory Units: (A) Yukon-Koyukuk River Drainages;
   (B) Sagavanirktok River Drainage
Number of Locations: 46

FISHING THE DALTON HIGHWAY

The Dalton Highway crosses the Yukon River and parallels two other large drainages—Koyukuk and Sagavanirktok—and thus provides extensive roadside access to a multitude of lakes and tributary streams. Grayling inhabit virtually every watershed along the road, with whitefish, pike, and burbot also being abundant in some locations - particularly south of the Brooks Range. Char are common north of the Brooks Range with sizable populations found in deep lakes and the Sagavanirktok River. Limited numbers of salmon are present in some of the larger watersheds. Angler success is fair to good in both lakes and streams.

Angling pressure is very light by most standards, with most of it occurring between mid-June and mid-September. Jim River and surrounding waters are popular for grayling and pike in summer and early fall, while the Sagavanirktok River is the focal point during the late summer and fall sea-run char migrations.

Recommended Hot Spots: South Fork Bonanza, North Fork Bonanza, No Name, Fish, and Prospect creeks; Jim and Sagavanirktok rivers; Grayling, Galbraith, Toolik Access, Toolik, and Slope Mountain lakes.

Content

Pages

QUICK REFERENCE

 Road Condition   **P** Parking Area   **A** Camp Sites   Hiking Trails   Boat Launch   Handicap Access   Fishing Pressure

■ - Good to Highly developed/conditions, intense pressure
● - Fair to Moderately developed/conditions, moderate pressure
◆ - Poor to marginally developed/conditions, limited pressure
✕ - Prohibited

#	LOCATION	MILE POST		**P**	**A**					PAGE
J1.	Jct.: Elliott Highway	0								
1.	Hess Creek	23.8	●	●					◆	72
2.	Isom Creek	33.7	●						◆	72
3.	Yukon River (Middle)	55.6	●	●			●	●	◆	72
4.	Ray River	70.0	●	●	◆				◆	72
5.	Ft. Hamlin Hills Creek	72.6	●	●					◆	72
6.	No Name Creek	79.1	●	●					◆	72
7.	Dall Creek	91.1	●	●					◆	72
8.	Kanuti River	105.8	●	●	◆		■	◆	◆	72

Map 1: Unit A: Yukon-Koyukuk River Drainages

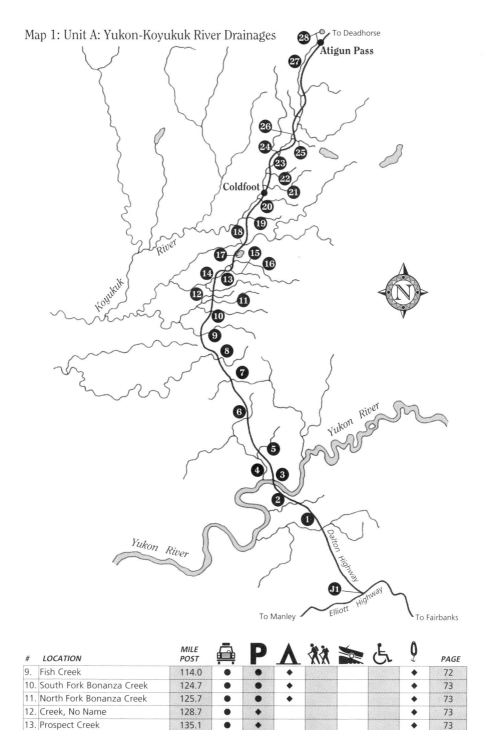

#	LOCATION	MILE POST	🚗	P	Λ	🚶	🎣	♿	⚓	PAGE
9.	Fish Creek	114.0	●	●	◆				◆	72
10.	South Fork Bonanza Creek	124.7	●	●	◆				◆	73
11.	North Fork Bonanza Creek	125.7	●	●	◆				◆	73
12.	Creek, No Name	128.7	●	◆					◆	73
13.	Prospect Creek	135.1	●	◆					◆	73
14.	Jim River (Middle)	135.8/140.1	●	●	◆				●	73

Map 2: Unit B: Sagavanirktok River Drainage

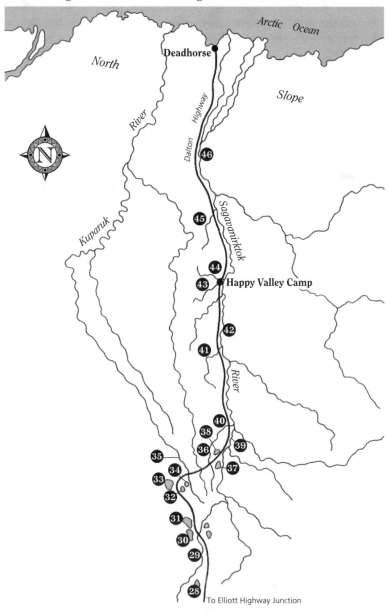

#	LOCATION	MILE POST	🚐	**P**	Λ	🚶	🛶	♿	🎣	PAGE
15.	Douglas Creek	141.8	●	◆					◆	73
16.	Jim River (Upper)	144.0	●	●	◆				●	73
17.	Grayling Lake	150.9	●	●				◆	◆	74
18.	South Fork Koyukuk River	156.1	●	●	◆		●	◆	●	74
19.	Rosie Creek	169.8	●	●					◆	74

#	LOCATION	MILE POST	🚗	P	A	🚶	⛵	♿	🎣	PAGE
20.	Slate Creek	175.2	●	◆					◆	74
21.	Marion Creek	179.9	●	●	■				◆	74
22.	Minnie Creek	187.2	●	●	◆				◆	74
23.	Middle Fork Koyukuk River	188.5/190.8	●	●	◆		●	◆	◆	74
24.	Hammond River	190.6	●	●					◆	74
25.	Gold Creek	197.0	●	◆					◆	75
26.	Middle Fork Koyukuk River	204.3/204.5	●	●	◆				◆	75
27.	Dietrich River	207.0	●	●	◆				◆	75
28.	Tea Lake	270.2	●	◆		◆			◆	75
29.	Atigun River	270.9	●	●					◆	75
30.	Galbraith Lake	274.0	●	◆		◆			◆	76
31.	Island Lake	276.5	●	◆		◆			◆	76
32.	Toolik Access Lake	284.3	●	◆		◆			◆	76
33.	Toolik Lake	284.4	●	◆		◆			◆	76
34.	Horizon Lake	287.7	●	◆		◆			◆	76
35.	Kuparuk River	288.9	●	◆					◆	76
36.	Oksrukuyik (Oxbow) Creek	297.8	●	●					◆	76
37.	Cutoff Lake	298.7	●	◆		◆			◆	76
38.	Slope Mountain Lake	303.0	●	◆		◆			◆	77
39.	Sagavanirktok River (Upper)	309.5-325.0	●	●	◆			◆	●	77
40.	Oksrukuyik Creek	313.9	●	●					◆	77
41.	Dan Creek	330.7	●	●	◆				◆	77
42.	Sagavanirktok River (Middle)	333.9-348.2	●	●	◆			◆	●	77
43.	Happy Valley Creek	334.4	●	●					◆	77
44.	Creek, No Name	335.3	●	◆					◆	77
45.	Creek, No Name	345.5	●	◆					◆	78
46.	Sagavanirktok River (Lower)	368.0-414.0	●	●	◆			◆	◆	78

Unit A: Yukon-Koyukuk River Drainages

Includes all roadside waters flowing into and surrounding Yukon and Koyukuk rivers.

UNIT REGULATIONS:

* Salmon fishing prohibited: All waters (except Ray River), year-round.

UNIT TIMING

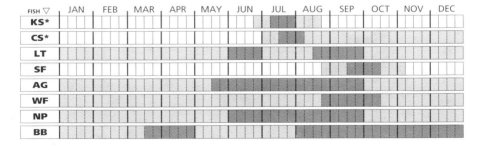

FISH ▽	JAN	FEB	MAR	APR	MAY	JUN	JUL	AUG	SEP	OCT	NOV	DEC

Rows: KS*, CS*, LT, SF, AG, WF, NP, BB

*Note: Timing shown for salmon indicates fish in all stages of maturity.

1. Hess Creek
Access: MP 23.8; road crosses stream.
Fishing: Slow-flowing tannic stream supporting decent fall action for grayling.
Arctic Grayling / fair-good / mid September – mid October / 7-14 in. / spinners, flies.

2. Isom Creek
Access: MP 33.7; road crosses stream.
Fishing: Small clearwater stream supporting a small population of grayling in summer.
Arctic Grayling / fair / mid June – late August / 7-12 in. / spinners, flies.

3. Yukon River
Access: MP 55.6; road crosses river.
Fishing: Large, glacial river with limited opportunities for burbot in spring and fall.
Burbot / good / March – April, September – December / 3-8 lbs. / bait.

4. Ray River
Access: MP 70.0; road parallels river, turnout. Park and hike 0.75 mile W to river.
Fishing: A fairly large stream with decent opportunities for grayling, pike, and burbot
Arctic Grayling / fair-good / early September – mid October / 7-14 in. / spinners, flies.
Northern Pike / fair-good / mid June – late September / 2-6 lbs. / spoons, plugs, bait.
Burbot / fair / late June – mid October / 2-6 lbs. / bait.

5. Ft. Hamlin Hills Creek
Access: MP 72.6; road crosses stream.
Fishing: Small clearwater stream supporting a small population of grayling in summer.
Arctic Grayling / fair / mid June – late August / 7-12 in. / spinners, flies.

6. No Name Creek
Access: MP 79.1; road crosses stream.
Fishing: Clearwater stream supporting a small population of grayling in summer, fall.
Arctic Grayling / good / late May – mid September / 7-12 in. / spinners, flies.

7. Dall Creek
Access: MP 91.1; road crosses stream.
Fishing: Clearwater stream supporting a small population of grayling in summer, fall.
Arctic Grayling / fair-good / early June – mid September / 7-12 in. / spinners, flies.

8. Kanuti River
Access: MP 105.8; road crosses river.
Fishing: Slow-flowing stream with decent opportunities for grayling in summer.
Arctic Grayling / fair-good / mid June – late September / 7-12 in. / spinners, flies.
Burbot / fair / late June – late September / 2-4 lbs. / bait.

9. Fish Creek
Access: MP 114.0; road crosses stream.
Fishing: Clearwater stream supporting a healthy population of grayling in summer.
Arctic Grayling / good / mid-June – late August / 7-12 in. / spinners, flies.

10. South Fork Bonanza Creek

Access: MP 124.7; road crosses stream.
Fishing: Slow-flowing tannic stream with decent opportunities for grayling and burbot.
Arctic Grayling / good / mid June – late September / 7-12 in. / spinners, flies.
Whitefish / poor / mid July – early October / 10-20 in. / flies, bait.
Burbot / fair / late June – late September / 2-4 lbs. / bait.

11. North Fork Bonanza Creek

Access: MP 125.7; road crosses stream.
Fishing: Slow-flowing tannic stream with decent opportunities for grayling and burbot.
Arctic Grayling / good / mid June – late September / 7-12 in. / spinners, flies.
Whitefish / poor / mid July – early October / 10-20 in. / flies, bait.
Northern Pike / fair / mid June – mid September / 2-4 lbs. / spoons, plugs, flies.

12. Creek, No Name

Access: MP 128.7; road crosses stream.
Fishing: Small tannic stream containing a small population of grayling in summer.
Arctic Grayling / fair / mid June – late August / 7-10 in. / spinners, flies.

13. Prospect Creek

Access: MP 135.1; road crosses stream.
Fishing: Slow-flowing tannic stream with decent opportunities for grayling and pike.
Arctic Grayling / good / mid June – late September / 7-12 in. / spinners, flies.
Whitefish / poor / mid July – early October / 10-20 in. / flies, bait.
Northern Pike / fair / mid June – mid September / 2-4 lbs. / spoons, plugs, flies.

14. Jim River (Middle)

Access A: MP 135.8; W on access road 1.1 mile to 3-way split, middle fork leads 0.2 mile to river, right fork 0.3 mile to river.
Access B: MP 140.1 and 141.0; road crosses river in two locations.
Fishing: One of the more popular clearwater streams in the area, known for its productive grayling fishery. Pike and burbot in slower sections. Salmon spawning area.
Arctic Grayling / good / early June – mid Sept. / 7-14 in. / spinners, flies.
Whitefish / poor / late August – early October/ 10-20 in. /attractors, flies, bait.
Northern Pike / fair / mid June – early September / 2-5 lbs. / spoons, plugs, flies.
Burbot / poor / early August – mid October / 2-4 lbs. / bait.

15. Douglas Creek

Access: MP 141.8; road crosses stream.
Fishing: Productive summer and fall fishery for grayling.
Arctic Grayling / fair-good / mid June – late September / 7-12 in. / spinners, flies.

16. Jim River (Upper)

Access: MP 144.0; road crosses river. *(continues on next page)*

Fishing: River supports a healthy population of grayling in summer and fall.
Arctic Grayling / good / mid June – late September / 7-14 in. / spinners, flies.
Whitefish / poor / late July – early October / 10-20 in. / flies, bait.

17. Grayling Lake
Access: MP 150.9; road parallels lake.
Fishing: Lake contains grayling in summer. Use canoe/float tube, cast from shore.
Arctic Grayling / good / June – August / 7-12 in. / spinners, flies.

18. South Fork Koyukuk River
Access: MP 156.1; road crosses river.
Fishing: Large, glacial river with limited fall opportunities for grayling.
Arctic Grayling / good / mid September – mid October / 7-14 in. / spinners, flies.
Whitefish / poor / mid September – mid October / 10-20 in. / flies, bait.

19. Rosie Creek
Access: MP 169.8; road crosses stream.
Fishing: Stream supports a small population of grayling in summer.
Arctic Grayling / fair / mid June – late August / 7-12 in. / spinners, flies.

20. Slate Creek
Access: MP 175.2; road crosses stream.
Fishing: Stream supports a small population of grayling in summer.
Arctic Grayling / fair / mid June – late August / 7-12 in. / spinners, flies.

21. Marion Creek
Access: MP 179.9; road crosses stream.
Fishing: Stream supports a small population of grayling in summer.
Arctic Grayling / fair / mid June – late August / 7-12 in. / spinners, flies.

22. Minnie Creek
Access: MP 187.2; road crosses stream.
Fishing: Stream supports a small population of grayling in summer.
Arctic Grayling / fair / mid June – late August / 7-12 in. / spinners, flies.

23. Middle Fork Koyukuk River
Access: MP 188.5 and 190.8; road parallels and crosses river.
Fishing: Large, glacial river with limited fall opportunities for grayling
Arctic Grayling / fair-good / mid September – mid October / 7-14 in. / spinners, flies.
Whitefish / poor / mid September – mid October / 10-20 in. / flies, bait.

24. Hammond River
Access: MP 190.6; road crosses river.
Fishing: Large glacial river with limited fall opportunities for grayling.
Arctic Grayling / fair / mid September – early October / 7-12 in. / spinners, flies.

25. Gold Creek

Access: MP 197.0; road crosses stream.
Fishing: Stream supports a small population of grayling in summer.
Arctic Grayling / fair / mid June – late August / 7-12 in. / spinners, flies.

26. Middle Fork Koyukuk River

Access: MP 204.3 – 204.8; road parallels river, crossing it at MP 204.3 and 204.5.
Fishing: Large glacial river with limited fall opportunities for grayling.
Arctic Grayling / fair-good / mid September – mid October / 7-14 in. / spinners, flies.
Whitefish / poor / mid September – mid October / 10-20 in. / flies, bait.

27. Dietrich River

Access: MP 207.0; road crosses river, paralleling it at MP 206.2.
Fishing: River supports a moderate population of grayling in summer.
Arctic Grayling / fair-good / mid June – late August / 7-12 in. / spinners, flies.

28. Tea Lake

Access: MP 270.2; hike through open terrain 0.5 mile W to lake.
Fishing: Lake supports decent numbers of char, grayling, burbot. Use canoe/flot tube.
Lake Trout / fair-good / June, August – September / 2-4 lbs. / spoons, plugs, bait.
Arctic Grayling / fair-good / June – September / 7-12 in. / spinners, flies.
Burbot / fair / April – May, October – November / 2-4 lbs. / bait.

Unit B: Sagavanirktok River Drainage

Includes all roadside waters flowing into and surrounding the Sagavanirktok River.

UNIT REGULATIONS:

* Salmon fishing prohibited: All waters, year-round.
* Lake trout fishing: Catch-and release only, all watrs, year-round.

UNIT TIMING:

FISH ▽	JAN	FEB	MAR	APR	MAY	JUN	JUL	AUG	SEP	OCT	NOV	DEC
PS*							▓	▓				
CS*						▓	▓	▓	▓			
LT	░	░	░	░	░	▓	▓	▓	░	░	░	░
AC	░	░	░	░	░	▓	▓	▓	▓	░	░	░
DV	░	░	░	░	░	▓	▓	▓	▓	░	░	░
AG						▓	▓	▓	▓			
WF	░	░	░	░	░			▓	▓	░	░	░
BB	░	░	▓	▓	▓	▓	▓	▓	▓	▓	▓	▓

29. Atigun River

Access: MP 271.0; road crosses river.
Fishing: Small river supporting decent numbers of grayling in summer.
Arctic Grayling / fair-good / late June – mid August / 7-12 in. / spinners, flies.

30. Galbraith Lake

Access: MP 274.0; hike through open terrain 0.5 mile W to lake.
Fishing: Lake contains large numbers of fish. Use canoe/float tube, cast from shore.
Lake Trout / good / June, August – September / 2-5 lbs. / spoons, plugs.
Arctic Char / good / May – September / 2-4 lbs. / spoons, plugs, bait.
Arctic Grayling / good / June – August / 7-14 in. / spinners, flies.
Burbot / fair / April – May, October – December / 2-4 lbs. / bait.

31. Island Lake

Access: MP 276.5; hike through open terrain 0.25 mile W to lake.
Fishing: Lake contains moderate numbers of fish. Use canoe/float tube.
Lake Trout / fair / June, August – September / 2-5 lbs. / spoons, plugs.
Arctic Char / fair / May – September / 2-4 lbs. / spoons, plugs, bait.
Arctic Grayling / fair-good / June – August / 7-14 in. / spinners, flies.

32. Toolik Access Lake

Access: MP 284.3; hike through open terrain 100 yards E to lake.
Fishing: Lake contains large numbers of grayling. Use canoe/float tube.
Arctic Grayling / good / June – August / 7-12 in. / spinners, flies.

33. Toolik Lake

Access: MP 284.4; W on access road 1.0 mile to lake.
Fishing: Lake contains large numbers of grayling. Use canoe/float tube, cast from shore.
Lake Trout / good / June, August – September / 2-5 lbs. / spoons, plugs.
Arctic Grayling / good / June – August / 7-14 in. / spinners, flies.

34. Horizon Lake

Access: MP 287.7; hike through open terrain 200 yards SE to lake.
Fishing: Lake contains moderate numbers of char. Use canoe/float tube.
Arctic Char / fair-good / May – September / 10-20 in. / spoons, plugs, bait.

35. Kuparuk River

Access: MP 288.9; road crosses river.
Fishing: Small, slow-flowing stream with limited opportunities in summer for grayling.
Arctic Grayling / fair-good / mid June – mid August / 7-12 in. / spinners, flies.
Burbot / poor / late June – late August / 10-20 in. / bait.

36. Oksrukuyik (Oxbow) Creek

Access: MP 297.8; road crosses stream.
Fishing: Stream supports a decent populatin of grayling during summer months.
Arctic Grayling / fair-good / mid June – mid August / 7-12 in. / spinners, flies.

37. Cutoff Lake

Access: MP 298.7; hike through open terrain 0.25 mile S to lake.
Fishing: Lake contains a moderate number of char. Use canoe/float tube.
Arctic Char / fair-good / May – September / 10-20 in. / spoons, plugs, bait.

38. Slope Mountain Lake

Access: MP 303.0; hike through open terrain 200 yards W to lake.
Fishing: Lake contains a moderate number of grayling. Use canoe/float tube.
Arcitc Grayling / good / June – August / 7-12 in. / spinners, flies.

39. Sagavanirktok River (Upper)

Access: MP 309.5 – 314.0, 316.7 – 318.1, and 320.3 – 325.0; road parallels river.
Fishing: The premier angling destination in the area, known for its population of large sea-run char that may reach 15 pounds or more. Healthy numbers of grayling also inhabit the clear waters of the river. Look for schools of whitefish in fall.
Dolly Varden / good / mid September – early October / 2-6 lbs. / spinners, flies.
Arctic Grayling / excellent / late June – late September / 7-14 in. / spinners, flies.
Whitefish / fair / mid August – late September / 10-18 in. / attractors, flies, bait.
Burbot / fair / early June – mid October / 2-4 lbs. / bait.

40. Oksrukuyik Creek / Sagavanirktok River Confluence

Access: MP 313.9; road crosses stream.
Fishing: Decent numbers of grayling and burbot present during summer months.
Arctic Grayling / fair-good / early June – late August / 7-12 in. / spinners, flies.
Burbot / fair-good / late June – late August / 2-4 lbs. / bait.

41. Dan Creek

Access: MP 330.7; road crosses stream.
Fishing: Clearwater stream with decent action for grayling in summer.
Arctic Grayling / fair-good / early June – late August / 7-12 in. / spinners, flies.

42. Sagavanirktok River (Middle)

Access: MP 333.9 – 335.3 and 347.6 – 348.2; road parallels river.
Fishing: The premier angling destination in the area, known for its population of large sea-run char that may reach 15 pounds or more. Healthy numbers of grayling also inhabit the clear waters of the river. Look for schools of whitefish in late summer and fall.
Dolly Varden / good / early September – late September / 2-6 lbs. / spinners, flies.
Arctic Grayling / excellent / late June – late Sept. / 7-14 in. / spinners, flies.
Whitefish / fair / early August – late Sept. / 10-18 in. / attractors, flies, bait.
Burbot / fair / early July – mid October / 2-4 lbs. / bait.

43. Happy Valley Creek

Access: MP 334.4; road crosses stream.
Fishing: Small clearwater stream supporting decent numbers of graying in summer.
Arctic Grayling / fair-good / early June – late August / 7-12 in. / spinners, flies.

44. Creek, No Name

Access: MP 335.3; road crosses stream.
Fishing: Small clearwater stream supporting decent numbers of graying in summer.
Arctic Grayling / fair-good / early June – late August / 7-12 in. / spinners, flies.

45. Creek, No Name

Access: MP 345.5; road crosses stream.
Fishing: Small clearwater stream supporting decent numbers of graying in summer.
Arctic Grayling / fair-good / early June – late August / 7-12 in. / spinners, flies.

46. Sagavanirktok River (Lower)

Access: MP 368.0 – 371.0, 378.5 – 380.0, 382.6 – 388.0, 403.0 – 414.0; road parallels river.
Fishing: The premier angling destination in the area, known for its population of large sea-run char that may reach 15 pounds or more. Healthy numbers of grayling also inhabit the clear waters of the river. Look for schools of whitefish in late summer and fall.
Dolly Varden / good / mid August – mid September / 2-6 lbs. / spinners, flies.
Arctic Grayling / good-excellent / late June – late September / 7-14 in. / spinners, flies.
Whitefish / poor-fair / early August – mid September / 10-18 in. / attractors, flies, bait.
Burbot / poor-fair / early July – mid October / 2-4 lbs. / bait.

Other Locations

Unit A: Yukon-Koyukuk River Drainages:

Creek, No Name - MP 33.7; AG Creek, No Name - MP 93.6; AG Creek, No Name - MP 100.0; AG Creek, No Name - MP 102.6; AG Creek, No Name - MP 121.1; AG Creek, No Name - MP 128.7; AG Creek, No Name - MP 140.1; AG Creek, No Name - MP 143.3; AG Creek, No Name - MP 161.7; AG Creek, No Name - MP 163.1; AG Creek, No Name - MP 202.7; AG Snowden Creek - MP 216.0; AG Creek, No Name - MP 225.6; AG

LOCATION & SPECIES APPENDIX

● - Wild/Native fish, fishable numbers.
◆ - Present in small numbers and/or only occasionally caught.
▲ - Stocked/Hatchery fish, fishable numbers.
■ - Mix of Wild and Hatchery fish, fishable numbers.
✕ - Indicated species present but currently protected by law (PROHIBITED).

#	LOCATION	KING SALMON	RED SALMON	PINK SALMON	CHUM SALMON	SILVER SALMON	LANDLOCKED SALMON	KOKANEE	STEELHEAD TROUT	RAINBOW TROUT	LAKE TROUT	ARCTIC CHAR	DOLLY VARDEN	SHEEFISH	ARCTIC GRAYLING	WHITEFISH	NORTHERN PIKE	BURBOT	PACIFIC HALIBUT	LING COD	ROCKFISH
1.	Hess Creek													◆	●	◆	◆				
2.	Isom Creek														●						
3.	Yukon River (Middle)	◆			◆	◆								◆	◆	◆	◆	●			
4.	Ray River													◆	●	◆	●	●			
5.	Ft. Hamlin Hills Creek														●		◆	◆			
6.	No Name Creek														●	◆		◆			
7.	Dall Creek														●						
8.	Kanuti River														●	◆		●			
9.	Fish Creek														●	◆					
10.	South Fork Bonanza Creek	✕			✕										●	●	◆	●			
11.	North Fork Bonanza Creek	✕			✕										●	●	●	◆			
12.	Creek, No Name														●	◆					
13.	Prospect Creek	✕													●	●	●				
14.	Jim River (Middle)	✕			✕										●	●	●	●			
15.	Douglas Creek														●						
16.	Jim River (Upper)														●	●	◆	◆			
17.	Grayling Lake														●						
18.	South Fork Koyukuk River	✕			✕									◆	●	●	◆	◆			
19.	Rosie Creek														●	◆					
20.	Slate Creek	✕			✕								◆		●	◆					
21.	Marion Creek				✕								◆		●	◆					
22.	Minnie Creek												◆		●	◆		◆			
23.	Middle Fork Koyukuk River	✕			✕								◆	◆	●	●	◆	◆			
24.	Hammond River	✕													●	◆					
25.	Gold Creek																				
26.	Middle Fork Koyukuk River	✕			✕								◆	◆	●	●	◆				
27.	Dietrich River												◆		●	◆		◆			
28.	Tea Lake										●	◆			●			●			
29.	Atigun River												◆		●	◆					
30.	Galbraith Lake										●	●			●	◆		●			
31.	Island Lake										●	●			●	◆					
32.	Toolik Access Lake														●						
33.	Toolik Lake										●				●	◆					
34.	Horizon Lake											●									
35.	Kuparuk River														●			●			
36.	Oksrukuyik Creek												◆		●	◆					
37.	Cutoff Lake											●									
38.	Slope Mountain Lake														●						
39.	Sagavanirktok River			✕	✕								●		●	●		●			
40.	Oksrukuyik (Oxbow) Creek												◆		●	◆		●			
41.	Dan Creek												◆		●						
42.	Sagavanirktok River			✕	✕								●		●	●	●	●			
43.	Happy Valley Creek												◆		●	◆		◆			
44.	Creek, No Name												◆		●						
45.	Creek, No Name												◆		●						
46.	Sagavanirktok River			✕	✕								●		●	●	●				

Denali Highway

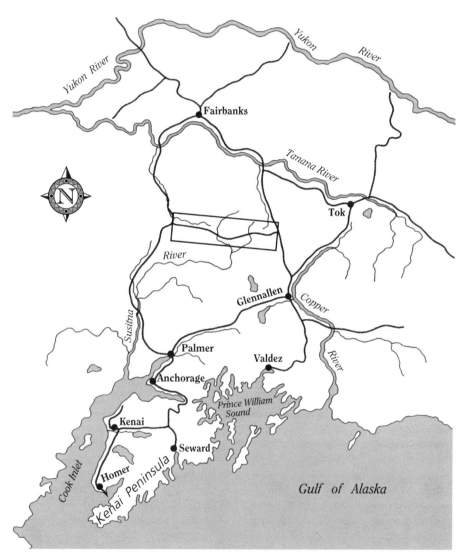

Area Covered: Paxson to Cantwell; 135.5 miles
Regulatory Units: (A) Gulkana River Drainage; (B) Delta River Drainage; (C) Susitna River Drainage; (D) Nenana River Drainage
Number of Locations: 34

FISHING THE DENALI HIGHWAY

The Denali Highway is unique in that the surrounding waters drain into three different regions of Alaska. The road crosses or parallels the major drainages of Copper, Delta, Maclaren, Susitna, and Nenana rivers. Some of the waters flow into Prince William Sound and the Gulf of Alaska through the Gulkana and Copper rivers, others into Cook Inlet by the way of Maclaren and Susitna rivers, and also into the Bering Sea through Delta or Nenana, Tanana, and, finally, Yukon rivers. The most common sport fish species along the road is without a doubt grayling, which inhabit just about any size lake or stream, but char and burbot are also frequently caught in some of the larger lakes. Anglers may also come across red salmon in lakes connected to the Gulkana River, and whitefish are abundant but oftentimes hard to catch. Angler success is good in streams and good to excellent in lakes.

Angling pressure is for the most part very light but can be light to moderate in a few locations in mid-summer or during weekend holidays. The Tangle lakes system receives the most angling pressure.

Recommended Hot Spots: Little Swede, Big Swede, Round Tangle, Upper Tangle, Landmark Gap, and Glacier lakes; Tangle River; Rock, Crooked, Clearwater, and Fish creeks.

Content

QUICK REFERENCE

 Road Condition   Parking Area   Camp Sites   Hiking Trails   Boat Launch   Handicap Access   Fishing Pressure

■ - Good to Highly developed/conditions, intense pressure
● - Fair to Moderately developed/conditions, moderate pressure
◆ - Poor to marginally developed/conditions, limited pressure
✕ - Prohibited

#	LOCATION	MILE POST	🚗	P	△	🏃	🛥	♿	𝥺	PAGE
J1.	Richardson Hwy.	0								
1.	East Fork Gulkana River	0.2	■	●					◆	85
2.	Mud Lake	0.3	●	●					◆	85
3.	Sevenmile Lake	6.9	●	●					◆	86
4.	Tenmile Lake	9.9	●	●			●		◆	86
5.	Teardrop Lake	10.4	●	●					◆	86
6.	Octopus Lake	11.1	●	◆		●			◆	86
7.	Little Swede Lake	16.8	●	●		●			◆	86
8.	Big Swede Lake	16.8	●	●		●			◆	86
9.	16.8-Mile Lake	16.8	●	◆		●			◆	87

Map 1: Unit A: Gulkana River Drainage
       Unit B: Delta River Drainage
       Unit C: Susitna River Drainage

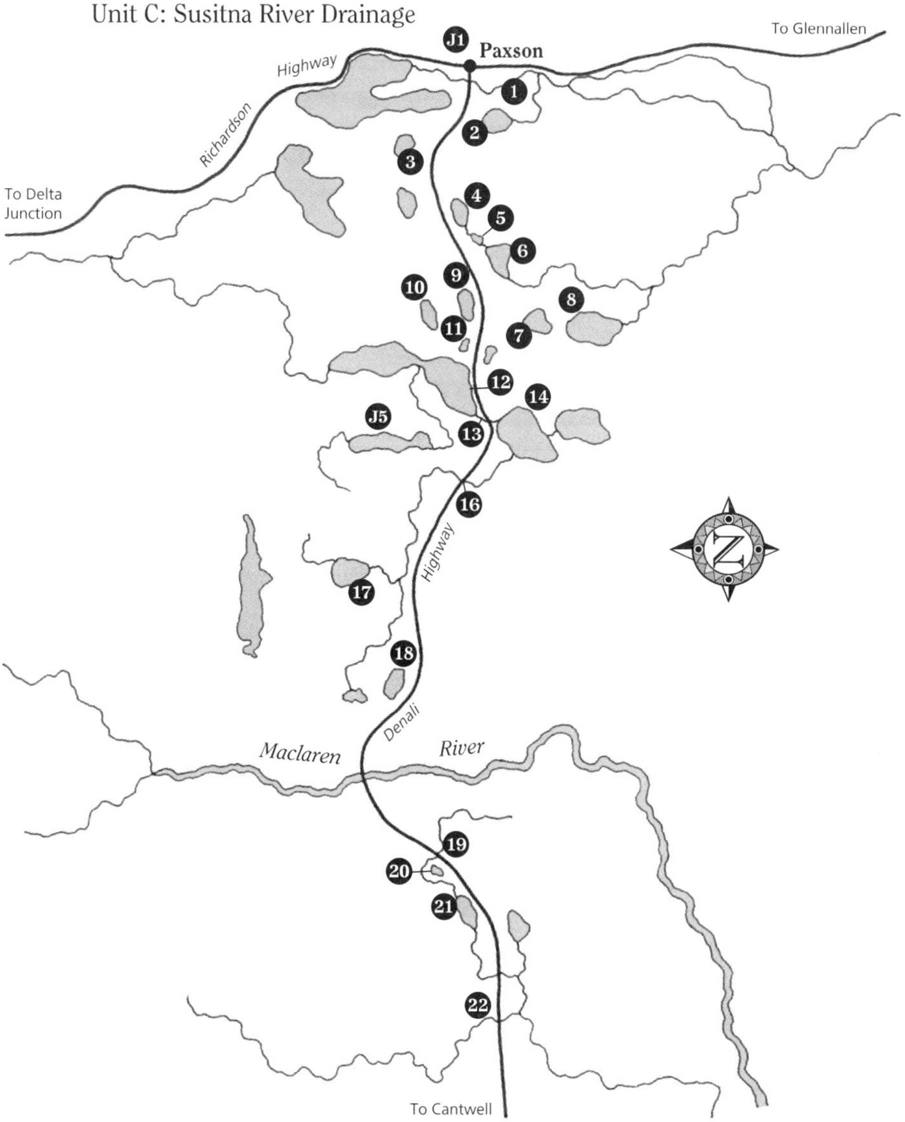

#	LOCATION	MILE POST	🚗	P	⛺	🥾	🛶	♿	🎣	PAGE
10.	Rusty Lake	16.8	●	◆		●			◆	87
11.	17-Mile Lake	17.0	●			●			◆	87
12.	Round Tangle Lake	21.5	●	●	●		●	●	●	87
13.	Tangle River	21.4	●	●					◆	87
14.	Upper Tangle Lake	21.7	●	●				●	◆	88
15.	Landmark Gap Lake	24.8	●	◆		●			◆	88

Map 2: Unit C: Susitna River Drainage
Unit D: Nenana River Drainage

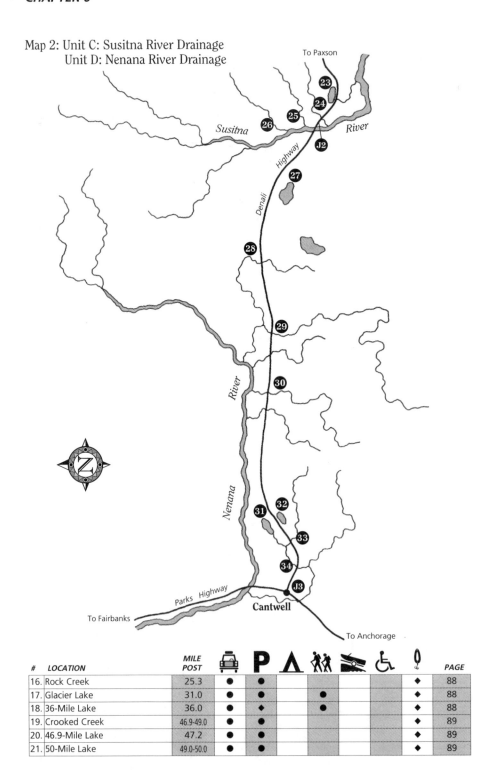

#	LOCATION	MILE POST		P	Λ	🚶	🛶	♿	♀	PAGE
16.	Rock Creek	25.3	●	●					◆	88
17.	Glacier Lake	31.0	●	●		●			◆	88
18.	36-Mile Lake	36.0	●	◆		●			◆	88
19.	Crooked Creek	46.9-49.0	●	●					◆	89
20.	46.9-Mile Lake	47.2	●	●					◆	89
21.	50-Mile Lake	49.0-50.0	●	●					◆	89

#	LOCATION	MILE POST	🚐	P	Δ	🚶	🛶	♿	🎣	PAGE
22.	Clearwater Creek	59.4	•	•					◆	89
23.	Lake, No Name	77.5	•	◆					◆	89
24.	Creek, No Name	79.2	•	◆					◆	89
J2.	Valdez Creek Rd.	78.8								
25.	Windy Creek	78.8	•	◆					◆	89
26.	Valdez Creek	78.8	•	•					◆	89
27.	Stevenson's Lake	84.0	•	◆		•			◆	90
28.	Canyon Creek	94.8	•	◆					◆	90
29.	Brushkana River	104.3	•	•	•				◆	90
30.	Seattle Creek	111.7	•	◆					◆	90
31.	Jerry Lake	125.4	•	•					◆	90
32.	Joe Lake	125.4	•	•					◆	90
33.	Fish Creek (Upper)	127.6	•	◆					◆	90
34.	Fish Creek (Lower)	132.3	•	◆					◆	90
J3.	Parks Hwy.	133.7								

DENALI HIGHWAY LOCATIONS

Unit A: Gulkana River Drainage

Includes all roadside waters flowing into and surrounding Gulkana River.

UNIT REGULATIONS:

* There are no general area-wide restrictions for waters in Unit A.

UNIT TIMING

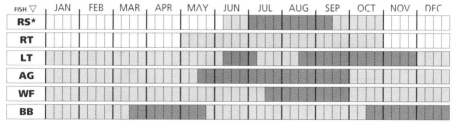

Note: Timing shown for salmon indicates fish in all stages of maturity.

1. East Fork Gulkana River

Access: MP 0.2; road crosses river.
Fishing: Salmon spawning stream supporting a good population of grayling.
Arctic Grayling / fair / mid-June – late September / 7-12 in. / spinners, flies.

2. Mud Lake

Access: MP 0.3; S on gravel road 0.6 mile to stream draining out of Mud Lake. Hike short distance upstream along creek to reach lake outlet.
Fishing: Lake contains a healty population of grayling. Outlet stream also has fish.
Arctic Grayling / good / June – September / 7-12 in. / spinners, flies.

3. Sevenmile Lake

Access: MP 6.9; N on gravel road 0.6 mile to lake.
Fishing: Decent number of char present. Use canoe/float tube.
Lake Trout / good / June, September – October / 2-5 lbs. / spoons, plugs, bait.

4. Tenmile Lake

Access: MP 9.9; S on gravel road 0.3 mile to lake.
Fishing: Lake contains a fair number of fish. Casting from shore can be productive.
Lake Trout / fair / June, September – October / 2-5 lbs. / spoons, plugs, bait.
Arctic Grayling / good / June – September / 7-12 in. / spinners, flies.
Burbot / fair / March – April, September – December / 2-4 lbs. / bait.

5. Teardrop Lake

Access: MP 10.4; hike short distance S down steep hill to lake.
Fishing: Small lake supporting a variety of fish. A few salmon also spawn here.
Lake Trout / fair / June, September – October / 2-5 lbs. / spoons, plugs, bait.
Arctic Grayling / good / June – September / 7-12 in. / spinners, flies.
Burbot / fair / March – April, September – December / 2-4 lbs. / bait.

6. Octopus Lake

Access: MP 11.1; hike 0.3 mile S through open terrain to lake.
Fishing: Mainly a char and grayling fishery. Casting from shore can be productive.
Lake Trout / fair / June, September – October / 2-5 lbs. / spoons, plugs, bait.
Arctic Grayling / good / June – September / 7-12 in. / spinners, flies.

7. Little Swede Lake

Access: MP 16.8; S on gravel road 0.2 mile to parking area on right next to sign. Cat trail leads S 1.7 mile to fork, right fork 0.8 mile to lake.
Fishing: Very productive lake for char in summer and fall. Use canoe/float tube.
Lake Trout / good / June, September – November / 2-6 lbs. / spoons, plugs, bait.

8. Big Swede Lake

Access: MP 16.8; S on gravel road 0.2 mile to parking area on right next to sign. Cat trail leads S 1.7 mile to fork, left/straight fork 1.3 mile to lake.
Fishing: Semi-remote lake with great char and grayling opportunities. Salmon present.
Lake Trout / good / June, September – November / 2-6 lbs. / spoons, plugs, bait.
Arctic Grayling / good-excellent / June – September / 7-14 in. / spinners, flies.
Burbot / fair / March – April, September – December / 2-5 lbs. / bait.

Unit B: Delta River Drainage

Includes all roadside waters flowing into and surrounding Delta River.

UNIT REGULATIONS:

* There are no general area-wide restrictions for waters in Unit B.

UNIT TIMING:

FISH ▽	JAN	FEB	MAR	APR	MAY	JUN	JUL	AUG	SEP	OCT	NOV	DEC
LT												
AG												
WF												
BB												

9. 16.8-Mile Lake

Access: MP 16.8; hike 200 yards N up creek to lake.
Fishing: Lake contains decent numbers of char and grayling. Use canoe/float tube.
Lake Trout / fair / June, September – October / 2-5 lbs. / spoons, plugs, bait.
Arctic Grayling / good / June – September / 7-12 in. / spinners, flies.

10. Rusty Lake

Access: MP 16.8; hike 0.6 mile N up creek to lake, about 0.5 mile beyond 16.8-Mile Lake.
Fishing: Lake contains decent numbers of char and grayling. Use canoe/float tube.
Lake Trout / fair / June, September – October / 2-5 lbs. / spoons, plugs, bait.
Arctic Grayling / good / June – September / 7-12 in. / spinners, flies.

11. 17-Mile Lake

Access: MP 17.0; trail leads 0.2 mile N to lake.
Fishing: Lake contains decent numbers of char, grayling, burbot. Use canoe/float tube.
Lake Trout / fair / June, September – October / 2-5 lbs. / spoons, plugs, bait.
Arctic Grayling / good / June – September / 7-12 in. / spinners, flies.
Burbot / fair / March – April, September – December / 2-5 lbs. / bait.

12. Round Tangle Lake

Access: MP 21.5; road parallels lake.
Fishing: Lake contains large population of fish. Use canoe/float tube or cast from shore.
Lake Trout / good / 2-5 lbs. (20 lbs.) / spoons, plugs, bait.
Arctic Grayling / excellent / 7-14 in. (20 in.) / spinners, flies.
Burbot / fair / 2-4 lbs. (1 lbs.) / bait.

FISH ▽	JAN	FEB	MAR	APR	MAY	JUN	JUL	AUG	SEP	OCT	NOV	DEC
LT												
AG												
BB												

13. Tangle River

Access: MP 21.4; road crosses river.
Fishing: Short river with great fall opportunities for grayling. Scout for holes and runs.
Arctic Grayling / good / mid-August – late September / 7-12 in. / spinners, flies.

14. Upper Tangle Lake
Access: MP 21.7; road parallels lake.
Fishing: Lake contains decent populations of fish. Use canoe/float tube, cast from shore.
Lake Trout / fair / June, September – November / 2-4 lbs. / spoons, plugs, bait.
Arctic Grayling / good / June – September / 7-14 in. / spinners, flies.
Burbot / fair / March – April, September – December / 2-4 lbs. / bait.

15. Landmark Gap Lake
Access: MP 24.8; BLM trail leads 3.0 miles N to lake.
Fishing: One of the better angling spots on the highway. Great for char and grayling.
Lake Trout / good / June, September – October / 2-5 lbs. / spoons, plugs, bait.
Arctic Grayling / excellent / June – September / 7-14 in. / spinners, flies.
Burbot / fair / March – April, September – December / 2-4 lbs. / bait.

16. Rock Creek
Access: MP 25.3; road crosses stream.
Fishing: Small clearwater stream with prodcutive spring and fall grayling opportunities.
Arctic Grayling / fair-good / June, September / 7-12 in. / spinners, flies.

17. Glacier Lake
Access: MP 31.0; cat trail leads 2.0 miles N to lake.
Fishing: Semi-remote lake with superb potential for char and grayling.
Lake Trout / good / June, September – November / 2-6 lbs. / spoons, plugs, bait.
Arctic Grayling / excellent / June – September / 7-14 in. / spinners, flies.

18. 36-Mile Lake
Access: MP 36.0; hike 0.5 mile N to lake.
Fishing: Lake supports a decent population of char and grayling. Use canoe/float tube.
Lake Trout / fair / June, September – October / 2-5 lbs. / spoons, plugs, bait.
Arctic Grayling / good / June – September / 7-14 in. / spinners, flies.

Unit C: Susitna River Drainage
Includes all roadside waters draining into and surrounding Susitna River.

UNIT REGULATIONS:

* There are no general area-wide restrictions for waters inUnit C.

UNIT TIMING:

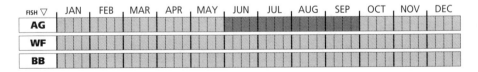

FISH ▽	JAN	FEB	MAR	APR	MAY	JUN	JUL	AUG	SEP	OCT	NOV	DEC
AG												
WF												
BB												

19. Crooked Creek
Access: MP 46.9 – 49.0; road parallels stream.
Fishing: Clearwater stream supporting a decent number of grayling in summer, fall.
Arctic Grayling / good / early June – mid-September / 7-12 in. / spinners, flies.

20. 46.9-Mile Lake
Access: MP 47.2; hike short distance N to lake.
Fishing: Lake supports a large populaton of grayling. Use canoe/float tube.
Arctic Grayling / good-excellent / June – September / 7-12 in. / spinners, flies.

21. 50-Mile Lake
Access: MP 49.0 – 50.0; road parallels lake.
Fishing: Lake supports a moderate number of grayling. Use canoe/float tube.
Arctic Grayling / fair / June – September / 7-12 in. / spinners, flies.

22. Clearwater Creek
Access: MP 59.4; road crosses stream.
Fishing: Decent number of grayling available throughout the summer months.
Arctic Grayling / good / mid-June – mid-September / 7-12 in. / spinners, flies.

23. Lake, No Name
Access: MP 77.5; road parallels lake and crosses outlet stream.
Fishing: Little-fished lake containing a fair population of grayling.
Arctic Grayling / fair / June – September / 7-12 in. / spinners, flies.

24. Creek, No Name
Access: MP 79.2; road crosses stream.
Fishing: Small clearwtaer stream supporting a late spring/early summer grayling fishery.
Arctic Grayling / fair / mid-June – mid-September / 7-12 in. / spinners, flies.

25. Windy Creek
Access: MP 78.8; N on Valdez Creek Rd. 0.6 mile to stream crossing.
Fishing: Small number of grayling available during the summer months.
Arctic Grayling / fair / mid-June – early September / 7-14 in. / spinners, flies.

26. Valdez Creek
Access: MP 78.8; N on Valdez Creek Rd. 4.5 miles to stream on left.
Fishing: Small number of grayling available during the summer months.
Arctic Grayling / fair-good / mid-June – early September / 7-14 in. / spinners, flies.

Unit D: Nenana River Drainage
Includes all roadside waters flowing into and surrounding Nenana River.

UNIT REGULATIONS: *There are no general area-wide restrictions for waters in Unit D.
UNIT TIMING:

FISH ▽	JAN	FEB	MAR	APR	MAY	JUN	JUL	AUG	SEP	OCT	NOV	DEC
DV												
AG												
WF												

27. Stevenson's Lake
Access: MP 84.0; hike 0.5 mile S through open terrain to lake.
Fishing: Lake supports a decent population of grayling. Use canoe/float tube.
Arctic Grayling / good / June – September / 7-14 in. / spinners, flies.

28. Canyon Creek
Access: MP 94.8; road crosses stream.
Fishing: Small stream supporting a summer fishery for grayling. Look for deep holes.
Arctic Grayling / fair-good / mid-June – late August / 7-12 in. / spinners, flies.

29. Brushkana River
Access: MP 104.3; road crosses river.
Fishing: Clearwater stream supporting large grayling population. Hike away from road.
Dolly Varden / fair / mid-July – mid-September / 7-12 in. / flies, bait.
Arctic Grayling / good / early June – mid-September / 7-12 in. / spinners, flies.

30. Seattle Creek
Access: MP 111.7; road crosses stream.
Fishing: Small stream supporting a summer fishery for char and grayling. Scout holes.
Dolly Varden / fair / mid-July – mid-September / 7-12 in. / flies, bait.
Arctic Grayling / fair-good / mid-June – late August / 7-12 in. / spinners, flies.

31. Jerry Lake
Access: MP 125.4; trail leads short distance N to lake.
Fishing: Lake contains a small population of grayling. Casting from shore possible.
Arctic Grayling / fair-good / June – September / 7-12 in. / spinners, flies.

32. Joe Lake
Access: MP 125.4; trail leads short distance S to lake.
Fishing: Lake contains a small population of grayling. Casting from shore possible.
Arctic Grayling / fair-good / June – September / 7-12 in. / spinners, flies.

33. Fish Creek (Upper)
Access: MP 127.6; road crosses stream.
Fishing: Small clearwater stream supporting a decent number of grayling in summer.
Arctic Grayling / fair-good / mid-June – mid-September / 7-12 in. / spinners, flies.

34. Fish Creek (Lower)
Access: MP 132.3; road crosses stream.
Fishing: Clearwater stream supporting a healthy population of grayling in summer, fall.
Arctic Grayling / excellent / early June – late September / 7-12 in. / spinners, flies.

Other Locations

Unit C: Susitna River Drainage:
Maclaren River - MP 42.0; AG,(WF) Susitna River - MP 79.3; AG,(WF)
Unit D: Nenana River Drainage:
Stickwan Creek - MP 107.2; AG

LOCATION & SPECIES APPENDIX

● - Wild/Native fish, fishable numbers.

◆ - Present in small numbers and/or only occasionally caught.

▲ - Stocked/Hatchery fish, fishable numbers.

■ - Mix of Wild and Hatchery fish, fishable numbers.

✕ - Indicated species present but currently protected by law (PROHIBITED).

#	LOCATION	KING SALMON	RED SALMON	PINK SALMON	CHUM SALMON	SILVER SALMON	LANDLOCKED SALMON	KOKANEE	STEELHEAD TROUT	RAINBOW TROUT	LAKE TROUT	ARCTIC CHAR	DOLLY VARDEN	SHEEFISH	ARCTIC GRAYLING	WHITEFISH	NORTHERN PIKE	BURBOT	PACIFIC HALIBUT	LING COD	ROCKFISH
1.	East Fork Gulkana River	✕								◆					●	◆					
2.	Mud Lake	◆								◆					●						
3.	Sevenmile Lake										●				●						
4.	Tenmile Lake										●				●	◆		●			
5.	Teardrop Lake			◆							●				●	◆		●			
6.	Octopus Lake			◆							●				●	◆					
7.	Little Swede Lake										●				●						
8.	Big Swede Lake			◆							●				●	◆		●			
9.	16.8-Mile Lake										●				●						
10.	Rusty Lake										●				●						
11.	17-Mile Lake										●				●	◆		●			
12.	Round Tangle Lake										●				●	◆		●			
13.	Tangle River														●						
14.	Upper Tangle Lake										●				●	◆		●			
15.	Landmark Gap Lake										●				●	◆		●			
16.	Rock Creek														●						
17.	Glacier Lake										●				●	◆					
18.	36-Mile Lake										●				●						
19.	Crooked Creek														●						
20.	46.9-Mile Lake														●						
21.	50-Mile Lake														●						
22.	Clearwater Creek														●						
23.	Lake, No Name														●						
24.	Creek, No Name														●						
25.	Windy Creek														●						
26.	Valdez Creek														●						
27.	Stevenson's Lake														●						
28.	Canyon Creek														●						
29.	Brushkana River												●		●						
30.	Seattle Creek												●		●						
31.	Jerry Lake														●						
32.	Joe Lake														●						
33.	Fish Creek (Upper)														●						
34.	Fish Creek (Lower)														●						

Edgerton Highway

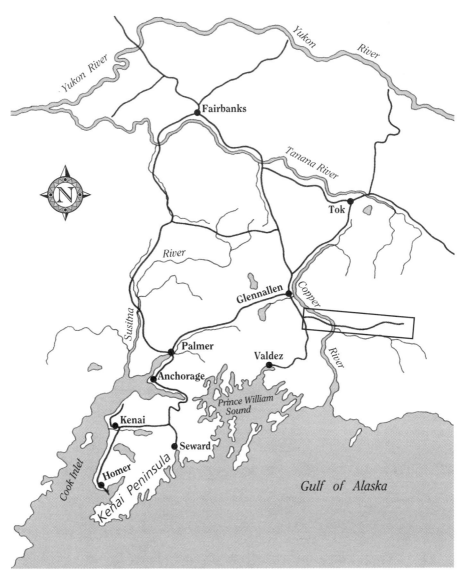

Area Covered: Richardson Highway Junction to Kennicott River; 93.4 miles
Regulatory Unit: Copper River Drainage
Number of Locations: 17

FISHING THE EDGERTON HIGHWAY

The Edgerton Highway has a few limited stream fishing opportunities (mainly for grayling) and a couple of small, yet very productive, lakes containing stocked trout and grayling. The McCarthy Road, however, has more variety to offer and provides access to several larger lakes with healthy populations of stocked land-locked salmon and trout and lesser numbers of native char, grayling, and burbot. Sea-run salmon are mainly present in area rivers, but no significant sport fishery exists due to the glacial nature of some of these waters. However, an important personal use dip net fishery takes place along the Copper River during the summer months. Angler success is fair in streams, good to excellent in lakes.

Angling pressure is usually light throughout the year, though some lakes, particularly along the McCarthy Road, may receive a fair amount of attention in fall and winter by fishers seeking trout.

Recommended Hot Spots: 2-Mile, 3-Mile, Strelna, Silver, Van, and Sculpin lakes.

Content
Pages

QUICK REFERENCE

 Road Condition   Parking Area   Camp Sites   Hiking Trails   Boat Launch   Handicap Access   Fishing Pressure

■ - Good to Highly developed/conditions, intense pressure
● - Fair to Moderately developed/conditions, moderate pressure
◆ - Poor to marginally developed/conditions, limited pressure
✕ - Prohibited

#	LOCATION	MILE POST	🚗	P	⋀	🚶	🚤	♿	🎣	PAGE
J1.	Richardson Hwy.	0								
1.	Willow Creek	5.5	■	◆					◆	96
2.	Tonsina River (Lower)	19.2	■	◆					◆	96
3.	Liberty Falls Creek	23.6	■	●	●				◆	96
4.	3-Mile Lake	29.6-30.0	■	●	◆				◆	96
5.	2-Mile Lake	30.1-30.7	■	●					◆	97
6.	Chitina (Town) Lake	33.4	●	●				◆	◆	97
J2.	McCarthy Rd.	35.1								
	McCarthy Road									
J2.	Edgerton Hwy.	0								
7.	Strelna (Nelson) Lake	8.3	●	●		●			◆	97
8.	Silver Lake	9.3	●	●	●			◆	◆	97
9.	Van Lake	9.3	●	●		●			◆	97
10.	Sculpin Lake	10.8	●	●	●			◆	◆	97
11.	Strelna Creek	13.3	●	●	●				◆	97

Map: Unit: Copper River Drainage

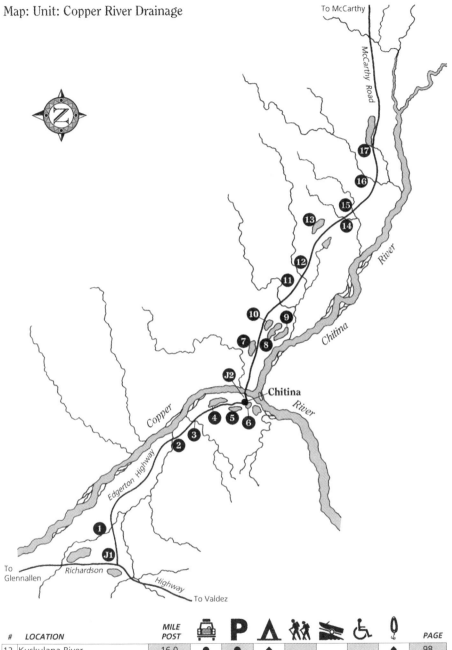

#	LOCATION	MILE POST	🚐	P	△	🥾	🛶	♿	⚓	PAGE
12.	Kuskulana River	16.0	●	●	◆				◆	98
13.	Lou' s Lake	23.5	●	●		●			◆	98
14.	Chokosna River	25.5	●	●	●				◆	98
15.	Gilahina River	27.7	●	●	◆			●	◆	98
16.	Lakina River	42.9	●	●					◆	98
17.	Long Lake	44.7-46.9	●	●					◆	98

EDGERTON HIGHWAY LOCATIONS

Unit: Copper River Drainage

Includes all roadside waters flowing into and surrounding Copper River.

UNIT REGULATIONS:

* There are no general area-wide restrictions for waters in this unit.

UNIT TIMING

FISH ▽	JAN	FEB	MAR	APR	MAY	JUN	JUL	AUG	SEP	OCT	NOV	DEC
KS												
RS												
SS												
LS												
ST												
RT												
LT												
DV												
AG												
WF												
BB												

1. Willow Creek

Access: MP 5.5; highway crosses stream.
Fishing: Slow-flowing clearwater stream supporting a spring run of grayling.
Arctic Grayling / fair-good / early May – early June / 7-12 in. / spinners, flies.

2. Tonsina River

Access: MP 19.2; highway crosses river.
Fishing: Glacial river offereing limited angling opportunities for salmon, char, and grayling. Seek out calm sections of water away from fast current. Use bait.
Silver Salmon / poor-fair / late August – mid-September / 6-10 lbs. / attractors, bait.
Dolly Varden / poor-fair / mid-July – mid-October / 7-15 in. / spinners, attractors.
Arctic Grayling / poor-fair / May, September / 7-14 in. / spinners, attractors.

3. Liberty Falls Creek

Access: MP 23.6; highway crosses stream.
Fishing: Very small, shallow stream containing a few grayling during summer months.
Arctic Grayling / poor / mid-June – mid-August / 7-10 in. / spinners, flies.

4. 3-Mile Lake

Access: MP 29.6 – 30.0; highway parallels lake.
Fishing: Small lake stocked with trout and grayling. Cast from shore or float tube.
Rainbow Trout / good / June, September – December / 7-15 in. / spinners, flies, bait.
Arctic Grayling / good / June – September / 7-12 in. / spinners, flies.

5. 2-Mile Lake

Access: MP 30.1 – 30.7; highway parallels lake.
Fishing: Small lake stocked with trout and grayling. Cast from shore or float tube.
Rainbow Trout / good / June, September – December / 7-15 in. / spinners, flies, bait.
Arctic Grayling / good / June – September / 7-12 in. / spinners, flies.

6. Town (Chitina) Lake

Access: MP 33.4; road parallels lake.
Fishing: Small lake stocked with grayling. Cast from shore or float tube.
Arctic Grayling / fair / June – September / 7-10 in. / spinners, flies.

McCarthy Road

Road begins in Chitina (Mile 0) and ends at Kennicott River (Mile 58.2).

7. Strelna (Nelson) Lake

Access: Mile 8.3; trail leads 0.3 mile due N to lake.
Fishing: Lake contains a healthy population of stocked salmon and trout.
Landlocked Salmon / excellent / June – March / 7-12 in. / spinners, jigs, flies, bait.
Rainbow Trout / good / June, September – December / 8-16 in. / spoons, flies, bait.

8. Silver Lake

Access: Mile 9.3; S on access road to lake.
Fishing: Lake contains a healthy population of stocked trout. Big fish possible.
Rainbow Trout / good / June, September – December / 8-16 in. / spoons, flies, bait.

9. Van Lake

Access: Mile 9.3; park at Silver Lake access site on right. Trail leads 1.25 mile due S to lake.
Fishing: Lake contains a healthy population of stocked trout. Big fish possible.
Rainbow Trout / good / June, September – December / 7-16 in. / spoons, flies, bait.

10. Sculpin Lake

Access: Mile 10.8; S on access road to lake.
Fishing: Lake contains a healthy population of stocked trout, some char.
Rainbow Trout / excellent / June, September – December / 7-16 in. / spoons, flies, bait.
Dolly Varden / fair / September – December / 7-12 in. / spinners, flies, bait.

11. Strelna Creek

Access: Mile 13.3; road crosses stream.
Fishing: Small clearwater stream supporting a population of char in summer and fall.
Dolly Varden / fair / mid-July – mid-September / 7-15 in. / spinners, flies, bait.

12. Kuskulana River

Access: Mile 16.0; road crosses river. Road W of bridge leads short distance to parking area with access to river.
Fishing: Glacial drainage with limited opportunities for char and grayling in fall.
Dolly Varden / fair / mid-September – mid-October / 7-15 in. / spinners, flies, bait.
Arctic Grayling / fair / mid-September – mid-October / 7-12 in. / spinners, flies.

13. Lou's Lake

Access: Mile 23.5; trail leads 0.75 mile N to lake.
Fishing: Lake supports a decent population of grayling. Use canoe/float tube.
Arctic Grayling / good / June – September / 7-14 in. / spinners, flies.

14. Chokosna River

Access: Mile 25.5; road crosses stream.
Fishing: Small river with limited opportunities for char and grayling in summer and fall.
Dolly Varden / poor-fair / mid-July – mid-September / 7-15 in. / spinners, bait.
Arctic Grayling / poor-fair / mid-June – mid-September / 7-12 in. / spinners, flies.

15. Gilahina River

Access: Mile 27.7; road crosses stream.
Fishing: Small river with limited opportunities for char and grayling in summer and fall.
Dolly Varden / poor-fair / mid-July – mid-September / 7-15 in. / spinners, bait.
Arctic Grayling / poor-fair / mid-June – mid-September / 7-12 in. / spinners, flies.

16. Lakina River

Access: Mile 42.9; road crosses river.
Fishing: Small river with limited opportunities for char and grayling in fall.
Dolly Varden / fair / late August – mid-October / 7-15 in. / spinners, flies, bait.
Arctic Grayling / fair / late August – mid-October / 7-12 in. / spinners, flies.

17. Long Lake

Access: Mile 44.7 – 46.9; road parallels lake.
Fishing: Large lake containing decent populations of various species. Use a canoe.
Lake Trout / fair / June, September – November / 2-6 lbs. / spoons, plugs, bait.
Dolly Varden / fair / September – December / 7-15 in. / spoons, spinners, bait.
Arcitc Grayling / fair-good / June – September / 7-14 in. / spinners, flies.
Burbot / fair / March – April, September – December / 2-4 lbs. / bait.

Other Locations

Unit: Copper River Drainage:
Edgerton Highway: Copper River - MP 34.7; BB, (KS, RS, SS, ST, RT, DV, AG, WF)
McCarthy Road: Swift Creek - MP 54.9; AG, (DV) Kennicott River - MP 58.2; DV, AG, (SS)

LOCATION & SPECIES APPENDIX

● - Wild/Native fish, fishable numbers.

◆ - Present in small numbers and/or only occasionally caught.

▲ - Stocked/Hatchery fish, fishable numbers.

■ - Mix of Wild and Hatchery fish, fishable numbers.

✕ - Indicated species present but currently protected by law (PROHIBITED).

#	LOCATION	KING SALMON	RED SALMON	PINK SALMON	CHUM SALMON	SILVER SALMON	LANDLOCKED SALMON	STEELHEAD TROUT	KOKANEE	RAINBOW TROUT	LAKE TROUT	ARCTIC CHAR	DOLLY VARDEN	ARCTIC GRAYLING	SHEEFISH	WHITEFISH	NORTHERN PIKE	BURBOT	PACIFIC HALIBUT	LING COD	ROCKFISH
1.	Willow Creek													●							
2.	Tonsina River (Lower)	◆	◆			●							◆	●		●	◆	◆			
3.	Liberty Falls Creek													●							
4.	3-Mile Lake									▲											
5.	2-Mile Lake									▲											
6.	Town (Chitina) Lake													●							
	McCarthy Road																				
7.	Strelna Lake						▲			▲											
8.	Silver Lake									▲											
9.	Van Lake									▲											
10.	Sculpin Lake									▲			●								
11.	Strelna Creek												●								
12.	Kuskulana River					◆							●	●							
13.	Lou's Lake													●							
14.	Chokosna River	✕	◆										●	●							
15.	Gilahina River	✕	◆			◆							●	●							
16.	Lakina River		◆			◆				◆			●	●							
17.	Long Lake		◆			◆				◆	◆	●	●	●				●			

Elliott Highway

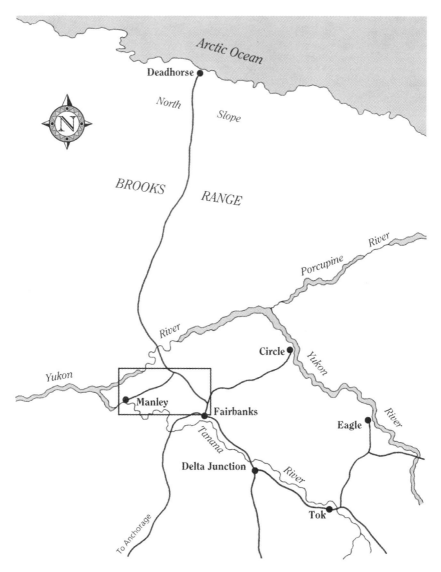

Area Covered: Fox to Manley Hot Springs; 152 miles
Regulatory Unit: Tanana River Drainage
Number of Locations: 11

FISHING THE ELLIOTT HIGHWAY

The Elliott Highway offers extensive access to the Tolovana River drainage and a few clearwater tributaries of Tanana River. Grayling is the major sport fish species here and are present in most all lakes and streams along the highway, followed by lesser numbers of whitefish, pike, and burbot that are chiefly present in larger area lakes and rivers. Runs of salmon (mostly kings and some chums) occur primarily in the Chatanika River, which also hosts a small population of sheefish - a rather rare roadside species. The salmon, however, are in or near spawning condition and usually not suitable for consumption. Stocked trout are available, too. Angler success is fair to good in both lakes and streams.

Boaters do well exploring the Minto Flats area and parts of Manley Hot Springs Slough.

Angling pressure is light throughout the summer season, with the Chatanika River receiving some moderate effort during the summer king salmon run.

Recommended Hot Spots: Olnes Pond; Chatanika and West Fork Tolovana rivers; Hutlinana Creek.

Content

QUICK REFERENCE

 Road Condition
 Parking Area
 Camp Sites
 Hiking Trails
 Boat Launch
Handicap Access
Fishing Pressure

■ - Good to Highly developed/conditions, intense pressure
● - Fair to Moderately developed/conditions, moderate pressure
◆ - Poor to marginally developed/conditions, limited pressure
✕ - Prohibited

#	LOCATION	MILE POST	🚗	P	⛺	Hiking	Boat	♿	Fishing	PAGE
J1.	Steese Highway	0								
1.	Olnes Pond	10.6	●	●	◆			■	◆	104
2.	Chatanika River (Middle)									
	Access A	10.6	●	■	●	●			●	104
	Access B	11.0	■	●	◆			◆	●	104
3.	Washington Creek	18.3	●	●					◆	105
4.	Globe Creek	37.0	●	●					◆	105
5.	Tatalina Creek	44.8	●	●					◆	105
6.	Tolovana River (Upper)	57.0	●	●					◆	105
J2.	Dalton Highway	73.1								
7.	West Fork Tolovana R.	74.9	●	●					◆	105
8.	Tolovana R. / Minto Flats	109.8	●	●	◆		●	■	◆	105
9.	Hutlinana Creek	129.3	●	●					◆	105
10.	Baker Creek	137.3	●	●					◆	105
11.	Hot Springs Slough	152.0	●	●			●	■	◆	106

Map: Unit: Tanana River Drainage

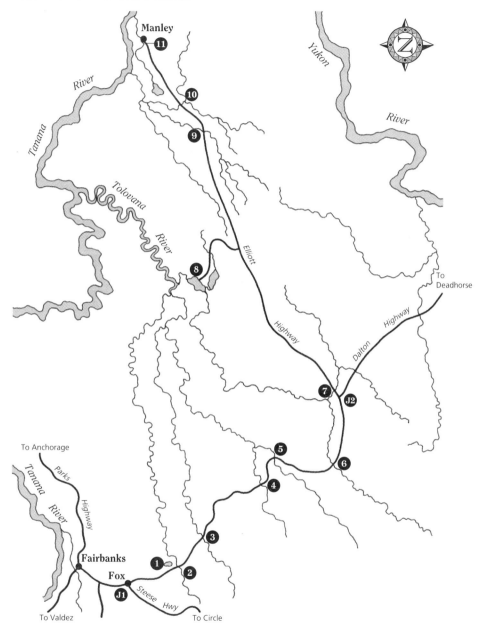

ELLIOTT HIGHWAY LOCATIONS

Unit: Tanana River Drainage

Includes all roadside waters flowing into and surrounding Tanana River.

UNIT REGULATIONS:

* There are no general area-wide restrictions for waters in this unit.

UNIT TIMING:

FISH ▽	JAN	FEB	MAR	APR	MAY	JUN	JUL	AUG	SEP	OCT	NOV	DEC
KS*							▓					
CS*							▓					
SS*								▓	▓			
RT	▓	▓	▓			▓		▓	▓	▓	▓	▓
DV						▓	▓	▓	▓			
SF						▓	▓		▓			
AG				▓	▓	▓	▓	▓	▓	▓		
WF	▓	▓	▓						▓	▓	▓	▓
NP						▓	▓	▓				
BB	▓	▓	▓	▓		▓	▓	▓	▓	▓		

* **Note:** *Timing shown for salmon indicates fish in all stages of maturity.*

1. Olnes Pond

Access: MP 10.6; W on gravel road 1.0 mile to access road on right, short distance to parking area and pond.
Fishing: Small pond stocked with trout and grayling. Good shore fishing.
Rainbow Trout / fair-good / June, September – December / 7-15 in. / spinners, flies, bait.
Arctic Grayling / fair-good / June – September / 7-12 in. / spinners, flies.

2. Chatanika River

Access A: MP 10.6; W on gravel road 1.0 mile to access road on right, short distance to parking area by Olnes Pond. Locate one of two trails leading to river.
Access B: MP 11.0; highway crosses stream.
Fishing: Salmon spawning river offering a variety of species. Grayling most abundant.
King Salmon / fair-good / mid-July – late July / 8-20 lbs. / spoons, spinners, flies.
Chum Salmon / poor / mid-July – late July / 5-10 lbs. / spoons, spinners, flies.
Sheefish / poor / mid-September – late September / 4-8 lbs. / spoons, spinners, flies.
Arctic Grayling / good / early September – early October / 10-18. / spoons, spinners, flies.
Whitefish / poor-fair / mid-June – mid-September / 8-20 lbs. / flies, bait.
Northern Pike / poor-fair / mid-June – mid-September / 2-5 lbs. / spoons, plugs, flies.
Burbot / poor / mid-June – mid-October / 10-20 in. / bait.

3. Washington Creek
Access: MP 18.3; highway crosses stream.
Fishing: Small stream supporting a decent population of grayling in summer and fall.
Arctic Grayling / fair / early June – mid-September / 7-12 in. / spinners, flies.

4. Globe Creek
Access: MP 37.0; highway crosses stream.
Fishing: Small stream supporting a decent population of grayling in summer and fall.
Arctic Grayling / fair / early June – mid-September / 7-12 in. / spinners, flies.

5. Tatalina Creek
Access: MP 44.8; highway crosses stream.
Fishing: Small stream supporting a decent population of grayling in summer and fall.
Arctic Grayling / fair / early June – mid-September / 7-12 in. / spinners, flies.

6. Tolovana River
Access: MP 57.0; highway crosses stream.
Fishing: Small river supporting a decent population of grayling in summer and fall.
Arctic Grayling / fair / early June – mid-September / 7-12 in. / spinners, flies.

7. West Fork Tolovana River
Access: MP 74.9; highway crosses stream.
Fishing: Small river supporting a decent population of grayling in summer and fall.
Arctic Grayling / fair-good / early June – late September / 7-12 in. / spinners, flies.

8. Tolovana River / Minto Flats
Access: MP 109.8; S on Minto Rd. 10.8 miles to Minto Village and the flats.
Fishing: Some fish available from shore but best action is accessed by boat.
Arctic Grayling / fair / June – September / 7-14 in. / spinners, flies.
Northern Pike / fair / June – October / 2-6 lbs. / spoons, plugs, attractors.
Burbot / fair / March – April, September – December / 2-6 lbs. / bait.

9. Hutlinana Creek
Access: MP 129.3; highway crosses stream.
Fishing: Stream supports summer and fall populations of char and grayling.
Dolly Varden / fair-good / mid-July – late September / 7-12 in. / flies, bait.
Arctic Grayling / fair-good / early June – mid-September / 7-12 in. / spinners, flies.

10. Baker Creek
Access: MP 137.3; highway crosses stream.
Fishing: Stream supports summer and fall populations of char and grayling.
Dolly Varden / fair / mid-July – late September / 7-12 in. / flies, bait.
Arctic Grayling / fair-good / early June – mid-September / 7-12 in. / spinners, flies.

11. Hot Springs Slough

Access: MP 152.0; highway crosses slough.
Fishing: Some fish available from shore but best action is accessed by boat.
Northern Pike / fair / June – September / 2-6 lbs. / spoons, plugs, bait.
Burbot / fair / March – April, September – December / 2-4 lbs. / bait.

Other Locations

None

LOCATION & SPECIES APPENDIX

● - Wild/Native fish, fishable numbers.
◆ - Present in small numbers and/or only occasionally caught.
▲ - Stocked/Hatchery fish, fishable numbers.
■ - Mix of Wild and Hatchery fish, fishable numbers.
✕ - Indicated species present but currently protected by law (PROHIBITED).

#	LOCATION	KING SALMON	RED SALMON	PINK SALMON	CHUM SALMON	SILVER SALMON	LANDLOCKED SALMON	KOKANEE	STEELHEAD TROUT	RAINBOW TROUT	LAKE TROUT	ARCTIC CHAR	DOLLY VARDEN	SHEEFISH	ARCTIC GRAYLING	WHITEFISH	NORTHERN PIKE	BURBOT	PACIFIC HALIBUT	LING COD	ROCKFISH
1.	Olnes Pond									▲					▲	◆		◆			
2.	Chatanika River (Middle)	●			●	◆									●	●	●	●	●		
3.	Washington Creek														●	◆		◆			
4.	Globe Creek														●	◆					
5.	Tatalina Creek														●	◆		◆			
6.	Tolovana River (Upper)														●	◆		◆			
7.	West Fork Tolovana River														●	◆					
8.	Tolovana R. / Minto Flats	◆			◆	◆									◆	●	◆	●	●		
9.	Hutlinana Creek				◆								●		●	◆					
10.	Baker Creek				◆								●	◆	●	◆	◆	◆			
11.	Hot Springs Slough														◆	◆	◆	●	●		

Fairbanks Area

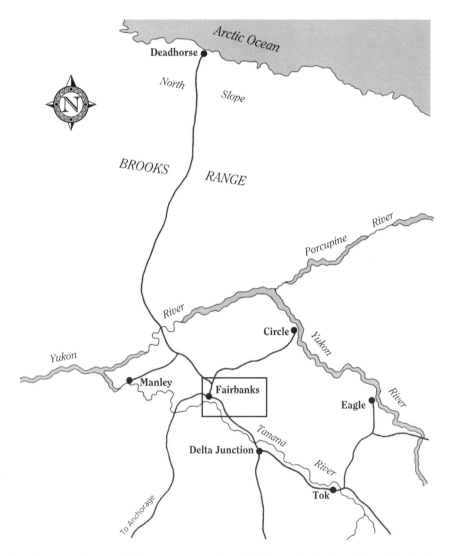

Area Covered: Greater Fairbanks area roads and highways, including Chena Hot Springs Road and military bases
Regulatory Units: (A) Fairbanks City Drainages; (B) Tanana River Drainage; (C) Chena River Drainage
Number of Locations: 37

FISHING THE FAIRBANKS AREA

The Fairbanks Area roads and highways provide excellent access to lakes, ponds, and the Tanana River drainage in and around the city of Fairbanks and surrounding military installations. Permits are required to access the bases. Rivers and streams in the area contain primarily grayling, yet healthy populations of native king and chum salmon, whitefish, pike, and burbot are also present. Extensive stocking efforts have created popular lake fisheries for land-locked salmon, trout, char, and grayling. Angler success is fair to good in both lakes and streams.

Angling pressure is for the most part fairly light with the brunt of it occurring on the Chena River during the brief king salmon run.

Recommended Hot Spots: Chena River; Chena Lake; Piledriver and Badger sloughs; 45.5-Mile, 48-Mile, North Pole, and Bathing Beauty ponds.

Content   *Pages*

QUICK REFERENCE

Road Condition	**P** Parking Area	**A** Camp Sites	Hiking Trails	Boat Launch	Handicap Access	Fishing Pressure

■ - Good to Highly developed/conditions, intense pressure
● - Fair to Moderately developed/conditions, moderate pressure
◆ - Poor to marginally developed/conditions, limited pressure
× - Prohibited

#	LOCATION	MILE POST		**P**	**A**	Hiking	Boat	Handicap	Fishing	PAGE
	Fairbanks City									
1.	Chena River (Lower)	(City)	■	●	●		●	●	◆	112
2.	Ballaine Lake	358.0	■	●				◆	◆	112
	Ft. Wainwright									
3.	Chena River (Lower)	(Base)								
	Access A			●	●				◆	113
	Access B			■	●				◆	113
	Access C			●	●				◆	113
4.	Monterey Lake	(Base)	■	◆					◆	113
5.	Wainwright #6 Pond	(Base)	●	●					◆	113
6.	Lundgren Pond	(Base)	●	●					◆	113

Map 1: Unit A: Fairbanks City Drainages
Unit B: Tanana River Drainage

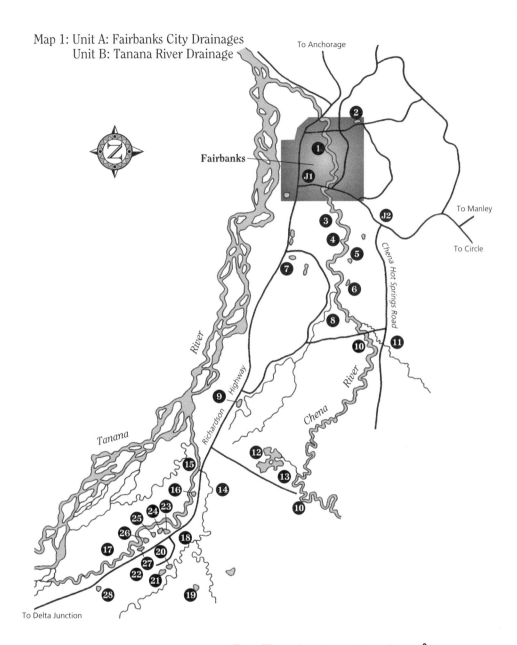

#	LOCATION	MILE POST	🚗	P	△	🥾	🛶	♿	⚓	PAGE
	Richardson Highway									
J1.	Jct.: Steese Expressway	363.9								
7.	Sirlin Drive Pond	357.1	●	●					◆	114
8.	Badger (Chena) Slough	357.1/349.5	■	●					●	114
9.	North Pole Pond	349.5	●	●					◆	115

Map 2: Unit C: Chena River Drainage

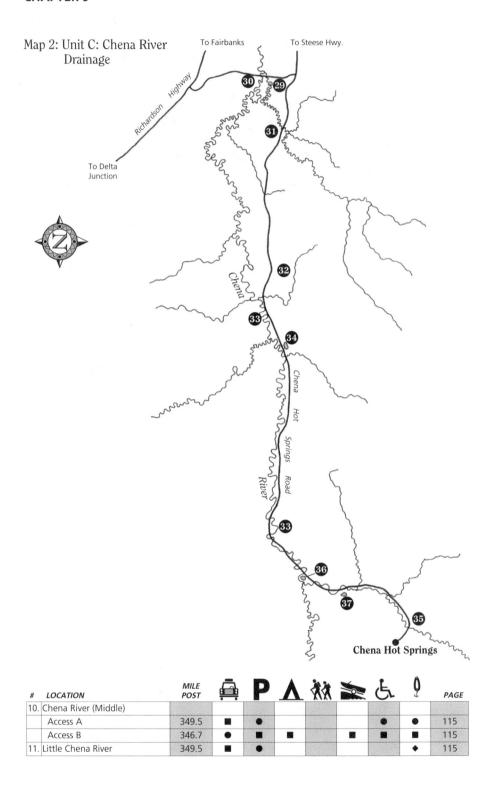

To Fairbanks

To Steese Hwy.

Richardson Highway

To Delta Junction

Chena

Chena Hot Springs Road

River

Chena Hot Springs

#	LOCATION	MILE POST		P	A	🚶	🛶	♿	𝄆	PAGE
10.	Chena River (Middle)									
	Access A	349.5	■	●				●	●	115
	Access B	346.7	●	■	■		■	■	■	115
11.	Little Chena River	349.5	■	●					◆	115

#	LOCATION	MILE POST	🚗	P	Λ	👥	🚤	♿	⚓	PAGE
12.	Chena Lake	346.7	●	■	■		■	■	■	115
13.	North Chena Pond	346.7	●	◆					◆	116
14.	Moose Creek	344.7	■	●					◆	116
15.	Piledriver Slough									
	Access A	344.7	●	●					●	116
	Access B	343.7	●	●					●	116
	Access C	343.0	■	●		●			●	116
	Access D	342.6	●	●					●	116
16.	Bathing Beauty Pond	343.7	●	●				■	●	116
	Eielson AFB									
17.	Piledriver Slough									
	Access A	338.7	●	●					●	117
	Access B	338.4	●	◆		●			◆	117
18.	Bear Lake	341.0	■	●					◆	117
19.	Manchu Lake	341.0	●	●					◆	117
20.	Polaris Lake	341.0	■	●			●		◆	117
21.	Moose Lake	341.0	■	●			●		◆	117
22.	Mullins Pond	341.0	■	◆					◆	118
23.	Hidden Lake	341.0	●	●			■		◆	118
24.	Pike Lake	341.0	●	●			■		◆	118
25.	Rainbow Lake	341.0	●	●			●		◆	118
26.	Scout Lake	339.6	●	●			■		◆	118
27.	Grayling Lake	339.6	●	■	◆		■		◆	119
28.	25-Mile Pond	335.1	●	●			●			119
	Chena Hot Springs Road									
J2	Jct.: Steese Expressway	0								
29.	Little Chena River	6.3	■	●					◆	119
30.	Chena River (Middle)	6.3	■	●			■		●	120
31.	Little Chena River	11.9	■	◆					◆	120
32.	25-Mile Pond	25.0	■	●	◆				◆	120
33.	Chena River (Upper)	27.0-32.8	■	●	●				●	120
34.	Twin Bears Lake (30 Mile Pond)	30.0	■	●			●		◆	120
35.	North Fork Chena River	37.9-55.3	■	●					◆	121
36.	45.5-Mile Pond	45.5	■	●			●		◆	121
37.	47.9-Mile Pond	47.9	■	●			●		◆	121

FAIRBANKS AREA LOCATIONS

Unit A: Fairbanks City Drainages

Includes all roadside waters within the city of Fairbanks.

UNIT REGULATIONS:

* Northern pike fishing prohibited: All waters, April 1 – May 31.

(continues on next page)

UNIT TIMING

FISH ▽	JAN	FEB	MAR	APR	MAY	JUN	JUL	AUG	SEP	OCT	NOV	DEC
KS*												
CS*												
SS*												
LS												
RT												
AC												
SF												
AG												
WF												
NP												
BB												

Note: Timing shown for salmon indicates fish in all stages of maturity

---

Fairbanks City

1. Chena River (Lower)

Access: There are a multitude of roads that cross or parallel the river within the city of Fairbanks. A few of the larger access points include Parks Hwy., University Av., Peger Rd., Cushman St., Wendell St./Old Richardson Hwy., and Steese Exprswy.

Fishing: This portion of the river, due to the abundance of slackwater, is better suited for targeting burbot. The river mouth is a local hot spot during the winter months. Some grayling present in spring and fall. Salmon pass through the area.

King Salmon / poor-fair / mid-July / 12-25 lbs. / spinners, plugs, attractors.
Arctic Grayling / fair / mid-September – mid-October / 7-14 in. / spinners, flies.
Northern Pike / poor-fair / mid-June – mid-September / 2-5 lbs. / spoons, plugs, bait.
Burbot / good / March – May, September – mid-December / 2-8 lbs. / bait.

2. Ballaine Lake

Access: MP 358.0 Parks Highway; E on Airport Way 1.0 mile, left on University Av. 3.5 miles to parking area and lake on left.

Fishing: Lake is stocked with trout but suffers from winterkill. Summer and fall best.

Rainbow Trout / fair-good / June, September – October / 7-12 in. / spinners, flies, bait.

Fort Wainwright

Area locations on military base – Directions originate from Main Gate/Visitor Center, except where indicated. **Note:** A permit is required to fish on base. Public must check in at Ft. Wainwright main gate prior to entering area. Call 353-7595 for information.

3. Chena River (Lower)

Note: There are numerous access points to the river, most of them along Gaffney Rd. (south shore) and River Rd. (north shore).

Access A: Mile 1.5 - River Road Bridge #1; left on River Rd. 0.1 mile to river crossing.
Access B: Mile 2.4 - Trainor Gate Road Bridge; left on Swanson Lp. 0.8 mile to river crossing.
Access C: Mile 4.2 - River Road Bridge #2; left on Kinney Rd. 0.1 mile, left on River Rd. 0.1 mile to river crossing.
Fishing: This portion of the river, due to the abundance of slackwater, is better suited for targeting burbot. Some grayling present in spring and fall. Salmon pass through the area.
King Salmon / fair / mid-July / 12-25 lbs. / spinners, plugs, attractors.
Arctic Grayling / fair / mid-September – mid-October / 7-14 in. / spinners, flies.
Northern Pike / poor-fair / mid-June – mid-September / 2-6 lbs. / spoons, plugs, bait.
Burbot / fair / March – early May, September – mid-December / 2-5 lbs. / bait.

4. Monterey Lake

Access: Mile 1.5; right on Meridian Rd. 0.4 mile, left on Montgomery Rd. 0.4 mile, right on Santiago Ave. 0.7 mile, left on Rhineland Ave. 0.2 mile to lake access on right.
Fishing: Lake is stocked with salmon and trout. Productive seasonal fishery.
Landlocked Salmon / excellent / June – March / 7-12 in. / spinners, jigs, flies, bait.
Rainbow Trout / good / May, September – December / 7-15 in. / spinners, flies, bait.

5. Wainright #6 Pond

Access: Mile 1.5, left on River Rd. 5.1 miles, left on Sage Hill Rd. 0.1 mile, left on access road 0.1 mile to pond
Fishing: Pond is stocked with trout. Productive seasonal fishery, low angling pressure.
Rainbow Trout / good / May, September – December / 715 in. / spinners, flies, bait.

6. Lundgren Pond

Access: Mile 4.2; left on Kinney Rd. 0.1 mile, left on River Rd. 0.2 mile, right on Nautilus Dr. 0.6 mile to pond on left.
Fishing: Pond is stocked with trout. Productive seasonal fisher, low angling pressure.
Rainbow Trout / fair / May, September – December / 7-15 in. / spinners, flies, bait.

Unit B: Tanana River Drainage

Includes all roadside waters in and around Eielson AFB, North Pole, and along the Richardson Highway.

UNIT REGULATIONS:

* Northern pike fishing prohibited: All waters, April 1 – May 31.

UNIT TIMING:

FISH ▽	JAN	FEB	MAR	APR	MAY	JUN	JUL	AUG	SEP	OCT	NOV	DEC
KS*												
CS*												
SS*												
LS												
RT												
AC												
SF												
AG												
WF												
NP												
BB												

Note: Timing shown for salmon indicates fish in all stages of maturity.

Richardson Highway

Highway section within the greater Fairbanks area begins in city of Fairbanks and ends by Eielson AFB. Badger Road begins at MP 357.1 Richardson Hwy. (Mile 0) and ends at MP 349.5 Richardson Hwy. (Mile 11.2).

7. Sirlin Drive Pond

Access: MP 357.1; N on Badger Rd. 0.5 mile, right on Sirlin Dr. 100 yards to pond on right.
Fishing: Pond is stocked with trout. Productive seasonal fishery, low angling pressure.
Rainbow Trout / good / May, September – December / 7-14 in. / spinners, flies, bait.

8. Badger (Chena) Slough

Access: MP 357.1 (N) and 349.5 (S); N on Badger Rd. **Note:** There are numerous access roads within 0.5 mile east of Badger Rd. Main access points include Persinger, Peede, Nordale, Repp, Plack, and Hurst roads.
Fishing: One of the top locations in the area for spring-run grayling. Local favorite.
Arctic Grayling / good-excellent / late April – mid-May / 7-12 in. / spinners, flies.
Northern Pike / poor-fair / early June – late August / 2-4 lbs. / spoons, plugs, bait.
Burbot / poor-fair / mid-September – late October / 2-4 lbs. / bait.

9. North Pole Pond

Access: MP 349.5 ; N on Badger Rd. 0.2 mile, right on Doughchee Av. 0.5 mile, right on Singa Rd. to pond on left.

Fishing: Pond is stocked with landlocked salmon and trout. Productive seasonal fishery.

Landlocked Salmon / good / November – April / 7-12 in. / jigs, bait.

Rainbow Trout / good / May, September – December / 7-15 in. / spinners, flies, bait.

Arctic Grayling / good / June – September / 7-12 in. / spinners, flies.

10. Chena River (Middle)

Access A: MP 349.5; N on Badger Rd. 4.7 miles, right on Nordale Rd. 2.3 miles to river crossing.

Access B: MP 346.7; NE on Laurence Rd. 5.1 miles, left on access road 0.8 mile to river.

Fishing: Productive king and chum salmon action in mid-summer, the best on the entire stretch of river. Solid opportunities casting from shore and boat.

King Salmon / fair-good / 12-25 lbs. (50 lbs.) / spoons, spinners, attractors.

Chum Salmon / fair / 5-10 lbs. (15 lbs.) / spoons, spinners.

Arctic Grayling / fair-good / 7-14 in. (20 in.) / spinners, flies.

Northern Pike / fair / 2-5 lbs. (15 lbs.) / spoons, plugs, bait.

Burbot / fair / 2-4 lbs. (15 lbs.) / bait.

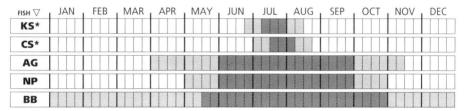

Note: Timing shown for salmon indicates fish in all stages of maturity

11. Little Chena River

Access: MP 349.5; N on Badger Rd. 4.7 miles, right on Nordale Rd. 3.0 miles to stream crossing.

Fishing: Stream supports a decent population of grayling. Catch-and-release only.

Arctic Grayling / fair-good / mid-June – mid-September / 7-12 in. / spinners, flies.

12. Chena Lake

Access: MP 346.7; NE on Laurence Rd. 3.7 miles, left on access road to recreation area and lake, 1.4 mile to end of road. Numerous access points along road.

Fishing: Lake is stocked with fish. A local hot spot, productive year-round.

Landlocked salmon / excellent / 7-12 in. (20 in.) / spinners, jigs, flies, bait.

Rainbow trout / good / 8-16 in. (8 lbs.) / spoons, spinners, flies, bait.

Arctic char / fair-good / 8-20 in. (10 lbs.) / spoons, jigs, bait.

(chart shown on next page)

FISH ▽	JAN	FEB	MAR	APR	MAY	JUN	JUL	AUG	SEP	OCT	NOV	DEC
LS												
RT												
AC												

13. North Chena Pond

Access: MP 346.7; NE on Laurence Rd. 5.1 miles, left on access road 2.2 miles. Pond is adjacent to road.
Fishing: Pond is stocked with trout. Productive seasonal fishery, low angling pressure.
Rainbow Trout / good / May, September – December / 7-15 in. / spinners, flies, bait.

14. Moose Creek

Access: MP 344.7; highway crosses stream. Rough dirt road parallels stream from SW side of bridge 0.2 mile to mouth and Piledriver Slough.
Fishing: Slow-flowing stream with limited seasonal fishery, low angling pressure.
Arctic Grayling / fair / late April – mid-May / 7-12 in. / spinners, flies.
Northern Pike / fair / mid-September – late October / 2-4 lbs. / spoons, plugs, bait.
Burbot / fair / mid-September – late October / 2-4 lbs. / bait.

15. Piledriver Slough

Note: There are numerous access points along highway, some with trails leading to slough. Main access below.

Access A: MP 344.7; S on rough dirt road next to Moose Creek bridge 0.2 mile to slough.
Access B: MP 343.7; S on Eielson Farm Rd. 0.4 mile to slough crossing.
Access C: MP 343.0; pull-off S of highway. Trail leads short distance to slough.
Access D: MP 342.6; SW on dirt road 0.2 mile to slough.
Fishing: Slough is stocked with trout. Productive seasonal fishery and a local favorite.
Rainbow Trout / excellent / late May – mid-September / 7-15 in. / spinners, flies, bait.
Arctic Grayling / excellent / late April – mid-May / 7-12 in. / spinners, flies.

16. Bathing Beauty Pond

Access: MP 343.7; S on Eielson Farm Rd. 50 yards to pond on right.
Fishing: Pond is stocked with landlocked salmon, trout, and char. Productive seasonal fishery and one of the most popular spots in the area.
Landlocked Salmon / excellent / June – March / 7-12 in. / spinners, jigs, flies, bait.
Rainbow Trout / good / May, September – December / 7-15 in. / spinners, flies, bait.
Arctic Char / fair / May – June, September – January / 7-15 in. / spoons, jigs, bait.
Arctic Grayling / good / June – September / 7-12 in. / spinners, flies.

Eielson AFB

Area locations on military base – Directions originate from Main Gate/Visitor Center, except where indicated. **Note:** A permit is required to fish on base. Public must check in at Eielson AFB main gate prior to entering area. Call 377-5182 for information.

17. Piledriver Slough

Note: There are numerous access points along highway, some with trails leading to slough. Main access below.

Access A: MP 338.7; W on access road 0.5 mile to slough.
Access B: MP 338.4; W on dirt road 0.1 mile. Trail along powerline leads 0.3 mile S to slough.
Fishing: Slough is stocked with trout. Productive seasonal fishery and a local favorite.
Rainbow Trout / excellent / late May – mid-September / 7-15 in. / spoons, flies, bait.
Arctic Grayling / excellent / late April – mid-May / 7-14 in. / spinners, flies.

18. Bear Lake

Access: MP 341.0; NE on Central Dr. 0.2 mile, left on Flightline Dr. 0.9 mile to intersection, right on Arctic Ave. 0.3 mile to lake on left. Road parallels lake next half mile.
Fishing: Lake is stocked with trout. Productive seasonal fishery, low angling pressure.
Rainbow Trout / good / May, September – December / spinners, flies, bait.

19. Manchu Lake

Access: MP 341.0; NE on Central Dr. 1.2 mile, left on Manchu Rd. 0.1 mile to Arctic Ave. intersection, continue left short distance to another intersection, right on Manchu Rd. Trail 1.4 mile, left at intersection 0.3 mile to lake on right.
Fishing: Lake is stocked with trout and char. Productive seasonal fishery.
Rainbow Trout / good / May, September – December / 7-16 in. / spinners, flies, bait.
Arctic Char / fair-good /May, September – January / 7-20 in. / spoons, jigs, bait.

20. Polaris Lake

Access: MP 341.0; N on Central Dr. 1.2 mile, left on Manchu Rd. 0.1 mile, right on Arctic Av. 0.1 mile, left on Glacier Blvd. 0.4 mile to French Creek (Industrial) Dr., proceed straight ahead 0.1 mile to lake.
Fishing: Lake is stocked with fish. Productive seasonal fishery, low angling pressure.
Landlocked Salmon / excellent / June – March / 7-12 in. / spinners, jigs, flies, bait.
Rainbow Trout / good / May, September – December / 7-15 in. / spinners, flies, bait.
Arctic Char / fair / May – June, September – January / 7-20 in. / spoons, jigs, bait.

21. Moose Lake

Access: MP 341.0; NE on Central Dr. 1.2 mile, left on Manchu Rd. 0.1 mile, right on Arctic Av. 0.1 mile, left on Glacier Blvd. 0.4 mile, right on French Creek (Industrial) Dr. 0.1 mile to Moose Lake Dr./Polaris St. intersection. Numerous access points left of French Creek Dr. next 0.5 mile. Additional access also off Moose Lake Dr.

Fishing: Lake is stocked with trout and char. A few pike present, low angling pressure.
Rainbow Trout / good / May, September – December / 7-15 in. / spinners, flies, bait.
Arctic Char / fair-good / May, September – January / 7-20 in. / spoons, jigs, bait.
Arctic Grayling / poor / June – September / 10-15 in. / spinners, flies.
Northern Pike / poor / June – September / 2-4 lbs. / spoons, plugs, bait.

22. Mullins Pond

Access: MP 341.0; NE on Central Dr. 0.5 mile, right on Flight Line Ave. 2.8 miles, left on Quarry Rd. 0.1 mile to lake access on right.

Fishing: Pond is stocked with salmon and char. Productive seasonal fishery.
Landlocked Salmon / excellent / June – March / 7-12 in. / spinners, jigs, flies, bait.
Arctic Char / fair-good / May, September – January / 7-20 in. / spoons, jigs, bait.
Arctic Grayling / poor / June – September / 10-15 in. / spinners, flies.

23. Hidden Lake

Access: MP 341.0; SW on gravel road 0.4 mile to four-way intersection. *Option A:* Right 0.1 mile, right short distance to lake on left. *Option B:* Right 0.2 mile to end of road and lake on right.

Fishing: Lake is stocked with trout and char. Productive seasonal fishery.
Landlocked Salmon / excellent / June – March / 7-12 in. / spinners, jigs, flies, bait.
Rainbow Trout / good / May, September – December / 7-15 in. / spinners, flies, bait.
Arctic Char / fair / May, September – December / 7-20 in. / spoons, jigs, bait.
Arctic Grayling / poor / June – September / 10-15 in. / spinners, flies.

24. Pike Lake

Access: MP 341.0; SW on gravel road 0.4 mile to four-way intersection. *Option A:* Straight 0.1 mile to lake on right. *Option B:* Right 0.2 mile to end of road and lake on left.

Fishing: Lake supports a small number of pike.
Northern Pike / poor / June – September / 2-4 lbs. / spoons, plugs, bait.

25. Rainbow Lake

Access: MP 341.0; SW on gravel road 0.4 mile to four-way intersection, left 0.3 mile, right on access road 0.2 mile to cul-de-sac and lake on left.

Fishing: Lake supports a small number of pike and burbot.
Northern Pike / poor / June – September / 2-4 lbs. / spoons, plugs, bait.
Burbot / poor / March – April, October – December / bait.

26. Scout Lake

Access: MP 339.6; SW on gravel road 0.2 mile to four-way intersection. *Option A:* Straight short distance to lake on right. *Option B:* Right 0.3 mile, left on access road short distance to lake.

Fishing: Lake supports a small number of pike and burbot.
Northern Pike / poor / June – September / 2-4 lbs. / spoons, plugs, bait.
Burbot / poor / March – April, October – December / bait.

27. Grayling Lake

Access: MP 339.6; SW on gravel road 0.2 mile to four-way intersection, left on access road short distance to lake.
Fishing: Lake is stocked with trout and char. A few pike present, low angling pressure.
Rainbow Trout / good / May, September – December / 7-15 in. / spinners, flies, bait.
Arctic Char / fair / May, September – January / 7-20 in. / spoons, jigs, bait.
Arctic Grayling / poor / June – September / 10-15 in. / spinners, flies.
Northern Pike / poor / June – September / 2-4 lbs. / spoons, plugs, bait.

28. 28-Mile Pond

Access: MP 335.1; N on access road 0.1 mile to pond.
Fishing: Pond is stocked with trout and char. A few pike present, low angling pressure.
Rainbow Trout / good / May, September – December / 7-15 in. / spinners, flies, bait.
Arctic Char / fair / May, September – January / 7-15 in. / spoons, jigs, bait.
Northern Pike / poor / June – September / 2-4 lbs. / spoons, plugs, bait.

Unit C: Chena River Drainage

Includes all roadside waters flowing into and surrounding the Chena River along the Chena Hot Springs Road.

UNIT REGULATIONS:

* Northern pike fishing prohibited: All waters, April 1 – May 31.

UNIT TIMING:

*Note: Timing shown for salmon indicates fish in all stages of maturity

Chena Hot Springs Road

The road begins at MP 4.9 Steese Hwy. (MP 0) and ends in Chena Hot Springs (MP 56.5).

29. Little Chena River

Access: MP 6.3; S on Nordale Rd. 2.6 miles to stream crossing.
Fishing: Stream supports a decent population of grayling. Catch-and-release only.
Arctic Grayling / fair-good / mid-June – mid-September / 7-12 in. / spinners, flies.

30. Chena River (Middle)

Access: MP 6.3; S on Nordale Rd. 3.3 miles to river crossing.
Fishing: Productive king and chum salmon action in mid-summer, the best on the entire stretch of river. Solid opportunities casting from shore and boat.
King Salmon / fair-good / 12-25 lbs. (50 lbs.) / spoons, spinners, attractors.
Chum Salmon / poor / 5-10 lbs. (15 lbs.) / spoons, spinners.
Arctic Grayling / fair-good / 7-14 in. (20 in.) / spinners, flies.
Northern Pike / poor-fair / 2-6 lbs. (15 lbs.) / spoons, plugs
Burbot / fair / 2-5 lbs. (15 lbs.) / bait.

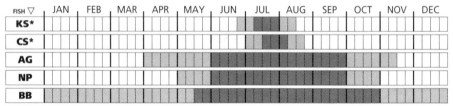

Note: Timing shown for salmon indicates fish in all stages of maturity

31. Little Chena River

Access: MP 11.9; road crosses river.
Fishing: Stream supports a decent population of graling. Catch-and-release only.
Arctic Grayling / fair-good / mid-June – mid-September / 7-12 in. / spinners, flies.

32. 25-Mile Pond

Access: MP 25.0; N on gravel road short distance to pond.
Fishing: Pond is stocked with fish. Productive seasonal fishery, low angling pressure.
Rainbow Trout / good / May, September – December / 7-15 in. / spinners, flies, bait.
Arctic Grayling / good / June – September / 7-12 in. / spinners, flies.

33. Chena River (Upper)

Access: MP 27.0 – 32.8; road parallels river, numerous turnouts.
Fishing: One of the best grayling waters on the road system, known for fish up to 20 inches. Catch-and-release only. Salmon spawning area.
Arctic Grayling / good / mid-June – mid-September / 7-14 in. / spinners, flies.

34. Twin Bears Lake (30-Mile Pond)
Access: MP 30.0; N on Twin Bears Camp access road short distance to pond.
Fishing: Lake is stocked with trout. Productive seasonal fishery, low angling pressure.
Rainbow Trout / good / May, September – December / 7-15 in. / spinners, flies, bait.
Arctic Grayling / good / June – September / 7-12 in. / spinners, flies.

35. North Fork Chena River
Access: MP 37.9, 39.5, 44.0, 49.0, and 55.3; road crosses river, numerous turnouts.
Fishing: Clearwater stream supporting a decent population of grayling.
Arctic Grayling / fair-good / mid-June – mid-September / 7-14 in. / spinners, flies.

36. 45.5-Mile Pond
Access: MP 45.5; E on gravel road 0.2 mile to pond.
Fishing: Pond is stocked with fish. Productive seasonal fishery, low angling pressure.
Rainbow Trout / good / May, September – December / 7-15 in. / spinners, flies, bait.
Arctic Grayling / good / June – September / 7-12 in. / spinners, flies.

37. 47.9-Mile Pond
Access: MP 47.9; E on gravel road short distance to pond. Pond on right is stocked with fish; pond on left is not.
Fishing: Pond is stocked with fish. A few burbot present. Productive seasonal fishery.
Rainbow Trout / good / May, September – December / 7-15 in. / spinners, flies, bait.
Arctic Grayling / good / June – September / 7-12 in. / spinners, flies.

Other Locations
Unit A: Fairbanks City Drainages:
Goldstream Creek - (Fairbanks); AG,(NP)

Unit C: Chena River Drainage:
Chena Hot Springs Road: Colorado Creek - MP 31.3; AG Angel Creek - MP 49.9; AG

LOCATION & SPECIES APPENDIX
● - Wild/Native fish, fishable numbers.
◆ - Present in small numbers and/or only occasionally caught.
▲ - Stocked/Hatchery fish, fishable numbers.
■ - Mix of Wild and Hatchery fish, fishable numbers.
✕ - Indicated species present but currently protected by law (PROHIBITED).

(continues on next page)

#	LOCATION	KING SALMON	RED SALMON	PINK SALMON	CHUM SALMON	SILVER SALMON	LANDLOCKED SALMON	KOKANEE	STEELHEAD TROUT	RAINBOW TROUT	LAKE TROUT	ARCTIC CHAR	DOLLY VARDEN	ARCTIC GRAYLING	SHEEFISH	WHITEFISH	NORTHERN PIKE	BURBOT	PACIFIC HALIBUT	LING COD	ROCKFISH
	Fairbanks City																				
1.	Chena River (Lower)	●			◆	◆								◆	●	◆	●	●			
2.	Ballaine Lake									▲											
	Ft. Wainwright																				
3.	Chena River (Lower)	●			◆	◆								◆	●	◆	●	●			
4.	Monterey Lake							▲		▲											
5.	Wainright # 6 Pond									▲											
6.	Lundgren Pond									▲											
	Richardson Highway																				
7.	Sirlin Drive Pond									▲											
8.	Badger (Chena) Slough													●		◆	●	●			
9.	North Pole Pond							▲		▲				◆							
10.	Chena River (Middle)	●			●									◆	●	◆	●	●			
11.	Little Chena River	×			×									●		◆	◆	◆			
12.	Chena Lake							▲		▲		▲		◆							
13.	North Chena Pond									▲											
14.	Moose Creek													■		◆	●	●			
15.	Piledriver Slough	◆			◆					▲				◆	■	●	◆	◆			
16.	Bathing Beauty Pond							▲		▲		▲		◆							
	Eielson AFB																				
17.	Piledriver Slough	◆			◆					▲				◆	●	◆	◆	◆			
18.	Bear Lake									▲											
19.	Manchu Lake									▲		▲									
20.	Polaris Lake							▲		▲		▲									
21.	Moose Lake									▲		▲		◆			●				
22.	Mullins Pond							▲		▲				◆							
23.	Hidden Lake									▲		▲		◆							
24.	Pike Lake																●				
25.	Rainbow Lake																●	●			
26.	Scout Lake																●	●			
27.	Grayling Lake									▲		▲		◆			●				
28.	28-Mile Pond									▲		▲					●				
	Chena Hot Springs Road																				
29.	Little Chena River	×			×									●		◆	◆	◆			
30.	Chena River (Middle)	●			●									◆	●	◆	●	●			
31.	Little Chena River	×			×									●		◆	◆	◆			
32.	25-Mile Pond									▲				◆							
33.	Chena River (Upper)	×			×									●		◆	◆	◆			
34.	Twin Bears Lake (30-Mile)									▲				◆							
35.	North Fork Chena River	×			×									●		◆	◆	◆			
36.	45.5-Mile Pond									▲				◆							
37.	47.9-Mile Pond									▲				◆							

Glenn Highway

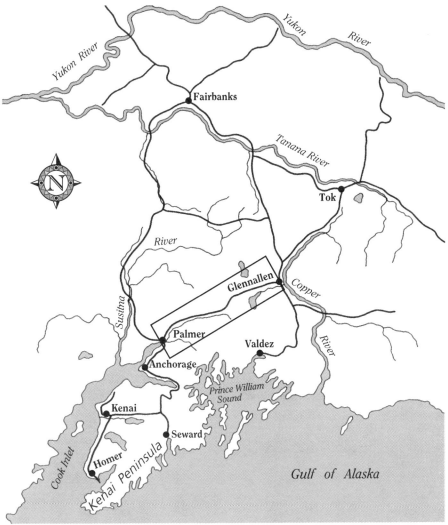

## CHAPTER 10

Area Covered: Palmer to Glennallen; 189 miles.

Note: For fishing information along the Glenn Highway south of Palmer (Palmer-Wasilla Area), see chapter 12 on page 147; or north of Anchorage (Anchorage Area), chapter 4 on page 59.

Regulatory Units: (A) Matanuska River Drainage; (B) Tazlina Lake/River Drainage; (C) Lake Louise Road Drainages

Number of Locations: 55

FISHING THE GLENN HIGHWAY

The Glenn Highway parallels two large river systems, the Matanuska and Tazlina, crossing several of their tributaries and accessing many lakes in the region. Salmon (usually chum and silver) and char are the prevalent kinds of fish in streams flowing into the Matanuska, while the lakes contain a good mixture of both stocked and wild populations of trout (both rainbow and lake), grayling, and burbot. Although many of the streams may look prime for sport fishing, wild runs of salmon are generally very small. On the Tazlina portion of the highway, however, grayling are by far the most numerous species in both lakes and streams with small, scattered runs of king and red salmon. The spring grayling fisheries in area creeks can be very productive. In the larger lakes, such as Lake Louise, anglers can in addition find huge char. Stocked trout are common in lakes along Lake Louise Road and in locations closer to Glennallen. Angler success is fair to good in both lakes and streams.

Angling pressure is fairly light overall, with some moderate effort occurring in the Lake Louise area.

Recommended Hot Spots: Wishbone, Seventeenmile, Ida, Lower Bonnie, Ryan, Arizona, Forgotten, Caribou, Connor, Louise, Tex Smith, Lost Cabin, Kay, and Tolsona lakes; Cache, Mendeltna, Tolsona, and Moose creeks.

Content

QUICK REFERENCE

 Road Condition   Parking Area   Camp Sites   Hiking Trails   Boat Launch   Handicap Access   Fishing Pressure

■ - Good to Highly developed/conditions, intense pressure
● - Fair to Moderately developed/conditions, moderate pressure
◆ - Poor to marginally developed/conditions, limited pressure
✕ - Prohibited

#	LOCATION	MILE POST	🚗	P	⛰	🚶	🛥	♿	🎣	PAGE
1.	Moose Creek (Upper)	53.0	◆	●	◆			◆	◆	129
2.	Wishbone Lake	53.0	◆	●	◆				◆	129
3.	Moose Creek (Lower)									
	Access A	54.6	■	■	■		●		◆	129
	Access B	55.3	◆	◆	◆				◆	129
4.	Seventeenmile Lake	57.9	●	■	◆		●	●	◆	130
5.	Eska Creek	60.8	■	●					◆	130
6.	Slipper (Eska) Lake	60.9	●	■	◆				◆	130

Map 1: Unit A: Matanuska River Drainage

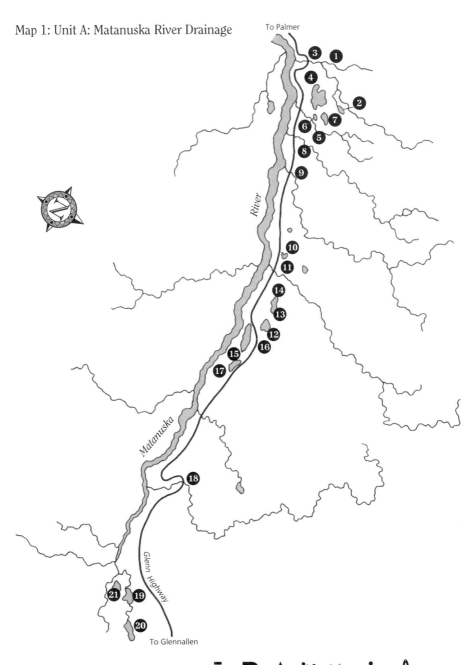

To Palmer

To Glennallen

#	LOCATION	MILE POST		P	Δ	🚶	🛶	♿	🎣	PAGE
7.	Coyote Lake	60.9	♦	●	♦			●	♦	130
8.	Granite Creek	62.4	■	●	●				♦	130
9.	Kings River	66.5	■	■	♦			♦	♦	130
10.	Ida Lake	73.0	●	●	♦				♦	130

#	LOCATION	MILE POST	🚗	P	Λ	🚶	🛶	♿	🎣	PAGE
11.	Chickaloon River	78.0	■	●					♦	130
12.	Ravine Lake	83.3	●	●	♦			♦	♦	131
13.	Lower Bonnie Lake	83.3	●	■	●	●			♦	131
14.	Upper Bonnie Lake	83.3	●	■	●				♦	131
15.	Long Lake	85.4	■	■	●	●	●		♦	131
16.	Buck (Spider) Lake	87.5	■	♦		●			♦	131
17.	Weiner Lake	88.5	■	●	♦		♦	●	♦	131
18.	Caribou Creek	106.9	■	♦					♦	131
19.	Knob Lake	118.5	●	♦					♦	131
20.	North Knob Lake	118.5	●	♦					♦	132
21.	Trail Lake	118.5	●	♦					♦	132
22.	Leila Lake	121.2	■	●	♦				♦	132
23.	Tahneta Lake	122.0	■	●	♦		●		♦	132
24.	Startup Creek	123.5	■	♦					♦	132
25.	Little Nelchina River	137.6	■	■	■			●	♦	133
26.	Cache Creek	147.1	■	♦					♦	133
27.	Alabama Lake	147.7	■	●	♦	●			♦	133
28.	Ryan (Mirror) Lake	149.0	●	●	♦	●			♦	133
29.	Mendeltna Creek	152.8	■	■	♦			●	♦	133
30.	Gergie Lake	155.2	■	●	♦	●			♦	133
31.	Arizona Lake	155.8	■	●	♦	●			♦	133
32.	Buffalo Lake	156.2	■	●	♦	●			♦	133
33.	D-J Lake	156.7	■	●	♦	●			♦	133
34.	Little Junction Lake	159.8	■	♦		●			♦	134
J1.	Jct.: Lake Louise Road	159.9								
35.	Tex Smith Lake	162.0	■	●	♦		♦	●	♦	134
36.	Lost Cabin Lake	165.9	■	●	♦	●			♦	134
37.	Kay Lake	168.0	■	●	♦	●			♦	134
38.	Mae West Lake	169.3	■	●	♦	●			♦	134
39.	Tolsona Lake	170.5	●	●	●		●	●	♦	134
40.	Tolsona Creek									
	Access A	172.9	■	●	♦			♦	♦	134
	Access B	173.0	●	●	■			♦	♦	134
41.	Moose Creek	186.0	■	♦				♦	♦	134
	Lake Louise Road									
J1.	Jct.: Glenn Hwy.	0								
42.	Junction Lake	0.5	●	●				●	♦	135
43.	Crater Lake	1.3	●	●		●			♦	135
44.	Little Crater Lake	1.5	●			●			♦	135
45.	Old Road Lake	5.1	●	●				●	♦	135
46.	Round Lake	5.1	●	●				●	♦	135
47.	Peanut Lake	6.7	♦	♦		●			♦	136
48.	Mendeltna Creek	6.7	♦	●	♦			♦	♦	136
49.	Forgotten Lake	7.0	●	●		●			♦	136
50.	Elbow Lake	11.6	●	♦					♦	136
51.	Caribou Lake	11.6	●	♦					♦	136
52.	Connor Lake	16.9	●	♦		●			♦	136
53.	Lake Louise	17.3	●	●	●		●	●	●	136
54.	George Lake	17.6	●	●		●			♦	136
55.	Dinty Lake	19.3	●	●	♦		●	●	♦	136

Map 2: Unit B: Tazlina Lake/River Drainages

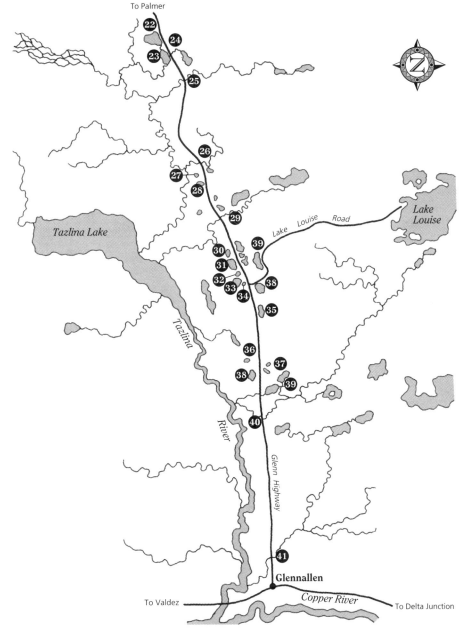

Map 3: Unit C: Lake Louise Road
         Drainages

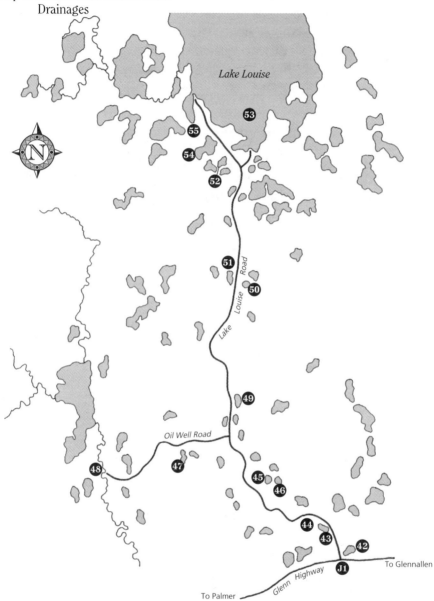

Lake Louise

GLENN HIGHWAY LOCATIONS

Unit A: Matanuska River Drainage

Includes all roadside waters flowing into and surrounding Matanuska River.

UNIT REGULATIONS:

* King salmon fishing prohibited: All waters, year-round.
* All flowing waters: Only unbaited, artificial lures September 1 – May 15.

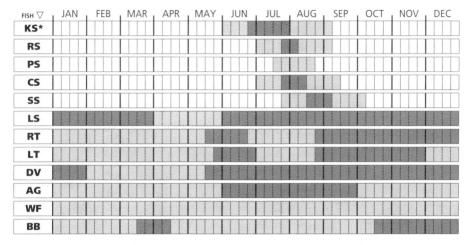

Note: Timing shown for king salmon indicates fish in all stages of maturity.

1. Moose Creek (Upper)

Access: MP 53.0; N on Buffalo Mine Rd. 3.7 miles to a "Y," right fork 0.4 mile to stream.
Fishing: Some trout and char available in summer and fall. Salmon spawning area.
Rainbow Trout / poor / early June – late August / 7-15 in. / spinners, flies, bait.
Dolly Varden / poor-fair / mid-July – late August / 7-15 in. / flies, bait.

2. Wishbone Lake

Access: MP 53.0; N on Buffalo Mine Rd. 3.7 miles to a "Y," right on dirt road 0.4 mile to
Moose Creek bridge, cross stream 0.6 mile to a "Y," left fork 1.5 mile to another "Y," right
fork 0.5 mile, left on access road 1.0 mile to lake. *Note:* Rough road - 4WD vehicles only
recommended beyond Moose Creek bridge.
Fishing: Lake is stocked with trout. Use canoe/float tube
Rainbow Trout / good / June, September – October / 7-16 in. / spoons, spinners, flies.

3. Moose Creek (Lower)

Access A: MP 54.6; highway crosses stream.
Access B: MP 55.3; S on rough dirt road 0.5 mile to small parking area and Matanuska
River confluence.
Fishing: Bright salmon available primarily at stream mouth. Some trout, char present.
Red Salmon / poor-fair / late July – early August / 4-7 lbs. / spinners, flies.
Chum Salmon / poor-fair / early August / 5-10 lbs. / spoons, spinners.
Silver Salmon / fair / late August – early September / 5-10 lbs. / spinners, bait.
Rainbow Trout / poor-fair / early June – late August / 7-12 in. / flies, bait.
Dolly Varden / fair-good / early July – late August / 7-10 in. / flies, bait.

4. Seventeenmile Lake

Access: MP 57.9; N on 58 Mile Rd. 0.5 mile, right 1.7 mile, left on Twin Hills Ln. 0.3 mile, right on Seventeen Mile Blvd. 0.2 mile, right on Wishbone Pl. 0.2 mile to parking area and lake.
Fishing: Lake is stocked with trout and char. Use canoe/float tube.
Rainbow Trout / good / May, September – December / 7-16 in. / spinners, flies, bait.
Arctic Char / fair-good / May – June, September – January / 7-16 in. / spoons, jigs, bait.

5. Eska Creek

Access: MP 60.8; highway crosses stream.
Fishing: Small and shallow stream supporting small numbers of char. Look for holes.
Dolly Varden / poor-fair / mid-July – late August / 7-10 in. / spinners, flies, bait.

6. Slipper (Eska) Lake

Access: MP 60.9; N on Jonesville Rd. 2.0 miles to access road on left, 0.2 mile to parking area and lake.
Fishing: Lake is stocked with trout. Use canoe/float tube, cast from shore.
Rainbow Trout / fair / May, September – October / 7-15 in. / spinners, flies, bait.

7. Coyote Lake

Access: MP 60.9; N on Jonesville Rd. 2.9 miles to end of road and parking next to lake.
Fishing: Lake is stocked with trout. Use canoe/float tube, cast from shore.
Rainbow Trout / fair / May, September – October / 7-14 in. / spinners, flies, bait.

8. Granite Creek

Access: MP 62.4; highway crosses stream.
Fishing: Clearwater stream with limited opportunities for trout and char.
Rainbow Trout / poor-fair / mid-May – mid-June / 7-12 in. / flies, bait.
Dolly Varden / poor-fair / mid-July – mid-August / 7-10 in. / flies, bait.

9. Kings River

Access: MP 66.5; highway crosses river.
Fishing: Limited opportunities for trout and char. Salmon spawning area.
Rainbow Trout / poor-fair / mid-May – mid-June / 7-12 in. / flies, bait.
Dolly Varden / poor-fair / mid-July – mid-August / 7-10 in. / flies, bait.

10. Ida Lake

Access: MP 73.0; W on Fish Lake Rd. 0.2 mile, left on Granvold Dr. 0.4 mile, left on Ida Dr. 0.2 mile, left on Oline Cir. 0.1 mile to parking area. Trail leads down steep hill to lake.
Fishing: Lake is stocked with trout and grayling. Kokanee present. Use canoe/float tube.
Kokanee / poor-fair / May – June, August – Sept. / 7-14 in. / spinners, flies, bait
Arctic Grayling / good / May – Sept. / 7-12 in. / spinners, flies.
Rainbow Trout / good / May, September – December / 7-16 in. / spinners, flies, bait.

11. Chickaloon River

Access: MP 78.0; highway crosses river.
Fishing: Turbid river with limited opportunties for char.
Dolly Varden / poor-fair / mid-July – mid-September / 7-12 in. / attractors, bait.

12. Ravine Lake
Access: MP 83.3; N on Bonnie Lake Rd. 0.9 mile to lake on right.
Fishing: Lake is stocked with trout. Use canoe/float tube, cast from shore.
Rainbow Trout / good / June, September – December / 7-15 in. / spinners, flies, bait.

13. Lower Bonnie Lake
Access: MP 83.3; N on Bonnie Lake Rd. 1.1 mile to a "Y," right fork 0.9 mile to parking area and lake.
Fishing: Lake supports a moderate population of trout. Use canoe/float tube.
Rainbow Trout / fair / June, September – December / 7-16 in. / spinners, flies, bait.

14. Upper Bonnie Lake
Access: MP 83.3; N on Bonnie Lake Rd. 1.1 mile to a "Y," right fork 0.9 mile to Lower Bonnie Lake and trailhead. Trail leads 2 miles E to lake.
Fishing: Lake supports a decent population of native trout. Use canoe/float tube.
Rainbow Trout / good / June, August – October / 8-20 in. / spinners, flies, bait.

15. Long Lake
Access: MP 85.4; S into parking area next to lake.
Fishing: Lake is stocked with trout and char. Burbot present. Use canoe/float tube.
Rainbow Trout / fair / June, September – October / 8-18 in. / spinners, flies, bait.
Arctic Char / fair / June, September – January / 8-20 in. / spoons, jigs, bait.
Burbot / fair / March – April, September – December / 10-20 in. / bait.

16. Buck (Spider) Lake
Access: MP 87.5; pullout. Trail leads 1.0 mile to lake.
Fishing: Lake is stocked with trout. Use canoe/float tube.
Rainbow Trout / good / June, August – October / 7-15 in. / spinners, flies, bait.

17. Weiner Lake
Access: MP 88.5; highway parallels lake.
Fishing: Lake is stocked with trout. Use canoe/float tube, cast from shore.
Rainbow Trout / fair-good / June, September – December / 7-15 in. / spinners, flies, bait.

18. Caribou Creek
Access: MP 106.9; highway crosses stream.
Fishing: Turbid stream with limited opportunties for char.
Dolly Varden / poor-fair / mid-July – mid-September / 7-12 in. / attractors, bait.

19. Knob Lake
Access: MP 118.5; SE on gravel road 2.0 miles to access site on right and lake.
Fishing: Lake is stocked with trout. Use canoe/float tube.
Rainbow Trout / fair-good / June, August – October / 7-15 in. / spinners, flies, bait.

20. North Knob Lake
Access: MP 118.5; SE on gravel road 1.8 miles to access site on right and lake.
Fishing: Lake is stocked with trout. Use canoe/float tube.
Rainbow Trout / fair-good / June, August – October / 7-15 in. / spinners, flies, bait.

21. Trail Lake
Access: MP 118.5; SE on gravel road 2.9 miles to lake on left.
Fishing: Lake supports a decent population of grayling and burbot.
Arctic Grayling / fair / June – September / 7-12 in. / spinners, flies.
Burbot / fair / March – April, September – December / 10-20 in. / bait.

Unit B: Tazlina Lake/River Drainages
Includes all roadside waters flowing into and surrounding Tazlina Lake and River.

UNIT REGULATIONS:
* King salmon fishing prohibited: All waters, year-round.

UNIT TIMING:

FISH ▽	JAN	FEB	MAR	APR	MAY	JUN	JUL	AUG	SEP	OCT	NOV	DEC
KS*						▓	▓	▓				
RS*						▓	▓	▓				
RT					▓	▓	▓	▓	▓	▓	▓	▓
LT					▓	▓	▓	▓	▓	▓	▓	▓
AG	▓	▓	▓	▓	▓	▓	▓	▓	▓	▓	▓	▓
WF	▓	▓	▓	▓	▓	▓	▓	▓	▓	▓	▓	▓
BB	▓	▓	▓	▓	▓	▓	▓	▓	▓	▓	▓	▓

Note: Timing shown for salmon indicates fish in all stages of maturity.

22. Leila Lake
Access: MP 121.2; SE on dirt road 0.2 mile to lake.
Fishing: Lake supports a decent population of grayling and burbot.
Arctic Grayling / fair / June – September / 7-12 in. / spinners, flies.
Burbot / fair / March – April, September – December / 10-20 in. / bait.

23. Tahneta Lake
Access: MP 122.0; highway parallels lake.
Fishing: Lake supports a decent population of grayling.
Arctic Grayling / fair-good / June – September / 7-12 in. / spinners, flies.

24. Startup Creek
Access: MP 123.5; highway crosses stream.
Fishing: Small stream with spring opportunities for spawn-bound grayling.
Arctic Grayling / fair-good / early, mid-May / 7-12 in. / spinners, flies.

25. Little Nelchina River
Access: MP 137.6; N on gravel road E of bridge 0.3 mile to campground and river.
Fishing: Clearwater stream with limited opportunties for grayling.
Arctic Grayling / poor-fair / late May – late September / 7-12 in. / spinners, flies.

26. Cache Creek
Access: MP 147.1; highway crosses stream.
Fishing: Small stream with spring opportunitites for spawn-bound grayling.
Arctic Grayling / good / early, mid-May / 7-12 in. / spinners, flies.

27. Alabama Lake
Access: MP 147.7; lake is located 200 feet SE of highway.
Fishing: Lake supports a moderate population of native grayling.
Arctic Grayling / fair / June – September / 7-12 in. / spinners, flies.

28. Ryan (Mirror) Lake
Access: MP 149.0; S on access road 0.25 mile to lake.
Fishing: Lake is stocked with trout. Use canoe/float tube.
Rainbow Trout / good / June, September – December / 7-15 in. / spoons, flies, bait.

29. Mendeltna Creek (Middle)
Access: MP 152.8; highway crosses stream.
Fishing: Clearwater stream with late-season opportunities for grayling.
Arctic Grayling / good / mid- September – early October / 7-12 in. / spinners, flies.

30. Gergie Lake
Access: MP 155.2; trail leads 1.25 mile S to lake.
Fishing: Lake is stocked with trout. Use canoe/float tube.
Rainbow Trout / good / June, September – December / 7-15 in. / spoons, flies, bait.

31. Arizona Lake
Access: MP 155.8; trail leads 0.5 mile S to lake.
Fishing: Lake is stocked with grayling. Use canoe/float tube.
Arctic Grayling / good / June – September / 7-12 in. / spinners, flies.

32. Buffalo Lake
Access: MP 156.2; S on dirt road 0.2 mile to lake.
Fishing: Lake is stocked with trout. Use canoe/float tube.
Rainbow Trout / fair / June, September – December / 7-15 in. / spoons, flies, bait.

33. D-J Lake
Access: MP 156.9; trail leads 0.5 mile S to lake.
Fishing: Lake is stocked with trout. Use canoe/float tube.
Rainbow Trout / fair / June, September – December / 7-15 in. / spinners, flies, bait.

34. Little Junction Lake
Access: MP 159.8; trail leads 0.25 mile S to lake.
Fishing: Lake is stocked with grayling. Use canoe/float tube, cast from shore.
Arctic Grayling / fair-good / June – September / 7-12 in. / spinners, flies.

35. Tex Smith Lake
Access: MP 162.0; lake is adjacent to N side of highway.
Fishing: Lake is stocked with trout. Use canoe/float tube.
Rainbow Trout / good / June, September – December / 7-15 in. / spinners, flies, bait.

36. Lost Cabin Lake
Access: MP 165.9; trail leads 0.75 mile S to lake.
Fishing: Lake supports a decent population of native grayling. Use canoe/float tube.
Arctic Grayling / good / June – September / 7-12 in. / spinners, flies.

37. Kay Lake
Access: MP 168.0; trail leads 0.75 mile N to lake.
Fishing: Lake supports a decent population of native grayling. Use canoe/float tube.
Arctic Grayling / good / June – September / 7-12 in. / spinners, flies.

38. Mae West Lake
Access: MP 169.3; trail leads 0.25 mile S to lake.
Fishing: Lake supports a decent population of native grayling. Use canoe/float tube.
Arctic Grayling / fair-good / June – September / 7-12 in. / spinners, flies.

39. Tolsona Lake
Access: MP 170.5; N on gravel road 0.7 mile to a lodge and lake.
Fishing: Lake supports a decent population of native grayling. Use canoe/float tube.
Arctic Grayling / good / June – September / 7-14 in. / spinners, flies.

40. Tolsona Creek
Access A: MP 172.9; highway crosses stream.
Access B: MP 173.0; N on gravel road 0.7 mile to campground and stream.
Fishing: Small clearwater stream with great opportunties for grayling.
Arctic Grayling / good / mid-May – late September / 7-12 in. / spinners, flies.

41. Moose Creek
Access: MP 186.0; highway crosses stream.
Fishing: Small, tannic stream with spring opportunities for spawn-bound grayling.
Arctic Grayling / good / early, mid-May / 7-12 in. / spinners, flies.

Unit C: Lake Louise Road Drainages

Includes all roadside waters along and surrounding Lake Louise Road.

UNIT REGULATIONS:

* Salmon fishing prohibited All flowing waters, year-round.

UNIT TIMING:

FISH ▽	JAN	FEB	MAR	APR	MAY	JUN	JUL	AUG	SEP	OCT	NOV	DEC
RS*												
RT												
LT												
AG												
WF												
BB												

***Note:** Timing shown for red salmon indicates fish in all stages of maturity.*

Lake Louise Road

Road begins at MP 159.8 Glenn Highway (MP 0) and ends at Lake Louise (MP 19.3).

42. Junction Lake

Access: MP 0.5; lake is adjacent to E side of road.
Fishing: Lake is stocked with grayling. Use canoe/float tube.
Arctic Grayling / fair-good / June – September / 7-12 in. / spinners, flies.

43. Crater Lake

Access: MP 1.3; trail leads 200 yards W to lake.
Fishing: Lake is stocked with trout. Use canoe/float tube.
Rainbow Trout / good / June, September – December / 7-16 in. / spoons, flies, bait.

44. Little Crater Lake

Access: MP 1.5; trail leads 200 yards W to lake.
Fishing: Lake is stocked with trout. Use canoe/float tube.
Rainbow Trout / fair / June, September – October / 7-15 in. / spoons, flies, bait.

45. Old Road Lake

Access: MP 5.1; E on Old Rd. 0.4 mile to lake on left.
Fishing: Lake is stocked with trout. Casting from bank possible.
Rainbow Trout / fair / June, September – October / 7-14 in. / spinners, flies, bait.

46. Round Lake

Access: MP 5.1; E on Old Rd. 0.4 mile to lake on right.
Fishing: Lake is stocked with trout. Casting from bank possible.
Rainbow Trout / fair / June, September – October / 7-14 in. / spinners, flies, bait.

47. Peanut Lake

Access: MP 6.7; W on Oil Well Rd. 1.8 miles to trailhead on left, 0.5 mile to lake.
Fishing: Lake is stocked with trout. Use canoe/float tube.
Rainbow Trout / fair-good / June, September – October / 7-15 in. / spinners, flies, bait.

48. Mendeltna Creek (Upper)

Access: MP 6.7; W on Oil Well Rd. 5.5 miles to end of road and stream.
Fishing: Late-season opportunties for migrating grayling. Salmon spawning area.
Arctic Grayling / good / early September – early October / 7-12 in. / spinners, flies.

49. Forgotten Lake

Access: MP 7.0; trail leads 0.25 mile E to lake.
Fishing: Lake supports a decent population of native grayling. Use canoe/float tube.
Arctic Grayling / good / June – September / 7-12 in. / spinners, flies.

50. Elbow Lake

Access: MP 11.6; lake is adjacent to road.
Fishing: Lake supports a decent populaton of native grayling. Use canoe/float tube.
Arctic Grayling / fair-good / June – September / 7-12 in. / spinners, flies.

51. Caribou Lake

Access: MP 11.6; W short distance to a "T," right on gravel road 0.7 mile to lake on left.
Fishing: Lake supports a decent population of native grayling. Use canoe/float tube.
Arctic Grayling / good / June – September / 7-12 in. / spinners, flies.

52. Connor Lake

Access: MP 16.9; trail leads 0.25 mile W to lake.
Fishing: Lake supports a decent population of native grayling. Use canoe/float tube.
Arctic Grayling / good / June – September / 7-12 in. / spinners, flies.

53. Lake Louise

Access A: MP 17.3; left at "Y" 0.2 mile, right on access road short distance to lake.
Access B: MP 17.3; right at "Y" 0.5 mile to lake.
Fishing: The most popular lake in the area, supporting large populations of char and grayling.
A boat/canoe is necessary to reach best spots. Char to 20-25 pounds possible.
Lake Trout / good / June, September – November / 3-8 lbs. / spoons, plugs, bait.
Arctic Grayling / good / June – September / 7-14 in. / spinners, flies.

54. George Lake

Access: MP 17.6; trail leads 0.25 mile W to lake.
Fishing: Lake supports a decent population of native grayling. Use canoe/float tube.
Arctic Grayling / good / June – September / 7-12 in. / spinners, flies.

55. Dinty Lake

Access: MP 19.3; end of road - Dinty Lake is located on left, Lake Louise on right.
Fishing: Small lake with limited opportunities for grayling and burbot.
Arctic Grayling / fair / June – September / 7-12 in. / spinners, flies.
Burbot / poor / March – April, September – December / 2-5 lbs. / bait.

Other Locations

NONE

LOCATION & SPECIES APPENDIX

● - Wild/Native fish, fishable numbers.

◆ - Present in small numbers and/or only occasionally caught.

▲ - Stocked/Hatchery fish, fishable numbers.

■ - Mix of Wild and Hatchery fish, fishable numbers.

× - Indicated species present but currently protected by law (PROHIBITED).

#	LOCATION	King Salmon	Red Salmon	Pink Salmon	Chum Salmon	Silver Salmon	Landlocked Salmon	Kokanee	Steelhead Trout	Rainbow Trout	Lake Trout	Arctic Char	Dolly Varden	Arctic Grayling	Sheefish	Whitefish	Northern Pike	Burbot	Pacific Halibut	Ling Cod	Rockfish
1.	Moose Creek (Upper)	×	◆		◆	◆							●	●		◆					
2.	Wishbone Lake													■							
3.	Moose Creek (Lower)	×	●	◆	●	●							●	●		◆	◆				
4.	Seventeenmile Lake											▲	▲	◆							
5.	Eska Creek	×	◆		◆	◆							◆	●		◆					
6.	Slipper (Eska) Lake													▲							
7.	Coyote Lake													▲							
8.	Granite Creek	×			◆	◆							●	●		◆	◆				
9.	Kings River	×			◆	◆							◆	●		◆	◆				
10.	Ida Lake							●						▲			▲				
11.	Chickaloon River	×			◆	◆							◆	●		◆	◆				
12.	Ravine Lake													▲							
13.	Lower Bonnie Lake													●		◆					
14.	Upper Bonnie Lake													●							
15.	Long Lake									▲	◆		▲	◆				●			
16.	Buck (Spider) Lake													▲							
17.	Weiner Lake													▲							
18.	Caribou Creek	×			◆	◆							◆	●		◆	◆				
19.	Knob Lake													▲							
20.	North Knob Lake													▲							
21.	Trail Lake													●		◆		●			
22.	Leila Lake													●		◆		●			
23.	Tahneta Lake													●		◆		◆			
24.	Startup Creek													●							
25.	Little Nelchina River													●							
26.	Cache Creek													●							
27.	Alabama Lake													●							
28.	Ryan (Mirror) Lake													▲		◆					
29.	Mendeltna Creek	×	×											◆			●	◆			
30.	Gergie Lake													▲							
31.	Arizona Lake																▲				
32.	Buffalo Lake													▲							
33.	D-J Lake													▲							
34.	Little Junction Lake																▲				
35.	Tex Smith Lake													▲							

#	LOCATION	KING SALMON	RED SALMON	PINK SALMON	CHUM SALMON	SILVER SALMON	LANDLOCKED SALMON	KOKANEE	STEELHEAD TROUT	RAINBOW TROUT	LAKE TROUT	ARCTIC CHAR	DOLLY VARDEN	SHEEFISH	ARCTIC GRAYLING	WHITEFISH	NORTHERN PIKE	BURBOT	PACIFIC HALIBUT	LING COD	ROCKFISH
36.	Lost Cabin Lake														●						
37.	Kay Lake														●						
38.	Mae West Lake														●						
39.	Tolsona Lake									◆					●			×			
40.	Tolsona Creek		◆							◆					●						
41.	Moose Creek														●						
	Lake Louise Road																				
42.	Junction Lake														▲						
43.	Crater Lake									▲											
44.	Little Crater Lake									▲											
45.	Old Road Lake									▲											
46.	Round Lake									▲											
47.	Peanut Lake									▲											
48.	Mendeltna Creek		×							◆					●	◆					
49.	Forgotten Lake														●						
50.	Elbow Lake									◆					●						
51.	Caribou Lake														●						
52.	Connor Lake														●						
53.	Lake Louise										●				●	◆		×			
54.	George Lake														●						
55.	Dinty Lake									◆					●	◆	●				

Kenai Spur
Highway

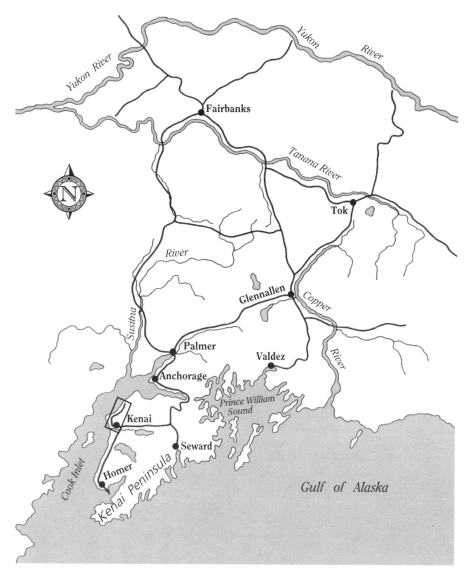

Area Covered: Soldotna to Swanson River; 39 miles
Regulatory Unit: Northern Kenai Peninsula Drainages
Number of Locations: 20

FISHING THE KENAI SPUR HIGHWAY*

The Kenai Spur Highway provides extensive access to the tidal-influenced areas of Kenai River, as well as to a few stocked lakes. Salmon are the most sought-after species here and are chiefly present in summer and fall. The North Kenai Road is better known for its lake fishing opportunities and has plenty of it to offer. Trout are stocked in many of them, and native fish abound as well. Char can also be caught. Sea-run salmon are available in the Swanson River, which also serves as a take-out point for anglers rafting the river down from Swanson River Road (accessed via Sterling Highway). Angler success is fair to excellent in both lakes and streams.

Angling pressure is heavy at times, particularly along the section of road between Soldotna and Kenai where it parallels Kenai River, with plenty of boat traffic and shore angling to be expected during the height of salmon runs. However, area lakes receive relatively little attention.

Recommended Hot Spots: Kenai and Swanson rivers; Sport, Elephant, Douglas, Cabin, Island, Daniels, and Stormy lakes.

*__*Note:__ That portion of the highway beyond Kenai is referred to as North Kenai Road, but the mileposts stay consistent throughout.*

Content
Pages

QUICK REFERENCE

 Road Condition   Parking Area   Camp Sites   Hiking Trails   Boat Launch   Handicap Access   Fishing Pressure

■ - Good to Highly developed/conditions, intense pressure
● - Fair to Moderately developed/conditions, moderate pressure
◆ - Poor to marginally developed/conditions, limited pressure
× - Prohibited

#	LOCATION	MILE POST	🚕	P	⛺	🚶	🚤	♿	🎣	PAGE
1.	Sport Lake	2.5	●	●			●	●	●	142
2.	Loon Lake	2.5	●	◆					◆	143
3.	Union Lake	2.5	●	●					◆	143
4.	Elephant (Spirit) Lake	4.7	●	●					●	143
5.	Kenai River (Lower)									
	Access A	5.1	■	■	●		■	●	■	143
	Access B	6.4	■	■	×		■	●	■	143
	Access C	10.5	■	■					■	143
6.	Beaver Creek	6.3	■	●					◆	144
	North Kenai Road									
7.	Douglas Lake	19.3	●	●					◆	144

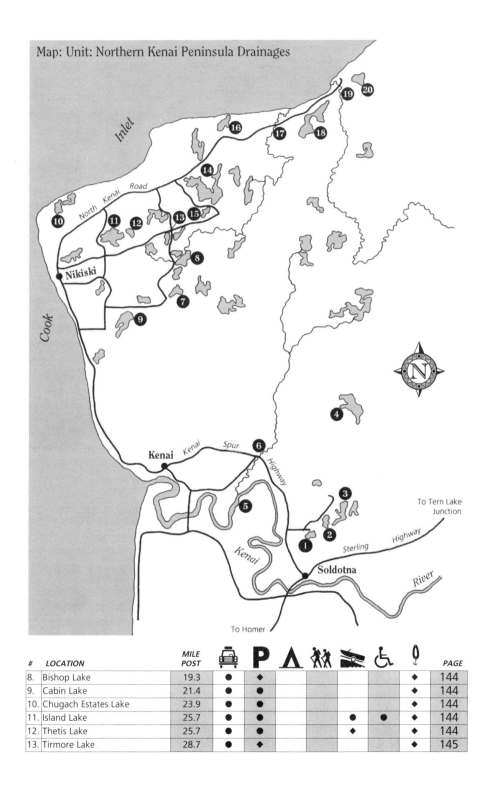

Map: Unit: Northern Kenai Peninsula Drainages

#	LOCATION	MILE POST	🚗	**P**	⛺	🥾	🛶	♿	⚓	PAGE
8.	Bishop Lake	19.3	●	◆					◆	144
9.	Cabin Lake	21.4	●	●					◆	144
10.	Chugach Estates Lake	23.9	●	●					◆	144
11.	Island Lake	25.7	●	●			●	●	◆	144
12.	Thetis Lake	25.7	●	●			◆		◆	144
13.	Tirmore Lake	28.7	●	◆					◆	145

#	LOCATION	MILE POST	🚗	P	⛺	🥾	🛶	♿	🎣	PAGE
14.	Daniels Lake	29.6	●	●					♦	145
15.	Barbara Lake	29.6	●	●					♦	145
16.	Cecille Lake	33.2	●	♦					♦	145
17.	Bishop Creek									
	Access A	35.1	■	●					♦	145
	Access B	35.9	■	●		●			♦	145
18.	Stormy Lake									
	Access A	36.9	●	●					●	145
	Access B	37.8	●	●				●	●	145
19.	Swanson River (Lower)									
	Access A	38.7	■	●					●	145
	Access B	39.0	■	■	●	●			●	145
20.	Salmo Lake	39.0	■	●		●			♦	146

KENAI SPUR HIGHWAY LOCATIONS

Unit: Northern Kenai Peninsula Drainages

Includes all roadside waters flowing into and surrounding upper Cook Inlet.

UNIT REGULATIONS:

* King salmon fishing prohibited: All waters (except Kenai River), year-round.
* Rainbow trout fishing prohibited: All flowing waters, April 15 – June 14.
Note: Consult sport fishing regulations closely for Kenai River.

UNIT TIMING:

FISH ▽	JAN	FEB	MAR	APR	MAY	JUN	JUL	AUG	SEP	OCT	NOV	DEC
KS												
RS												
PS												
CS												
SS												
LS												
RT												
DV												
AC												
WF												
NP												

1. Sport Lake

Access: MP 2.5; E. on Sport Lake Rd. 1.0 mile to a "Y," right on Moser Rd. 0.2 mile to access site on left.

Fishing: Lake is stocked with landlocked salmon and trout. Use canoe/float tube.
Landlocked Salmon / good / June – March / 7-12 in. / spinners, jigs, flies, bait.
Rainbow Trout / good / May, September – December / 7-16 in. / spinners, flies, bait.

2. Loon Lake

Access: MP 2.5; E. on Sport Lake Rd. 1.0 mile to a "Y," short distance and left on Conner Rd. 0.3 mile to lake on right. Access is where lake is closest to road.
Fishing: Lake is stocked with landlocked salmon. Use canoe/float tube.
Landlocked Salmon / good / June – March / 7-12 in. / spinners, flies, jigs, bait.

3. Union Lake

Access: MP 2.5; E. on Spots Lake Rd. 1.0 mile to a "Y," short distance and left on Conner Rd. 1.3 mile to Union 76 gate, right on gravel road short distance to access road on right.
Fishing: Lake supports a small population of pike. Spring and fall opportunities.
Northern Pike / fair / May – June, September – October / 2-4 lbs. / spoons, plugs.

4. Elephant Spirit Lake

Access: MP 4.7; E. on Strawberry Rd. 1.4 mile, right on Gene St. 0.4 mile to a "T," right on Carver Dr. 0.5 mile, left on Park St. 3.5 miles to a "T," left at sign 0.4 mile to end of road and lake.
Fishing: Lake is stocked with landlocked salmon and trout. Use canoe/float tube.
Landlocked Salmon / good / June – March / 7-12 in. / spinners, flies, jigs, bait.
Rainbow Trout / good / May, September – December / 7-16 in. / spinners, flies, bait.

5. Kenai River (Lower)

Access A: MP 5.1 - Eagle Rock; S. on Eagle Rock Dr. 0.4 mile to river.
Access B: MP 6.4 - Cunningham Park; S. on Beaver Loop Rd. 2.7 miles to access road on left leading to parking area and river.
Access C: MP 10.5 - Warren Ames Bridge; SW on River Access Rd. 1.0 mile to river crossing.
Fishing: Superb salmon fishing opportunities along with trout and sea-run char. Kings are ideally targeted from a boat and reds from shore. Best action for all species is from Cunningham Park upstream. This section of the Kenai is influenced by tidal activity.
King Salmon / Early Run: fair-good / 15-50 lbs. (100 lbs.) / plugs, attractors.
    Late Run: good / 25-60 lbs. (100 lbs.) / plugs, attractors, bait.
Red Salmon / Early Run: poor-fair / 4-8 lbs. (12 lbs.) / flies.
    Late Run: good-excellent / 4-10 lbs. (16 lbs.) / flies, bait.
Pink Salmon / fair-excellent / 2-6 lbs. (12 lbs.) / spoons, spinners.
Silver Salmon / Early Run: good-excellent / 5-12 lbs. (18 lbs.) / plugs, attractors, bait.
    Late Run: good-excellent / 6-15 lbs. (22 lbs.) / plugs, attractors, bait.
Rainbow Trout / fair / 8-20 in. (15 lbs.) / spinners, flies, bait.
Dolly Varden / good / 10-20 in. (15 lbs.) / spoons, flies, bait.

FISH ▽	JAN	FEB	MAR	APR	MAY	JUN	JUL	AUG	SEP	OCT	NOV	DEC
KS					▓	▓	▓	▓				
RS					▓	▓	▓	▓				
PS							▓	▓				
SS	▓						▓	▓	▓			
RT							▓	▓	▓			
DV				▓	▓	▓	▓	▓	▓			

6. Beaver Creek

Access: MP 6.3; road crosses stream.
Fishing: Small clearwater stream with limited seasonal opportunities for trout and char.
Silver Salmon / poor / mid-August – early September / 5-10 lbs. / spinners, bait.
Rainbow Trout / fair / mid-May – mid-June / 7-20 in. / spinners, flies, bait.
Dolly Varden / fair / mid-July – mid-September / 7-15 in. / flies, bait.

7. Douglas Lake

Access: MP 19.3; E. on Miller Rd. 2.1 miles, right on Holt Rd. 2.9 miles, right on Douglas Ln. 0.8 mile, right on Drew St. 100 yards to lake.
Fishing: Lake is stocked with trout. Use Canoe/float tube.
Rainbow Trout / good / May, September – December / 7-16 in. / spinners, flies, bait.

8. Bishop Lake

Access: MP 19.3; E. on Miller Rd. 2.1 miles, right on Holt Rd. 4.5 miles to access site on right, short hike to lake.
Fishing: Lake supports a moderate population of native trout. Use canoe/float tube.
Rainbow Trout / fair / May, September – December / 8-20 in. / spoons, flies, bait.

9. Cabin Lake

Access: MP 21.4; E. on Miller Rd. 1.2 mile, right on Cabin Lake Dr. 0.4 mile, left on Interlake Dr. 0.3 mile to access road on right leading short distance to lake.
Fishing: Lake is stocked with trout. Use canoe/float tube.
Rainbow Trout / good / May, September – December / 7-16 in. / spinners, flies, bait.

10. Chugach Estates Lake

Access: MP 23.9; NW on Tustumena St. 0.2 mile, left on McKinley Ave. 0.2 mile, right on Shumya Way short distance, left on Tyonek Cir. leading short distance to lake.
Fishing: Lake is stocked with trout. Use canoe/float tube.
Rainbow Trout / good / May, September – December / 7-16 in. / spinners, flies, bait.

11. Island Lake

Access: MP 25.7; S. on Island Lake Rd. 2.4 miles, left on Pipeline Rd. 0.7 mile, left on Moose Run Rd. 0.8 mile, left on access road short distance to lake.
Fishing: Lake is stocked with trout and char. Use canoe/float tube.
Rainbow Trout / good / May, September – December / 7-16 in. / spinners, flies, bait.
Arctic Char / fair-good / May, September – January / 7-20 in. / spoons, jigs, bait.

12. Thetis Lake

Access: MP 25.7; S. on Island Lake Rd. 2.4 miles, left on Pipeline Rd. 0.7 mile, left on Moose Run Rd. 0.8 mile, turn right and cross north end of airstrip, 150 yards to access road on left leading to lake.
Fishing: Lake is stocked with trout. Use canoe/float tube.
Rainbow Trout / good / May, September – December / 7-16 in. / spinners, flies, bait.

13. Tirmore Lake

Access: MP 28.7; S. on Lamplight Rd. 2.5 miles to lake on right, public easement located where lake is closest to road.
Fishing: Lake is stocked with trout. Use canoe/float tube.
Rainbow Trout / good / May, September – December / 8-16 in. / spinners, flies, bait.

14. Daniels Lake

Access: MP 29.6; S. on Halibouty Rd. 0.3 mile, left on Rappe Rd. 0.2 mile to lake area.
Fishing: Lake supports a population of native trout and char. Use canoe/float tube.
Rainbow Trout / fair / May, September – December / 8-18 in. / spinners, flies, bait.
Arctic Char / fair / May – June, September – January / 8-22 in. / spoons, jigs, bait.

15. Barbara Lake

Access: MP 29.6; S. on Halibouty Rd. 2.3 miles, right on Ramona Rd. 0.4 mile, right on Pipeline Rd. 0.4 mile to public access road on right.
Fishing: Lake is stocked with trout. Use canoe/float tube.
Rainbow Trout / good / May, September – December / 7-16 in. / spoons, flies, bait.

16. Cecille Lake

Access: MP 33.2; NW on Seascape Rd. 0.3 mile to lake on left.
Fishing: Lake is stocked with trout. Use canoe/float tube.
Rainbow Trout / fair-good / May, September – December / 7-16 in. / spinners, flies, bait.

17. Bishop Creek

Access A: MP 35.1; road crosses stream.
Access B: MP 35.9; N into parking area. Trails lead to stream.
Fishing: Small stream containing populations of trout and char. Salmon spawning area.
Rainbow Trout / fair / early August – mid-September / 7-15 in. / spinners, flies, bait.
Dolly Varden / poor / early August   mid-September / 7-12 in. / spoons, flies, bait.

18. Stormy Lake

Access A: MP 36.9; SE on access road leading to parking area. Trails lead short distance to lake.
Access B: MP 37.8; SE on gravel road leading to lake.
Fishing: Lake contains a decent population of native trout and char. Some pike present, a few up to 15 pounds. Char to 10 pounds available. Productive fall and winter fishery.
Rainbow Trout / good / May, September – December / 8-18 in. / spinners, flies, bait.
Arctic Char / good / May, September – January / 8-18 in. / spoons, jigs, bait.
Northern Pike / fair / May, September – January / 2-4 lbs. / plugs, flies, bait.

19. Swanson River (Lower)

Access A: MP 38.6; SE on gravel access road short distance to parking areas on left, or continue 0.6 mile to parking area and end of road. Trails lead 100 yards to river.
Access B: MP 38.7; road crosses over river.
Access C: MP 39.0; left fork at "Y" 0.4 mile, left on access road leading to campground. Trails lead to lower river.
Fishing: The best salmon spot in the area, especially for silvers in late summer and early fall. Other salmon species present in lesser numbers. Trout available above tidewater.
(Continued on next page)

N0. 19 - Swanson River continued.

Red Salmon / poor-fair / 4-7 lbs. (12 lbs.) / flies.
Pink Salmon / poor-fair / 2-4 lbs. (6 lbs.) / spoons, spinners.
Silver Salmon / good / 5-12 lbs. (18 lbs.) / spinners, plugs, bait.
Rainbow Trout / poor-fair / 7-12 in. (3 lbs.) / spinners, flies, bait.
Dolly Varden / fair / 7-15 in. (5 lbs.) / spoons, flies, bait.

FISH ▽	JAN	FEB	MAR	APR	MAY	JUN	JUL	AUG	SEP	OCT	NOV	DEC
RS						▓	█	▓				
PS							▓	█				
SS							▓	█	█	▓		
RT			▓	▓	▓	▓	▓	█	▓			
DV			▓	▓	▓	▓	▓	▓	▓			

20. Salmo Lake

Access: MP 39.0; right fork at "Y" to parking area. Trail leads 0.3 mile to lake.
Fishing: Lake contains a small population of native trout. Use canoe/float tube.
Rainbow Trout / fair / May, September – December / 8-18 in. / spoons, flies, bait.

LOCATION & SPECIES APPENDIX

● - Wild/Native fish, fishable numbers.
◆ - Present in small numbers and/or only occasionally caught.
▲ - Stocked/Hatchery fish, fishable numbers.
■ - Mix of Wild and Hatchery fish, fishable numbers.
✕ - Indicated species present but currently protected by law (PROHIBITED).

#	LOCATION	KING SALMON	RED SALMON	PINK SALMON	CHUM SALMON	SILVER SALMON	LANDLOCKED SALMON	KOKANEE	STEELHEAD TROUT	RAINBOW TROUT	LAKE TROUT	ARCTIC CHAR	DOLLY VARDEN	SHEEFISH	ARCTIC GRAYLING	WHITEFISH	NORTHERN PIKE	BURBOT	PACIFIC HALIBUT	LING COD	ROCKFISH
1.	Sport Lake							▲		▲											
2.	Loon Lake							▲													
3.	Union Lake																	●			
4.	Elephant (Spirit) Lake							▲		▲											
5.	Kenai River (Lower)	●	■	●	◆	●			◆	●			●				◆				
6.	Beaver Creek	✕	◆	◆		●				●			●								
	North Kenai Road																				
7.	Douglas Lake									▲											
8.	Bishop Lake			✕		✕				●			◆								
9.	Cabin Lake									▲											
10.	Chugach Estates Lake									▲											
11.	Island Lake									▲											
12.	Thetis Lake									▲											
13.	Tirmore Lake									▲											
14.	Daniels Lake			✕		✕				●			●								
15.	Barbara Lake									▲											
16.	Cecille Lake									▲											
17.	Bishop Creek			✕	✕	✕				●			●								
18.	Stormy Lake									▲		●					●				
19.	Swanson River (Lower)	✕	●	●	◆	●				●			●								
20.	Salmo Lake									●											

Palmer - Wasilla Area

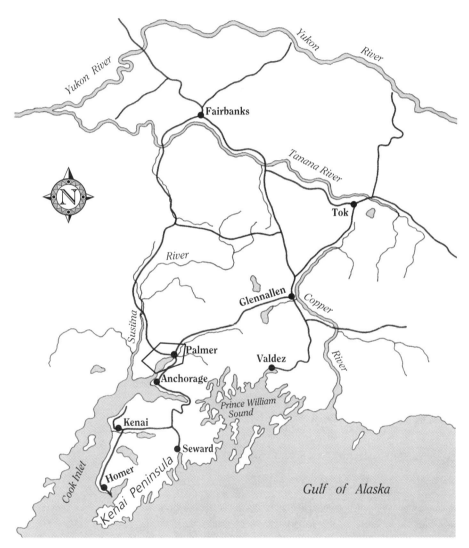

Area Covered: Old Glenn Highway, sections of Glenn Highway and Parks Highway, Palmer-Wasilla vicinity roads, Knik-Goose Bay Road, and Big Lake Road
Regulatory Units: (A) East Knik Arm Drainages; (B) Central Knik Arm Drainages; (C) West Knik Arm Drainages
Number of Locations: 80

FISHING THE PALMER-WASILLA AREA

The Palmer-Wasilla area roads and highways provide anglers with excellent access opportunities for a multitude of fish species. Lakes contain both wild and stocked populations of land-locked salmon, trout, char, grayling, and burbot, while rivers and streams support healthy runs of all five species of salmon, and trout and char. The Big Lake drainage and Kepler/Bradley Recreation Area are two of the more popular and rewarding fishing grounds. Salmon are taken at the mouths or lower reaches of many streams throughout most of the Little Susitna and Knik river drainages. While angling in or near the communities of Palmer and Wasilla can have an urban feel to it, there are many locations only minutes away that offer a truly rural experience. Angler success is good to excellent in both lakes and streams.

Boaters have limited choices but have established fisheries on the Little Susitna River and Big Lake among other larger lakes.

Angling pressure is typically light to moderate, at times heavy during the peak of salmon runs, locations off Old Glenn Highway (Eklutna Tailrace and Jim Creek) and the Knik-Goose Bay Road (Cottonwood and Fish creeks, Little Susitna River) receiving the most effort.

Recommended Hot Spots: Wasilla, Cottonwood, Fish, and Jim creeks; Little Susitna River; Eklutna Tailrace; Kepler/Bradley Lakes Recreation Area; Finger, Echo, Kalmbach, Prator, Bear Paw, Memory, Knik, Carpenter, Diamond, Big, Marion, Lorraine, Beverly, Seymour, Visnaw, Lalen, Dawn, Morvro, Loon, Walby, Wolf, Lucille, Twin Island, and Meirs lakes.

Content

QUICK REFERENCE

 Road Condition   Parking Area   Camp Sites   Hiking Trails   Boat Launch   Handicap Access   Fishing Pressure

■ - Good to Highly developed/conditions, intense pressure
● - Fair to Moderately developed/conditions, moderate pressure
◆ - Poor to marginally developed/conditions, limited pressure
✕ - Prohibited

Map 1: Unit A: East Knik Arm Drainages

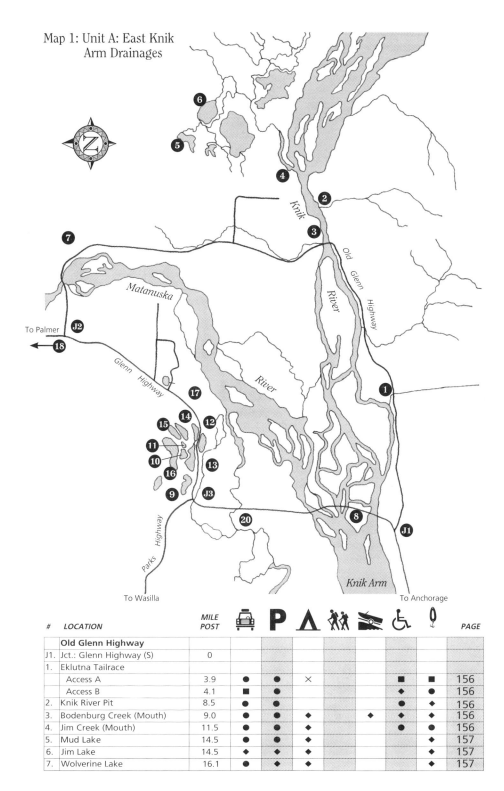

#	LOCATION	MILE POST	🚐	P	⛺	🚶	🛶	♿	🪝	PAGE
	Old Glenn Highway									
J1.	Jct.: Glenn Highway (S)	0								
1.	Eklutna Tailrace									
	Access A	3.9	●	●	✕			■	■	156
	Access B	4.1	■	●				◆	●	156
2.	Knik River Pit	8.5	●	●				●	◆	156
3.	Bodenburg Creek (Mouth)	9.0	●	●	◆		◆	◆	◆	156
4.	Jim Creek (Mouth)	11.5	●	●	◆			●	●	156
5.	Mud Lake	14.5	●	●	◆				◆	157
6.	Jim Lake	14.5	◆	◆	◆				◆	157
7.	Wolverine Lake	16.1	●	◆	◆				◆	157

#	LOCATION	MILE POST	🚗	P	Λ	🚶	⛵	♿	⚓	PAGE
J2.	Jct.: Glenn Highway (N)	35.3								
	Glenn Highway									
J1.	Jct.: Old Glenn Highway	29.6								
8.	No Name Lake	30.6	●	●	◆				◆	157
9.	Matanuska Lake	36.4	■	■	◆	■		■	●	157
J3.	Jct: Parks Highway	35.3								
10.	Victor Lake									
	Access A	36.4	●	●		●			◆	157
	Access B	37.3	●	●		●			◆	157
11.	Klaire Lake	36.4	●	●		●			◆	158
12.	Echo Lake	37.0	■	■		●			◆	158
13.	Kepler/Bradley Lakes	37.3	●	●	◆		◆	◆	●	158
14.	Canoe Lake	38.0	●	●		■		●	◆	158
15.	Irene Lake	38.0	●	●		●		●	◆	158
16.	Long Lake	38.0	●	●	◆	■			◆	158
17.	Meirs (McLeod) Lake	39.2	●	●	◆				◆	159
18.	Little Susitna River (Upper)									
	Access A	49.5	●	●					◆	159
	Access B	49.5	■	●	◆				◆	159
J2.	Jct.: Old Glenn Highway	42.1								
	Parks Highway									
J3.	Jct.: Glenn Highway	35.0								
19.	Loberg (Junction) Lake	35.7	■	●			◆	◆	◆	160
20.	Wasilla Creek (Lower)	34.7	●	●	◆		◆	●	◆	160
21.	Wasilla Creek (Middle)									
	Access A	37.8	●	●					◆	160
	Access B	37.8	■	◆					◆	160
22.	Cottonwood Creek (Upper)									
	Access A	40.9	■	◆					◆	160
	Access B	41.1	●	◆					◆	160
23.	Wasilla Lake	41.7	■	●			●		◆	160
J4.	Jct.: Knik-Goose Bay Rd.	42.2								
24.	Memory Lake	42.2	●	●	×		◆	●	◆	160
25.	Little Susitna River (Upper)									
	Access A	42.2	●	●	◆		◆	■	◆	161
	Access B	42.2	■	●	●			■	◆	161
26.	Reed Lake	42.2	●	◆					◆	161
27.	Golden Lake	48.7	●	●					◆	161
28.	Kalmbach Lake	48.7	●	●		●			◆	161
29.	Beverly Lake	48.7	●	●		●			◆	161
30.	Bruce Lake	48.7	●	●		●			◆	161
31.	Lalen Lake	48.8	●	●			◆	●	◆	162
32.	Seymour Lake	48.8	●	●			◆	◆	◆	162
33.	Visnaw Lake	48.8	●	●				◆	◆	162
34.	Dawn Lake	51.6	●	●		●			◆	162
J5.	Jct.: Big Lake Road	52.3								
35.	Little Meadow Creek	52.3	■	●					◆	162
36.	Morvro Lake	54.3	●	●	◆				◆	162
37.	Loon Lake	54.8	●	●				◆	◆	162
38.	Prator Lake	54.8	●	●			◆	◆	◆	162
39.	Bear Paw Lake	57.0	●	●					◆	163
	Palmer-Wasilla Highway									
40.	Walby Lake	10.2	●	●	◆		●	●	◆	163

Map 2: Unit B: Central Knik Arm Drainages

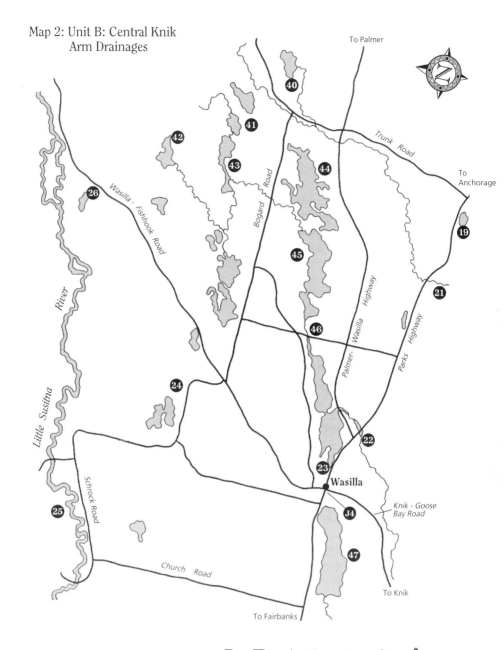

#	LOCATION	MILE POST	🚐	P	⛺	🥾	🛶	♿	🎣	PAGE
41.	Cornelius Lake	10.2	●	●				■	◆	163
42.	Wolf Lake	10.2	●	●	●	■		●	◆	163
43.	Neklason Lake	10.2	●	●	✕		●	◆	◆	163
44.	Finger Lake	10.2	●	■	■		●	■	●	163
45.	Cottonwood Lake	10.2	●	■	✕		●	■	◆	164

Map 3: Unit B: Central Knik
    Arm Drainages

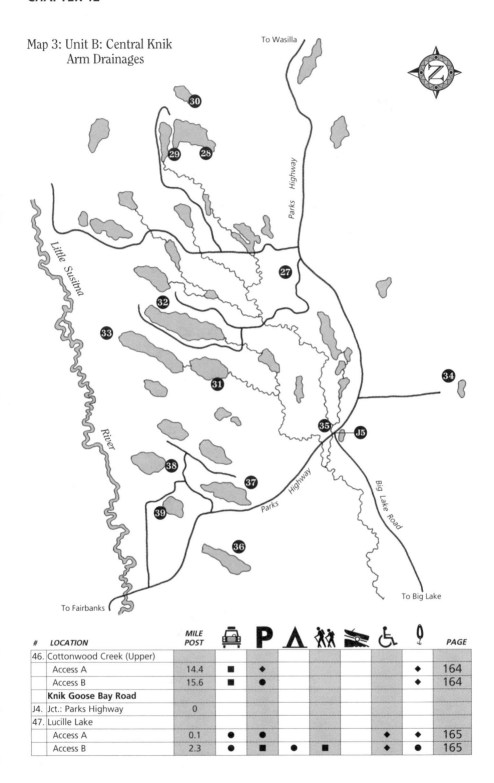

#	LOCATION	MILE POST	🚗	**P**	**Λ**	🥾	⛵	♿	🍴	PAGE
46.	Cottonwood Creek (Upper)									
	Access A	14.4	■	◆					◆	164
	Access B	15.6	■	●					◆	164
	Knik Goose Bay Road									
J4.	Jct.: Parks Highway	0								
47.	Lucille Lake									
	Access A	0.1	●	●				◆	◆	165
	Access B	2.3	●	■	●	■		◆	●	165

Map4: Unit C: West Knik Arm Drainages

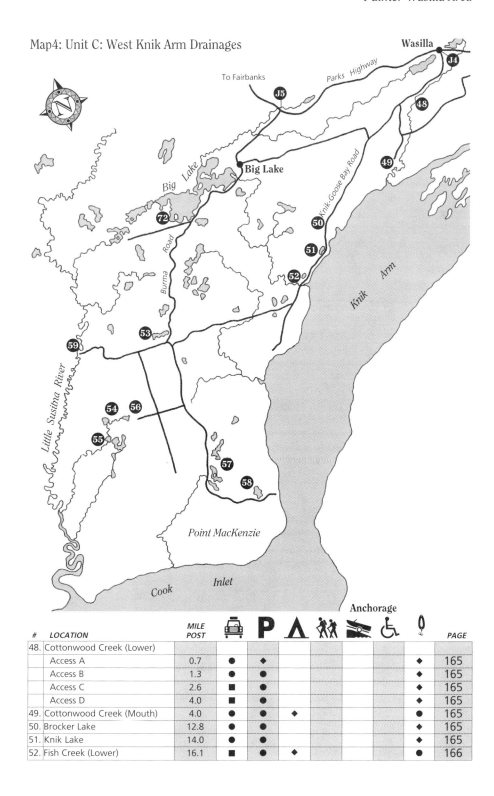

#	LOCATION	MILE POST	🚐	**P**	**⋀**	🚶🚶	🚣	♿	🎣	PAGE
48.	Cottonwood Creek (Lower)									
	Access A	0.7	●	◆					◆	165
	Access B	1.3	●	●					◆	165
	Access C	2.6	■	●					◆	165
	Access D	4.0	■	●					◆	165
49.	Cottonwood Creek (Mouth)	4.0	●	●	◆				●	165
50.	Brocker Lake	12.8	●	●					◆	165
51.	Knik Lake	14.0	●	●					◆	165
52.	Fish Creek (Lower)	16.1	■	●	◆				●	166

Map 5: Unit C: West Knik Arm Drainages

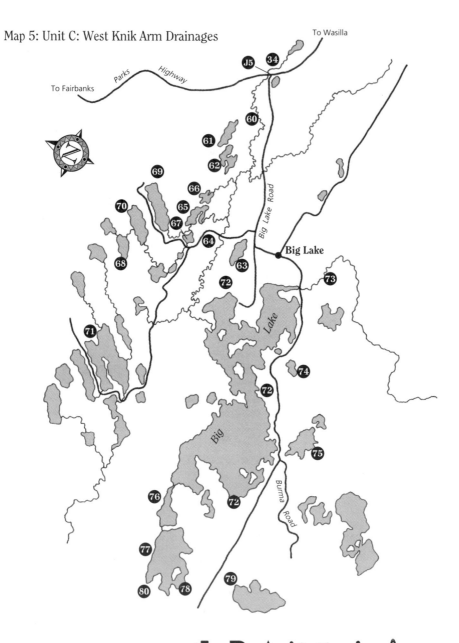

#	LOCATION	MILE POST		P	A	🚶🚶	🛶	♿	🎣	PAGE
53.	Carpenter Lake	17.2	●	●					◆	166
54.	Farmer Lake	17.2	●	●		●			◆	166
55.	Butterfly Lake	17.2	●	●					◆	166
56.	Barley Lake	17.2	●	●		●			◆	166
57.	Twin Island Lake	17.2	●	●		●			◆	166
58.	Lorraine Lake	17.2	●	●					◆	167
59.	Little Susitna River (Lower)	17.2	●	●	●		■	●	■	167

#	LOCATION	MILE POST	🚗	P	△	🥾	🛥	♿	🎣	PAGE
	Big Lake Road									
J5.	Jct.: Parks Highway	0								
60.	Little Meadow Creek	1.4	●	◆					◆	167
61.	Long Lake	1.4	●						◆	168
62.	Twin Lake	1.4	●	●	×		◆		◆	168
63.	Rocky Lake	3.4	●	●	■		◆	◆	◆	168
64.	Meadow Creek	3.4	■	●				◆	◆	168
65.	Stepan Lake	3.4	●	◆					◆	168
66.	Lazy Lake	3.4	●	◆	×	◆			◆	168
67.	Lynda Lake	3.4	●	◆					◆	168
68.	Little Beaver Lake	3.4	●	●					◆	168
69.	Big Beaver Lake	3.4	●	●	×		●	●	◆	169
70.	West Beaver Lake	3.4	●						◆	169
71.	Horseshoe Lake	3.4	●	●					◆	169
72.	Big Lake									
	Access A	3.5	■	■	●		■	●	●	169
	Access B	3.5	■	■	●		■	●	●	169
73.	Fish Creek (Upper)	3.5	■	●					◆	169
74.	Homestead Lake	3.5	●	●				◆	◆	169
75.	Marion Lake	3.5	●	●	◆	●			◆	169
76.	Mirror (Mud) Lake	3.5	●	●					◆	170
77.	Flat Lake	3.5	●	●					◆	170
78.	Sara Lake	3.5	●	●					◆	170
79.	Diamond Lake	3.5	●	●		●			◆	170
80.	Crooked Lake	3.5	●	●	◆			◆	◆	170

PALMER-WASILLA AREA LOCATIONS

Unit A: East Knik Arm Drainages

Includes all roadside waters flowing into and surrounding the eastern part of Knik Arm.

UNIT REGULATIONS:

* King salmon fishing prohibited: All waters, year-round, except Eklutna Tailrace.

UNIT TIMING:

FISH ▽	JAN	FEB	MAR	APR	MAY	JUN	JUL	AUG	SEP	OCT	NOV	DEC
KS*												
RS												
PS												
CS												
SS												
LS												
RT												
AC												
DV												
AG												
WF												
BB												

Note: Timing shown for king salmon indicates fish in all stages of maturity.

Old Glenn Highway

Highway begins at MP 29.6 Glenn Highway (MP 0) and ends at MP 42.1 Glenn Highway (MP 18.6) in the town of Palmer.

1. Eklutna Tailrace

Access A: MP 3.9; N on dirt road 0.1 mile to Knik River confluence.

Access B: MP 4.1; road crosses stream. Trail leads 0.2 mile downstream along tailrace to confluence area.

Fishing: This slow-flowing, glacial stream is home to large early runs of hatchery king and silver salmon, and thus a very popular local angling spot during the summer months. Some chums and char present as well. High-visibility lures and bait are best.

King Salmon / good-excellent / 12-30 lbs. (50 lbs.) / spinners, attractors, flies, bait.
Pink Salmon / poor / 2-4 lbs. (6 lbs.) / spoons, spinners, attractors.
Chum Salmon / fair-good / 6-12 lbs. (18 lbs.) / spoons, attractors.
Silver Salmon / good-excellent / 5-10 lbs. (15 lbs.) / spinners, attractors, bait.
Dolly Varden / fair / 7-12 in. (5 lbs.) / spinners, attractors, bait.

FISH ▽	JAN	FEB	MAR	APR	MAY	JUN	JUL	AUG	SEP	OCT	NOV	DEC
KS					▨	▓						
PS								▓				
CS							▨	▓				
SS							▨	▓				
DV					▨	▓	▓					

2. Knik River Pit

Access: MP 8.5; E on Knik River Road 3.2 miles, left on gravel road short distance to clear-water area and Knik River confluence.

Fishing: A moderately productive intercept fishery for salmon in summer, early fall.

Red Salmon / poor-fair / late July – early August / 4-6 lbs. / spinners, flies, bait.
Chum Salmon / fair / late July – mid-August / 6-10 lbs. / spinners, flies, bait.
Silver Salmon / fair-good / mid-August – early September / 5-10 lbs. / spinners, bait.
Dolly Varden / poor / mid-July – late August / 7-15 in. / spinners, flies, bait.

3. Bodenburg Creek / Knik River Confluence

Access: MP 9.0; N on gravel access road 0.1 mile to confluence area.

Fishing: Clearwater stream with limited opportunities for char. Salmon staging area.

Dolly Varden / poor-fair / early July – late August / 7-12 in. / flies, bait.

4. Jim Creek / Knik River Confluence

Access: MP 11.5; E on Plumley Rd. 1.2 miles to a "T," right on Caudill Rd. 0.7 mile, left on gravel road 1.8 miles to flats.

Fishing: A local salmon hot spot in summer and fall, supporting large native runs of various species. This slow-flowing, clearwater stream is reputed as being one of the best locations for reds and silvers in the area.

Red Salmon / fair-good / 4-7 lbs. (12 lbs.) / spinners, flies, bait.
Chum Salmon / good-excellent / 6-12 lbs. (18 lbs.) / spoons, attractors.

(Continues on next page)

No. 4 - Jim Creek / Knik River continued

Silver Salmon / good / 5-10 lbs. (15 lbs.) / spinners, attractors, bait.
Dolly Varden / fair / 7-15 in. (5 lbs.) / spinners, attractors, bit.

FISH ▽	JAN	FEB	MAR	APR	MAY	JUN	JUL	AUG	SEP	OCT	NOV	DEC
RS							▓	▓	▒			
CS							▓	▓	▒			
SS							▒	▓	▒			
DV					▒	▒	▓	▒	▒			

5. Mud Lake

Access: MP 14.5; E on Maud Rd. 4.0 miles to access site on right.
Fishing: Lake supports a small population of native char. Use a canoe/float tube.
Dolly Varden / fair / August – October / 7-12 in. / spinners, flies, bait.

6. Jim Lake

Access: MP 14.5; E on Maud Rd. 5.0 miles to access site and lake.
Fishing: Lake supports a small population of native char. Use canoe/float tube.
Dolly Varden / poor-fair / May, September – October / 7-12 in. / spinners, flies, bait.

7. Wolverine Lake

Access: MP 16.1; N on Clark-Wolverine Rd. 7.5 miles. Access east end of lake, closest to road.
Fishing: Lake contains a small population of native trout. Use a canoe/float tube.
Rainbow Trout / fair-good / June, September – October / 8-16 in. / spinners, flies, bait.

Glenn Highway

Highway begins in Anchorage and ends in Glennallen. The section covered in this chapter is from Eklutna (MP 26.3) to Fishhook-Willow Rd. junction (MP 49.5).

8. No Name Lake

Access: MP 30.6 — Knik River Access Exit; W. on access road 0.2 mile to gravel road on right and fence. Park and hike around fence short distance to lake.
Fishing: Shallow lake contains small numbers of native landlocked salmon and char.
Landlocked Salmon / fair / June – March / 7-10 in. / spinners, jigs, flies, bait.
Dolly Varden / poor / August – October / 7-12 in. / spinners, flies, bait.

9. Matanuska Lake

Access: MP 36.4; N on access road 0.2 mile to Kepler-Bradley Lakes State Recreation Area and lake.
Fishing: Lake supports a large population of stocked fish. Use a canoe/float tube.
Rainbow Trout / good / May, September – December / 7-18 in. / spinners, flies, bait.
Arctic Char / fair-good / May, September – January / 10-20 in. / spoons, jigs, bait.

10. Victor Lake

Access A: MP 36.4; N on access road 0.2 mile to Kepler-Bradley Lakes State Recreation Area.
Trail leads 0.4 mile to lake on right.

Access B: MP 37.3; N on gravel road ending at parking area by Kepler/Bradley Lakes, cross bridge, 4-wheel drive trail leads 0.5 mile to lake on left.
Fishing: Lake supports a large population of stocked salmon. Use a canoe/float tube.
Landlocked Salmon / excellent / June - March / 7-12 in. / spinners, jigs, flies, bait.

11. Klaire Lake
Access: MP 36.4; N on access road 0.2 mile to Kepler-Bradley Lakes State Recreation Area. Trail leads 0.4 mile to lake on left.
Fishing: Lake is stocked with landlocked salmon, but suffers from winterkill.
Landlocked Salmon / excellent / June – December / 7-12 in. / spinners, jigs, flies, bait.

12. Echo Lake
Access: MP 37.1; turnout. Lake is located S of highway.
Fishing: Lake supports a large population of stocked fish. Use a canoe/float tube.
Landlocked Salmon / excellent / June – April / 7-12 in. / jigs, bait.
Rainbow Trout / good / May, September – December / 8-18 in. / spinners, flies, bait.
Arctic Char / fair-good / May, September – January / 7-16 in. / spoons, jigs, bait.

13. Kepler / Bradley Lakes
Access: MP 37.3; N on Kepler Rd. short distance to lakes. Kepler Lake is on left, Bradley Lake on right.
Fishing: Lake supports a large population of stocked fish. Use a canoe/float tube.
Rainbow Trout / good / May, September – December / 8-20 in. / spinners, flies, bait.
Arctic Grayling / good / June – September / 7-12 in. / spinners, flies.

14. Canoe Lake
Access: MP 38.0; N on Colleen St. short distance, left on Bradley Lake Ave. 0.2 mile, right on Green Jade Pl. short distance, left on Killarney Dr. 0.2 mile to access site on right. Short hike to lake.
Fishing: Lake is stocked with fish, but occasionally winterkills.
Rainbow Trout / good / May, September – December / 7-16 in. / spinners, flies, bait.
Arctic Grayling / good / June – September / 7-12 in. / spinners, flies.

15. Irene Lake
Access: MP 38.0; N on Colleen St. short distance, left on Bradley Lake Ave. 0.2 mile, right on Green Jade Pl. short distance, left on Killarney Dr. 0.4 mile to parking area. Trail leads 50 yards to lake.
Fishing: Lake supports a large population of stocked fish. Char to 8 lbs. present.
Rainbow Trout / good / May, September – December / 7-18 in. / spinners, flies, bait.
Arctic Char / fair-good / May – June, September – January / 10-24 in. / spoons, flies, bait.

16. Long Lake
Access: MP 38.0; N on Colleen St. short distance, left on Bradley Lake Ave. 0.2 mile, right on Green Jade Place short distance, left on Killarney Dr. 0.6 mile, left on access road 0.1 mile to parking area. Trail leads 0.25 mile to lake.
Fishing: Population of stocked trout, a few up to 25 inches. Catch-and-release only.
Rainbow Trout / good / May, September – October / 7-20 in. / spoons, spinners, flies.

17. Meirs (McLeod) Lake
Access: MP 39.2; E on Outer Springer Loop 0.3 mile to access site on left. Trail leads short distance to lake.
Fishing: Lake supports a large population of stocked fish. Popular spot in winter.
Rainbow Trout / good / May, September – December / 7-15 in. / spinners, flies, bait.
Arctic Grayling / fair / June – September / 7-12 in. / spinners, flies.

18. Little Susitna River (Upper)
Access A: MP 49.5; W on Fishhook Willow (Hatcher Pass) Rd. to MP 7.2, left on Edgerton Park Rd. 0.2 mile to river crossing.
Access B: MP 49.5; W on Fishhook Willow (Hatcher Pass) Rd. to MP 8.5 and river crossing. Road parallels river next 5.3 miles.
Fishing: Rocky, fast-flowing river with opportunities for char in calm holes and pools.
Dolly Varden / poor-fair / mid-July – mid-September / 7-12 in. / flies, bait.

GLENN HIGHWAY fishing information continues on page 123, chapter 10.

Unit B: Central Knik Arm Drainages
Includes all roadside waters flowing into and surrounding the central part of Knik Arm.

UNIT REGULATIONS:
* Fishing prohibited: All flowing waters, April 15 – June 14.
* Salmon fishing prohibited: All flowing waters (except Wasilla Creek), year-round.
* King salmon fishing prohibited: All waters, yearround.

UNIT TIMING:

FISH ▽	JAN	FEB	MAR	APR	MAY	JUN	JUL	AUG	SEP	OCT	NOV	DEC
KS*						███	███					
RS*						█	███	███	█			
PS*							███	███	█			
CS*							███	███	█			
SS*							███	███	███	█		
LS	███	███	███	███	███	███	███	███	███	███	███	███
RT	███	███	███	███	███	███	███	███	███	███	███	███
AC	███	███	███	███	███				███	███	███	███
DV	███	███	███	███	███	███	███	███	███	███	███	███
AG	███	███	███	███	███	███	███	███	███	███	███	███

*****Note:** Timing shown for salmon indicates fish in all stages of maturity.*

Parks Highway

Highway begins at junction with Glenn Highway and ends in Fairbanks. The section covered in this chapter is from the junction (MP 35.0) to Houston (MP 57.5).

19. Loberg (Junction) Lake

Access: *Northbound* - MP 35.8; right on Trunk Rd. exit 0.2 mile, left on Trunk Rd. short distance, left on E. Fireweed Rd. 0.5 mile, right on gravel road and immediate right again to small parking area and lake. *Southbound* - MP 36.2; right on Trunk Rd. exit ramp 0.2 mile, right on Trunk Rd. short distance, left on E. Fireweed Rd. 0.5 mile, right on gravel road and immediate right again to small parking area and lake.

Fishing: Lake supports a large population of stocked fish. Use a canoe/float tube.

Rainbow Trout / good / May, September – December / 8-16 in. / spinners, flies, bait.

20. Wasilla Creek (Lower)

Access: *Northbound* - MP 35.8; right on Trunk Rd. exit ramp 0.2 mile, left on Trunk Rd. short distance to E. Fireweed Rd. From here, see Main Access below. *Southbound* - MP 36.2; right on Trunk Rd. exit ramp 0.2 mile, right on Trunk Rd. short distance to E. Fireweed Rd. From here see following information. *Main Access* - Left on E. Fireweed Rd. 1.4 miles to sharp turn and Nelson Rd., left on gravel road 0.7 mile to parking area.

Fishing: Vegetated, slow-moving stream supporting small runs of salmon, primarily silvers in late summer. Open to fishing on weekends only.

Pink Salmon / fair / mid – late July / 2-4 lbs. / spoons, spinners, flies.
Silver Salmon / good / early – mid-August / 4-8 lbs. / spinners, flies, bait.
Rainbow Trout / poor-fair / mid-July – late August / 7-12 in. / spinners, flies, bait.
Dolly Varden / fair / mid-July – mid-August / 7-12 in. / spinners, flies, bait.

21. Wasilla Creek (Middle)

Access: Northbound - MP 37.5; right on Fairview Loop exit, left on Hyer Rd. 0.1 mile, right on S. Frontage Rd. short distance to stream crossing. Southbound - MP 38.8; right on S. Frontage Rd. 1.0 mile to stream crossing.

Fishing: Weekend-only fishery, primarily silver salmon and char in late summer.

Silver Salmon / fair / mid – late August / 4-8 lbs. / spinners, flies, bait.
Rainbow Trout / poor / mid-July – late September / 7-12 in. / spinners, flies, bait.
Dolly Varden / fair / mid-July – late September / 7-12 in. / spinners, flies, bait.

22. Cottonwood Creek

Access A: MP 40.9; highway crosses stream.
Access B: MP 41.1; S on Palmer-Wasilla Hwy. short distance, first road on left 0.1 mile, right on Matanuska Rd. short distance to stream crossing.

Fishing: Very slow-flowing stream with opportunities for trout and char.

Rainbow Trout / fair / mid-July – mid-October / 7-15 in. / spinners, flies, bait.
Dolly Varden / poor / mid-August – mid-October / 7-14 in. / spinners, flies, bait.

23. Wasilla Lake

Access: MP 41.7; lake is located NE of road.

Fishing: Lake contains a healthy population of trout, a few fish up to eight pounds.

Rainbow Trout / fair / May, September – December / 8-18 in. / spinners, flies, bait.
Dolly Varden / poor / August – October / 8-16 in. / spoons, flies, bait.

24. Memory Lake

Access: MP 42.2; N on Main St. (Wasilla Fishhook Rd.) 3.0 miles, W on Schrock Rd. 1.1 mile, right on Hebrides Dr. 0.2 mile to a "T," left on Inverness Dr. short distance to access road on right leading to lake.

Fishing: Lake supports a large population of stocked fish. A few pike are present.
Landlocked Salmon / excellent / June – March / 7-12 in. / spinners, jigs, flies, bait.
Rainbow Trout / good / May, September – December / 8-20 in. / spinners, flies, bait.
Arctic Char / fair / May, September – January / 7-18 in. / spoons, jigs, bait.
Northern Pike / poor / May, September – October / 2-4 lbs. / spoons, plugs, bait.

25. Little Susitna River (Upper)

Access A: MP 42.2; N on Main St. (Wasilla Fishhook Rd.) 3.0 miles, left on Schrock Rd. 4.3 miles, right on North Sushana St. 0.6 mile to river crossing.
Access B: MP 42.2; N on Main St. (Wasilla Fishhook Rd.) 3.0 miles, left on Schrock Rd. 6.8 miles to river crossing.
Fishing: Little-fished stretch of water for trout, char, whitefish. Salmon spawning area.
Rainbow Trout / fair / mid-June – mid-September / 7-15 in. / spinners, flies, bait.
Dolly Varden / fair-good / mid-July – mid-September / 7-15 in. / flies, bait.
Arctic Grayling / fair / mid-June – mid-September / 7-12 in. / spinners, flies.
Whitefish / poor-fair / late September – mid-October / 10-15 in. / flies, bait.

26. Reed Lake

Access: MP 42.2; N on Main St. (Wasilla Fishhook Rd.) 7.3 miles, left on Welch Rd. 0.4 mile. Trail on right leads short distance to lake.
Fishing: Lake supports a large population of stocked fish. Popular spot late in season.
Rainbow Trout / good / May, September – December / 7-16 in. / spinners, flies, bait.
Arctic Grayling / fair / June – September / 7-12 in. / spinners, flies.

27. Golden Lake

Access: MP 48.7; N on Pittman Rd. 0.3 mile, left on Golden Ave. 0.3 mile, left on gravel access road 0.1 mile to lake.
Fishing: Lake supports a large population of stocked trout. Use a canoe/float tube.
Rainbow Trout / good / May, September – December / 7-16 in. / spinners, flies, bait.

28. Kalmbach Lake

Access: MP 48.7; E on Pittman Rd. 1.3 mile, right on Beverly Lake Rd. 3.1 miles to small parking area on right. Trail on left leads 100 yards to lake.
Fishing: Lake supports a large population of stocked salmon and trout.
Landlocked Salmon / excellent / June – March / 7-12 in. / spinners, jigs, flies, bait.
Rainbow Trout / good / May, September – December / 7-16 in. / spinners, flies, bait.

29. Beverly Lake

Access: MP 48.7; N on Pittman Rd. 1.3 mile, right on Beverly Lake Rd. 3.1 miles. Trail on right leads 0.2 mile to lake.
Fishing: Lake supports a large populaton of stocked torut. Use a canoe/float tube.
Rainbow Trout / good / May, September – December / 7-16 in. / spinners, flies, bait.

30. Bruce Lake

Access: MP 48.7; E on Pittman Rd. 1.4 miles, right on Beverly Lake Rd. 3.1 miles to Kalmbach/Beverly Lake access, left on Windy Bottom Dr. 0.2 mile. Trail on left leads 0.2 mile to lake.
Fishing: Lake supports a large population of stocked trout. Use a canoe/float tube.
Rainbow Trout / good / May, September – December / 8-16 in. / spinners, flies, bait.

31. Lalen Lake

Access: MP 48.8; E on Meadow Lakes Dr. 2.5 miles, left on Meadow Lakes Dr. 0.5 mile, left on Skyview Dr. 0.4 mile to access road on right, 0.1 mile to lake.
Fishing: Lake supports a large population of stocked trout. Use a canoe/float tube.
Rainbow Trout / good / May, September – December / 7-16 in. / spinners, flies, bait.

32. Seymour Lake

Access: MP 48.8; E on Meadow Lakes Dr. 2.5 miles, left on Meadow Lakes Dr. 1.6 mile, right on access road 0.1 mile to lake.
Fishing: Lake supports a large population of stocked trout. Use a canoe/float tube.
Rainbow Trout / good / May, September – December / 7-16 in. / spinners, flies, bait.

33. Visnaw Lake

Access: MP 48.8; E on Meadow Lakes Dr. 2.5 miles, left on Meadow Lakes Dr. 1.6 mile to Sylvia-Denise Ave. on left opposite Seymour Lake access, 0.3 mile to lake.
Fishing: Lake supports a large population of stocked trout. Use a canoe/float tube.
Rainbow Trout / good / May, September – December / 7-16 in. / spinners, flies, bait.

34. Dawn Lake

Access: MP 51.6; S on Johnson Rd. 1.5 mile, left on Dawn Lake Dr. 0.5 mile, right on Dawn Lake Crt. 0.1 mile to cul-de-sac. Access trail left of private drive leads short distance to lake.
Fishing: Lake supports a moderate population of stocked trout. Use a canoe/float tube.
Rainbow Trout / fair / May, September – December / 7-14 in. / spinners, flies, bait.

35. Little Meadow Creek

Access: MP 52.3; highway crosses stream.
Fishing: Small clearwater stream offering trout and char in summer and early fall.
Rainbow Trout / fair / mid-June – mid-September / 7-12 in. / spinners, flies, bait.
Arctic Char / fair / late June – mid-September / 7-12 in. / spinners, flies, bait.

36. Morvro Lake

Access: MP 54.3; W on Delroy Rd. 0.7 mile to section line access and lake.
Fishing: Lake supports a moderate population of stocked trout. Use a canoe/float tube.
Rainbow Trout / good / May, September – December / 7-14 in. / spinners, flies, bait.

37. Loon Lake

Access: MP 54.8; E on Cheri Lake Dr. 0.4 mile, right on Ray St. 0.2 mile, right on access road short distance to lake.
Fishing: Lake supports a large population of stocked trout. Use a canoe/float tube.
Rainbow Trout / good / May, September – December / 7-16 in. / spinners, flies, bait.

38. Prator Lake

Access: MP 54.8; E on Cheri Lake Dr. 1.0 mile, left on Karen Ave. 0.3 mile, left on Frog St. 0.3 mile, left on Prince Charming Dr. 0.2 mile, left on Duke St. 0.1 mile, right on access road short distance to lake.
Fishing: Lake supports a moderate population of stocked char. Some pike present.
Northern Pike / fair / May – June, September – October / 2-4 lbs. / spoons, plugs, bait.
Arctic Char / fair-good / May, September – January / 7-16 in. / spoons, jigs, bait.

39. Bear Paw Lake

Access: MP 57.0; E on King Arthur Dr. 1.4 mile, right on Magic Ave. 0.5 mile, right on 4-wheel drive access road 0.1 mile to lake.
Fishing: Lake supports a moderate population of stocked salmon and trout.
Landlocked Salmon / good / June – March / 7-12 in. / spinners, jigs, flies, bait.
Rainbow Trout / fair / May, September – December / 7-14 in. / spinners, flies, bait.

PARKS HIGHWAY fishing information continues on page 173, chapter 13.

Palmer-Wasilla Highway

Highway begins at MP 41.8 Glenn Highway in Palmer and ends at MP 41.1 Parks Highway in Wasilla (MP 16.3). It is intersected by Trunk Road at MP 10.2 and Seward Meridian Road at MP 14.4, both of which connect with Parks Highway at MP 35.4 and 39.4, respectively.

40. Walby Lake

Access: MP 10.2; N on Trunk Rd. 2.2 miles, right on Tern Dr. 0.6 mile to short access road on right.
Fishing: Lake supports a moderate population of stocked trout. Use canoe/float tube.
Rainbow Trout / good / May, September – December / 7-14 in. / spinners, flies, bait.

41. Cornelius Lake

Access: MP 10.2; N on Trunk Rd. 1.3 mile, left on Bogard Rd. 0.4 mile, right on Engstrom Rd. 1.0 mile to lake on right.
Fishing: Lake contains a healty population of trout and char, some up to five pounds.
Rainbow Trout / fair / May, September – December / 8-16 in. / spinners, flies, bait.
Dolly Varden / poor-fair / August – October / 7-15 in. / spoons, flies, bait.

42. Wolf Lake

Access: MP 10.2; N on Trunk Rd. 1.3 mile, left on Bogard Rd. 0.4 mile, right on Engstrom Rd. 2.6 miles to end of road. Trail leads 100 yards to lake.
Fishing: Lake supports a moderate population of stocked trout. Use canoe/float tube.
Rainbow Trout / fair / May, September – December / 7-16 in. / spinners, flies, bait.

43. Neklason Lake

Access: MP 10.2; N on Trunk Rd. 1.3 mile, left on Bogard Rd. 0.4 mile, right on Engstrom Rd. 0.8 mile, left on Zephyr Dr. 0.3 mile, right on Breezewood Rd. 0.4 mile to end of road and lake.
Fishing: Lake contains a healthy population of trout and char, some up to five pounds.
Rainbow Trout / fair / May, September – December / 8-16 in. / spinners, flies, bait.
Dolly Varden / poor / August – October / 7-15 in. / spoons, flies, bait.

44. Finger Lake

Access: MP 10.2; N on Trunk Rd. 1.3 mile, left on Bogard Rd. 0.9 mile, left on access road at sign 0.4 mile to lake.
Fishing: Lake supports a large population of stocked fish. One of the most popular ice fishing spots in the valley. Char up to 10 pounds or more possible. A few pike present.
Landlocked Salmon / excellent / June – March / 7-12 in. / spinners, jigs, flies, bait.
Rainbow Trout / good / May, September – December / 7-16 in. / spinners, flies, bait.

Arctic Char / good / May, September – January / 8-16 in. / spoons, jigs, bait.
Arctic Grayling / fair / May – September / 7-14 in. / spinners, flies.

45. Cottonwood Lake

Access: MP 10.2; N on Trunk Rd. 1.3 mile, left on Bogard Rd. 2.3 miles, left on Cottonwood
Loop 0.8 mile, left on Spruce Dr. 0.3 mile to lake. **Alternate Access:** MP 14.4; N on Seward
Meridian Rd. 1.0 mile, right on Bogard Rd. 1.7 mile to intersection, continue right on Bogard
Rd. 0.8 mile, right on Cottonwood Loop 0.8 mile, left on Spruce Dr. 0.3 mile to lake.
Fishing: Lake contains a healthy population of trout and char, a few up to eight pounds.
Rainbow Trout / fair / May, September – December / 8-16 in. / spinners, flies, bait.
Dolly Varden / poor / August – October / 7-15 in. / spoons, flies, bait.

46. Cottonwood Creek (Upper)

Access A: MP 14.4; N on Seward Meridian Rd. 0.8 mile to stream crossing.
Access B: MP 15.6; road crosses stream.
Fishing: Mainly a salmon spawning area with opportunities for trout and char.
Rainbow Trout / fair / mid-July – mid-October / 7-15 in. / spinners, flies, bait.
Dolly Varden / poor / mid-August – mid-October / 7-15 in. / spinners, flies, bait.

Unit C: West Knik Arm Drainages

Includes all roadside waters flowing into and surrounding the western part of Knik Arm.

UNIT REGULATIONS:

* Fishing prohibited: All flowing waters, April 15 – June 14 (except Little Susitna River).

* King salmon fishing prohibited: All waters, yearround (except Little Susitna River).

UNIT TIMING:

FISH ▽	JAN	FEB	MAR	APR	MAY	JUN	JUL	AUG	SEP	OCT	NOV	DEC
KS*												
RS*												
PS*												
CS*												
SS*												
LS												
RT												
LT												
AC												
DV												
AG												
WF												
NP												
BB												

***Note:** Timing shown for salmon indicates fish in all stages of maturity.*

Knik-Goose Bay Road

Road begins at MP 42.2 Parks Highway (MP 0) and ends at Goose Bay (MP 18.5).

47. Lucille Lake

Access A: Short distance on Main St., right on Susitna Ave. 0.3 mile to lake.
Access B: MP 2.3; N on Endeavor St. 0.5 mile to Mat-Su Borough Campground. Short hike on Boardwalk Trail to lake.
Fishing: Lake supports a large population of stocked trout. Popular spot in winter.
Rainbow Trout / good / May, September – December / 7-16 in. / spinners, flies, bait.

48. Cottonwood Creek (Middle)

Access A: MP 0.7; E on Glenwood Ave. 0.7 mile to stream crossing.
Access B: MP 1.3; SE on Fern St. 0.1 mile to stream crossing.
Access C: MP 2.6; S on Edlund Rd. 0.2 mile to stream crossing.
Access D: MP 4.0; S on Fairview Loop Rd. 2.4 mile to stream crossing.
Fishing: Slow-flowing stream with decent action for trout in summer and fall.
Rainbow Trout / good / early July – early October / 7-15 in. / flies, bait.
Dolly Varden / poor / mid-July – early October / 7-15 in. / flies, bait.

49. Cottonwood Creek (Lower)

Access: MP 4.0; S on Fairview Loop Rd. 1.9 mile to sharp turn in road, straight on Hayfield Rd. 1.3 mile, left on dirt road 0.5 mile to parking area and stream.
Fishing: Weekend-only summer fishery for primarily red and silver salmon. Lower stream is influenced by tides. High-visibility lures and bait are favored.
Red Salmon / fair-good / 4-7 lbs. (12 lbs.) / flies, bait.
Silver Salmon / good / 5-10 lbs. (15 lbs.) / attractors, flies, ait.
Dolly Varden / poor / 7-14 in. (3 lbs.) / attractors, bait.

FISH ▽	JAN	FEB	MAR	APR	MAY	JUN	JUL	AUG	SEP	OCT	NOV	DEC
RS							▓	▓				
SS								▓	▓			
DV					▓	▓	▓					

50. Brocker Lake

Access: MP 12.8; NW on Horizon Dr. 0.8 mile, right on Twilight Dr. 0.8 mile, right on Ogard 0.2 mile, left on Peterson Dr. 0.8 mile to public access on left and lake.
Fishing: Lake supports a large population of stocked trout. Use a canoe/float tube.
Rainbow Trout / good / May, September – December / 7-16 in. / spinners, flies, bait.

51. Knik Lake

Access: MP 14.0; NW on gravel road by Knik Museum 0.1 mile to lake.
Fishing: Lake supports a large population of stocked fish. Popular spot late in season.
Landlocked Salmon / excellent / June – March / 7-12 in. / spinners, jigs, flies, bait.
Rainbow Trout / good / May, September – December / 8-16 in. / spinners, flies, bait.
Arctic Grayling / fair / May – September / 7-15 in. / spinners, flies.

52. Fish Creek (Lower)

Access: MP 16.1; road crosses stream.
Fishing: Weekend-only fishery targeting primarily silver salmon in late summer. Resident species found upstream of road crossing. Lower stream is influenced by tides.
Red Salmon / poor-fair / 4-7 lbs. (12 lbs.) / flies.
Pink Salmon / poor-fair / 2-4 lbs. (6 lbs.) / spoons, spinners, flies.
Chum Salmon / poor / 6-12 lbs. (16 lbs.) / spoons, spinners, flies.
Silver Salmon / good / 5-10 lbs. (15 lbs.) / spinners, flies, bait.
Rainbow Trout / fair / 7-15 in. (5 lbs.) / spinners, flies, bait.
Dolly Varden / fair / 7-15 in. (5 lbs.) / spinners, flies, bai.

FISH ▽	JAN	FEB	MAR	APR	MAY	JUN	JUL	AUG	SEP	OCT	NOV	DEC
RS						■	■	■	■			
PS							■	■	■			
CS							■	■				
SS							■	■	■	■		
RT					■	■	■	■	■	■		
DV					■	■	■	■	■	■		

53. Carpenter Lake

Access: MP 17.2; W on Point Mackenzie Rd. 7.6 miles to a "T," turn right, then left on Ayrshire Rd. 1.2 mile, right on dirt road 0.5 mile to lake.
Fishing: Lake supports a large population of stocked fish. Use a canoe/float tube.
Landlocked Salmon / fair-good / June – March / 7-12 in. / spinners, jigs, flies, bait.
Rainbow Trout / good / May, September – December / 7-16 in. / spinners, flies, bait.
Arctic Char / fair / May, September – January / 7-16 in. / spoons, jigs, bait.

54. Farmer Lake

Access: MP 17.2; W on Point Mckenzie Rd. 7.6 miles to a "T," turn left, 3.4 miles to Holstein Ave., turn right, 2.7 miles to access on left. Locate short trail to lake.
Fishing: Lake supports a large population of stocked trout. Use a canoe/float tube.
Rainbow Trout / fair / May, September – December / 7-16 in. / spinners, flies, bait.

55. Butterfly Lake

Access: MP 17.2; W on Point Mckenzie Rd. 7.6 miles to a "T," turn left, 3.4 miles to Holstein Ave., right 3.2 miles to access on right. Short trail on boardwalk to lake.
Fishing: Lake supports a large population of stocked trout. Use a canoe/float tube
Rainbow Trout / good / May, September – December / 7-16 in. / spinners, flies, bait.

56. Barley Lake

Access: MP 17.2; W on Point Mckenzie Rd. 7.6 miles to a "T," turn left, 3.4 miles to Holstein Ave., turn right, 1.6 miles to Guernsey Rd., left at 4-way intersection on Guernsey Rd. for 1.1 miles, right at second farm lane 0.1 mile. Locate short trail to lake.
Fishing: Lake supports a large population of stocked fish. Use a canoe/float tube
Landlocked Salmon / good / June – March / 7-12 in. / spinners, jigs, flies, bait.
Rainbow Trout / good / May, September – December / 7-16 in. / spinners, flies, bait.

57. Twin Island Lake

Access: MP 17.2; W on Point Mckenzie Rd. 7.6 miles to a "T," turn left, 8.0 miles to unimproved seismic trail on left, 0.3 mile to SW corner of Mat-Su Borough lot, E 0.1 mile to lake.

Fishing: Lake supports a large population of stocked trout. Use a canoe/float tube

Rainbow Trout / good / May, September – December / 7-16 in. / spinners, flies, bait.

58. Lorraine Lake

Access: MP 17.2; W on Point Mckenzie Rd. 7.6 miles to a "T," turn left, 12.3 miles to pullout on left, 0.2 mile by 4-wheel drive or hike to lake.

Fishing: Lake supports a large population of stocked fish. Use a canoe/float tube

Rainbow Trout / good / May, September – December / 7-16 in. / spinners, flies, bait.

Arctic Grayling / fair / June – September / 7-12 in. / spinners, flies.

59. Little Susitna River (Lower)

Access: MP 17.2; W on Point Mackenzie Rd. 7.6 miles to a "T," right short distance to another "T," turn on Ayrshire Rd. 2.7 miles to a "Y," right on Little Su Access Rd. 3.3 miles to campground and river.

Fishing: The most popular angling spot in the Matanuska Valley area, with superb runs of bright kings, pinks, chums, and silvers along with added opportunity for reds. Some trout and char also available. Casting from shore is very productive as is fishing from boat.

King Salmon / good-excellent / 15-45 lbs. (75 lbs.) / plugs, attractors.

Red Salmon / Early Run: poor / 3-6 lbs. (10 lbs.) / spinners, flies, bait.

    Late Run: poor-fair / 4-7 lbs. (12 lbs.) / spinners, flies, bait.

Pink Salmon / good-excellent / 2-5 lbs. (7 lbs.) / spoons, spinners.

Chum Salmon / good-excellent / 6-12 lbs. (18 lbs.) / spoons, spinners, bait.

Silver Salmon / good-excellent / 5-12 lbs. (18 lbs.) / spinners, plugs, bait.

Rainbow Trout / fair / 7-15 in. (5 lbs.) / spinners, flies, bait.

Dolly Varden / fair / 7-15 in. (4 lbs.) / spinners, flies, bait.

Whitefish / poor / 10-15 in. (3 lbs.) /attractors, flies, bait.

Burbot / poor / 12-20 in. (6 lbs.) / bait.

FISH ▽	JAN	FEB	MAR	APR	MAY	JUN	JUL	AUG	SEP	OCT	NOV	DEC
KS						■						
RS						■	■					
PS							■					
CS							■					
SS								■				
RT								■	■			
DV							■	■				
WF								■	■			
BB						■	■	■				

Big Lake Road

Road begins at MP 52.3 Parks Highway (MP 0) and ends at Big Lake (MP 6.5).

60. Little Meadow Creek

Access: MP 1.4; N on Kenlar Rd. 0.3 mile to stream crossing.

Fishing: Stream contains a small number of trout and char during summer months.

Rainbow Trout / fair / mid-July – late September / 7-12 in. / spinners, flies, bait.

Arctic Char / fair / mid-July – late September / 7-12 in. / spinners, flies, bait.

61. Long Lake

Access: MP 1.4; N on Kenlar Rd. 0.8 mile, left on Birch Rd. 0.5 mile to section line access on right.
Fishing: Lake supports a small population of native trout. Use a canoe/float tube.
Rainbow Trout / fair / May, September – October / 8-15 in. / spinners, flies, bait.

62. Twin Lake

Access: MP 1.4; N on Kenlar Rd. 0.8 mile, left on Birch Rd. 0.7 mile, left on dirt road 0.2 mile, right on access road 0.1 mile to cul-de-sac. Short trail on left leads to lake.
Fishing: Lake supports a small population of native trout. Use a canoe/float tube.
Rainbow Trout / fair / May, September – October / 8-15 in. / spinners, flies, bait.

63. Rocky Lake

Access: MP 3.4; N on Beaver Lake Rd. 0.4 mile, left by sign on Rocky St., take first left to Rocky Lake Wayside and lake access.
Fishing: Lake supports a moderate population of native trout. Use a canoe/float tube.
Rainbow Trout / fair / May, September – December / 7-14 in. / spinners, flies, bait.

64. Meadow Creek

Access: MP 3.4; N on Beaver Lake Rd. 0.8 mile to stream crossing.
Fishing: Salmon spawning stream with potential catches of trout and char in summer.
Rainbow Trout / fair / mid-June – mid-September / 7-15 in. / spinners, flies, bait.
Arctic Char / fair / mid-June – mid-September / 7-12 in. / spinners, flies, bait.

65. Stepan Lake

Access: MP 3.4; N on Beaver Lake Rd. 1.1 mile, right on Ryan Creek Dr. 0.6 mile, left on Lazy Lake Dr. 0.2 mile to section line access on left.
Fishing: Lake supports a small population of native trout. Use a canoe/float tube.
Rainbow Trout / fair / May, September – October / 8-15 in. / spinners, flies, bait.

66. Lazy Lake

Access: MP 3.4; N on Beaver Lake Rd. 1.1 mile, right on Ryan Creek Dr. 0.6 mile, left on Lazy Lake Dr. 0.6 mile, right on Old Toby Rd. 0.3 mile, right on Ashley Row Rd. 0.7 mile to cul-de-sac and lake access on left.
Fishing: Lake supports a small population of native trout. Use a canoe/float tube.
Rainbow Trout / fair / May, September – October / 8-15 in. / spinners, flies, bait.

67. Lynda Lake

Access: MP 3.4; N on Beaver Lake Rd. 1.7 mile, lake is adjacent to right side of road.
Fishing: Lake supports a small population of native trout. Use a canoe/float tube.
Rainbow Trout / fair / May, September – October / 8-15 in. / spinners, flies, bait.

68. Little Beaver Lake

Access: MP 3.4; N on Beaver Lake Rd. 0.8 mile, left on Lakes blvd. 1.8 mile, right on Rogers Rd. 2.0 miles, left on section line access road 0.2 mile to lake.
Fishing: Lake supports a large population of stocked trout. Use a canoe/float tube.
Rainbow Trout / good / May, September – December / 7-16 in. / spinners, flies, bait.

69. Big Beaver Lake

Access: MP 3.4; N on Beaver Lake Rd. 2.3 miles to 4-way intersection, right on Beaver Lake Rd. continuation short distance, right on access road to lake.
Fishing: Lake supports a large population of population of trout. Fish to 5 lbs. present.
Rainbow Trout / fair / May, September – December / 8-16 in. / spinners, flies, bait.

70. West Beaver Lake

Access: MP 3.4; N on Beaver Lake Rd. 2.3 miles to 4-way intersection, right on Beaver Rd. continuation 0.3 mile, left on West Beaver Dr. 0.2 mile to section line access on left.
Fishing: Lake supports a large population of trout. Use a canoe/float tube.
Rainbow Trout / fair / May, September – December / 8-15 in. / spinners, flies, bait.

71. Horseshoe Lake

Access: MP 3.4; N on Beaver Lake Rd. 1.0 mile, left on North Big Lake Blvd. 3.6 miles, right on Horseshoe Lake Rd. 2.4 miles to access road on right.
Fishing: Lake supports a small population of native trout. Use a canoe/float tube.
Rainbow Trout / fair / May, September – October / 8-16 in. / spinners, flies, bait.

72. Big Lake

Access A: MP 3.5; right fork at "Y" on North Shore Dr. 1.5 mile to North Big Lake Wayside and lake access.
Access B: MP 3.5; left fork at "Y" on South Big Lake Rd. 1.7 mile to gravel road on right leading short distance to South Big Lake Wayside and lake access.
Fishing: Lake contains a moderate population of native trout and char along with whitefish and burbot. Char known to reach 12 pounds. Pike to 10 pounds present.
Rainbow Trout / fair / May, September – December / 8-18 in. / spinners, flies, bait.
Arctic Char / fair / May, September – January / 10-26 in. / spoons, jigs, bait.

73. Fish Creek (Upper)

Access: MP 3.5; left fork at "Y" on South Big Lake Rd. 1.6 miles to stream crossing.
Fishing: Anglers catch some trout, char, and whitefish here. Salmon spawning area.
Rainbow Trout / fair / mid-August – late October / 7-16 in. / spinners, flies, bait.
Arctic Char / fair / mid-August – late October / 7-16 in. / spinners, flies, bait.
Whitefish / poor-fair / mid-October – late November / 10-15 in. / flies, bait.

74. Homestead Lake

Access: MP 3.5; left fork at "Y" on South Big Lake Rd. 2.1 miles, left on Echo Lake Rd. 0.8 mile, right on Sun Dr. 0.3 mile to a "T," right on Alta Dr. 0.1 mile to another "T," left and immediate right short distance to lake.
Fishing: Lake supports a moderate population of stocked trout. Use a canoe/float tube.
Rainbow Trout / fair / May, September – December / 7-14 in. / spinners, flies, bait.

75. Marion Lake

Access: MP 3.5; left fork at "Y" on South Big Lake Rd. 5.2 miles, left on Marion Dr. short distance, left 0.5 mile to lake access on right by sign. Trail leads 100 yards to lake.
Fishing: Lake supports a large population of stocked fish. Use a canoe/float tube.
Rainbow Trout / good / May, September – December / 7-16 in. / spinners, flies, bait.
Arctic Char / fair / May, September – January / 8-24 in. / spoons, jigs, bait.

76. Mirror (Mud) Lake

Access: MP 3.5; left fork at "Y" on South Big Lake Rd. 5.2 miles to 4-way intersection, right on South Big Lake Rd. continuation 2.5 miles, right on Purington Rd. 1.6 miles to end of road. Winter foot access only. Follow center of canal short distance to lake on right. Flat Lake is on left.

Fishing: Lake supports a population of native trout and char. Use a canoe/float tube.
Rainbow Trout / fair / May, September – October / 7-16 in. / spinners, flies, bait.
Arctic Char / fair / May, September – October / 7-18 in. / spoons, jigs, bait.

77. Flat Lake

Access: MP 3.5; left fork at "Y" on South Big Lake Rd. 5.2 miles to 4-way intersection, right on South Big Lake Rd. continuation 2.5 miles, right on Purington Rd. 1.6 miles to end of road. Winter foot access only. Follow center of canal short distance to lake on left. Mirror Lake is on right.

Fishing: Lake supports a population of native char. Use a canoe/float tube.
Rainbow Trout / fair / May, September – October / 7-16 in. / spinners, flies, bait.
Arctic Char / fair / May, September – October / 7-18 in. / spoons, jigs, bait.

78. Sara Lake

Access: MP 3.5; left fork at "Y" on South Big Lake Rd. 5.2 miles to 4-way intersection, right on South Big Lake Rd. continuation 2.5 miles, right on Purington Rd. 1.6 miles to end of road. Winter foot access only. Follow center of canal short distance to Flat Lake on left, continue along left shoreline 0.3 mile to public easement on left. Undefined trail leads 50 feet to lake.

Fishing: Lake supports a small population of native char. Use a canoe/float tube.
Arctic Char / fair / May, September – October / 7-18 in. / spoons, jigs, bait.

79. Diamond Lake

Access: MP 3.5; left fork at "Y" on South Big Lake Rd. 5.2 miles to four-way intersection, right on South Big Lake Rd. continuation 3.4 miles, left on Raines Dr. 1.1 mile to section line access. Trail leads 100 yards to lake.

Fishing: Lake supports a large population of stocked salmon and trout.
Landlocked Salmon / excellent / June – March / 7-12 in. / spinners, jigs, flies, bait.
Rainbow Trout / good / May, September – December / 7-16 in. / spinners, flies, bait.

80. Crooked Lake

Access: MP 3.5; left fork at "Y" on South Big Lake Rd. 5.2 miles to four-way intersection, right on South Big Lake Rd. continuation 3.8 miles, right on access road by sign 0.6 mile to end of road and lake.

Fishing: Lake supports a large population of trout. Fish to five pounds present
Rainbow Trout / good / May, September – October / 7-16 in. / spinners, flies, bait.

Other Locations

Unit A: East Knik Arm Drainages:

Old Glenn Highway: Goat Creek - MP 6.1; DV, (PS, CS, SS) Knik River - MP 8.7; (KS, RS, PS, CS, SS, DV, WF, BB) Bodenburg Creek - MP 9.0/12.9; DV, (RS,CS,SS) Matanuska River

- MP 16.8; (KS, RS, PS, CS, SS, DV, WF, BB) **Glenn Highway:** Knik River - MP 29.7/30.8; (KS, RS, PS, CS, SS, DV, WF, BB) Matanuska River - MP 31.5; (KS, RS, PS, CS, SS, DV, WF, BB) Spring Creek - MP 35.1; DV, (SS, RT)

Unit B: Central Knik Arm Drainages:

Palmer-Wasilla Roads: Wasilla Creek - (M 10.4 Palmer-Wasilla Hwy./Bogard Rd.); RT, DV, (KS, RS, PS, CS, SS) Cottonwood Creek - (Bogard Rd.); RT, DV, (RS, SS)

Unit C: West Knik Arm Drainages:

Big Lake Road: Lucille Creek - MP 2.1; RT, Arctic Char, (RS, SS)

LOCATION & SPECIES APPENDIX

● - Wild/Native fish, fishable numbers.
◆ - Present in small numbers and/or only occasionally caught.
▲ - Stocked/Hatchery fish, fishable numbers.
■ - Mix of Wild and Hatchery fish, fishable numbers.
× - Indicated species present but currently protected by law (PROHIBITED).

#	LOCATION	KING SALMON	RED SALMON	PINK SALMON	CHUM SALMON	SILVER SALMON	LANDLOCKED SALMON	KOKANEE	STEELHEAD TROUT	RAINBOW TROUT	LAKE TROUT	ARCTIC CHAR	DOLLY VARDEN	ARCTIC GRAYLING	SHEEFISH	WHITEFISH	NORTHERN PIKE	BURBOT	PACIFIC HALIBUT	LING COD	ROCKFISH
	Old Glenn Highway																				
1.	Eklutna Tailrace	■	◆	●	●	■							●				◆		◆		
2.	Knik River Pit	×	●	◆	●	●							●								
3.	Bodenburg Creek (mouth)	×	×	×	×	×							●				◆		◆		
4.	Jim Creek (mouth)	×	●	◆	●	●							●				◆	◆	◆		
5.	Mud Lake					◆							●					◆			
6.	Jim Lake		◆										●				◆	◆			
7.	Wolverine Lake		◆			◆						●	◆								
	Glenn Highway																				
8.	No Name Lake									●			●								
9.	Matanuska Lake									▲	▲	▲									
10.	Victor Lake									▲											
11.	Klaire Lake									▲											
12.	Echo Lake									▲	▲	▲									
13.	Kepler/Bradley Lakes									▲				▲							
14.	Canoe Lake									▲				▲							
15.	Irene Lake									▲		▲									
16.	Long Lake									▲											
17.	Meirs Lake									▲				▲							
18.	Little Susitna River	×		×	×	×				◆			●				◆	◆			
	Parks Highway																				
19.	Loberg (Junction) Lake						▲			▲											
20.	Wasilla Creek (Lower)	×	◆	●	◆	●				●			●								
21.	Wasilla Creek	×	×	×	×	×				●			●								
22.	Cottonwood Creek			×	×	×				●			●				◆	◆			
23.	Wasilla Lake				×	×				●			●				◆	◆			
24.	Memory Lake						▲			■		▲							●		
25.	Little Susitna River	×		×	×	×			×	●			●				●	●	◆		
26.	Reed Lake									▲				▲							
27.	Golden Lake									▲											
28.	Kalmbach Lake						▲			■											
29.	Beverly Lake									■											
30.	Bruce Lake									▲											

#	LOCATION	KING SALMON	RED SALMON	PINK SALMON	CHUM SALMON	SILVER SALMON	LANDLOCKED SALMON	KOKANEE	STEELHEAD TROUT	RAINBOW TROUT	LAKE TROUT	ARCTIC CHAR	DOLLY VARDEN	SHEEFISH	ARCTIC GRAYLING	WHITEFISH	NORTHERN PIKE	BURBOT	PACIFIC HALIBUT	LING COD	ROCKFISH
31.	Lalen Lake									▲											
32.	Seymour Lake									■											
33.	Visnaw Lake									■											
34.	Dawn Lake									▲											
35.	Little Meadow Creek	×	×	×	×	×				●			●				◆	◆			
36.	Morvro Lake									▲											
37.	Loon Lake									▲											
38.	Prator Lake											▲						●			
39.	Bear Paw Lake								▲	▲											
	Palmer-Wasilla Roads																				
40.	Walby Lake									▲											
41.	Cornelius Lake		×			×				●			●				◆	◆			
42.	Wolf Lake									■											
43.	Neklason Lake		×			×				●			●				◆	◆			
44.	Finger Lake								▲	▲		▲			▲			◆			
45.	Cottonwood Lake		×			×				●			●				◆	◆			
46.	Cottonwood Creek		×			×				●			●				◆	◆			
	Knik Goose Bay Road																				
47.	Lucille Lake									■											
48.	Cottonwood Creek	×	×	×	×	×				●			●				◆				
49.	Cottonwood Creek	×	●	◆	◆	●				◆			●				◆				
50.	Brocker Lake																				
51.	Knik Lake								▲	▲					▲		◆				
52.	Fish Creek (Lower)	×	■	●	◆	■				●			●				◆				
53.	Carpenter Lake								▲	▲		▲									
54.	Farmer Lake									▲											
55.	Butterfly Lake									▲											
56.	Barley Lake								▲	▲											
57.	Twin Island Lake									▲											
58.	Lorraine Lake									▲					▲						
59.	Little Susitna River	●	■	●	●	■				●			◆		●		◆	●	◆	●	
	Big Lake Road																				
60.	Little Meadow Creek	×	×	×	×	×				●			●				◆	◆			
61.	Long Lake					×				●			◆				◆	◆			
62.	Twin Lake					×				●			◆				◆	◆			
63.	Rocky Lake									▲											
64.	Meadow Creek	×	×	×	×	×				●			●				◆	◆			
65.	Stepan Lake					×				●			◆				◆	◆			
66.	Lazy Lake					×				●			◆				◆	◆			
67.	Lynda Lake					×				●			◆				◆	◆			
68.	Little Beaver Lake									▲											
69.	Big Beaver Lake					×				■			◆				◆	◆			
70.	West Beaver Lake					×				■			◆				◆	◆			
71.	Horseshoe Lake					×				●			◆				◆	◆			
72.	Big Lake	×	×	×	×	×				●		◆	●				◆	◆	●		
73.	Fish Creek (Upper)	×	×	×	×	×				●			●				●	◆			
74.	Homestead Lake									▲											
75.	Marion Lake									▲		▲									
76.	Mirror (Mud) Lake	×				×				●			●				◆	◆	◆		
77.	Flat Lake	×				×				●			●				◆	◆	◆		
78.	Sara Lake												●								
79.	Diamond Lake								▲	▲											
80.	Crooked Lake									■											

Parks Highway

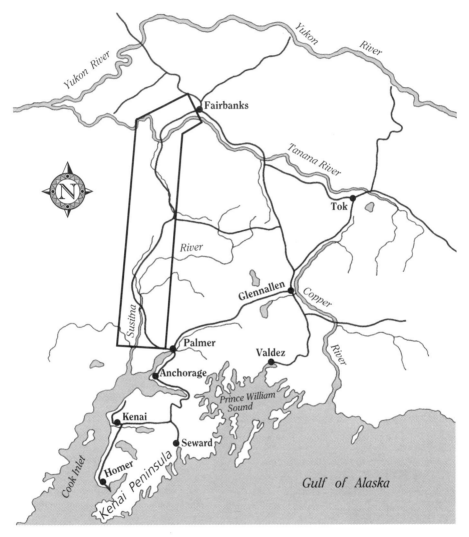

Area Covered: Houston to Fairbanks; 301.9 miles

Note: For fishing information along the Parks Highway between Glenn Highway Junction and Houston (Palmer-Wasilla Area), see chapter 12, page 147

Regulatory Units: (A) Susitna Valley Drainages; (B) Chulitna River Drainage; (C) Nenana River Drainage

Number of Locations: 95

FISHING THE PARKS HIGHWAY

The Parks Highway crosses and parallels three major glacial river systems; the Susitna, Chulitna, and Nenana. From the road there are a multitude of lakes and streams to fish, many with easy access and excellent fishing. All five species of salmon as well as trout, char, and grayling are present with some of the best fishing occurring in tributaries of the Susitna River during the summer and fall months. King and silver salmon typically attract the most attention in area streams, but angling in the various lakes is tops in fall and early winter, with land-locked salmon, trout, char, and grayling being the species most frequently encountered. Whitefish, pike, and burbot are also quite common in certain locations. Angler success is good to excellent in both lakes and streams.

Boaters can launch from areas along the Susitna, Talkeetna, and Nenana rivers to reach more remote, lesser fished locations.

Angling pressure is generally moderate to light during the open water season, but can be very heavy in some of the major salmon fisheries (such as Willow, Sheep, and Montana creeks) between Willow and Talkeetna.

Recommended Hot Spots: Little Susitna River; Willow, Little Willow, Caswell, Sheep, Goose, Montana, Sunshine, Byers, and Peters creeks; Nancy Lake Parkway lakes; Lynne, Honeybee, Crystal, Little Lonely, Florence, Vera, Benka, Christansen, and Sansing lakes.

Content Pages

QUICK REFERENCE

- ■ - Good to Highly developed/conditions, intense pressure
- ● - Fair to Moderately developed/conditions, moderate pressure
- ◆ - Poor to marginally developed/conditions, limited pressure
- ✕ - Prohibited

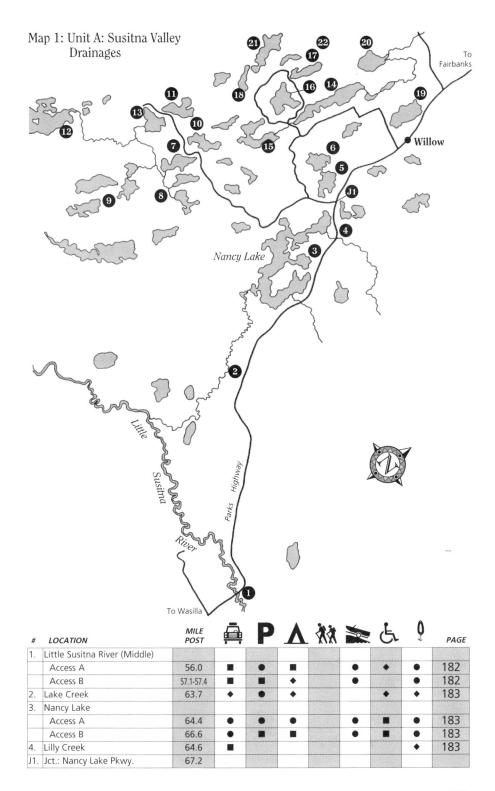

Map 1: Unit A: Susitna Valley Drainages

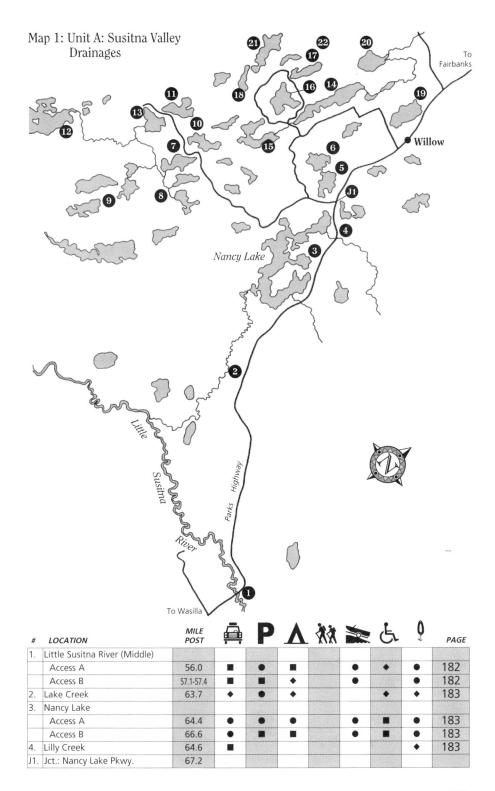

#	LOCATION	MILE POST	🚐	**P**	⛺	🚶	🛶	♿	🎣	PAGE
1.	Little Susitna River (Middle)									
	Access A	56.0	■	●	■		●	◆	●	182
	Access B	57.1-57.4	■	■	◆		●		●	182
2.	Lake Creek	63.7	◆	●	◆			◆	◆	183
3.	Nancy Lake									
	Access A	64.4	●	●	●		●	■	●	183
	Access B	66.6	●	■	■		●	■	●	183
4.	Lilly Creek	64.6	■						◆	183
J1.	Jct.: Nancy Lake Pkwy.	67.2								

#	LOCATION	MILE POST	🚗	P	⛺	🥾	🛶	♿	⚓	PAGE
	Nancy Lake Parkway									
J1.	Jct.: Parks Hwy.	0								
5.	Lynne Lake	0.7	●	◆	×				◆	183
6.	Honeybee Lake	0.7	●	◆	×				◆	183
7.	Tanaina (Denaina) Lake	4.6	●	■	×				◆	184
8.	Nancy Lake Rec. Area, East Lp.	4.6	●	■	×	●			◆	184
9.	Nancy Lake Rec. Area, West Lp.	4.6	●	■	×	●			◆	184
10.	Rhein Lake	5.1	●	●		●			◆	184
11.	North Rolly Lake	6.0	●	●		●			◆	184
12.	Red Shirt Lake	6.5	●	■		■			●	184
13.	South Rolly Lake	6.5	●	■	■		●	◆	●	185
	Parks Highway (cont.)	67.2								
14.	Long Lake	69.2	●	◆					◆	185
15.	Rainbow Lake	69.2	●	■	×				◆	185
16.	Crystal Lake	69.2	●	●	×		◆	◆	◆	185
17.	Florence Lake	69.2	●	◆					◆	185
18.	Little Lonely Lake	69.2	●	●	×			◆	◆	185
19.	Willow Lake	69.7	●	●	◆				◆	185
20.	Shirley Lake	70.7	●	●	×				◆	186
21.	Vera Lake	70.7	●	◆					◆	186
22.	Boot Lake	70.7	●	●	×				◆	186
23.	Willow Creek (Mouth)	70.7	●	■	●	■		●	■	186
J2.	Jct.: Hatcher Pass Road	71.2								
	Hatcher Pass Road									
J2.	Jct.: Parks Hwy.	49.1								
24.	Willow Creek (Middle)	48.2	●	■	●			◆	●	187
25.	Deception Creek	48.1	■	■	●				●	187
26.	Willow Creek (Upper)									
	Access A	34.5	●	●					◆	187
	Access B	30.0	●	●					◆	187
	Parks Highway (cont.)	71.2								
27.	Willow Creek	71.4	■	■	●		●	■	■	188
28.	Little Willow Creek	74.7	■	●				●	●	188
29.	Kashwitna Lake	76.4	■	●				●	◆	189
30.	Grey's Creek	81.0	■	●				●	◆	189
31.	Kashwitna River (Mouth)	82.5	●	●			●		●	189
32.	Kashwitna River (Middle)	83.2	■	●					◆	189
33.	Caswell Creek (Mouth)	84.1	●	●	●				■	190
34.	Caswell Creek (Upper)	84.9	■	◆				◆	◆	190
35.	Sheep Creek Slough	85.8	●	■	●			■	■	190
36.	Sheep Creek (Middle)									
	Access A	88.1	●	●	◆				◆	191
	Access B	88.6	■	●	●			■	●	191
37.	Caswell #3 Lake	88.1	●						◆	192
38.	Goose Creek	92.7	■	●	◆				●	192
39.	Montana Creek (Lower)	96.5	■	■	■			●	■	192
J3.	Jct.: Talkeetna Spur Hwy.	98.7								
	Talkeetna Spur Highway									
J3.	Jct.: Parks Hwy.	0								
40.	Benka Lake	3.1	●	●	◆		●	◆	◆	193
41.	Montana Creek (Upper)	3.1	●	■	◆			●	◆	193
42.	West Sunshine Lake	3.6	●	●	◆				◆	193
43.	Question Lake									
	Access A	6.7	■	◆					◆	193

Map 2: Unit A: Susitna Valley Drainages

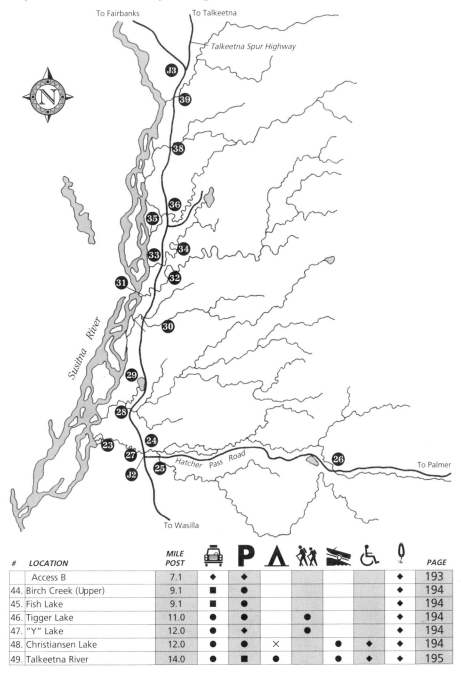

#	LOCATION	MILE POST	🚐	**P**	**Λ**	🥾	🛶	♿	🎣	PAGE
	Access B	7.1	◆	◆					◆	193
44.	Birch Creek (Upper)	9.1	■	●					◆	194
45.	Fish Lake	9.1	■	●					◆	194
46.	Tigger Lake	11.0	●	●		●			◆	194
47.	"Y" Lake	12.0	●	◆		●			◆	194
48.	Christiansen Lake	12.0	●	●	✕		●	◆	◆	194
49.	Talkeetna River	14.0	●	■	●		●	◆	◆	195

Map 3: Unit A: Susitna Valley Drainages

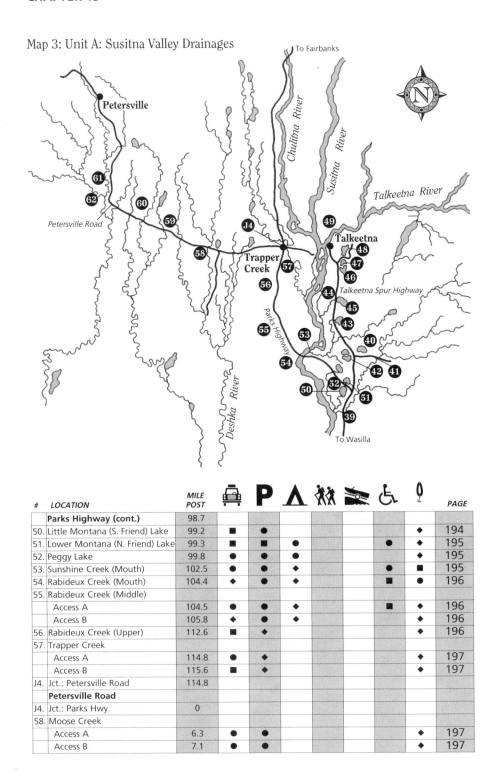

#	LOCATION	MILE POST	🚐	P	⋀	🥾	🛶	♿	⚓	PAGE
	Parks Highway (cont.)	98.7								
50.	Little Montana (S. Friend) Lake	99.2	■	●					◆	194
51.	Lower Montana (N. Friend) Lake	99.3	■	■	●		●		◆	195
52.	Peggy Lake	99.8	●	●	●				◆	195
53.	Sunshine Creek (Mouth)	102.5	●	●	◆		●		■	195
54.	Rabideux Creek (Mouth)	104.4	◆	●	◆		■		●	196
55.	Rabideux Creek (Middle)									
	Access A	104.5	●	●	◆		■		◆	196
	Access B	105.8	◆	●	◆				◆	196
56.	Rabideux Creek (Upper)	112.6	■	◆					◆	196
57.	Trapper Creek									
	Access A	114.8	●	◆					◆	197
	Access B	115.6	■	◆					◆	197
J4.	Jct.: Petersville Road	114.8								
	Petersville Road									
J4.	Jct.: Parks Hwy.	0								
58.	Moose Creek									
	Access A	6.3	●	●					◆	197
	Access B	7.1	●	●					◆	197

Map 4: Unit B: Chulitna River Drainages

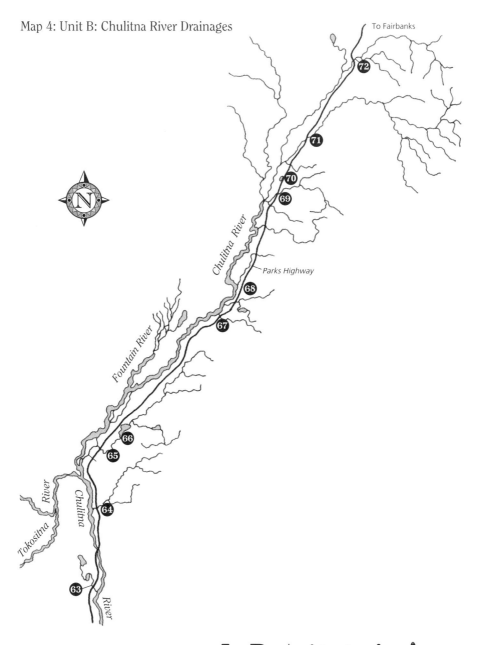

To Fairbanks

#	LOCATION	MILE POST	🚙	P	Λ	🚶	🛶	♿	🎣	PAGE
59.	Gate Lake	10.75	●	●					◆	197
60.	Kroto Creek	14.0	●	●					◆	197
61.	Peters Creek									
	Access A	18.7	●	■	◆				●	197-8
	Access B	19.5	●	●					◆	197-8
62.	Martin Creek	18.7	●	■		●			◆	198

Map 5: Unit C: Nenana River
    Drainages

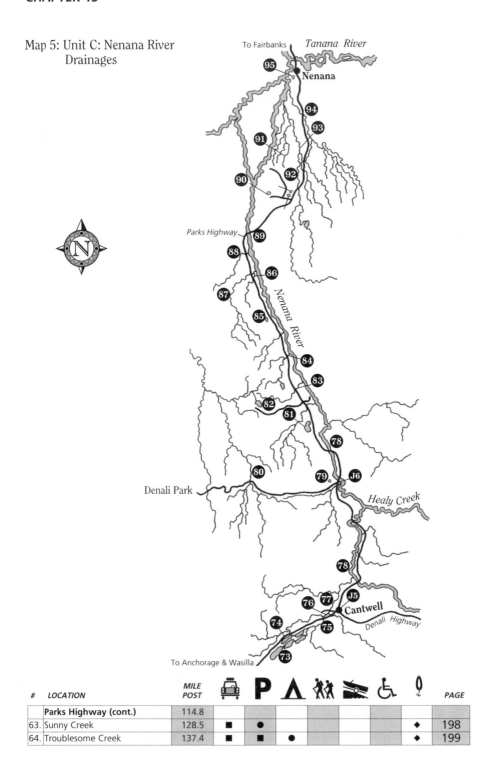

#	LOCATION	MILE POST		**P**	⋀	🥾	🛶	♿	☿	PAGE
	Parks Highway (cont.)	114.8								
63.	Sunny Creek	128.5	■	●					◆	198
64.	Troublesome Creek	137.4	■	■	●				◆	199

#	LOCATION	MILE POST	🚗	P	▲	👣	⛵	♿	🎣	PAGE
65.	Byers Creek (Middle)	143.9	■	◆				●	◆	199
66.	Byers Lake	147.2	●	●	■			●	◆	199
67.	Horseshoe Creek	159.8	■	◆					◆	199
68.	Creek, No Name	161.3	■	●	◆				◆	200
69.	Honolulu Creek	178.1	■	●				●	◆	200
70.	Mile 180 Lake	180.0	■	■	●			◆	◆	200
71.	East Fork Chulitna River	184.8	■	●	●				◆	200
72.	Middle Fork Chulitna River	194.5	■	●					◆	200
73.	Summit Lake	200.1	●	●					◆	200
74.	Mirror Lake	202.0	●	◆		●			◆	201
75.	Pass Creek	208.0	■	●					◆	201
76.	Mile 209 Pond	208.9	■	●	◆			◆	◆	201
77.	Jack River									
	Access A	209.6	■	●					◆	201
	Access B	209.9	●	●					◆	201
J5.	Jct.: Denali Highway	209.9								
78.	Nenana River (Middle)	215.3-242.9	■	●	●				◆	202
J6.	Jct.: McKinley Park Rd	237.3								
79.	Horseshoe Lake	237.3	●	●		●			◆	202
80.	Savage River	237.3	●	●	●				◆	202
81.	Otto Lake	247.0	●	●					◆	202
82.	Eightmile Lake	251.2	●	●		●			◆	202
83.	Panguingue Creek	252.4	■	●					◆	202
84.	Slate Creek	257.8	■	◆					◆	202
85.	Parks 261 Pond	261.1	■	●					◆	202
86.	June Creek	269.0	■	●	●				◆	203
87.	Bear Creek	269.3	■	●					◆	203
88.	Birch Creek	272.5	■	◆					◆	203
89.	Nenana River (Lower)	275.8	■	●					◆	203
90.	Sansing Lake	283.5	●	●				◆	◆	203
91.	Wood Creek	283.5	●	●		●			◆	203
92.	Julius Creek	285.6	■	◆					◆	204
93.	Julius Creek	295.2	●	●					●	204
94.	Fish Creek	296.6	■	◆					◆	204
95.	Nenana City Pond	303.4	●	●				◆	◆	204

Unit A: Susitna Valley Drainages

Includes all roadside waters flowing into and surrounding Susitna River and upper Cook Inlet.

UNIT REGULATIONS:

* There are no general area-wide regulations for waters in this unit.

Note: Consult sport fishing regulations closely regarding legal species, seasons, areas, gear, and bag limits for all flowing waters within this unit.

(continues on next page)

UNIT TIMING:

FISH ▽	JAN	FEB	MAR	APR	MAY	JUN	JUL	AUG	SEP	OCT	NOV	DEC
KS					▨	■	■	▨				
RS							▨	▨				
PS						▨	■	■	▨			
CS						▨	■	■	▨			
SS							■	■	▨			
RT	▨	▨	▨	▨	■	■	■	■	■	■	■	■
LT	▨	▨	▨	▨	■	▨	▨	▨	■	■	▨	▨
AC	■	▨	▨	▨	▨	▨	▨	▨	▨	■	■	■
DV	■	▨	▨	▨	▨	▨	▨	▨	▨	■	■	■
AG	▨	▨	▨	▨	▨	▨	▨	▨	▨	■	■	▨
WF	▨	▨	▨	▨	▨	▨	▨	▨	■	■	▨	▨
NP	▨	▨	▨	▨	■	■	▨	▨	■	■	▨	▨
BB	▨	▨	■	▨	■	■	■	■	■	■	▨	▨

1. Little Susitna River (Middle)

Access A: MP 56.0 – Miller's Reach; SW on Millers Reach Rd. 2.0 miles to sharp bend in road where it joins Rapalla St., proceed 0.4 mile to a "Y," continue straight 0.1 mile to small parking area. Trail leads 100 yards to river.

Access B: MP 57.1 – Parks Highway Bridge; highway crosses river. Large parking area with trails leading short distance to and along river.

Access C: MP 57.4; S on gravel access road at commercial area, proceed to the left on road leading 0.3 mile to parking area. Short trail leads to river.

Fishing: Clearwater river with abundant opportunities in summer for several salmon species along with trout, char, and grayling. Schools of whitefish in fall. River is easily affected by adverse weather conditions. Closed to salmon fishing upstream of highway.

King Salmon / fair-good / 15-45 lbs. (75 lbs.) / spinners, attractors, flies.
Red Salmon / poor / 3-6 lbs. (12 lbs.) / flies, bait.
Pink Salmon / fair-good / 2-5 lbs. (7 lbs.) / spoons, spinners.
Chum Salmon / good / 6-12 lbs. (18 lbs.) / spoons, spinners, bait.
Silver Salmon / fair-good / 5-12 lbs. (18 lbs.) / spinners, attractors, bait.
Rainbow Trout / fair / 7-15 in. (3 lbs.) / spinners, flies, bait.
Dolly Varden / fair / 8-15 in. (4 lbs.) / spinners, flies, bait.
Arctic Grayling / fair / 7-12 in. (17 in.) / spinners, flies.
Whitefish / poor-fair / 10-15 in. (3 lbs.) / attractors, flies, bait.

FISH ▽	JAN	FEB	MAR	APR	MAY	JUN	JUL	AUG	SEP	OCT	NOV	DEC
KS					▨	■	▨					
RS						▨	■	▨				
PS							▨	■	▨			
CS						▨	■	■	▨			
SS						▨	■	▨	▨			
RT				▨	▨	■	■	■	■	▨		
DV				▨	▨	■	■	■	■	▨		
AG			▨	▨	▨	▨	▨	▨	■	▨		
WF					▨	▨	▨	▨	■	▨		

2. Lake Creek

Access: MP 63.7; W on N. Lynx Lake Rd. 0.9 mile to stream crossing.
Note: Nancy Lake outlet is located a few hundred yards upstream of crossing.

Fishing: Slow-flowing stream with opportunities for trout, char. Salmon present.
Rainbow Trout / fair / late June – late August / 7-12 in. / spinners, flies, bait.
Dolly Varden / fair / mid-July – late August / 7-12 in. / spinners, flies, bait.

3. Nancy Lake

Access A: MP 64.4 - Nancy Lake Marina; W on Mike Ardaw Rd. 0.2 mile to lake.
Access B: MP 66.6 - Nancy Lake State Recreation Area; S on Buckingham Palace Rd. 0.2 mile, right on access road 0.1 mile to lake.
Fishing: Popular recreation lake supporting runs of salmon as well as resident trout and char. Target schools of salmon at lake outlet or near inlets. Use boat or canoe.
Red Salmon / poor-fair / early August / 4-8 lbs. / spinners, flies.
Silver Salmon / fair / early September / 5-12 lbs. / spinners, flies, bait.
Rainbow Trout / fair-good / May, September – December / 7-18 in. / spoons, flies, bait.
Dolly Varden / fair / May, September – December / 7-15 in. / spoons, flies, bait.

4. Lilly Creek

Access: MP 64.6; highway crosses stream.
Fishing: Very small stream with limited opportunities for trout and char.
Rainbow Trout / fair / mid-September – mid-October / 7-12 in. / spinners, flies, bait.
Dolly Varden / fair / mid-September – mid-October / 7-12 in. / spinners, flies, bait.

PARKS HIGHWAY log continues on page 185.

Nancy Lake Parkway

Road begins at MP 67.2 Parks Highway (MP 0) and ends at South Rolly Lake (MP 6.6).

5. Lynne Lake

Access: MP 0.7; W on Long Lake Rd. 0.9 mile, right on gravel road 0.6 mile and park. Lake is adjacent to right side of road.
Fishing: Lake is stocked with trout and char. Use canoe/float tube.
Rainbow Trout / good / May, September – December / 7-18 in. / spinners, flies, bait.
Arctic Char / good / May, September – January / 7-18 in. / spoons, plugs, bait.

6. Honeybee Lake

Access: MP 0.7; W on Long Lake Rd. 0.9 mile, right on gravel road 0.7 mile and park. Lake is adjacent to left side of road.
Fishing: Lake is stocked with trout. Use canoe/float tube.
Rainbow Trout / good / May, September – December / 7-18 in. / spinners, flies, bait.

7. Tanaina (Denaina) Lake

Access: MP 4.6; access road on left leads short distance to parking area and lake.
Note: Tanaina Lake represents the starting point of the Tanaina Lake Canoe Trail with access to several area lakes.

Fishing: Lake is stocked with trout. Some pike available. Use canoe/float tube.
Rainbow Trout / good / May, September – December / 8-18 in. / spinners, flies, bait.
Northern Pike / fair / May, September – December / 2-4 lbs. / spoons, plugs, bait.

8. Nancy Lake Recreation Area Lakes, East Loop

Note: Locations are on the Nancy Lake Canoe Trail system. They are accessible in winter on foot and mechanical means of transportation following the same general pattern of lake crossing and portaging as in summer.

Access: MP 4.6 - Tanaina Lake; SE across lake to marked starting point with access to Milo (Mile 0.5), Ardaw (Mile 1.0), Frazier (2.0), Little Frazier (2.8), Lynx (3.3), and Charr (4.0) lakes.
Fishing: Lakes contain moderate to large populations of pike. Use canoe/float tube.
Northern Pike / good / May, September – December / 2-6 lbs. / plugs, flies, bait.

9. Nancy Lake Recreation Area Lakes, West Loop

Note: Locations are on the Nancy Lake Canoe Trail system. They are accessible in winter on foot and mechanical means of transportation following the same general pattern of lake crossing and portaging as in summer.

Access: MP 4.6 - Tanaina Lake; S across lake to marked starting point with access to Little No Luck (Mile 1.4), Big No Luck (Mile 2.2), Chicken (Mile 2.7), James (Mile 3.6), and Owl (Mile 4.0) lakes.
Fishing: Lakes contain moderate to large populations of pike. Use canoe/float tube.
Northern Pike / good / May, September – December / 2-6 lbs. / plugs, flies, bait.

10. Rhein Lake

Access: MP 5.1; pullout. Trail leads 0.1 mile N to lake.
Fishing: Lake supports a moderate population of pike. Use canoe/float tube.
Rainbow Trout / poor / May, September – October / 7-18 in. / spinners, flies, bait.
Northern Pike / fair / May, September – December / 2-4 lbs. / spoons, plugs, bait.

11. North Rolly Lake

Access: MP 6.0; trail leads 200 yards N to lake.
Fishing: Lake supports a moderate population of pike. Use canoe/float tube.
Rainbow Trout / poor / May, September – December / 8-16 in. / spoons, flies, bait.
Northern Pike / poor-fair / May, September – December / 2-4 lbs. / spoons, plugs, bait.

12. Red Shirt Lake

Access: MP 6.5; near end of road. Park at South Rolly Lake, trail leads 3.0 miles to lake.
Fishing: Lake supports a healthy population of pike. Popular hike-in fishery; pike may occasionally reach 10 pounds. A few char and burbot present. Use canoe/float tube
Lake Trout / poor / May – June, September – January / 2-6 lbs. / spoons, plugs, bait.

Northern Pike / good / May, September – December / 2-6 lbs. / spoons, plugs, bait.
Burbot / poor-fair / March – April, September – December / 2-4 lbs. / bait.

13. South Rolly Lake

Access: MP 6.6; end of road. Lake is located on left.
Fishing: Lake is stocked with trout. Use canoe/float tube or cast from shore.
Rainbow Trout / good / May, September – December / 8-16 in. / spinners, flies, bait.
Northern Pike / fair / May, September – December / 2-4 lbs. / spoons, plugs, bait.

PARKS HIGHWAY log continues.

14. Long Lake

Access: MP 69.2; W on Long Lake Rd. 3.2 miles to where it becomes Crystal Lake Rd., 0.2 mile to stream crossing. Follow stream 50 yards N to lake.
Fishing: Lake is stocked with trout. Pike present. Use canoe/float tube.
Rainbow Trout / fair / May, September – December / 8-18 in. / spinners, flies, bait.
Northern Pike / poor-fair / May, September – December / 2-6 lbs. / plugs, flies, bait.

15. Rainbow Lake

Access: MP 69.2; W on Long Lake Rd. 3.2 miles to where it becomes Crystal Lake Rd., 0.1 mile to unnamed road on left, 0.1 mile to large boulder blocking vehicle access. Trail leads 0.2 mile to lake.
Fishing: Lake supports a small population of pike, a few trout. Use canoe/float tube.
Rainbow Trout / poor / May, September – October / 7-15 in. / spinners, flies, bait.
Northern Pike / fair / May, September – December / 2-6 lbs. / plugs, flies, bait.

16. Crystal Lake

Access: MP 69.2; W on Long Lake Rd. 3.2 miles to where it becomes Crystal Lake Rd., 0.3 mile to Crystal Lake Alt. on right, 1.1 mile to Crystal View Dr., 0.9 mile to Crystal Lake access.
Fishing: Lake is stocked with trout. Pike present. Use canoe/float tube.
Rainbow trout / fair-good / May, September – December / 7-15 in. / spinners, flies, bait.
Northern Pike / poor-fair / May, September – December / 2-6 lbs. / plugs, flies, bait

17. Florence Lake

Access: MP 69.2; W on Long Lake Rd. 3.2 miles to where it becomes Crystal Lake Rd., 0.3 mile to Crystal Lake Alt. on right, 1.4 mile to lake access on right. Short trail leads to lake.
Fishing: Lake is stocked with trout and grayling. Use canoe/float tube.
Rainbow Trout / good / May, September – December / 7-18 in. / spinners, flies, bait.
Arctic Grayling / good / May – September / 7-12 in. / spinners, flies.

18. Little Lonely Lake

Access: MP 69.2; W on Long Lake Rd. 3.2 miles to where it becomes Crystal Lake Rd., 1.7 mile to gravel road on left, 0.2 mile to dirt road on left, 0.1 mile and park. Trail leads to lake.
Fishing: Lake is stocked with trout. Use canoe/float tube.
Rainbow Trout / good / May, September – December / 7-18 in. / spinners, flies, bait.

19. Willow Lake

Access: MP 69.8; W at Willow Community Center Cir. 0.1 mile to parking area and lake.
Fishing: Lake is stocked with trout. Use canoe/float tube.
Rainbow Trout / good / May, September – December / 7-15 in. / spinners, flies, bait.

20. Shirley Lake

Access: MP 70.7; W on Willow Creek Pkwy. 2.0 miles to Crystal Lake Rd. 1.8 mile to Shirley Lake Rd., left 0.4 mile to Michigan St., right 0.2 mile to South Lake Cr., left 0.2 mile to Canoe Way, left 0.1 mile to end of road. Short trail leads to lake.
Fishing: Lake supports a small population of pike, a few trout. Use canoe/float tube.
Rainbow Trout / poor / May, September – December / 7-18 in. / spinners, flies, bait.
Northern Pike / fair / May, September – December / 2-6 lbs. / plugs, flies, bait.

21. Vera Lake

Access: MP 70.7; W on Willow Creek Pkwy. 2.0 miles to Crystal Lake Rd., left 2.4 miles to Deshka Landing Rd., right 1.0 mile to 4-wheel drive section line trail on left leading 0.1 mile to lake.
Fishing: Lake is stocked with trout. Use canoe/float tube.
Rainbow Trout / good / May, September – December / 7-18 in. / spinners, flies, bait.

22. Boot Lake

Access: MP 70.7; W on Willow Creek Pkwy. 2.0 miles, left on Crystal Lake Rd. 2.6 miles, right on Verjo Rd. 0.2 mile to access site on left.
Fishing: Lake is stocked with trout. Use canoe/float tube.
Rainbow Trout / good / May, September – December / 7-15 in. / spinners, flies, bait.

23. Willow Creek / Susitna River Confluence

Access: MP 70.7; W on Willow Creek Pkwy. 3.9 miles to campground and parking area. Trails lead 0.25 mile to confluence area.
Fishing: One of the very best angling spots in the entire Susitna Valley, famed for its superb salmon action. Large schools of salmon gather at the stream mouth throughout the summer months. Trout and grayling present in spring and fall, few burbot all season.
King Salmon / good-excellent / 15-45 lbs. (80 lbs.) / spoons, spinners, attractors.
Pink Salmon / good-excellent / 2-5 lbs. (7 lbs.) / spoons, spinners.
Chum Salmon / good-excellent / 6-12 lbs. (18 lbs.) / spoons, spinners, bait.
Silver Salmon / good-excellent / 5-10 lbs. (15 lbs.) / spoons, spinners, bait.
Rainbow Trout / fair-good / 8-18 in. (12 lbs.) / spinners, attractors, flies.
Dolly Varden / fair / 8-15 in. (5 lbs.) / spoons, flies, bait.
Arctic Grayling / fair-good / 7-14 in. (18 in.) / spinners, flies.
Whitefish / poor / 10-15 in. (17 in.) / flies, bait.
Burbot / fair / 2-4 lbs. (10 lbs.) / bait.

FISH ▽	JAN	FEB	MAR	APR	MAY	JUN	JUL	AUG	SEP	OCT	NOV	DEC
KS												
PS												
CS												
SS												
RT												
DV												
AG												
WF												
BB												

PARKS HIGHWAY log continues on page 188.

Hatcher Pass (Fishhook-Willow) Road

Road begins at MP 71.2 Parks Highway (MP 49.9) and ends at MP 49.5 Glenn Highway (MP 0) near Palmer.

Note: Hatcher Pass Road mileposts begin at Glenn Highway in Palmer and end at Parks Highway. Miles given in parenthesis in access information below is distance measured from Parks Highway.

24. Willow Creek (Middle)

Access: MP 48.2 (Mile 1.7); left at Deception Creek Wayside short distance to parking area. Trail leads 50 yards to river.

Fishing: Stream supports large runs of salmon and healthy populations of trout and grayling. Many pinks and chums but few bright specimens. Fresh silvers present early in season. Great fly-fishing for rainbows. Major salmon spawning area. Wade or float.

Pink Salmon / poor / 2-5 lbs. (7 lbs.) / spoons, spinners, flies.
Chum Salmon / poor / 6-12 lbs. (18 lbs.) / spoons, spinners, flies.
Silver Salmon / fair-good / 5-10 lbs. (15 lbs.) / spoons, spinners.
Rainbow Trout / good / 8-18 in. (12 lbs.) / spinners, attractors, flies.
Dolly Varden / poor-fair / 8-15 in. (5 lbs.) / spoons, flies.
Arctic Grayling / fair-good / 7-14 in. (18 in.) / spinners, flies.
Whitefish / poor / 10-15 in. (17 in.) / flies.

FISH ▽	JAN	FEB	MAR	APR	MAY	JUN	JUL	AUG	SEP	OCT	NOV	DEC
PS												
CS												
SS												
RT												
DV												
AG												
WF												

25. Deception Creek

Access: MP 48.1 (Mile 1.8); road crosses stream.
Fishing: Tannic stream with decent action for trout, grayling. Salmon spawning area.
Rainbow Trout / fair / mid-August – mid-September / 8-18 in. / spinners, flies, bait.
Arctic Grayling / fair / mid-August – mid-September / 7-14 in. / spinners, flies.

26. Willow Creek (Upper)

Access: MP 34.5-30.0 (Mile 14.6-19.1); road parallels stream, crossing it at MP 34.2 (Mile 15.0).
Fishing: Fast-flowing stream supporting a moderate population of small char.
Dolly Varden / fair / mid-July – mid-August / 7-10 in. / flies, bait.

PARKS HIGHWAY log continues.

27. Willow Creek (Middle)

Access: MP 71.4; highway crosses river.
Fishing: Popular stretch of water offering very productive action for salmon, trout, and grayling. Most salmon show a hint of color this far upstream, silvers being the brightest species. Great fly-fishing for rainbows. Major salmon spawning area. Wade or float.
King Salmon / fair-good / 15-45 lbs. (80 lbs.) / spinners, attractors, flies.
Pink Salmon / fair-good / 2-5 lbs. (7 lbs.) / spoons, spinners, flies.
Chum Salmon / fair-good / 6-12 lbs. (18 lbs.) / spoons, spinners, flies.
Silver Salmon / fair-good / 5-10 lbs. (15 lbs.) / spinners, flies, bait.
Rainbow Trout / good / 8-18 in. (12 lbs.) / spinners, attractors, flies.
Dolly Varden / poor-fair / 8-15 in. (5 lbs.) / spoons, flies, bait.
Arctic Grayling / fair-good / 7-14 in. (18 in.) / spinners, flies.
Whitefish / poor-fair / 10-15 in. (17 in.) / attractors, flies, bait

FISH ▽	JAN	FEB	MAR	APR	MAY	JUN	JUL	AUG	SEP	OCT	NOV	DEC
KS												
PS												
CS												
SS												
RT												
DV												
AG												
WF												

28. Little Willow Creek (Middle)

Access: MP 74.7; highway crosses stream.
Fishing: Tannic stream supporting decent runs of salmon along with productive action for trout, grayling, and whitefish. Hike away from road for best fishing. Most salmon show a hint of color this far upstream, silvers being the brightest species. Salmon spawning area.
King Salmon / fair / 15-45 lbs. (80 lbs.) / spinners, attractors, flies.

Pink Salmon / fair / 2-5 lbs. (7 lbs.) / spoons, spinners, flies.
Chum Salmon / fair / 6-12 lbs. (18 lbs.) / spoons, spinners, flies.
Silver Salmon / fair-good / 5-10 lbs. (15 lbs.) / spinners, flies, bait.
Rainbow Trout / fair-good / 8-18 in. (12 lbs.) / spinners, flies, bait.
Dolly Varden / poor / 8-15 in. (5 lbs.) / spoons, flies, bait.
Arctic Grayling / fair-good / 7-14 in. (18 in.) / spinners, flies.
Whitefish / fair / 10-15 in. (17 in.) / attractors, flies, bait.

FISH ▽	JAN	FEB	MAR	APR	MAY	JUN	JUL	AUG	SEP	OCT	NOV	DEC
KS						▓	▓					
PS							▓	▓				
CS							▓	▓				
SS								▓	▓			
RT					▓	▓			▓	▓		
DV						▓		▓	▓			
AG				▓	▓			▓	▓	▓		
WF						▓	▓	▓	▓			

29. Kashwitna Lake

Access: MP 76.4; lake is adjacent to W side of road.
Fishing: Lake is stocked with trout. Use canoe/float tube.
Rainbow Trout / good / May, September – December / 7-15 in. / spinners, flies, bait.

30. Grey's Creek

Access: MP 81.0; highway crosses stream.
Fishing: Small, tannic stream offering decent opportunities for grayling.
Arctic Grayling / poor-fair / mid-June– late August / 7-14 in. / spinners, flies.

31. Kashwitna River / Susitna River Confluence

Access: MP 82.5; W on Susitna Landing Rd. 0.6 mile to confluence area.
Fishing: Glacial stream supporting runs of salmon and opportunities for trout and grayling.
River is easily affected by adverse weather conditions. Best action in fall.
King Salmon / poor-fair / late June – early July / 15-45 lbs. / spinners, attractors.
Pink Salmon / poor-fair / mid-late July / 2-5 lbs. / spoons, spinners, attractors.
Chum Salmon / poor-fair / late July – early August / 7-12 lbs. / spinners, attractors.
Silver Salmon / fair / early, mid-August / 5-12 lbs. / spinners, attractors, bait.
Rainbow Trout / fair / mid-September – mid-October / 8-18 in. / spinners, flies, bait.
Dolly Varden / fair / late July – mid-October / 8-18 in. / attractors, flies, bait.
Arctic Grayling / fair-good / mid-September – mid-October / 7-14 in. / spinners, flies.
Whitefish / poor-fair / mid-July – mid-October / 10-15 in. / attractors, bait.
Burbot / fair / mid-May – mid-October / 2-4 lbs. / bait.

32. Kashwitna River (Middle)

Access: MP 83.2; highway crosses river.
Fishing: Glacial stream supporting runs of salmon and opportunities for trout and grayling.
River is easily affected by adverse weather conditions. Best action in fall.

King Salmon / poor / late June – early July / 15-45 lbs. / spoons, spinners, attractors.
Pink Salmon / poor / late July – early August / 2-5 lbs. / attractors.
Chum Salmon / poor / late July – early August / 6-12 lbs. / attractors, bait.
Silver Salmon / poor / mid-, late August / 5-10 lbs. / attractors, bait.
Rainbow Trout / fair / mid-September – early October / 8-18 in. / spinners, flies.
Dolly Varden / fair / mid-July – mid-September / 8-15 in. / attractors, flies, bait.
Arctic Grayling / fair-good / mid-September – early October / 7-14 in. / spinners, flies.
Whitefish / fair / mid-July – mid-October / 10-15 in. / attractors, flies, bait.

33. Caswell Creek / Susitna River Confluence

Access: MP 84.1; W on dirt road 0.4 mile to camping area. Short hike down bluff to confluence area.

Fishing: Slow-flowing stream with very productive salmon action. Fish gather in big schools at mouth. Some trout and grayling in spring and fall. Burbot present all season.
King Salmon / good / 15-45 lbs. (80 lbs.) / spoons, spinners, attractors.
Red Salmon / poor / 4-7 lbs. (12 lbs.) / spinners, flies.
Pink Salmon / good / 2-5 lbs. (7 lbs.) / spoons, spinners.
Chum Salmon / good / 6-12 lbs. (18 lbs.) / spoons, spinners, bait.
Silver Salmon / good-excellent / 5-10 lbs. (15 lbs.) / spoons, spinners, bait.
Rainbow Trout / fair-good / 8-18 in. (12 lbs.) / spinners, attractors, bait.
Arctic Grayling / fair-good / 7-14 in. (18 in.) / spinners, flies.
Burbot / fair / 2-4 lbs. (10 lbs.) / bait

FISH ▽	JAN	FEB	MAR	APR	MAY	JUN	JUL	AUG	SEP	OCT	NOV	DEC
KS						■						
RS							■					
PS							■					
CS								■				
SS								■				
RT									■			
AG					■							
BB				■								

34. Caswell Creek (Upper)

Access: MP 84.9; highway crosses stream.

Fishing: Clearwater stream with limited opportunities for trout and grayling.
Rainbow Trout / poor / mid-June – mid-September / 7-12 in. / spinners, flies, bait.
Arctic Grayling / poor-fair / mid-May – mid-September / 7-12 in. / spinners, flies.

35. Sheep Creek Slough

Access: MP 85.8; W on Resolute Dr. 1.4 mile to large parking area. Trail leads 150 yards to slough.

Fishing: One of the premier salmon streams in the area, offering superb action for kings, pinks, chums, and silvers. Fish school at mouth. Trout and grayling available early and late in season. Burbot present. Sheep is slow-flowing and often off-colored.

King Salmon / good-excellent / 15-45 lbs. (80 lbs.) / spoons, spinners, attractors.
Pink Salmon / good-excellent / 2-5 lbs. (7 lbs.) / spoons, spinners.
Chum Salmon / good-excellent / 6-12 lbs. (18 lbs.) / spoons, spinners, bait.
Silver Salmon / good-excellent / 5-10 lbs. (15 lbs.) / spoons, spinners, bait.
Rainbow Trout / fair-good / 8-18 in. (12 lbs.) / spinners, flies, bait.
Dolly Varden / poor / 8-15 in. (5 lbs.) / spoons, flies, bait.
Arctic Grayling / fair-good / 7-14 in. (18 in.) / spinners, flies.
Whitefish / poor-fair / 10-15 in. (17 in.) / flies, bait.
Burbot / fair / 2-4 lbs. (10 lbs.) / bait.

FISH ▽	JAN	FEB	MAR	APR	MAY	JUN	JUL	AUG	SEP	OCT	NOV	DEC
KS												
PS												
CS												
SS												
RT												
DV												
AG												
WF												
BB												

36. Sheep Creek (Middle)

Access A: From MP 88.1; E on Hidden Hill Access Rd. 0.7 mile to a "Y," left fork 0.2 mile, left on access road short distance to stream.

Access B: MP 88.6; highway crosses stream.

Fishing: Stream supports healthy runs of salmon along with very productive action for trout and grayling. Most salmon show a hint of color this far upstream, silvers being the brightest species. Salmon spawning area. Stream affected by adverse weather conditions.
King Salmon / fair-good / 15-45 lbs. (80 lbs.) / spoons, attractors, flies.
Pink Salmon / fair-good / 2-5 lbs. (7 lbs.) / spoons, spinners, flies.
Chum Salmon / good / 6-12 lbs. (18 lbs.) / spoons, spinners, flies, bait.
Silver Salmon / fair-good / 5-10 lbs. (15 lbs.) / spinners, flies, bait.
Rainbow Trout / good / 8-18 in. (12 lbs.) / spinners, attractors, flies.
Dolly Varden / poor / 8-15 in. (5 lbs.) / spoons, flies, bait.
Arctic Grayling / fair-good / 7-14 in. (18 in.) / spinners, attractors, flies.
Whitefish / fair / 10-15 in. (17 in.) / attractors, flies, bait.

FISH ▽	JAN	FEB	MAR	APR	MAY	JUN	JUL	AUG	SEP	OCT	NOV	DEC
KS												
PS												
CS												
SS												
RT												
DV												
AG												
WF												

37. Caswell #3 Lake

Access: MP 88.1; E on Hidden Hill Access Rd. 0.6 mile, left on East Caswell Lakes Road 3.0 miles to access site on right. Trail leads due S short distance to lake.
Fishing: Lake is stocked with trout. Use canoe/float tube.
Rainbow Trout / good / May, September – October / 7-15 in. / spinners, flies, bait.

38. Goose Creek

Access: MP 92.7; highway crosses stream. To reach Susitna River confluence, hike along N bank of creek about 1.0 mile W of highway.
Fishing: Tannic stream supporting runs of salmon along with decent action for trout and grayling. Hike downstream towards mouth for best salmon fishing, upstream for resident species. Salmon spawning area.
King Salmon / fair-good / 15-45 lbs. (80 lbs.) / spinners, attractors, flies.
Pink Salmon / fair-good / 2-5 lbs. (7 lbs.) / spoons, spinners, flies.
Chum Salmon / fair-good / 6-12 lbs. (18 lbs.) / spoons, spinners, flies.
Silver Salmon / fair-good / 5-10 lbs. (15 lbs.) / spinners, flies, bait.
Rainbow Trout / fair-good / 8-18 in. (12 lbs.) / spinners, flies, bait.
Dolly Varden / poor / 8-15 in. (5 lbs.) / spoons, flies, bait.
Arctic Grayling / fair-good / 7-14 in. (18 in.) / spinners, flies.

FISH ▽	JAN	FEB	MAR	APR	MAY	JUN	JUL	AUG	SEP	OCT	NOV	DEC
KS						▓	▓					
PS							▓	▓				
CS							▓	▓				
SS								▓	▓			
RT				▓	▓	▓	▓	▓	▓	▓		
DV						▓	▓	▓	▓	▓		
AG				▓	▓	▓	▓	▓	▓	▓		

39. Montana Creek (Lower)

Access: MP 96.5; highway crosses stream. Trails lead 0.5 mile along stream from bridge parking areas to Susitna River confluence.
Fishing: One of the top salmon producers in the area, known for its clear waters and very productive king and silver action. Pinks and chums also abundant. Salmon fishing is best at the mouth; for trout and grayling head upstream. Scout holes. Salmon spawning area.
King Salmon / good-excellent / 15-45 lbs. (80 lbs.) / spinners, attractors, flies.
Pink Salmon / good-excellent / 2-5 lbs. (7 lbs.) / spoons, spinners, flies.
Chum Salmon / good-excellent / 6-12 lbs. (18 lbs.) / spoons, flies, bait.
Silver Salmon / good-excellent / 5-10 lbs. (15 lbs.) / spinners, flies, bait.
Rainbow Trout / fair-good / 8-18 in. (12 lbs.) / spinners, attractors, flies.
Dolly Varden / poor / 8-15 in. (5 lbs.) / attractors, flies, bait.
Arctic Grayling / fair-good / 7-14 in. (18 in.) / spinners, flies.
Whitefish / poor-fair / 10-15 in. (17 in.) / flies, bait.
Burbot / fair / 2-4 lbs. (10 lbs.) / bait.

FISH ▽	JAN	FEB	MAR	APR	MAY	JUN	JUL	AUG	SEP	OCT	NOV	DEC
KS												
PS												
CS												
SS												
RT												
DV												
AG												
WF												
BB												

PARKS HIGHWAY log continues on page 194.

Talkeetna Spur Highway

Road begins at MP 98.7 Parks Highway (MP 0) and ends in town of Talkeetna (MP 14.5).

40. Benka Lake

Access: MP 3.1; E on Yoder Rd. 0.5 mile to Lakeview St. on left, 0.4 mile to lake.
Fishing: Lake is stocked with trout and char. Use canoe/float tube or cast from shore.
Rainbow Trout / good / May, September – December / 7-15 in. / spinners, flies, bait.
Arctic Char / good / May, September – January / 7-18 in. / spoons, plugs, bait.

41. Montana Creek (Upper)

Access: MP 3.1; E on Yoder Rd. 2.7 miles to stream crossing.
Fishing: Clearwater stream supporting a healthy population of trout and grayling.
Rainbow Trout / fair-good / early June – mid-September / 8-18 in. / spinners, flies.
Arctic Grayling / fair-good / early June – mid-September / 7-14 in. / spinners, flies.

42. West Sunshine Lake

Access: MP 3.5; W on Sheldon Ave. 0.2 mile to a "T," left on West Sunshine Lake Dr. 0.1 mile, right on East Sunshine Lake Dr. 0.3 mile to cul-de-sac. Locate short trail to lake on right.
Fishing: Lake is stocked with trout. Use canoe/float tube.
Rainbow Trout / good / May, September – December / 7-18 in. / spinners, flies, bait.

43. Question Lake

Access A: MP 6.7; lake outlet is E of road.
Access B: MP 7.1; E on dirt road 0.2 mile to lake.
Fishing: Lake contains a small population of native trout. Use canoe/float tube.
Rainbow Trout / poor-fair / May, September – October / 7-16 in. / spinners, flies, bait.

44. Birch Creek (Upper)
Access: MP 9.1; road crosses stream.
Fishing: Stream supports a small population of trout in summer and fall.
Rainbow Trout / poor-fair / mid-June – mid-September / 7-14 in. / spinners, flies.

45. Fish Lake
Access: MP 9.1; lake outlet is adjacent to E side of road.
Fishing: Lake contains a small population of native trout. Use canoe/float tube.
Rainbow Trout / poor-fair / May, September – October / 7-14 in. / spinners, flies, bait

46. Tigger Lake
Access: MP 11.0; park E of road at gravel pit access blocked by locked chain, cross pit staying to the left side. Trail on far side of pit leads 0.3 mile to lake.
Fishing: Lake is stocked with trout. Use canoe/float tube.
Rainbow Trout / good / May, September – December / 7-18 in. / spinners, flies, bait.

47. "Y" Lake
Access: MP 12.0; E on Comsat Rd. 0.8 mile, park on left side of road. Locate public access trail on right side leading to lake.
Fishing: Lake is stocked with trout. Use canoe/float tube.
Rainbow Trout / good / May, September – December / 7-18 in. / spinners, flies, bait.

48. Christiansen Lake
Access: MP 12.0; E on Comsat Rd. 0.8 mile, left on Christiansen Lake Rd. 0.7 mile, right on Botner Rd. 0.1 mile to a "Y," right on access road short distance to lake.
Fishing: Lake is stocked with salmon and trout. Use canoe/float tube.
Landlocked Salmon / excellent / June – March / 7-12 in. / spinners, jigs, flies, bait.
Rainbow Trout / good / May, September – December / 7-18 in. / spinners, flies, bait.

49. Talkeetna River (Lower)
Access: MP 14.0; end of road at a "T," left on Main St. 0.2 mile to river banks.
Fishing: Glacial drainage with limited opportunities for trout, char, and grayling. Best in spring and fall. A few king salmon may be caught early in the season.
King Salmon / poor-fair / mid-June / 15-35 lbs. / spoons, spinners, attractors.
Rainbow Trout / fair / late September – mid-October / 8-18 in. / attractors, flies.
Dolly Varden / fair / late September – mid-October / 8-16 in. / attractors, flies.
Arctic Grayling / fair / late September – early October / 7-14 in. / spinners, flies.
Whitefish / poor / late September – mid-October / 10-15 in. / attractors.
Burbot / poor-fair / mid-April – late October / 2-4 lbs. / bait.

PARKS HIGHWAY log continues.

50. Little Montana (South Friend) Lake
Access: MP 99.2; lake is adjacent to SW side of highway.

Fishing: Lake is stocked with trout. Use canoe/float tube.
Rainbow Trout / good / May, September – December / 7-16 in. / spinners, flies, bait.

51. Lower Montana (North Friend) Lake

Access: MP 99.3; lake is adjacent to NE side of highway.
Fishing: Lake is stocked with trout. Use canoe/float tube.
Rainbow Trout / good / May, September – December / 8-16 in. / spinners, flies, bait.

52. Peggy Lake

Access: MP 99.8; W on gravel road 1.0 mile to YMCA camp and lake.
Fishing: Lake is stocked with trout. Use canoe/float tube.
Rainbow Trout / good / May, September – December / 7-15 in. / spinners, flies, bait.

53. Sunshine Creek / Susitna River Confluence

Access: MP 102.5; NE on dirt road 0.6 mile to parking area. Trail leads 100 yards to confluence area.
Fishing: Small, slow-flowing stream providing very productive salmon action at its mouth, especially for silvers. Find big schools of fish in early morning. Some trout and grayling available late in the season, burbot all summer.
King Salmon / good / 15-45 lbs. (70 lbs.) / spoons, spinners, attractors.
Red Salmon / Early Run: poor / 4-7 lbs. (12 lbs.) / spoons, spinners.
     Late Run: fair / 3-7 lbs. (12 lbs.) / spoons, spinners, flies.
Pink Salmon / good-excellent / 2-5 lbs. (7 lbs.) / spoons, spinners.
Chum Salmon / good / 6-12 lbs. (18 lbs.) / spoons, spinners, bait.
Silver Salmon / good-excellent / 5-10 lbs. (15 lbs.) / spinners, bait.
Rainbow Trout / fair / 8-18 in. (7 lbs.) / spinners, flies, bait.
Dolly Varden / poor / 8-15 in. (3 lbs.) / spoons, flies, bait.
Arctic Grayling / fair / 7-14 in. (18 in.) / spinners, flies.
Whitefish / poor / 10-15 in. (17 in.) / bait.
Burbot / fair / 2-4 lbs. (10 lbs.) / bait.

FISH ▽	JAN	FEB	MAR	APR	MAY	JUN	JUL	AUG	SEP	OCT	NOV	DEC
KS						▓	▓					
RS						▓	▓					
PS							▓					
CS							▓					
SS								▓				
RT					▓	▓	▓	▓	▓			
DV					▓	▓	▓	▓	▓			
AG					▓	▓	▓	▓	▓			
WF					▓	▓	▓	▓	▓			
BB	▓	▓	▓		▓	▓	▓	▓	▓		▓	▓

54. Rabideux Creek / Susitna River Confluence

Access: MP 104.4; W on gravel road 0.7 mile to confluence area.
Note: Access road is often in poor condition and may at times be impassable due to flooding from the Susitna River.

Fishing: Slow flowing, tannic stream supporting healthy runs of king and silver salmon along with lesser numbers of reds, pinks, and chums. Search for schools of fish. Some trout, grayling, and burbot available in season.
King Salmon / fair-good / 15-40 lbs. (65 lbs.) / spoons, spinners, attractors.
Red Salmon / poor-fair / 4-7 lbs. (12 lbs.) / spoons, spinners.
Pink Salmon / fair-good / 2-4 lbs. (6 lbs.) / spoons, spinners.
Chum Salmon / fair / 6-12 lbs. (16 lbs.) / spoons, attractors, bait.
Silver Salmon / good / 5-10 lbs. (15 lbs.) / spinners, attractors, bait.
Rainbow Trout / fair / 7-16 in. (6 lbs.) / spinners, attractors, bait.
Arctic Grayling / fair / 7-12 in. (18 in.) / spinners, flies.
Whitefish / poor / 10-15 in. (17 in.) / bait.
Burbot / fair / 2-4 lbs. (10 lbs.) / bait.

FISH ▽	JAN	FEB	MAR	APR	MAY	JUN	JUL	AUG	SEP	OCT	NOV	DEC
KS					▓	▓						
RS							▓	▓				
PS							▓	▓				
CS							▓	▓				
SS								▓	▓			
RT	▓	▓	▓	▓	▓	▓	▓	▓	▓	▓	▓	▓
AG	▓	▓	▓	▓	▓	▓	▓	▓	▓	▓	▓	▓
WF	▓	▓	▓	▓	▓	▓	▓	▓	▓	▓	▓	▓
BB	▓	▓	▓	▓	▓	▓	▓	▓	▓	▓	▓	▓

55. Rabideux Creek (Middle)

Access A: MP 104.5; W on dirt road 0.3 mile to stream.
Access B: MP 105.8; highway crosses stream.
Fishing: Slow flowing, tannic stream offers opportunities for salmon, particularly silvers. Most fish are semi-bright. Trout and grayling available in spring and fall.
Pink Salmon / poor / late July – early August / 2-4 lbs. / spoons, spinners.
Silver Salmon / fair-good / mid-, late August / 5-10 lbs. / spinners, bait.
Rainbow Trout / fair / late August – late September / 7-15 in. / spinners, flies.
Arctic Grayling / fair / May, late August – late September / 7-12 in. / spinners, flies.

56. Rabideux Creek (Upper)

Access: MP 112.6; highway crosses stream.
Fishing: Slow flowing, tannic stream with limited opportunities for trout and grayling.
Rainbow Trout / fair / mid-June – mid-August / 7-15 in. / spinners, flies.
Arctic Grayling / fair / late May – mid-August / 7-12 in. / spinners, flies.

57. Trapper Creek (Middle)

Access A: MP 114.8; E on gravel road 0.5 mile to stream crossing.
Access B: MP 115.6; highway crosses stream.
Fishing: Small stream supporting limited opportunities for salmon, trout, grayling.
Silver Salmon / fair / mid-, late August / 5-10 lbs. / spinners, flies, bait.
Rainbow Trout / poor-fair / late August – mid-September / 7-15 in. / spinners, flies.
Arctic Grayling / fair / June, late August – mid-September / 7-12 in. / spinners, flies.

PARKS HIGHWAY log continues on page 198.

Petersville Road

Road begins at MP 114.9 Parks Highway (Mile 0) and ends in settlement of Petersville (Mile 40).

58. Moose Creek

Access A: MP 6.3; S on Oil Well Rd. 6.0 miles to end of road and stream.
Access B: MP 7.1; road crosses stream.
Fishing: Tannic stream with salmon, trout, grayling opportunities.
Silver Salmon / fair / mid-, late August / 5-10 lbs. / spoons, spinners, flies.
Rainbow Trout / fair / June, late August – mid-September / 7-16 in. / spinners, flies.
Arctic Grayling / fair / June, mid-August – mid-September / 7-14 in. / spinners, flies.

59. Gate Lake

Access: Mile 10.75; pullout on N side of road. Trail leads short distance to lake.
Fishing: Lake is stocked with trout. Use canoe/float tube.
Rainbow trout / fair-good / June, August – September / 7-15 in. / spinners, flies, bait.

60. Kroto Creek

Access: MP 14.0; road crosses stream.
Fishing: Slow flowing stream with limited opportunities for salmon, trout, and grayling.
Silver Salmon / poor / mid-, late August / 5-10 lbs. / spoons, spinners, flies.
Rainbow Trout / poor / June, late August – mid-September / 7-16 in. / spinners, flies.
Arctic Grayling / fair / June, mid-August – mid-September / 7-12 in. / spinners, flies.

61. Peters Creek

Access A: MP 18.7; take left fork 0.2 mile to parking area next to bridge crossing river.
Access B: MP 18.7; take right fork 0.8 mile to pull-off on left. Hike down hill due W to river.
Fishing: Clearwater stream with productive action for silver salmon, trout, and grayling. Most salmon are semi-bright this far upstream in the drainage. Salmon spawning area.
Silver Salmon / good / 5-10 lbs. (15 lbs.) / spinners, flies, bait.
Rainbow Trout / fair-good / 8-18 in. (7 lbs.) / spinners, flies, bait.

Arctic Grayling / good / 7-14 in. (18 in.) / spinners, flies.

Whitefish / poor / 10-1 in. (3 lbs.) / flies, bait.

FISH ▽	JAN	FEB	MAR	APR	MAY	JUN	JUL	AUG	SEP	OCT	NOV	DEC
SS												
RT												
AG												
WF												

62. Martin Creek

Access: MP 18.7; left fork in road 0.2 mile to parking area by Peters Creek. Walk over bridge spanning river and hike upstream 0.25 mile to mouth of Martin Creek.

Fishing:Small clearwater stream offering silver salmon, trout, and grayling action.

Silver Salmon / fair / mid-, late August / 5-10 lbs. / spoons, spinners, flies.

Rainbow Trout / fair / June, mid-August – mid-September / 7-16 in. / spinners, flies.

Arctic Grayling / fair-good / mid-June – mid-September / 7-12 in. / spinners, flies.

Unit B: Chulitna River Drainage

Includes all roadside waters flowing into and surrounding Chulitna River.

UNIT REGULATIONS:

* King salmon fishing prohibited: All waters (except East Fork Chulitna River), year-round.

* Only unbaited, artificial lures: All flowing waters, September 1 – July 13.

UNIT TIMING:

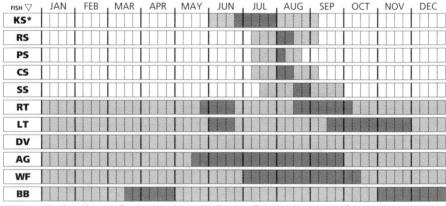

FISH ▽	JAN	FEB	MAR	APR	MAY	JUN	JUL	AUG	SEP	OCT	NOV	DEC
KS*												
RS												
PS												
CS												
SS												
RT												
LT												
DV												
AG												
WF												
BB												

***Note**: Timing shown for king salmon indicates fish in all stages of maturity.*

63. Sunny Creek

Access: MP 128.5; highway crosses stream.

Fishing: Small stream with limited opportunities fro salmon, trout, char, and grayling.

Red Salmon / poor-fair / early August / 4-7 lbs. / spinners, flies.

Pink Salmon / poor / early August / 2-4 lbs. / spoons, spinners, flies.

Silver Salmon / fair / mid-, late August / 5-10 lbs. / spinners, flies, bait.
Rainbow Trout / poor-fair / mid-August – mid-September / 7-15 in. / spinners, flies.
Dolly Varden / poor-fair / mid-August – mid-September / 7-15 in. / flies, bait.
Arctic Grayling / fair / June, mid-August – mid-September / 7-12 in. / spinners, flies.

64. Troublesome Creek (Lower)

Access: MP 137.4; highway crosses stream. Trail leads along S bank 0.6 mile to Chulitna River confluence.

Fishing: Clearwater stream with opportunities for salmon, trout, and grayling. Salmon fishing best at mouth, other species above highway.
Red Salmon / poor-fair / early August / 4-7 lbs. / spoons, spinners, flies.
Pink Salmon / fair / early August / 2-4 lbs. / spoons, spinners, flies.
Chum Salmon / fair / early August / 6-12 lbs. / spoons, spinners, flies.
Silver Salmon / fair-good / mid-, late August / 5-10 lbs. / spoons, spinners, bait.
Rainbow Trout / fair / mid-August – late September / 7-18 in. / spinners, flies, bait.
Arctic Grayling / fair-good / mid-June – mid-September / 7-14 in. / spinners, flies.

65. Byers Creek (Middle)

Access: MP 143.9; highway crosses stream.
Fishing: Limited opportunities for red and silver salmon. Productive trout stream.
Red Salmon / fair / early, mid-August / 4-7 lbs. / spinners, flies.
Pink Salmon / poor / early August / 2-4 lbs. / spoons, spinners, flies.
Chum Salmon / poor / early August / 6-12 lbs. / spoons, spinners, flies.
Silver Salmon / fair / late August – early September / 5-10 lbs. / spinners, flies, bait.
Rainbow Trout / fair-good / mid-August – late September / 7-18 in. / spinners, flies.
Arctic Grayling / fair-good / mid-June – mid-September / 7-14 in. / spinners, flies.

66. Byers Lake

Access: MP 147.2; E on gravel road 0.3 mile to campground and lake.
Fishing: Some opportunities for char and grayling near lake outlet. Salmon present.
Rainbow Trout / poor / June, September / 7-18 in. / spoons, spinners, flies.
Lake Trout / poor-fair / June, September / 2-5 lbs. / spoons, bait.
Dolly Varden / poor-fair / August – September / 8-15 in. / spoons, flies, bait.
Arctic Grayling / fair / June, September / 7-14 in. / spinners, flies.
Whitefish / poor / September – October / 10-15 in. / flies, bait.
Burbot / poor / March – April, September – December / 2-4 lbs. / bait.

67. Horseshoe Creek

Access: MP 159.8; highway crosses stream.
Fishing: Limited opportunities for salmon; trout and grayling available in summer.
Red Salmon / poor / mid-August / 4-7 lbs. / spinners, flies.
Silver Salmon / poor-fair / late August / 5-10 lbs. / spinners, flies, bait.
Rainbow Trout / fair / mid-August – mid-September / 7-18 in. / spinners, flies, bait.
Arctic Grayling / fair-good / mid-June – mid-September / 7-12 in. / spinners, flies.

68. Creek, No Name

Access: MP 161.3; highway crosses stream.
Fishing: Tannic stream supporting a small population of grayling, a few salmon, trout.
Silver Salmon / poor / late August / 5-10 lbs. / spinners, flies, bait.
Rainbow Trout / poor / mid-August – mid-September / 7-16 in. / spinners, flies, bait.
Arctic Grayling / fair / mid-June – mid-September / 7-12 in. / spinners, flies.

69. Honolulu Creek

Access: MP 178.1; highway crosses stream.
Fishing: Clearwater stream with productive trout and grayling action. Salmon present.
Rainbow Trout / fair-good / mid-June – mid-September / 7-16 in. / spinners, flies.
Arctic Grayling / fair-good / late May – mid-September / 7-14 in. / spinners, flies.

70. Mile 180 Lake

Access: MP 180.0; two pullouts. Lake is adjacent to NW side of highway.
Fishing: Lake is stocked with trout. Use canoe/float tube or cast from shore.
Rainbow Trout / good / June, September – December / 7-14 in. / spinners, flies, bait.

71. East Fork Chulitna River

Access: MP 184.8; highway crosses river.
Fishing: Semi-glacial stream. Mainly a trout and grayling fishery in summer and early fall.
A few salmon may be caught; fish will be blushing.
King Salmon / poor-fair / early July / 15-40 lbs. / attractors, flies.
Silver Salmon / poor / early September / 5-10 lbs. / attractors, flies.
Rainbow Trout / fair / mid-June – mid-September / 8-18 in. / spinners, flies, bait.
Arctic Grayling / good / mid-June – mid-September / 7-14 in. / spinners, flies.
Whitefish / poor / mid-July – late September / 10-15 in. / flies, bait.

72. Middle Fork Chulitna River

Access: MP 194.5; highway crosses river.
Fishing: Semi-glacial stream. Mainly a trout and grayling fishery in summer and early fall.
A few salmon may be caught; fish will be blushing.
Silver Salmon / poor / early September / 5-10 lbs. / attractors, flies.
Rainbow Trout / fair-good / mid-June – mid-September / 8-18 in. / spinners, flies.
Arctic Grayling / fair-good / mid-June – mid-September / 7-14 in. / spinners, flies.

73. Summit Lake

Access: MP 200.1; E on gravel road short distance to parking area. Trail leads 50 yards E
to lake.
Fishing: Fairly large lake with opportunities for char, grayling, and burbot.
Lake Trout / good / June, September – October / 2-6 lbs. / spoons, plugs, bait.
Arctic Char / fair / June, September – October / 8-20 in. / spoons, jigs, bait.
Arctic Grayling / fair-good / June – September / 7-12 in. / spinners, flies.
Burbot / fair / March – April, September – December / 2-5 lbs. / bait.

74. Mirror Lake

Access: MP 202.0; hike 0.25 mile E through low brush to lake.
Fishing: Lake contains populations of char, grayling, and burbot. Use canoe/float tube.
Lake Trout / fair / June, September – October / 2-6 lbs. / spoons, plugs, bait.
Arctic Grayling / fair-good / June – September / 7-12 in. / spinners, flies.
Burbot / fair / March – April, September – December / 2-5 lbs. / bait.

Unit C: Nenana River Drainage

Includes all roadside waters flowing into and surrounding Nenana River.

UNIT REGULATIONS:

* Northern pike fishing prohibited: All lakes, April 21 – May 31.

UNIT TIMING:

FISH ▽	JAN	FEB	MAR	APR	MAY	JUN	JUL	AUG	SEP	OCT	NOV	DEC
KS*							▓	▓				
CS*							▓	▓	▓	▓		
SS*									▓	▓		
LS	▓	▓	▓	▓	▓	▓	▓	▓	▓	▓	▓	▓
RT					▓	▓			▓	▓		
DV						▓	▓	▓	▓			
AG					▓	▓	▓	▓	▓			
WF												
NP					▓	▓	▓	▓	▓	▓		
BB			▓	▓						▓	▓	▓

Note: Timing shown for salmon indicates fish in all stages of maturity.

75. Pass Creek

Access: MP 208.0; highway crosses stream.
Fishing: Small stream with limited opportunities for grayling.
Arctic Grayling / poor-fair / mid-June – mid-September / 7-12 in. / spinners, flies.

76. Mile 209 Pond

Access: MP 208.9; pullout. Lake is adjacent to W side of highway.
Fishing: Pond is stocked with trout. Use canoe/float tube or cast from shore.
Arctic Grayling / poor-fair / mid-June – mid-September / 7-12 in. / spinners, flies.

77. Jack River

Access A: MP 209.6; highway crosses river.
Access B: MP 209.9; W on paved road 0.7 mile to river crossing.
Fishing: Larger clearwater drainage with opportunities for grayling.
Arctic Grayling / fair / mid-June – early October / 7-14 in. / spinners, flies.

78. Nenana River (Middle)

Access: MP 215.3 – 242.9; highway parallels river, crossing it at MP 215.7, 231.3, 238.0, and 242.9.
Fishing: Glacial drainage with limited opportunities for char and grayling.
Dolly Varden / poor / late September – mid-October / 7-12 in. / spinners, flies, bait.
Arctic Grayling / poor-fair / late September – mid-October / 7-14 in. / spinners, flies.

79. Horseshoe Lake

Access: MP 237.3; NW on Denali Park Rd. 1.5 mile to parking area on right. Trail leads 1.0 mile to lake.
Fishing: Lake supports a small population of grayling. Use a canoe/float tube.
Arctic Grayling / poor-fair / June – September / 7-12 in. / spinners, flies.

80. Savage River

Access: MP 237.3; W on McKinley Rd. 12.5 miles to campground and Savage River Checkpoint. River is located W of checkpoint.
Fishing: Glacial drainage with early-season opportunities for grayling.
Arctic Grayling / fair-good / mid-, late May / 7-14 in. / spinners, flies.

81. Otto Lake

Access: MP 247.0; W on gravel road 1.0 mile to lake on left.
Fishing: Lake is stocked with landlocked salmon and trout. Use canoe/float tube.
Landlocked Salmon / good-excellent / July – March / 7-12 in. / spinners, jigs, bait.
Rainbow Trout / fair / June, September – October / 8-15 in. / spinners, flies, bait.

82. Eightmile Lake

Access: MP 251.2; SW on Stampede Rd. 8.2 miles to parking area. Hike 0.25 mile NE through open terrain to lake.
Fishing:Lake contains a moderate population of grayling. Use canoe/float tube.
Arctic Grayling / fair-good / June – September / 7-12 in. / spinners, flies.

83. Panguingue Creek

Access: MP 252.4; highway crosses stream.
Fishing: Small, tannic stream with limited opportunities for grayling in summer.
Arctic Grayling / poor-fair / early June – mid-September / 7-12 in. / spinners, flies.

84. Slate Creek

Access: MP 257.8; highway crosses stream.
Fishing: Small stream with limited opportunities for grayling in late spring.
Arctic Grayling / poor-fair / mid-, late May / 7-12 in. / spinners, flies.

85. Parks 261 Pond

Access: MP 261.1; pullout. Pond is adjacent to W side of highway.
Fishing: Pond is stocked with trout. Use canoe/float tube or cast from shore.
Rainbow Trout / good / June, August – October / 7-12 in. / spinners, flies, bait.

86. June Creek

Access: MP 269.0; highway crosses stream.
Fishing: Small stream with limited opportunities for grayling in late spring.
Arctic Grayling / poor-fair / mid-, late May / 7-12 in. / spinners, flies.

87. Bear Creek

Access: MP 269.3; highway crosses stream.
Fishing: Small stream with limited opportunities for grayling in late spring.
Arctic Grayling / poor-fair / mid-, late May / 7-12 in. / spinners, flies.

88. Birch Creek

Access: MP 272.5; highway crosses stream.
Fishing: Small stream with limited opportunities for grayling in late spring.
Arctic Grayling / poor-fair / mid-, late May / 7-12 in. / spinners, flies.

89. Nenana River (Lower)

Access: MP 275.8; highway crosses river.
Fishing: Glacial drainage with limited opportunities for grayling and burbot.
Arctic Grayling / fair / late September – early November / 7-14 in. / spinners, flies.
Burbot / fair / late September – early November / 2-5 lbs. / bait.

90. Sansing Lake

Access: MP 283.5; W on Clear Highway 1.9 mile to Clear Air Force Station gate, continue on right-of-way 1.3 mile, right on access road 0.4 mile to parking area and lake.
Fishing: Lake is stocked with trout. Use a canoe/float tube or cast from shore.
Arctic Char / fair-good / May, September – January / 7-15 in. / spoons, jigs, bait.

91. Wood Creek

Access: MP 283.5; W on Clear Hwy. 1.2 mile, right on Anderson Rd. 4.4 miles, right on Clear Creek Rd. 0.25 mile, left on dirt road 0.1 mile and park. ATV trail leads 1.5 to 2.5 miles to stream area. Several points of access off to the right from main trail.
Fishing: Slow-flowing stream supporting a decent run of salmon. Grayling present.
Silver Salmon / fair / late September – early October / 5-8 lbs. / spinners, flies.
Arctic Grayling / fair / mid-June – mid-September / 7-12 in. / spinners, flies.

92. Julius Creek (Upper)

Access: MP 285.6; highway crosses stream.
Fishing: Slow-flowing stream with limited opportunities for grayling.
Arctic Grayling / poor-fair / mid-May – mid-June / 7-12 in. / spinners, flies.

93. Julius Creek / Clear Creek Confluence

Access: MP 295.2; W on rough road 0.9 mile to parking area and railroad tracks. Trail begins on other side of tracks leading 1.5 mile to confluence area.

Fishing: Stream area supports small runs of salmon in addition to grayling action. The majority of salmon are in pre-spawn condition.

King Salmon / poor-fair / mid-July – late July / 8-25 lbs. / spoons, spinners, flies.
Chum Salmon / poor / mid-July – early August / 5-10 lbs. / spoons, spinners, flies.
Silver Salmon / fair-good / mid-September – early October / 5-8 lbs. / spinners, flies.
Arctic grayling / fair-good / mid-May – late September / 7-14 in. / spinners, flies.
Whitefish / poor / mid-September – early October / 8-16 in. / attractors, flies, bait.

94. Fish Creek

Access: MP 296.6; highway crosses stream.

Fishing: Small stream with limited opportunities for grayling in spring, early summer.

Arctic Grayling / poor-fair / mid-May – mid-June / 7-12 in. / spinners, flies.

95. Nenana City Pond

Access: MP 303.4; W on gravel road 0.7 mile to campground and pond.

Fishing: Pond is stocked with trout. Use canoe/float tube or cast from shore.

Rainbow Trout / fair-good / June, September – October / 8-16 in. / spinners, flies, bait.

Other Locations

Unit A: Susitna Valley Drainages:

Talkeetna Spur Road: Answer Creek - MP 5.3; SS,RT,DV, (RS,AG) Question Creek - MP 6.7; SS,RT,DV, (RS,AG) **Parks Highway (Cont.):** Susitna River - MP 104.3; RT,DV,AG,BB, (KS,RS,PS,CS,SS,WF,NP) Sawmill Creek - MP 109.8; AG, (KS,SS,RT,DV) **Petersville Road:** Kenny Creek - MP 15.6; AG, (SS)

Unit B: Chulitna River Drainage:

Chulitna River - MP 132.8; Rainbow Trout,AG,BB, (KS,RS,PS,CS,SS,DV,WF) Little Coal Creek - MP 163.2; Rainbow Trout,AG, (Dolly Varden) Mile 180 Lake - MP 180.0; Rainbow Trout

Unit C: Nenana River Drainage:

Slime Creek - MP 220.0; AG,(DV) Carlo Creek - MP 223.9; AG, (DV) Riley Creek - MP 237.2; AG Tanana River - MP 305.1; AG,BB, (KS,CS,SS,DV,SF,WF,NP) Little Goldstream Creek - MP 314.8; AG, (NP)

LOCATION & SPECIES APPENDIX

● - Wild/Native fish, fishable numbers.
◆ - Present in small numbers and/or only occasionally caught.
▲ - Stocked/Hatchery fish, fishable numbers.
■ - Mix of Wild and Hatchery fish, fishable numbers.
✕ - Indicated species present but currently protected by law (PROHIBITED).

(Chart shown on next page)

#	LOCATION	KING SALMON	RED SALMON	PINK SALMON	CHUM SALMON	SILVER SALMON	LANDLOCKED SALMON	KOKANEE	STEELHEAD TROUT	RAINBOW TROUT	LAKE TROUT	ARCTIC CHAR	DOLLY VARDEN	ARCTIC GRAYLING	SHEEFISH	WHITEFISH	NORTHERN PIKE	BURBOT	PACIFIC HALIBUT	LING COD	ROCKFISH
1.	Little Susitna River (Middle)	●	■	●	●	■				●			●			●	●	◆			
2.	Lake Creek	×	×	×	×	×				●			●				◆	◆			
3.	Nancy Lake	×	■	◆	◆	■				●		◆		●		◆	◆			×	
4.	Lilly Creek	×	◆	◆	◆	◆				●			●			◆					
	Nancy Lake Parkway																				
5.	Lynne Lake									▲		▲									
6.	Honeybee Lake									▲											
7.	Tanaina (Denaina) Lake							◆		■								●			
8.	Nancy Lake Rec. Area, East Lp.		◆					◆		◆			◆				◆	●			
9.	Nancy Lake Rec. Area, West Lp.		◆					◆		◆			◆				◆	●			
10.	Rhein Lake									●								●			
11.	North Rolly Lake									●								●			
12.	Red Shirt Lake		◆					◆		◆	●		◆				◆	●	●		
13.	South Rolly Lake							◆		■								●			
	Parks Highway (cont.)																				
14.	Long Lake									■								●			
15.	Rainbow Lake									●								●			
16.	Crystal Lake									▲								●			
17.	Florence Lake									▲						▲					
18.	Little Lonely Lake									▲											
19.	Willow Lake									▲											
20.	Shirley Lake									●								●			
21.	Vera Lake									▲											
22.	Boot Lake									▲											
23.	Willow Creek (Mouth)	■	◆	●	●	●				●			●			●	●	◆	●		
	Hatcher Pass Road																				
24.	Willow Creek (Middle)	×	◆	●	●	●				●			●			●	◆				
25.	Deception Creek	×	×	×	×	×				●			◆			●	◆				
26.	Willow Creek (Upper)									●											
	Parks Highway (cont.)																				
27.	Willow Creek (Middle)	■	◆	●	●	●				●			●			●	●	◆	◆		
28.	Little Willow Creek	●	◆	●	●	●				●			◆			●	◆		◆		
29.	Kashwitna Lake							◆		■								◆			
30.	Grey's Creek									◆			◆			●					
31.	Kashwitna River (Mouth)	●	◆	●	●	●				●			●			●	●	◆			
32.	Kashwitna River	×	◆	◆	◆	●				●			●			●	●				
33.	Caswell Creek (Mouth)	●	●	●	●	●				●			◆			●	●	◆	◆		
34.	Caswell Creek (Upper)		◆			◆				●			◆			●		◆			
35.	Sheep Creek Slough	●	◆	●	●	●				●			●			●	●	◆	●		
36.	Sheep Creek (Middle)	●	◆	●	●	●				●			●			●	●		◆		
37.	Caswell #3 Lake									▲											
38.	Goose Creek	●	◆	●	●	●				●			●			●	◆		◆		
39.	Montana Creek (Lower)	●	◆	●	●	●				●			●			●	●	◆	●		
	Talkeetna Spur Highway																				
40.	Benka Lake									▲		▲									
41.	Montana Creek (Upper)	×	×	×	×	×				●			◆			●	◆				
42.	West Sunshine Lake									▲											
43.	Question Lake		◆					◆		●			◆			◆					
44.	Birch Creek (Upper)	×	×	×	×	×				●			◆			◆	◆	◆			
45.	Fish Lake		×	×	×	×				●			◆			◆	◆	◆			
46.	Tigger Lake									▲											

#	LOCATION	KING SALMON	RED SALMON	PINK SALMON	CHUM SALMON	SILVER SALMON	LANDLOCKED SALMON	KOKANEE	STEELHEAD TROUT	RAINBOW TROUT	LAKE TROUT	ARCTIC CHAR	DOLLY VARDEN	ARCTIC GRAYLING	SHEEFISH	WHITEFISH	NORTHERN PIKE	BURBOT	PACIFIC HALIBUT	LING COD	ROCKFISH
	Parks Highway (cont.)																				
47.	"Y" Lake									▲							◆				
48.	Christiansen Lake						▲			▲											
49.	Talkeetna River	◆	◆	◆	◆	◆				●				●		●	●		●		
	Parks Highway (cont.)																				
50.	Little Montana Lake						◆			■			◆								
51.	Lower Montana Lake						◆			■			◆								
52.	Peggy Lake									▲											
53.	Sunshine Creek (Mouth)	●	●	●	●	●				●			◆			●	●	◆	●		
54.	Rabideux Creek (Mouth)	●	●	●	●	●				●			◆			●	●	◆	●		
55.	Rabideux Creek (Middle)	×	◆	●	◆	●				●			◆			●	◆	●			
56.	Rabideux Creek (Upper)	×	◆			◆				●			◆			●	◆	●			
57.	Trapper Creek	×	◆	◆	◆	●				●			◆			●		◆			
	Petersville Road																				
58.	Moose Creek	×	◆	◆		●				●			◆			●	◆	●			
59.	Gate Lake									▲											
60.	Kroto Creek	×	◆	◆	◆	●				●			◆			●	◆	●			
61.	Peters Creek	×	◆	◆	◆	●				●			◆			●	●				
62.	Martin Creek	×		◆	◆	●				●			◆			●					
63.	Sunny Creek	×	●	●	◆	●				●						●	◆				
64.	Troublesome Creek	×	●	●	●	●				●			◆			●			◆		
65.	Byers Creek (Middle)	×	●	●	●	●				●			◆			●					
66.	Byers Lake	×	×	×	×	×				●	●		◆			●	●				
67.	Horseshoe Creek	×	●	●	●	●				●			◆			●	◆				
68.	Creek, No Name	×		◆	●	●				●			◆			●	◆				
69.	Honolulu Creek	×			◆	●				●			◆			●	●				
70.	Mile 180 Lake									▲			◆								
71.	East Fork Chulitna River	●			◆	●				●			◆			●	●				
72.	Middle Fork Chulitna River	×			◆	●				●			◆			●	◆				
73.	Summit Lake										●	▲				●	◆		●		
74.	Mirror Lake										●					●	◆				≈
75.	Pass Creek												◆								
76.	Mile 209 Pond																				
77.	Jack River												◆			●	◆				
78.	Nenana River (Middle)													●		●	◆		◆		
79.	Horseshoe Lake															●					
80.	Savage River															●					
81.	Otto Lake						▲			▲											
82.	Eightmile Lake															●	◆				
83.	Panguingue Creek					◆							◆			●					
84.	Slate Creek															●					
85.	Parks 261 Pond									▲											
86.	June Creek												◆			●					
87.	Bear Creek												◆			●					
88.	Birch Creek															●					
89.	Nenana River (Lower)	◆			◆	◆							◆	◆		●	◆	◆	●		
90.	Sansing Lake											▲									
91.	Wood Creek					●										●					
92.	Julius Creek															●	◆		◆		
93.	Julius Creek (Mouth)	●			●	●										●	◆		◆		
94.	Fish Creek															●	◆				
95.	Nenana City Pond									▲						◆					

Richardson Highway

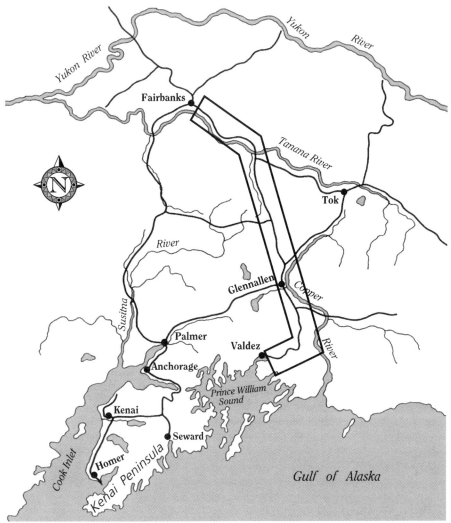

Area Covered: Valdez to Eielson AFB; 332 miles

Note: *For fishing information along the Richardson Highway between Eielson AFB and Fairbanks, see chapter 9, page 107.*

Regulatory Units: (A) Port Valdez Drainages; (B) Copper Valley Drainages; (C) Gulkana River Drainage; (D) Delta River Drainage; (E) Tanana Valley Drainages
Number of Locations: 87

FISHING THE RICHARDSON HIGHWAY

The Richardson Highway spans a very large portion of the state and provides rich and varied sport fishing opportunities along most its length. Major fisheries include the Valdez area marine waters for salmon (primarily pink and silver) and bottomfish. Farther north up the Copper River system, the Klutina and Gulkana rivers are good for salmon, char, and grayling. Although red salmon are the most abundant of the salmon species, it is the king that receives the most effort on the Copper and its tributaries. A multitude of lakes and ponds have been stocked with land-locked salmon, trout, char, and grayling, most notably in the Glennallen and Delta Junction area. North of Delta Junction in the Tanana River drainage, fishing is productive for king salmon, grayling, and burbot, with additional opportunities for pike. Angler success is good in both fresh and salt water.

Boaters are successful putting in at the larger rivers and lakes to access lesser fished areas, as well as increasing chances for bottomfish in northern Prince William Sound.

Angling pressure ranges from light to heavy, the bulk of it concentrated in areas of Port Valdez, at the highway crossings over Klutina and Gulkana rivers, and the mouth of Salcha River.

Recommended Hot Spots: Robe, Little Tonsina, Klutina, Gulkana, Delta Clearwater, and Salcha rivers; Sourdough and Shaw creeks; Port Valdez; Allison Point; Squirrel Creek Pit; Paxson, Summit, Fielding, Coal Mine Road, Meadows Road, Quartz, Birch, and Harding lakes.

Content

QUICK REFERENCE

■ - Good to Highly developed/conditions, intense pressure
● - Fair to Moderately developed/conditions, moderate pressure
◆ - Poor to marginally developed/conditions, limited pressure
× - Prohibited

Map 1: Unit A: Port Valdez
        Drainages

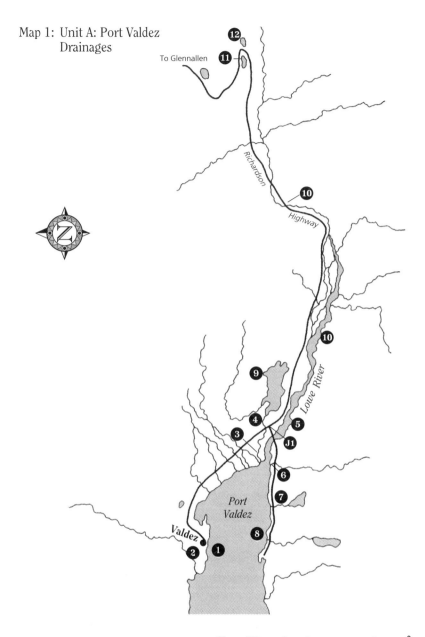

#	LOCATION	MILE POST	🚗	P	⛺	🚶	🛥	♿	🎣	PAGE
1.	Port Valdez	(Town)	■	■			■		●	218
2.	Ruth Pond	(Town)	■	●					◆	218
3.	Robe River (Lower)	1.5	●	●					●	218
4.	Robe River (Middle)	2.7	■	◆					◆	219
J1.	Jct.: Dayville Road	2.8								

Map 2: Unit B: Copper
Valley Drainages

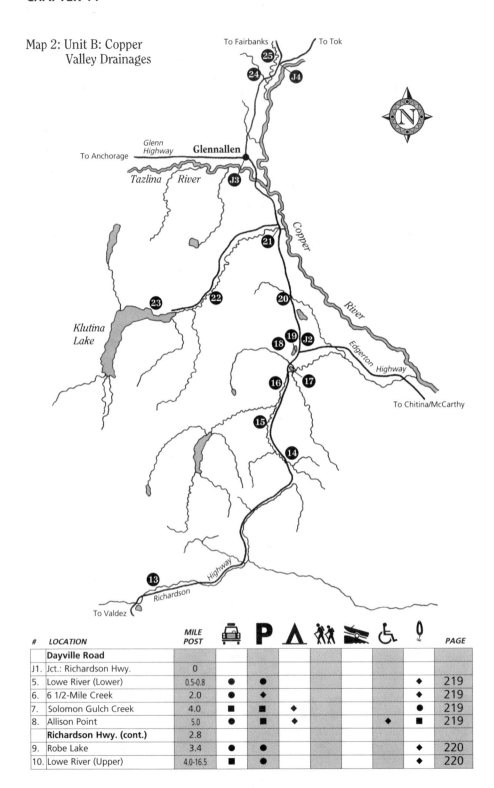

#	LOCATION	MILE POST		P	A	🚶	🛶	♿	🎣	PAGE
	Dayville Road									
J1.	Jct.: Richardson Hwy.	0								
5.	Lowe River (Lower)	0.5-0.8	●	●					◆	219
6.	6 1/2-Mile Creek	2.0	●	◆					◆	219
7.	Solomon Gulch Creek	4.0	■	■	◆				●	219
8.	Allison Point	5.0	●	■	◆			◆	■	219
	Richardson Hwy. (cont.)	2.8								
9.	Robe Lake	3.4	●	●					◆	220
10.	Lowe River (Upper)	4.0-16.5	■	●					◆	220

#	LOCATION	MILE POST	🚗	P	⛺	🚶	🛶	♿	⚓	PAGE
11.	Thompson Lake	23.5	●	●					◆	220
12.	Blueberry Lake	24.1	●	●	●				◆	220
13.	Tiekel River	46.8-61.4	■	●					◆	221
14.	Little Tonsina River (Middle)								◆	
	Access A	65.0	■	●	●				◆	221
	Access B	68.2	●	●					◆	221
15.	Little Tonsina River (Mouth)	74.5	●	●					◆	221
16.	Tonsina River (Middle)	79.2	■	◆					◆	222
17.	Squirrel Creek Pit	79.4	■	●	●			■	◆	222
18.	Squirrel Creek	79.4	■	●	●				◆	222
J2.	Jct.: Edgerton Highway	82.6								
19.	Pippin Lake	81.7-83.5	■	●					◆	222
20.	Willow Creek	90.7	■	◆					◆	222
21.	Klutina River (Lower)									
	Access A	100.4	■	■	●		●	◆	●	222
	Access B	101.1	■	●	●				◆	222
22.	Klutina River (Upper)	101.8	●	●	●		◆	◆	●	223
23.	Klutina Lake	101.8	◆	●	●		◆	◆	◆	223
J3.	Jct.: Glenn Highway	115.0								
24.	Bear Creek	125.9	■	●					◆	223
25.	Gulkana River (Lower)									
	Access A.	126.5	●	■	●			◆	■	223
	Access B.	126.9	■	◆					■	223
	Access C.	129.1	■	●		●			●	223
	Access D.	129.3	■	●		●			●	223
J4.	Jct.: Tok Cutoff	128.6								
26.	Poplar Grove Creek	138.3	■	●					◆	224
27.	Gulkana River (Middle)									
	Access A	136.7	■	●		■			●	224
	Access B	139.6	■	●		■			●	224
	Access C	141.4	■	●		■			●	224
	Access D	146.5	■	●		■			●	224
	Access E	147.6	●	■	■		●	◆	●	224
28.	Sourdough Creek									
	Access A	147.6	●	■	■				◆	224
	Access B	147.7	■	●					◆	224
29.	Haggard Creek	161.0	■	◆					◆	224
30.	June Lake	166.5	■	●		●			◆	224
31.	Nita Lake	166.5	■	●		●			◆	225
32.	Gillespie Lake	168.1	■	●	◆	●			◆	225
33.	Meiers Lake	170.8	■	●	◆				◆	225
34.	Dick Lake	173.3	■	●	◆				◆	225
35.	Paxson Lake	175.0-182.5								
	Access A	175.0	●	■	■		■	◆	●	225
	Access B	179.4-182.5	■	●					●	225
J5.	Jct.: Denali Highway	185.5								
36.	East Fork Gulkana River	186.5-191.0	■	■	◆				◆	226
37.	Fish Lake	190.5	■	●					◆	226
38.	Summit Lake	190.0-196.0	■	●	◆		●		●	226
39.	Gunn Creek	196.8	■	●	◆				◆	226
40.	Fielding Lake	200.5	■	●	●		■		◆	227
41.	Rapids Lake	225.2	■	●	◆				◆	227
42.	Donnelly Creek	238.0	■	●	■				◆	227

Map 3: Unit C: Gulkana
River Drainage

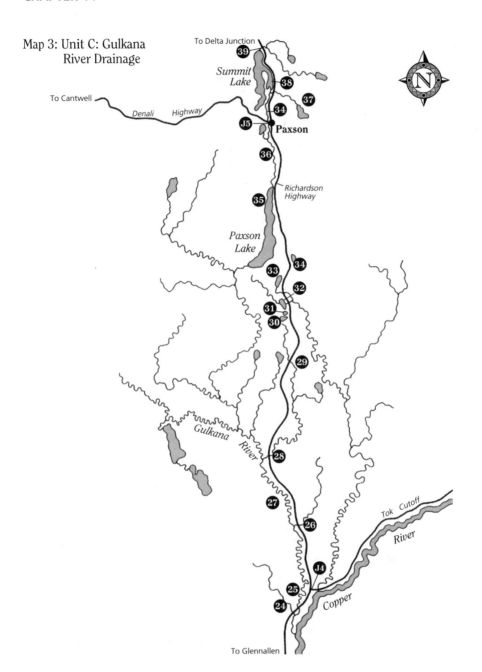

#	LOCATION	MILE POST		P	Λ	🏃	🛶	♿	🎣	PAGE
J6.	Jct.: Coal Mine Road	242.0								
	Coal Mine Road									
J6.	Jct.: Richardson Hwy.	0								
43.	Coal Mine #5 Lake	1.6	♦	●	♦	●			♦	227

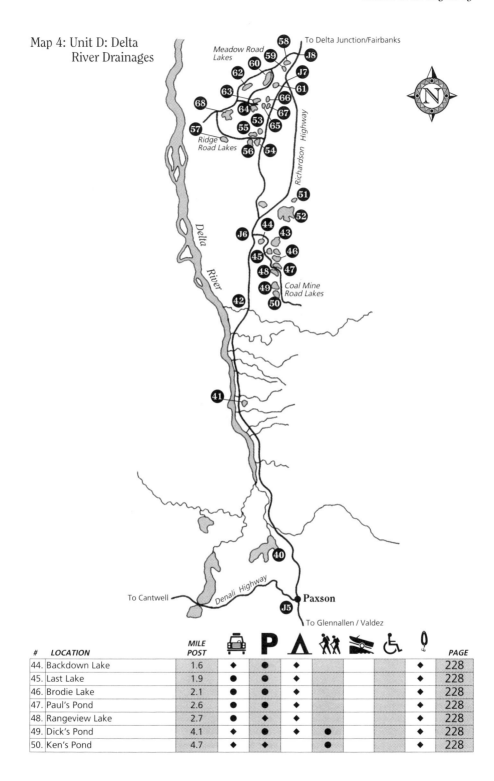

Map 4: Unit D: Delta
River Drainages

Meadow Road
Lakes

To Delta Junction/Fairbanks

Richardson Highway

Ridge
Road Lakes

Delta
River

Coal Mine
Road Lakes

Denali Highway

To Cantwell

Paxson

To Glennallen / Valdez

#	LOCATION	MILE POST	🚗	**P**	Δ	🚶	🛶	♿	🎣	PAGE
44.	Backdown Lake	1.6	♦	●	♦				♦	228
45.	Last Lake	1.9	●	●	♦				♦	228
46.	Brodie Lake	2.1	●	●	♦				♦	228
47.	Paul's Pond	2.6	●	●	♦				♦	228
48.	Rangeview Lake	2.7	●	♦	♦				♦	228
49.	Dick's Pond	4.1	♦	●	♦	●			♦	228
50.	Ken's Pond	4.7	♦	♦		●			♦	228

Map 5: Unit E: Tanana Valley Drainages

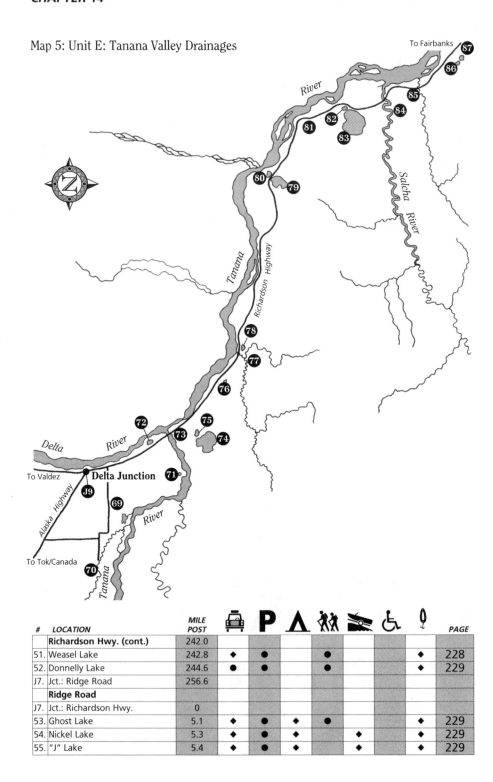

#	LOCATION	MILE POST	🚕	P	A	🥾	🛶	♿	♀	PAGE
	Richardson Hwy. (cont.)	242.0								
51.	Weasel Lake	242.8	◆	●		●			◆	228
52.	Donnelly Lake	244.6	●	●		●			◆	229
J7.	Jct.: Ridge Road	256.6								
	Ridge Road									
J7.	Jct.: Richardson Hwy.	0								
53.	Ghost Lake	5.1	◆	●	◆	●			◆	229
54.	Nickel Lake	5.3	◆	●	◆		◆		◆	229
55.	"J" Lake	5.4	◆	●	◆		◆		◆	229

#	LOCATION	MILE POST	🚐	P	▲	🚶	⛵	♿	⚓	PAGE
	Ridge Road (cont.)									
56.	Chet Lake	5.5	◆	●	◆				◆	229
57.	West Pond	6.8	●	◆					◆	230
J8.	Jct.: Meadows Road	257.6								
	Meadows Road									
J8.	Jct.: Richardson Hwy.	0								
58.	Sheefish Lake	1.5	●	●			●		◆	230
59.	Bullwinkle Lake	1.5	●	●			●		◆	230
60.	Bolio Lake	2.0	●	●	◆			●	◆	230
61.	Luke Pond	2.0	●	●			●		◆	230
62.	Mark Lake	5.3	●	●					◆	230
63.	North Twin Lake	5.6	●	●	●			●	◆	230
64.	South Twin Lake	5.6	●	●	●			●	◆	230
65.	No Mercy Lake	5.6	●	●			●		◆	231
66.	Rockhound Lake	5.6	●	●			●		◆	231
67.	Doc Lake	5.6	●	●			●		◆	231
68.	Big Lake	6.3	●	●					◆	231
	Richardson Hwy. (cont.)	257.6								
J9.	Jct.: Alaska Highway	266.0								
69.	Clearwater Lake	268.2	●	●	◆		●	●	◆	232
70.	Delta Clearwater River	268.2	■	●	●		●	◆	●	232
71.	Bluff Cabin Lake	271.8	●	●			●		◆	232
72.	Big D Pond	274.6	●	●					◆	233
73.	Tanana River (Middle)	275.4	■	●	◆		●	●	◆	233
74.	Quartz Lake	277.8	●	●	●		●		◆	233
75.	Little Lost Lake	277.8	●	◆					◆	233
76.	81-Mile Pond	284.5	■	●	◆				◆	233
77.	Shaw Creek	286.7	■	●			●		◆	233
78.	Shaw Pond	287.2	■	●	◆				◆	233
79.	Birch Lake	306.0	●	●				●	◆	234
80.	Lost Lake	306.2	●	◆			●		◆	234
81.	Mosquito Creek Lake	315.2	●	●					◆	234
82.	Little Harding Lake	319.5	●	●		●			◆	234
83.	Harding Lake	321.6	●	●	●		●	●	◆	234
84.	Salcha River (Middle)	324.1	■	●	●		●	●	◆	235
85.	Little Salcha River	327.8	■	◆					◆	235
86.	Johnson Road #1 Lake	330.4	●	●					◆	235
87.	31-Mile Pond	332.0	●	◆					◆	235

RICHARDSON HIGHWAY LOCATIONS

Unit A: Port Valdez Drainages

Includes all roadside waters flowing into and surrounding Port Valdez.

UNIT REGULATIONS:

* Salmon fishing prohibited: All fresh water, year-round (except Robe River and Solomon Gulch Creek).
* Halibut fishing prohibited: All salt water, January 1 – 31.
* Ling cod fishing prohibited: All salt water, January 1 – June 30.

Unit A: Port Valdez Drainages continued.

UNIT TIMING:

FISH ▽	JAN	FEB	MAR	APR	MAY	JUN	JUL	AUG	SEP	OCT	NOV	DEC
KS*						▓	▓	▓				
RS*					░	▓	▓	▓	░			
PS*						░	▓	▓	░			
CS*					░	▓	▓	▓	░			
SS*	▓						░	▓	▓	▓	▓	▓
RT	▓	▓	▓	▓	▓	▓	▓	▓	▓	▓	▓	▓
DV	▓	▓	▓	▓	▓	▓	▓	▓	▓	▓	▓	▓
AG	▓	▓	▓	▓	▓	▓	▓	▓	▓	▓	▓	▓

Note: Timing shown for salmon indicates fish in all stages of maturity.

1. Port Valdez

Access A: Harbor Breakwater – Downtown Valdez; From Egan Dr., S on Chitina Ave., left on Kennicott Way 0.2 mile to beach area and cove on left. Continue 0.5 mile to private campground/RV park and oceanfront.

Access B: City Docks – Downtown Valdez; From Egan Dr., S on Hazelet Ave. 0.2 mile to ferry terminal area and city dock at Port Valdez.

Fishing: Phenomenal catches of pink and silver salmon from both shore and boat. Some kings and chums and sea-run char also available. Try high-visibility lures for success.

Pink Salmon / good-excellent / 2-4 lbs. (7 lbs.) / spoons, spinners.

Chum Salmon / poor-fair / 6-12 lbs. (18 lbs.) / spoons, spinners.

Silver Salmon / good / 6-12 lbs. (20 lbs.) / spoons, spinners, bait.

Dolly Varden / poor-fair / 7-15 in. (7 lbs.) / spoons, bait.

FISH ▽	JAN	FEB	MAR	APR	MAY	JUN	JUL	AUG	SEP	OCT	NOV	DEC
PS						░	▓	░				
CS						░	▓	░				
SS							░	▓	░			
DV	▓	▓	▓	▓	▓	▓	▓	▓	▓			

2. Ruth Pond

Access: Downtown Valdez; From Egan Dr., S on Meals Ave. and continue along right-of-way (now Fidalgo Ave.) 0.2 mile to pond on right.

Fishing: Very small pond in city center that is stocked with trout. Bank fishing only.

Rainbow Trout / fair / June – August / 7-15 in. / spinners, flies, bait.

3. Robe River / Lowe River Confluence

Access: MP 1.5; W on dirt road 0.5 mile to a "Y," left fork leads 0.4 mile to lower stream, right fork 0.5 mile to confluence area.

Fishing: Good runs of salmon and sea-run char. Local hot spot in late summer and fall.

Red Salmon / poor / mid-late June / 4-6 lbs. / spinners, flies.

Pink Salmon / good-excellent / mid-July – early August / 2-4 lbs. / spoons, spinners, flies.

Chum Salmon / poor / late July – early August / 6-12 lbs. / spoons, spinners, flies, bait.
Silver Salmon / good / mid-September – early October / 6-12 lbs. / spinners, flies, bait.
Dolly Varden / good / early September – mid-October / 8-20 in. / spinners, flies, bait.

4. Robe River (Middle)
Access A: MP 1.5; W on dirt road 0.5 mile to "Y," left fork leads 0.4 mile to river, right fork 0.5 mile to river.
Access B: MP 2.7; highway crosses stream.
Fishing: Slow-flowing stream with decent opportunities for salmon and sea-run char.
Red Salmon / poor / mid-late June / 4-6 lbs. / spinners, flies.
Pink Salmon / poor-fair / late July – early August / 2-4 lbs. / spoons, spinners, flies.
Silver Salmon / good / mid-September – early October / 6-12 lbs. / spinners, flies, bait.
Dolly Varden / good / mid-September – mid-November / 8-20 in. / spinners, flies, bait..

RICHARDSON HIGHWAY log continues on page 220.

Dayville Road

Road begins at MP 2.9 Richardson Highway (Mile 0) and ends west of Allison Point at the Alaska Pipeline Valdez Marine Terminal (Mile 5.4).

5. Lowe River (Lower)
Access: MP 0.5-0.8; road crosses river.
Fishing: Glacial river with limited angling opportunities for char.
Dolly Varden / fair / mid-May, early July – late August / 8-20 in. / flies, bait.

6. 6 1/2-Mile Creek
Access: MP 2.0; road crosses stream.
Fishing: Salmon spawning stream supporting a small population of char in summer.
Dolly Varden / fair / early July – mid-August / 7-12 in. / spinners, flies, bait.

7. Solomon Gulch Creek Marine
Access: MP 4.0; road crosses stream.
Fishing: A major producer of pink and silver salmon. Cast off stream mouth. No fishing permitted within 300 feet of weir. Fish hatchery is located here.
Pink Salmon / excellent / mid-July – early August / 2-4 lbs. / spoons, spinners, flies.
Chum Salmon / poor / mid-July – early August / 6-12 lbs. / spoons, spinners, flies.
Silver Salmon / good / late August – mid-September / 6-12 lbs. / spinners, flies, bait.
Dolly Varden / poor / early June – mid-July / 7-15 in. / spoons, spinners, flies, bait.

8. Allison Point
Access: MP 5.0; large parking and primitive camping area on right next to bay.
Fishing: This is the premier angling spot in the Valdez area, offering superb action for pink and silver salmon. As water is very silty, use high-visibility lures for success.
Pink Salmon / excellent / 2-4 lbs. (7 lbs.) / spoons, spinners, bait.

Chum Salmon / poor / 6-12 lbs. (18 lbs.) / spoons, spinners.
Silver Salmon / good / 6-12 lbs. (20 lbs.) / spinners, bait.
Dolly Varden / poor-fair / 7-15 in. (7 lbs.) / spoons, bait.

FISH ▽	JAN	FEB	MAR	APR	MAY	JUN	JUL	AUG	SEP	OCT	NOV	DEC
PS						▓▓	▓▓	▓▓				
CS						░▓	▓▓	▓				
SS								░▓	▓			
DV			░▓	▓			▓▓	▓░		▓		

RICHARDSON HIGHWAY log continues.

9. Robe Lake

Access: MP 3.4; N on paved road 0.5 mile to lake.
Fishing: Lake is shallow and weedy along shoreline. A canoe is necessary to reach fish.
Dolly Varden / fair / May, October – November / 8-20 in. / spoons, flies, bait.

10. Lowe River (Upper)

Access: MP 4.0-16.5; highway parallels river, crossing it at MP 14.9, 15.3, and 16.3.
Fishing: Glacial river with angling opportunities for char in late fall and early spring.
Dolly Varden / fair / April, October – mid-November / 8-20 in. / flies, bait.

11. Thompson Lake

Access: MP 23.5; W on access road short distance to lake.
Fishing: Lake is stocked with grayling. Use a canoe/float tube.
Arctic Grayling / good / June – September / 7-12 in. / spinners, flies.

12. Blueberry Lake

Access: MP 24.1; E on access road 0.8 mile to campground and lake.
Fishing: Lake is stocked with trout. Casting from shore is productive.
Rainbow Trout / fair / June, September – October / 8-16 in. / spinners, flies, bait.

Unit B: Copper Valley Drainages

Includes all roadside waters in the Copper Valley.

UNIT REGULATIONS:

* There are no general area-wide restrictions for waters in Unit B.

UNIT TIMING:

FISH ▽	JAN	FEB	MAR	APR	MAY	JUN	JUL	AUG	SEP	OCT	NOV	DEC
KS						███	███	░░				
RS					░	███	███	███	░			
SS									░			
LS	███	███	███	███	███	███	███	███	███	███	███	███
ST	░	░	░	░	░							░
RT	░	░	░	░	███	███	███	███	███	░	░	░
LT	░	░	░	░	░	███	░	███	███	░	░	░
DV						███	███	███	███	░		
AG				███	███	███	███	███	███	░		
WF	░	░	░	░	░	███	░	███	███	░	░	░
BB			░	███	░					███	░	

13. Tiekel River

Access: MP 46.8-61.4; highway parallels river, crossing it at MP 46.9 and 50.7.
Fishing: Glacial river with limited opportunities in summer for small resident char.
Dolly Varden / fair / mid-June – early September / 7-10 in. / flies, bait.

14. Little Tonsina River (Middle)

Access A: MP 65.0; highway crosses stream.
Access B: MP 68.2; SW on gravel road 0.5 mile to small parking area. Stream is located beyond hill.
Fishing: Salmon spawning stream containing populations of silvers, char, and grayling.
Silver Salmon / fair / mid-, late September / 5-10 lbs. / spinners, bait.
Dolly Varden / fair / late July – mid-October / 7-15 in. / spinners, flies, bait.
Arctic Grayling / fair-good / mid-May – mid-September / 7-12 in. / spinners, flies.

15. Little Tonsina River / Tonsina River Confluence

Access: MP 74.5; W on gravel road short distance to a "Y," right fork 0.3 mile to confluence.
Fishing: The best spot for silvers in Copper Valley. Fish concentrate at mouth and below.
Red Salmon / poor / 3-6 lbs. (12 lbs.) / spinners, flies.
Silver Salmon / fair-good / 5-10 lbs. (15 lbs.) / spinners, flies, bait.
Dolly Varden / fair / 7-15 in. (3 lbs.) / spinners, flies, bait.
Arctic Grayling / fair-good / 7-12 in. (16 in.) / spinners, flies.

FISH ▽	JAN	FEB	MAR	APR	MAY	JUN	JUL	AUG	SEP	OCT	NOV	DEC
RS						░	███					
SS								░	███	░		
DV						███	███	███	███	░		
AG					███	███	███	███	███	░		

16. Tonsina River (Middle)

Access: MP 79.2; highway crosses river.
Fishing: Glacial drainage supporting runs of salmon, char, and grayling during summer and fall. Target quiet water away from main current using high-visibility lures or bait.
King Salmon / poor-fair / early, mid-July / 15-40 lbs. / attractors, bait.
Silver Salmon / poor-fair / mid-September / 5-10 lbs. / attractors, bait.
Dolly Varden / poor-fair / mid-June – mid-October / 7-15 in. / attractors, bait.
Arctic Grayling / poor / May, mid-September – mid-October / 7-12 in. / bait.

17. Squirrel Creek Pit

Access: MP 79.4; E on gravel road at Squirrel Creek Campground short distance to pond.
Fishing: Pond is stocked with trout. Casting from shore is productive.
Rainbow Trout / good / May, September – October / 7-15 in. / spoons, flies, bait.

18. Squirrel Creek

Access: MP 79.4; highway crosses stream. Short hike downstream to Tonsina River confluence.
Fishing: Limited opportunities for salmon, char, and grayling; try mouth.
Silver Salmon / poor-fair / mid-September / 5-10 lbs. / spinners, bait.
Dolly Varden / poor-fair / mid-July – late September / 7-12 in. / flies, bait.
Arctic Grayling / poor-fair / early June – mid-September / 7-10 in. / spinners, flies.

19. Pippin Lake

Access: MP 81.7-83.5; highway parallels lake, pullouts. Lake is situated approximately 100 to 200 yards W of highway.
Fishing: Lake is stocked with trout. Use a canoe/float tube.
Rainbow Trout / fair-good / June, September – December / 7-15 in. / spinners, flies, bait.

20. Willow Creek

Access: MP 90.7; highway crosses stream.
Fishing: Stream supports a small spawning run of grayling in spring and early summer.
Arctic Grayling / fair / 7-12 in. / mid-May – 0early June / spinners, flies.

21. Klutina River (Lower)

Access A: MP 100.4; E on Loop Rd. 0.4 mile to river crossing.
Access B: MP 101.1; highway crosses river.
Fishing: Fast-flowing glacial river offering some of the best salmon action in Copper Valley. Casting from shore is productive. Use high-visibility lures or bait.
King Salmon / fair-good / 15-45 lbs. (85 lbs.) / attractors, bait.
Red Salmon / good-excellent / 5-7 lbs. (14 lbs.) / flies.
Dolly Varden / fair / 7-15 in. (5 lbs.) / attractors, flies, bait.
Whitefish / poor / 8-15 in. (17 in.) / attractors, bait.
(continues on next page)

NO. 21 - Klutina River (Lower) continued.

FISH ▽	JAN	FEB	MAR	APR	MAY	JUN	JUL	AUG	SEP	OCT	NOV	DEC
KS												
RS												
DV												
WF												

22. Klutina River (Upper)

Access: MP 101.8; W on Brenwick-Craig (Klutina Lake) Rd. 13.4 miles. Road parallels river more or less next 12.5 miles to outlet of Klutina Lake. Very rough road last few miles – 4WD vehicle recommended.

Fishing: Hike along river to find places where salmon congregate in good numbers. Boaters have access to the best spots for kings. Use high-visibility lures or bait.

King Salmon / fair-good / 15-45 lbs. (85 lbs.) / attractors, bait.
Red Salmon / good-excellent / 5-7 lbs. (14 lbs.) / flies.
Dolly Varden / good / 7-18 in. (7 lbs.) / attractors, flies, bait.
Whitefish / poor-fair / 8-16 in. (4 lbs.) / attractors, flies, bait.

FISH ▽	JAN	FEB	MAR	APR	MAY	JUN	JUL	AUG	SEP	OCT	NOV	DEC
KS												
RS												
DV												
WF												

23. Klutina Lake

Access: MP 101.8; W on Brenwick-Craig (Klutina Lake) Rd. 25.9 miles to lake outlet. Very rough road last few miles - 4WD vehicle recommended.

Fishing: Glacial lake containing a good population of char as well as some grayling.

Lake Trout / poor-fair / June, September – November / 3-5 lbs. / bait.
Dolly Varden / good / July – October / 7-20 in. / attractors, bait.
Arctic Grayling / poor-fair / June – September / 7-12 in. / attractors, bait.

24. Bear Creek

Access: MP 125.9; highway crosses stream.

Fishing: Small stream supporting a spring spawning run of grayling.

Arctic Grayling / fair / early – late May / 7-12 in. / spinners, flies.

25. Gulkana River (Lower)

Access A: MP 126.7; E. on gravel road 0.1 mile, left on access road 0.1 mile to parking , beach area, and river.

Access B: MP 126.9; highway crosses river.

Access C: MP 129.1; trail leads W 1.2 mile to river.

Access D: MP 129.3; W on BLM access road 1.0 mile to river.

Fishing: Productive shore angling for early-run kings and two runs of red salmon. Sight

fishing is possible when water flows low and clear. Grayling are sometimes abundant.
King Salmon / fair-good / 15-30 lbs. (60 lbs.) / attractors, flies, bait.
Red Salmon / fair / 4-8 lbs. (14 lbs.) / flies.
Rainbow Trout / poor-fair / 8-20 in. (6 lbs.) / spinners, flies.
Arctic Grayling / good / 8-16 in. (3 lbs.) / spinners, flies.

FISH ▽	JAN	FEB	MAR	APR	MAY	JUN	JUL	AUG	SEP	OCT	NOV	DEC
KS						▓						
RS						▓	▓	▓				
RT					▓	▓	▓	▓	▓			
AG					▓	▓	▓	▓	▓			

26. Poplar Grove Creek
Access: MP 138.3; highway crosses stream.
Fishing: A fairly popular location for grayling during the spring spawning run.
Arctic Grayling / good-excellent / early – late May / 7-12 in. / spinners, flies.

27. Gulkana River (Middle)
Access A: MP 136.7; W on gravel road 1.2 mile to river.
Access B: MP 139.6; trail leads 0.6 mile W to river.
Access C: MP 141.4; turnout. Trail leads 1.0 mile W to river.
Access D: MP 146.5; trail leads 1.0 mile W to river.
Access E: MP 147.6; W on gravel road 0.5 mile to river.
Fishing: Scout river for deep holes and runs where kings can be found. Look for schools
of reds near shore. Trout and grayling action picks up in this stretch of the Gulkana.
King Salmon / fair-good / 15-30 lbs. (60 lbs.) / plugs, attractors, bait.
Red Salmon / fair / 4-8 lbs. (14 lbs.) / flies.
Rainbow Trout / fair / 8-20 in. (6 lbs.) / spinners, flies.
Arctic Grayling / good / 8-16 in. (3 lbs.) / spinners, flies.

FISH ▽	JAN	FEB	MAR	APR	MAY	JUN	JUL	AUG	SEP	OCT	NOV	DEC
KS						▓	▓					
RS						▓	▓	▓				
RT					▓	▓	▓	▓	▓			
AG					▓	▓	▓	▓	▓	▓		

28. Sourdough Creek
Access A: MP 147.6; W on gravel road 0.2 mile to stream crossing, continuing 0.3 mile
along stream to Gulkana River confluence.
Access B: MP 147.7; highway crosses stream.
Fishing: One of the top roadside fisheries for grayling in the area. Best in spring.
Arctic Grayling / good-excellent / early – late May / 7-14 in. / spinners, flies.

29. Haggard Creek
Access: MP 161.0; highway crosses stream.
Fishing: Small stream supporting a decent spring spawning run of grayling.
Arctic Grayling / good / mid-, late May / 7-14 in. / spinners, flies.

30. June Lake

Access: MP 166.5; trail leads 0.25 mile W to lake.
Fishing: Lake contains a moderate population of native grayling. Use a canoe/float tube.
Arctic Grayling / good / June – September / 7-12 in. / spinners, flies.

31. Nita Lake

Access: MP 166.5; trail leads 1.0 mile W to lake.
Fishing: Lake contains a moderate population of native grayling. Use a canoe/float tube.
Arctic Grayling / good / June – September / 7-12 in. / spinners, flies.

32. Gillespie Lake

Access: MP 168.1; hike up along Gillespie Creek 0.25 mile to lake.
Fishing: Lake contains a moderate population of native grayling. Use a canoe/float tube.
Arctic Grayling / good / June – September / 7-12 in. / spinners, flies.

33. Meiers Lake

Access: MP 170.8; lake is adjacent to highway.
Fishing: Lake contains a small population of native grayling and burbot.
Arctic Grayling / fair/ June – September / 7-14 in. / spinners, flies.
Burbot / fair / March – April, September – December / 2-4 lbs. / bait.

34. Dick Lake

Access: MP 173.3; E on dirt road short distance to lake.
Fishing: Lake is stocked with char. Use a canoe/float tube.
Arctic Char / fair-good / June, September – January / 7-16 in. / spoons, jigs, bait.

35. Paxson Lake

Access A: MP 175.0; W on gravel road next to sign 1.4 mile to a "Y," follow sign short distance to lake.
Access B: MP 179.4 – 182.5; highway parallels lake. Numerous turnouts present.
Fishing: Large clearwater lake best fished from a boat if targeting lake trout. Only fair opportunities from shore, mostly grayling. Productive ice fishing for char and burbot.
Red Salmon / poor / 4-8 lbs. (14 lbs.) / spinners, flies.
Rainbow Trout / fair / 8-18 in. (6 lbs.) / spoons, spinners, flies, bait.
Lake Trout / good / 3-10 lbs. (30 lbs.) / spoons, plugs, bait.
Arctic Grayling / good-excellent / 8-16 in. (3 lbs.) / spinners, flies.
Whitefish / poor / 8-16 in. (4 lbs.) / flies, bait.
Burbot / fair-good / 2-6 lbs. (27 lbs.) / bait.

FISH ▽	JAN	FEB	MAR	APR	MAY	JUN	JUL	AUG	SEP	OCT	NOV	DEC
RS						■	■	■	■			
RT						■	■		■	■		
LT					■	■			■			
AG						■	■	■	■			
WF					■	■						
BB			■	■						■	■	■

36. East Fork Gulkana River

Access: MP 186.5 – 191.0; highway parallels river.
Fishing: Mainly a salmon spawning stream with opportunities for grayling, a few trout.
Rainbow Trout / poor-fair / late June – early October / 7-18 in. / spoons, spinners, flies.
Arctic Grayling / fair / mid-May – late September / 7-14 in. / spinners, flies.

37. Fish Lake

Access: MP 190.5; turnout. Trail parallels Fish Creek 2.0 miles E to lake.
Fishing: Lake supports a large population of native grayling. Best in summer and fall.
Arctic Grayling / good / June – September / 7-12 in. / spinners, flies.

38. Summit Lake

Access: MP 191.0 – 196.0; highway parallels lake.
Fishing: Large and deep clearwater lake with healthy numbers of trout, char, grayling, and burbot. Angling can be good from shore but best from boat. Popular ice fishing spot.
Red Salmon / poor / 4-8 lbs. (14 lbs.) / spinners, flies.
Rainbow Trout / fair / 8-18 in. (7 lbs.) / spoons, spinners, flies, bait.
Lake Trout / fair-good / 3-10 lbs. (30 lbs.) / spoons, plugs, bait.
Arctic Grayling / good-excellent / 8-16 in. (3 lbs.) / spinners, flies.
Whitefish / poor / 8-16 in. (4 lbs.) / flies, bait.
Burbot / fair-good / 2-6 lbs. (27 lbs.) / bait.

FISH ▽	JAN	FEB	MAR	APR	MAY	JUN	JUL	AUG	SEP	OCT	NOV	DEC
RS							■	■				
RT						■			■	■		
LT					■				■	■		
AG					■	■	■	■	■	■		
WF						■						
BB				■						■		

39. Gunn Creek

Access: MP 196.8; highway crosses stream.
Fishing: Clearwater stream known for its great spring and fall runs of grayling.
Arctic Grayling / good-excellent / May, early Sept. – early Oct. / 7-16 in. / spinners, flies.

Unit C: Delta River Drainage

Includes all roadside waters flowing into and surrounding the Delta River.

UNIT REGULATIONS:

* Salmon fishing prohibited: All flowing waters, year-round.

(continues on next page)

Unit C: Delta River Drainages continued.

UNIT TIMING:

FISH ▽	JAN	FEB	MAR	APR	MAY	JUN	JUL	AUG	SEP	OCT	NOV	DEC
CS*								▓	▓	▓	▓	
SS*								▓	▓	▓	▓	
LS	▓	▓	▓	▓	▓	▓	▓	▓	▓	▓	▓	▓
RT	▓	▓	▓	▓	▓	▓	▓	▓	▓	▓	▓	▓
LT	▓	▓	▓	▓	▓	▓	▓	▓	▓	▓	▓	▓
AC	▓	▓	▓	▓	▓	▓	▓	▓	▓	▓	▓	▓
AG	▓	▓	▓	▓	▓	▓	▓	▓	▓	▓	▓	▓
WF						▓	▓	▓	▓	▓	▓	▓
BB	▓	▓	▓	▓	▓	▓	▓	▓	▓	▓	▓	▓

*Note: Timing shown for salmon indicates fish in all stages of maturity.

40. Fielding Lake

Access: MP 200.5; SW on gravel road 2.1 mile to lake outlet.
Fishing: Large and deep lake featuring char and grayling. Try casting near outlet.
Lake Trout / fair-good / June, August – October / 2-6 lbs. / spoons, plugs, bait.
Arctic Grayling / good / June, September – October / 7-14 in. / spinners, flies.

41. Rapids Lake

Access: MP 225.4; trail leads 0.25 mile N to lake.
Fishing: Lake is stocked with trout and char. Casting from shore is productive.
Rainbow Trout / good / June, September – October / 7-16 in. / spinners, flies, bait.
Lake Trout / fair / June, September – October / 2-6 lbs. / spoons, plugs, bait.

42. Donnelly Creek

Access: MP 238.0; highway crosses stream.
Fishing: Clearwater stream offering summer and fall opportunities for grayling.
Arctic Grayling / fair-good / early June – mid-September / 7-12 in. / spinners, flies.

RICHARDSON HIGHWAY log continues on page 228.

Coal Mine Road

Road begins at MP 242.1 Richardson Highway (Mile 0) and ends at coal mine (Mile 7.1).

43. Coal Mine #5 Lake

Access: Mile 1.7; left 0.4 mile on very rough 4-wheel-drive road to lake on left. Trail leads 200 yards to lake.
Fishing: Lake is stocked with trout. Seasonally productive, light angling pressure.
Rainbow Trout / good / June, September / 8-18 in. / spinners, spinners, flies.

44. Backdown Lake

Access: Mile 1.7; left 0.4 mile on very rough 4-wheel-drive road to lake on right. Trail leads 150 yards to lake.
Fishing: Lake is stocked with trout and char. Use a canoe/float tube.
Rainbow Trout / good / June, September – December / 7-15 in. / spinners, flies, bait.
Arctic Char / fair / June, September – January / 7-15 in. / spoons, jigs, bait.

45. Last Lake

Access: Mile 1.9; lake is located on left side of road. Trail leads 100 yards to lake.
Fishing: Lake is stocked with trout and char. Use a canoe/float tube.
Rainbow Trout / good / June, September – December / 7-15 in. / spinners, flies, bait.
Arctic Char / fair / June, September – January / 7-15 in. / spoons, jigs, bait.

46. Brodie Lake

Access: Mile 2.1; lake is located on left side of road. Trail leads 100 yards to lake.
Fishing: Lake is stocked with landlocked salmon, char, and grayling.
Landlocked Salmon / good / June – March / 7-12 in. / spinners, jigs, flies, bait.
Arctic Char / fair / June, September – January / 7-15 in. / spoons, jigs, bait.
Arctic Grayling / good / June – September / 7-12 in. / spinners, flies.

47. Paul's Pond

Access: Mile 2.5; lake is located on left side of road. Trail leads 50 yards to lake.
Fishing: Pond is stocked with grayling. Use a canoe/float tube.
Arctic Grayling / good / June – September / 7-12 in. / spinners, flies.

48. Rangeview Lake

Access: Mile 2.6; lake is located on right side of road. Short hike to lake.
Fishing: Lake is stocked with char and grayling. Use a canoe/float tube.
Arctic Char / fair / June, September – January / 7-15 in. / spoons, jigs, bait.
Arctic Grayling / good / June – September / 7-12 in. / spinners, flies.

49. Dick's Pond

Access: Mile 4.1; lake is located on right side of road. Trail leads 0.25 mile to lake.
Fishing: Lake is stocked with char. Seasonally productive, very little angling pressure.
Arctic Char / fair / June, September – January / 7-15 in. / spoons, jigs, bait.

50. Ken's Pond

Access: Mile 4.7; lake is located on right side of road. Trail leads 0.3 mile to lake.
Fishing: Pond is stocked with trout and char. Use a canoe/float tube.
Rainbow Trout / good / June, September – December / 7-15 in. / spinners, flies, bait.
Arctic Char / fair / June, September – January / 7-15 in. / spoons, jigs, bait.

RICHARDSON HIGHWAY log continues.

51. Weasel Lake

Access: MP 242.8; E on gravel road 0.7 mile. Lake is located 100 yards E of road. Lake is on military property. ***Note:*** A permit is required to fish on base. Public must check in at

Eielson AFB main gate (MP 341.0) prior to entering area. Call 873-1111 for information.

Fishing: Lake is stocked with trout. Seasonally productive, very little angling pressure.

Rainbow Trout / good / June, September – December / 7-15 in. / spinners, flies, bait.

52. Donnelly Lake

Access: MP 244.6; trail leads 0.5 mile E to lake.

Fishing: Lake is stocked with trout. A few char present. Use a canoe/float tube.

Rainbow Trout / good / June, September – December / 7-16 in. / spinners, flies, bait.

Arctic Char / poor / June, September – January / 10-20 in. / spoons, jigs, bait.

RICHARDSON HIGHWAY log continues on page 231.

Fort Greely Ridge Road

Road begins at MP 256.0 Richardson Highway (Mile 0) and extends into base area. Area locations on military base. *Note:* A permit is required to fish on base. Public must check in at Eielson AFB main gate (MP 341.0) prior to entering area. Call 873-1111 for information.

53. Ghost Lake

Access: MP 5.3; right 0.3 mile on very rough 4-wheel drive road to lake.

Fishing: Lake is stocked with trout and char. Use a canoe/float tube.

Rainbow Trout / good / June, September – December / 7-15 in. / spinners, flies, bait.

Arctic Char / fair-good / June, September – January / 7-16 in. / spoons, jigs, bait.

54. Nickel Lake

Access: MP 5.4; trail leads 100 yards S to lake.

Fishing: Lake is stocked with trout, char, and grayling. Use a canoe/float tube.

Rainbow Trout / good / June, September – December / 7-15 in. / spinners, flies, bait.

Arctic Char / fair-good / June, September – January / 7-16 in. / spoons, jigs, bait.

Arctic Grayling / fair / June – September / 7-12 in. / spinners, flies.

55. "J" Lake

Access: MP 5.4; trail leads 100 yards N to lake.

Fishing: Lake is stocked with char and grayling. Use a canoe/float tube

Arctic Char / fair-good / June, September – January / 7-16 in. / spoons, jigs, bait.

Arctic Grayling / good / June – September / 7-12 in. / spinners, flies.

56. Chet Lake

Access: MP 5.6; lake is adjacent to left side of road.

Fishing: Lake is stocked with trout and char. Use a canoe/float tube.

Rainbow Trout / good / June, September – December / 7-15 in. / spoons, flies, bait.

Arctic Char / fair-good / June, September – January / 7-16 in. / spoons, jigs, bait.

57. West Pond
Access: MP 6.8; lake is adjacent to left side of road. Use a canoe/float tube.
Fishing: Pond is stocked with trout. Use canoe/float tube, cast from shore.
Rainbow Trout / good / 7-15 in. / June, September – December / spinners, flies, bait.

Fort Greely Meadows Road
Road begins at MP 257.6 Richardson Highway (Mile 0) and extends into base area. Area locations on military base. *Note:* A permit is required to fish on base. Public must check in at Eielson AFB main gate (MP 341.0) prior to entering area. Call 873-1111 for information.

58. Sheefish Lake
Access: MP 2.5; trail leads 0.4 mile SW to a "Y," SE on left fork 0.25 mile to lake.
Fishing: Lake is stocked with char. Use a canoe/float tube.
Arctic Char / fair-good / June, September – January / 7-15 in. / spoons, jigs, bait.

59. Bullwinkle Lake
Access: MP 2.5; trail leads 0.5 mile SW to a "Y," SE fork leads 0.25 mile to lake.
Fishing: Lake is stocked with trout. Use a canoe/float tube.
Rainbow Trout / good / June, September – December / 7-15 in. / spinners, flies, bait.

60. Bolio Lake
Access: MP 2.3; left on Bolio Lake Rd. 1.0 mile to lake on right. Road parallels lake next 0.5 mile.
Fishing: Lake is stocked with fish. Hot spot for ice fishing. Use a canoe/float tube.
Landlocked salmon / good / June – March / 7-12 in. / spinners, jigs, flies, bait.
Rainbow Trout / good / June, September – December / 7-16 in. / spinners, flies, bait.
Arctic Grayling / good / June – September / 7-12 in. / spinners, flies.

61. Luke Pond
Access: MP 2.3; left on Bolio Lake Rd. 1.4 mile, 0.4 mile uphill from Bolio Lake test site.
Fishing: Pond is stocked with grayling. Use a canoe/float tube.
Arctic Grayling / good / June – September / 7-12 in. / spinners, flies.

62. Mark Lake
Access: MP 5.3; S on Mark Lake Rd. 0.3 mile to lake.
Fishing: Lake is stocked with landlocked salmon, trout, char. Use a canoe/float tube.
Landlocked Salmon / good / June – March / 7-12 in. / spinners, jigs, flies, bait.
Rainbow Trout / good / June, September – December / 7-15 in. / spinners, flies, bait.
Arctic Char / fair-good / June, September – January / 7-16 in. / spoons, jigs, bait.

63. North Twin Lake
Access: MP 5.7; left 0.6 mile to a "Y," right 0.8 mile to lake on left.
Fishing: Lake is stocked with trout and grayling. Use a canoe/float tube.
Rainbow Trout / good / June, September – December / 7-15 in. / spinners, flies, bait.
Arctic Grayling / good / June – September / 7-12 in. / spinners, flies.

64. South Twin Lake

Access: MP 5.7; left 0.6 mile to a "Y," right 0.8 mile to lake on right.
Fishing: Lake is stocked with trout. Use a canoe/float tube.
Rainbow Trout / good / June, September – December / 7-15 in. / spinners, flies, bait.

65. No Mercy Lake

Access: MP 5.7; left 0.6 mile to a "Y," right 0.8 mile to Twin Lakes parking area. Locate trail between lakes heading 0.5 mile E to a "Y," left fork leads 150 yards to lake.
Fishing: Lake is stocked with trout. Use a canoe/float tube.
Rainbow Trout / good / June, September – December / 7-15 in. / spinners, flies, bait.

66. Rockhound Lake

Access: MP 5.7; left 0.6 mile to a "Y," right 0.8 mile to Twin Lakes parking area. Locate trail between lakes heading 0.5 mile E to a "Y," left fork leads 250 yards to lake.
Fishing: Lake is stocked with trout. Use a canoe/float tube.
Rainbow Trout / good / June, September – December / 7-15 in. / spinners, flies, bait.

67. Doc Lake

Access: MP 5.7; left 0.6 mile to a "Y," right 0.8 mile to Twin Lakes parking area. Locate trail between lakes heading 0.5 mile E to a "Y," left fork leads 0.5 mile to lake.
Fishing: Lake is stocked with trout. Use a canoe/float tube
Rainbow Trout / good / June, September – December / 7-15 in. / spinners, flies, bait.

68. Big Lake

Access: MP 6.3; left on access road 0.3 mile to lake.
Fishing: Lake is stocked with trout. Use a canoe/float tube.
Rainbow Trout / good / 7-15 in. / June, September – December / spinners, flies, bait.

RICHARDSON HIGHWAY log continues.

Unit D: Tanana Valley Drainages

Includes all roadside waters in the Tanana Valley.

UNIT REGULATIONS:

* Northern pike fishing prohibited: All waters, April 1 – May 31.

(Timing chart on next page)

UNIT TIMING:

FISH ▽	JAN	FEB	MAR	APR	MAY	JUN	JUL	AUG	SEP	OCT	NOV	DEC
KS*												
CS*												
SS*												
LS												
RT												
AC												
SF												
AG												
WF												
NP												
BB												

Note: Timing shown for salmon indicates fish in all stages of maturity.

69. Clearwater Lake

Access: MP 268.2; E on Jack Warren Rd. to MP 9.3, left on Triple H Rd. 1.3 mile to parking area and lake.

Fishing: Lake supports small populations of fish. Use a canoe/float tube
Silver Salmon / fair / mid-October / 5-10 lbs. / spoons, spinners, bait.
Arctic Grayling / fair / June – September / 7-12 in. / spinners, flies.
Northern Pike / poor / June – September / 2-6 lbs. / spoons, plugs, bait.
Burbot / fair / March – April, September – December / 2-6 lbs. / bait.

70. Delta Clearwater River (Middle)

Access: Clearwater Campground - MP 268.2; E on Jack Warren Rd. 11.5 miles to sign, left on access road short distance to river.

Fishing: This spring-fed river enjoys the largest run of silver salmon in Interior as well as a healthy population of grayling, some specimens of which may reach trophy proportions. Good action from shore but a boat is necessary to reach river mouth or headwaters.
Silver Salmon / good-excellent / 5-10 lbs. (15 lbs.) / spinners, flies.
Arctic Grayling / fair-good / 7-14 in. (20 in.) / spinners, flies.

FISH ▽	JAN	FEB	MAR	APR	MAY	JUN	JUL	AUG	SEP	OCT	NOV	DEC
SS*												
AG												

Note: Timing shown for salmon indicates fish in all stages of maturity.

71. Bluff Cabin Lake

Access: MP 271.8; N on Tanana Loop Rd. 1.3 mile to junction, right fork 2.3 miles to ATV trailhead. Trail leads 4.0 miles N to lake.

Fishing: Lake is stocked with trout. Use a canoe/float tube.
Rainbow Trout / good / June, September – December / 7-16 in. / spinners, flies, bait.

72. Big D Pond

Access: MP 274.6; W on Old Richardson Hwy. 1.5 mile to pond.
Fishing: Pond is stocked with trout. Use a canoe/float tube.
Rainbow Trout / good / June, September – December / 7-15 in. / spinners, flies, bait.

73. Tanana River (Middle)

Access: MP 275.3; highway crosses river.
Fishing: Heavily silted glacial river with very limited angling opportunities. Some grayling and burbot may be caught in early spring and late fall when water clears up.
Arctic Grayling / fair / March – April, October – November / 7-14 in. / spinners.
Burbot / fair / March – April, September – December / 2-8 lbs. / bait.

74. Quartz Lake

Access: MP 277.8; E on Quartz Lake Rd. 2.6 miles to lake.
Fishing: Lake contains large numbers of stocked landlocked salmon, trout, and char. This is also one of the more popular ice fishing spots in the valley. Big fish possible.
Landlocked Salmon / good-excellent / 7-14 in. (20 in.) / jigs, bait.
Rainbow Trout / good-excellent / 8-20 in. (8 lbs.) / spoons, flies, bait.
Arctic Char / fair-good / 8-20 in. (12 lbs.) / spoons, jigs, bait.

FISH ▽	JAN	FEB	MAR	APR	MAY	JUN	JUL	AUG	SEP	OCT	NOV	DEC
LS												
RT												
AC												

75. Little Lost Lake

Access: MP 277.8; E on Quartz Lake Rd. 2.2 miles to lake on left.
Fishing: Lake is stocked with trout. Use a canoe/float tube.
Rainbow Trout / fair-good / June, September – December / 7-15 in. / spinners, flies, bait.

76. 81-Mile Pond

Access: MP 284.5; turnout. Pond is adjacent to NE side of highway.
Fishing: Pond is stocked with trout. Use a canoe/float tube, casting from shore possible.
Rainbow Trout / good / June, September – December / 7-15 in. / spinners, flies, bait.

77. Shaw Creek / Tenana River confluence

Access: MP 286.7; highway crosses stream.
Fishing: Salmon are best at mouth of stream. Large spring run of grayling.
Chum Salmon / poor / mid-September – mid-October / 5-10 lbs. / spoons, spinners.
Silver Salmon / fair / late September – early October / 5-10 lbs. / spinners, flies, bait.
Arctic Grayling / good-excellent / early April – early May / 7-14 in. / spinners, flies.
Burbot / fair-good / April – May, October – December / 2-8 lbs. / bait.

78. Shaw Pond

Access: MP 287.2; turnout. Pond is adjacent to NE side of highway.

Fishing: Pond is stocked with trout and char. Use a canoe/float tube.
Rainbow Trout / good / June, September – December / 7-15 in. / spinners, flies, bait.
Arctic Char / fair / June, September – January / 7-15 in. / spoons, jigs, bait.

79. Birch Lake

Access: MP 306.0; turnout. Lake is adjacent to N side of highway.
Fishing: Lake contains large numbers of stocked landlocked salmon, trout, char, and grayling. Popular spot for ice fishing. Some big fish caught here in spring and fall.
Landlocked Salmon / good-excellent / 7-12 in. (20 in.) / jigs, bait.
Rainbow Trout / good-excellent / 8-18 in. (6 lbs.) / spoons, flies, bait.
Arctic Char / fair-good / 8-20 in. (12 lbs.) / spoons, jigs, bait.
Arctic Grayling / poor / 10-16 in. (20 in.) / spinners, flies.

FISH ▽	JAN	FEB	MAR	APR	MAY	JUN	JUL	AUG	SEP	OCT	NOV	DEC
LS												
RT												
AC												
AG												

80. Lost Lake

Access: MP 306.2; S on Lost Lake Rd. 0.5 mile to a "Y," right fork leads short distance to lake.
Fishing: Lake is stocked with salmon, trout, and char. Use a canoe/float tube.
Landlocked Salmon / good / June – March / 7-12 in. / spinners, jigs, flies, bait.
Rainbow Trout / good / June, September – December / 7-15 in. / spoons, flies, bait.
Arctic Char / fair / June, September – January / 7-15 in. / spoons, jigs, bait.
Lake Trout / fair / June, September – January / 7-16 in. / spoons, plugs, bait.

81. Mosquito Creek Lake

Access: MP 315.2; E on Mosquito Creek Woodcutting Rd. 0.2 mile to lake on right.
Fishing: Lake is stocked with trout. Use a canoe/float tube.
Rainbow Trout / good / 7-15 in. / June, September – December / spinners, flies, bait.

82. Little Harding Lake

Access: MP 319.8; NE on paved road 0.4 mile to a "T," right fork 0.4 mile, right on access road next to sign, short distance to small parking area. Trail leads 100 yards to lake.
Fishing: Lake is stocked with trout. Use a canoe/float tube.
Rainbow Trout / good / June, September / 7-18 in. / spoons, spinners, flies.

83. Harding Lake

Access: MP 321.6; E on Harding Dr. 1.4 mile to a "Y," right fork leads to lake, left fork to campground.
Fishing: Lake supports decent population of char and burbot. Trophy lake trout fishery, known for catches up to 20-30 pounds. Char up to 15 pounds possible. A boat is recom-

mended to access best areas. Productive ice fishing.

Lake Trout / fair / June, September – November / 2-6 lbs. / spoons, plugs, bait.

Arctic Char / fair-good / June, September – January / 8-24 in. / spoons, jigs, bait.

Burbot / poor-fair / March – April, November – December / 2-5 lbs. / jigs, bait.

84. Salcha River (Middle)

Access: MP 323.4; highway crosses river. Campground and river is reached by gravel road from MP 323.1.

Fishing: Tannic river with mid-summer runs of king and chum salmon. Good grayling catches early and late in the season. A boat is necessary to access best holes.

King Salmon / fair / 15-30 lbs. (50 lbs.) / spinners, attractors, flies.

Chum Salmon / poor-fair / 5-10 lbs. (15 lbs.) / spoons, spinners, flies.

Arctic Grayling / fair-good / 7-14 in. (20 in.) / spinners, flies.

Whitefish / poor / 10-20 in. (5 lbs.) / flies, bait.

Northern Pike / poor / 2-5 lbs. (10 lbs.) / spoons, plugs, bait.

Burbot / poor / 2-4 lbs. (8 lbs.) / bait.

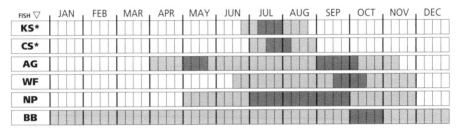

Note: Timing shown for salmon indicates fish in all stages of maturity.

85. Little Salcha River

Access: MP 327.8; highway crosses stream.

Fishing: Salmon spawning stream with opportunities for grayling in summer.

Arctic Grayling / fair / mid-June – mid-September / 7-12 in. / spinners, flies.

86. Johnson Road #1 Lake

Access: MP 330.4; N on Johnson Rd. 0.3 mile, turn left, then immediate right, 0.4 mile and left, short distance to pond.

Fishing: Lake is stocked with trout. Use a canoe/float tube.

Rainbow Trout / good / June, September – December / 7-15 in. / spinners, flies, bait.

87. 31-Mile Pond

Access: MP 332.0; NE on access road short distance to pond.

Fishing: Pond is stocked with trout and char. Use a canoe/float tube.

Rainbow Trout / good / June, September – December / 7-15 in. / spinners, flies, bait.

Arctic Char / fair / June, September – January / 7-15 in. / spoons, jigs, bait.

Other Locations

Unit A: Port Valdez Drainages:
Crooked Creek - (Valdez); *** Closed to Fishing *** **Dayville Road:** Solomon Gulch Creek - MP 4.1; PS,CS,SS,DV

Unit B: Copper Valley Drainages:
Tsina River - MP 32.0/37.3; (DV) Stuart Creek - MP 45.6; DV,AG Squaw Creek - 53.8; DV Tazlina River - MP 110.7; AG, (KS,RS,ST,RT,WF,BB) Dry Creek - MP 118.0; AG Gillespie Creek - MP 168.1; AG Fish Creek - MP 190.5; AG, (RS,RT)

Unit C: Delta River Drainage:
Phelan Creek - MP 201.5; AG Delta River - MP 214.0; AG,WF Jarvis Creek - MP 264.9; AG

LOCATION & SPECIES APPENDIX

● - Wild/Native fish, fishable numbers.
◆ - Present in small numbers and/or only occasionally caught.
▲ - Stocked/Hatchery fish, fishable numbers.
■ - Mix of Wild and Hatchery fish, fishable numbers.
× - Indicated species present but currently protected by law (PROHIBITED).

#	LOCATION	King Salmon	Red Salmon	Pink Salmon	Chum Salmon	Silver Salmon	Landlocked Salmon	Kokanee	Steelhead Trout	Rainbow Trout	Lake Trout	Arctic Char	Dolly Varden	Arctic Grayling	Sheefish	Whitefish	Northern Pike	Burbot	Pacific Halibut	Ling Cod	Rockfish
1.	Port Valdez	◆	◆	■	◆	■							●								
2.	Ruth Pond									▲											
3.	Robe River (Lower)	◆	●	●	●	●						◆	●								
4.	Robe River (Middle)	◆	●	●	◆	●						◆	●								
	Dayville Road																				
5.	Lowe River (Lower)	×	×	×	×	×							●								
6.	6 1/2-Mile Creek			×	×	×							●								
7.	Solomon Gulch Creek	◆	◆	■	●	■							●								
8.	Allison Point	◆	◆	■	●	■							●								
	Richardson Hwy. (cont.)																				
9.	Robe Lake		×	×	×	×						◆	●								
10.	Lowe River (Upper)	×	×	×	×	×							●								
11.	Thompson Lake													▲							
12.	Blueberry Lake									▲											
13.	Tiekel River												●								
14.	Little Tonsina River	×	◆							●			◆	●			●	◆			
15.	Little Tonsina River (Mouth)	×	●							●			◆	●			●	◆			
16.	Tonsina River (Middle)	●	◆							●			◆	●			●	◆			
17.	Squirrel Creek Pit													▲							
18.	Squirrel Creek	◆	◆							●				●			●				
19.	Pippin Lake													▲							
20.	Willow Creek																●				

#	LOCATION	KING SALMON	RED SALMON	PINK SALMON	CHUM SALMON	SILVER SALMON	LANDLOCKED SALMON	STEELHEAD TROUT	KOKANEE	RAINBOW TROUT	LAKE TROUT	ARCTIC CHAR	DOLLY VARDEN	SHEEFISH	ARCTIC GRAYLING	WHITEFISH	NORTHERN PIKE	BURBOT	PACIFIC HALIBUT	LING COD	ROCKFISH
21.	Klutina River (Lower)	●	●		◆					◆	◆				●		●	◆			
22.	Klutina River (Upper)	●	●		◆					◆	◆	◆			●		●	◆			
23.	Klutina Lake	●	◆		◆						◆				●		●	◆			
24.	Bear Creek														●						
25.	Gulkana River (Lower)	●	■							●	●				●		●	◆			
26.	Poplar Grove Creek														●						
27.	Gulkana River (Middle)	●	■							●	●				●		●	◆			
28.	Sourdough Creek		◆												●			◆			
28.	Haggard Creek														●						
30.	June Lake														●		◆				
31.	Nita Lake														●		◆				
32.	Gillespie Lake														●						
33.	Meiers Lake														●			●			
34.	Dick Lake										▲				◆			◆			
35.	Paxson Lake	×	■							●	●				●		●	●			
36.	East Fork Gulkana River		×							◆	◆				●		◆	◆			
37.	Fish Lake		◆							◆					●						
38.	Summit Lake		■							●	●				●		◆	●			
39.	Gunn Creek		◆							◆					●		◆				
40.	Fielding Lake										●				●		◆	×			
41.	Rapids Lake									▲	▲										
42.	Donnelly Creek														●						
	Coal Mine Road																				
43.	Coal Mine #5 Lake														▲						
44.	Backdown Lake														▲		▲				
45.	Last Lake														▲		▲				
46.	Brodie Lake						▲								▲		▲				
47.	Paul's Pond												◆				▲				
48.	Rangeview Lake														▲		▲				
49.	Dick's Pond														▲		◆				
50.	Ken's Pond														▲		▲				
	Richardson Hwy. (cont.)																				
51.	Weasel Lake														▲		●				
52.	Donnelly Lake														▲		▲				
	Ridge Road																				
53.	Ghost Lake														▲	◆	▲				
54.	Nickel Lake														▲	◆	▲	▲			
55.	"J" Lake														▲		▲				
56.	Chet Lake														▲	◆	▲				
57.	West Pond														▲						

#	LOCATION	KING SALMON	RED SALMON	PINK SALMON	CHUM SALMON	SILVER SALMON	LANDLOCKED SALMON	KOKANEE	STEELHEAD TROUT	RAINBOW TROUT	LAKE TROUT	ARCTIC CHAR	DOLLY VARDEN	SHEEFISH	ARCTIC GRAYLING	WHITEFISH	NORTHERN PIKE	BURBOT	PACIFIC HALIBUT	LING COD	ROCKFISH
	Meadows Road																				
58.	Sheefish Lake														▲						
59.	Bullwinkle Lake									▲					◆						
60.	Bolio Lake									▲					▲		▲				
61.	Luke Pond																▲				
62.	Mark Lake									▲					▲		▲				
63.	North Twin Lake														▲		◆				
64.	South Twin Lake														▲						
65.	No Mercy Lake														▲						
66.	Rockhound Lake														▲						
67.	Doc Lake														▲						
68.	Big Lake														▲						
	Richardson Hwy. (cont.)																				
69.	Clearwater Lake				◆	●									●	◆	●	●			
70.	Delta Clearwater River	◆			◆	●									●	◆	●	◆			
71.	Bluff Cabin Lake														▲						
72.	Tanana River	◆			◆	◆									●	◆	◆	●			
73.	Big D Pond														▲						
74.	Quartz Lake									▲					▲		▲				
75.	Little Lost Lake														▲						
76.	81-Mile Pond														▲			◆			
77.	Shaw Creek (Mouth)	◆			●	●									●	●	◆	●			
78.	Shaw Pond														▲		▲				
79.	Birch Lake									▲					▲		▲				
80.	Lost Lake									▲					▲	◆	▲				
81.	Mosquito Creek Lake														▲						
82.	Little Harding Lake														▲						
83.	Harding Lake											●			▲	◆	●	●			
84.	Salcha River (Middle)	●			●	◆									●	●	●	●			
85.	Little Salcha River	◆			◆										●	◆	◆				
86.	Johnson Road #1 Lake														▲		◆				
87.	31-Mile Pond														▲		▲				

Seward Highway

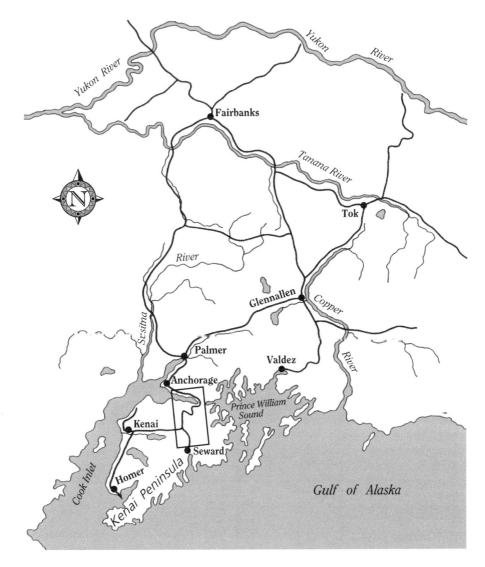

Area Covered: Anchorage - Seward; 127 miles
Regulatory Units: (A) Turnagain Arm Drainages; (B) Kenai Lake Drainage; (C) Resurrection Bay Drainages
Number of Locations: 66

FISHING THE SEWARD HIGHWAY

The Seward Highway serves as a link between Anchorage and coastal fishing communities on the Kenai Peninsula. It parallels or crosses a multitude of fish-rich streams, rivers, and lakes with additional access to ocean fishing. Salmon and sea-run char are plentiful in Turnagain Arm drainages and Resurrection Bay. King and silver salmon and halibut are the most sought-after species. Trout (both native and stocked rainbows) and char are more common in the central portion of Kenai Peninsula, especially in tributaries of Kenai and Trail lakes. Even grayling are frequently taken in a few locations as a result of past stocking efforts. Salt water species, like halibut and rockfish, are available in Resurrection Bay, though they are not, with few exceptions, caught consistently from shore. Angler success is good in both fresh and salt water.

Boaters have prime access to Portage area rivers (20-Mile and Placer) and their tributaries for salmon and char, and the outer parts of Passage Canal and Resurrection Bay for salmon and bottomfish.

Angling pressure is for the most part fairly light, except in a few locations (such as Bird and Resurrection creeks and Resurrection Bay waters) during the peak of salmon runs in summer and early fall when it becomes very heavy.

Recommended Hot Spots: Bird, California, lower Sixmile, Resurrection, Ptarmigan, and Salmon creeks; Trail River; Upper Summit, Carter, Crescent, Vagt, Ptarmigan, Long, Meridian, Troop, and Grouse lakes; Alder, Willow, Tangle, and Preacher ponds; Seward Harbor; West Resurrection Bay; Fourth of July Creek, Lowell Creek, and Tonsina Creek marine waters.

Content   Pages

QUICK REFERENCE

| Road Condition | Parking Area | Camp Sites | Hiking Trails | Boat Launch | Handicap Access | Fishing Pressure |

■ - Good to Highly developed/conditions, intense pressure
● - Fair to Moderately developed/conditions, moderate pressure
◆ - Poor to marginally developed/conditions, limited pressure
✕ - Prohibited

Map 1: Unit A: Turnagain Arm Drainages

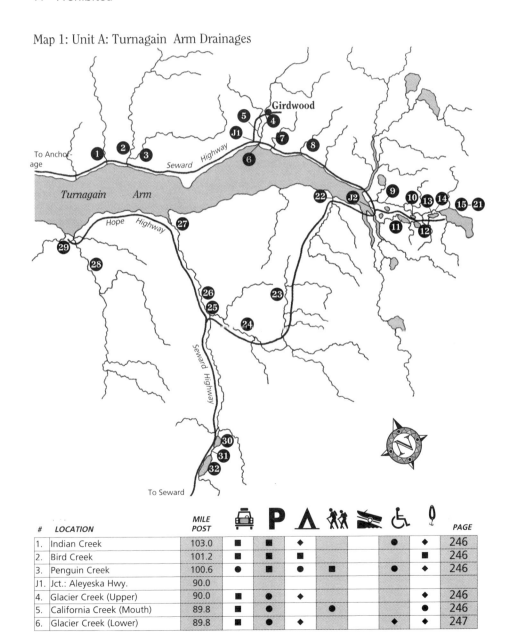

#	LOCATION	MILE POST	🚗	P	A	🚶	🚤	♿	Q	PAGE
1.	Indian Creek	103.0	■	■	◆			●	◆	246
2.	Bird Creek	101.2	■	■	■				■	246
3.	Penguin Creek	100.6	●	■	●	■		●	◆	246
J1.	Jct.: Aleyeska Hwy.	90.0								
4.	Glacier Creek (Upper)	90.0	■	●	◆				◆	246
5.	California Creek (Mouth)	89.8	■	●		●			●	246
6.	Glacier Creek (Lower)	89.8	■	●	◆		◆		◆	247

#	LOCATION	MILE POST	🚗	P	⛺	🥾	🚤	♿	⚓	PAGE
7.	Virgin Creek		■						◆	247
8.	Kern Creek	86.3	■	◆					◆	247
9.	Portage Creek (No. 2)	79.4	■	■	◆				◆	247
J2.	Jct.: Portage Glacier Rd.	79.2								
	Portage Glacier Road									
J2.	Jct.: Seward Hwy.	0								
10.	Willow Pond	1.2	●	■	■	■		●	◆	247
11.	Alder Pond	1.5	●	●	◆	■		■	◆	248
12.	Explorer Creek	1.8/2.4	●	●	◆	●		●	◆	248
13.	Tangle Pond	3.3	●	■	●			■	◆	248
14.	Williwaw Creek (Mouth)	3.6	■	◆					◆	248
	Whittier Access Road									
15.	Barge Creek	0	●	●	◆			●	●	248
16.	Shakespeare Creek Marine	0.4	■	■	◆			◆	●	249
17.	Passage Canal (West End)	0.6-1.0	■	◆					◆	249
18.	Whittier Creek	1.3	■	■	●				●	249
19.	Whittier Harbor	1.7	■	■			■	●	●	249
20.	Smitty's Cove	1.4	●	●			■	●	●	249
21.	Cove Creek Marine	1.4	●	●	◆			◆	●	250
	Seward Hwy. (cont.)	79.2								
22.	Ingram Creek	75.3	■	■	◆			●	◆	250
23.	Granite Creek									
	Access A	63.3	■	◆					◆	250
	Access B	62.5	■	■	■	●		◆	◆	250
24.	East Fork Sixmile Creek	61.6-56.7	■	●	◆				◆	250
J3.	Jct.: Hope Hwy.	56.1								
	Hope Highway									
J3.	Jct.: Seward Hwy.	0								
25.	Canyon Creek (Mouth)	0.2	●	■	◆				◆	251
26.	Sixmile Creek (Middle)									
	Access A	0.6-2.4	■	●	◆	●			◆	251
	Access B	3.8-6.5	■	●					◆	251
27.	Sixmile Creek (Lower)	7.1	●	●	◆		◆	●	◆	251
28.	Resurrection Cr. (Upper)	16.2	●	●				●	●	251
29.	Resurrection Creek (Lower)	16.3	●	■				●	●	252
	Seward Hwy. (cont.)	56.1								
30.	Lower Summit Lake	47.3	■	■	◆			●	◆	252
31.	Canyon Creek (Upper)	47.3-46.0	■	●					◆	252
32.	Upper Summit Lake									
	Access A	45.8	●	●	■			◆	◆	252
	Access B	46.0-44.6	■	●			◆	◆	◆	252
33.	Summit Creek	42.6	■	◆					◆	253
34.	Quartz Creek (Upper)									
	Access A	42.2-41.0	■	◆					◆	253
	Access B	39.5	■	■	◆	■			◆	253
35.	Jerome Lake	38.6	■	■				◆	◆	253
J4.	Jct.: Sterling Hwy.	37.0								
36.	Carter Lake	33.1	■	■	◆	●			◆	253
37.	Crescent Lake	33.1	■	■	◆	●			◆	254
38.	Moose Creek									
	Access A	32.9-32.2	■	●					◆	254
	Access B	32.3	●	■	◆			●	◆	254
39.	Upper Trail Lake									
	Access A	32.3	●	■	◆			◆	◆	254
	Access B	30.3	●	■	◆		●	■	◆	254

Map 2: Unit B: Kenai Lake Drainage

#	LOCATION	MILE POST	🚗	P	△	🥾	🚤	♿	⚓	PAGE
40.	Lower Trail Lake	25.3	■	●	◆			◆	◆	254
41.	Vagt Lake	25.3	●	●	◆	●			◆	254
42.	Trail River									
	Access A	25.3-25.1	■	●	◆			◆	◆	254
	Access B	24.1	●	■	■	●			●	254
43.	Kenai Lake									
	Access A	24.1	●	■	■	●			●	255
	Access B	23.5	●	■	✕		●	■	◆	255
	Access C	23.4	●	●	◆	●			●	255
	Access D	17.0	●	■	●		●	●	◆	255

Map 3: Unit C: Resurrection
   Bay Drainages

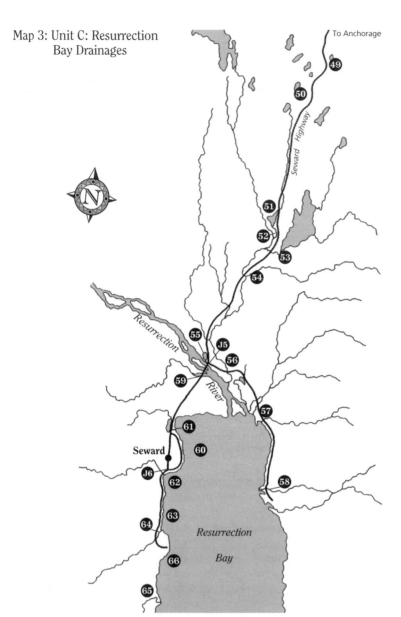

#	LOCATION	MILE POST	🚗	**P**	⛺	🥾	🛶	♿	🎣	PAGE
44.	Ptarmigan Creek									
	Access A	23.4	●	●	◆	●			●	255
	Access B	23.3	■	■	■	●		◆	●	255
45.	Ptarmigan Lake	23.2	■	■	■	●			◆	255
46.	Long Lake	16.1	■	●		●			◆	255
47.	Meridian Lake	13.3	■	●	◆	●			◆	255
48.	Grayling Lake	13.3	■	●	◆	●			◆	255
49.	Goldenfin Lake	11.6	■	●		●			◆	256
50.	Troop Lake	10.9	■	●		●			◆	256

#	LOCATION	MILE POST	🚗	P	⛺	🚶	🛥	♿	⚓	PAGE
51.	Grouse Lake	7.4	■	■	◆			◆	●	256
52	Grouse Creek (Lower)	7.3	■	◆				◆		256
53.	Bear Creek									
	Access A	6.6	●	◆				◆		256
	Access B	6.5	●	●	●		●	◆		256
54.	Salmon Creek (Upper)	5.9	■	◆				◆		257
55.	Preacher Pond	3.4	■	●	◆			●	●	257
J5.	Jct.: Nash Rd.	3.3								
	Nash Road									
J5.	Jct.: Seward Hwy.	0								
56.	Salmon Creek (Lower)	0.5	■	◆				◆		257
57.	Creek, No Name Marine	2.3	■	●				◆		257
58.	Fourth of July Creek Marine	5.1	●	■	●			●	●	257
	Seward									
59.	Resurrection River	2.8	■	●				◆		258
60.	Resurrection Bay (NW)	(Seward)								
	Access A		●	■	◆			●	●	258
	Access B		■	■	●				●	258
61.	Seward Lagoon Creek	(Seward)	●	■	◆			◆	■	259
	Lowell Point Road									
J6.	Jct.: 3rd Ave.	0								
62.	Lowell Creek Marine	0.3	●	●					■	259
63.	Resurrection Bay (W)	0.4-1.5	●	●					●	259
64.	Spruce Creek Marine	1.9	●	●					◆	260
65.	Tonsina Creek Marine	2.2	●	■		●			◆	260
66.	Lowell Point									
	Access A	2.3	●	●	×			◆	◆	260
	Access B	2.4	●	●	◆		●	◆	◆	260

SEWARD HIGHWAY LOCATIONS

Unit A: Turnagain Arm Drainages

Includes all roadside waters flowing into and surrounding Turnagain Arm.

UNIT REGULATIONS:

* King salmon fishing prohibited: All waters, year-round.

UNIT TIMING

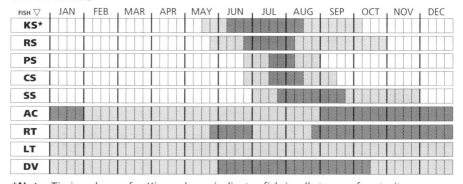

Note: *Timing shown for King salmon indicates fish in all stages of maturity.*

1. Indian Creek
Access: MP 103.0; highway crosses stream.
Fishing: Small clearwater stream with decent action for pink salmon and char.
Pink Salmon / fair-good / mid-, late July / 2-4 lbs. / spoons, spinners, flies.
Silver Salmon / poor / mid-, late August / 5-10 lbs. / spinners,flies, bait.
Dolly Varden / fair / early June – mid-July / 7-15 in. / spoons, spinners, bait.

2. Bird Creek
Access: MP 101.2; highway crosses stream. Parking areas located both sides of highway east of bridge with trails leading to creek.
Fishing: The premier roadside salmon sport fishery in Turnagain Arm. Superb opportunities for stocked silver salmon and wild runs of pink and chum salmon.
Pink Salmon / good-excellent / 2-4 lbs. (7 lbs.) / spoons, spinners, flies.
Chum Salmon / fair-good / 6-12 lbs. (18 lbs.) / spoons, spinners, flies.
Silver Salmon / excellent / 6-12 lbs. (18 lbs.) / spinners, flies, bait.
Dolly Varden / fair / 7-15 in. (5 lbs.) / spoons, spinners, bait.

FISH ▽	JAN	FEB	MAR	APR	MAY	JUN	JUL	AUG	SEP	OCT	NOV	DEC
PS						▓	▓	▓				
CS						▓	▓	▓				
SS						▓	▓	▓	▓			
DV					▓	▓	▓	▓	▓			

3. Penguin Creek
Access: MP 100.6; NE on Konikson Rd. 0.6 mile to parking area. Wide trail leads 0.25 mile to stream.
Fishing: Salmon spawning stream with decent action for char in late summer.
Dolly Varden / poor-fair / mid-July – mid-August / 7-12 in. / flies, bait.

4. Glacier Creek (Upper)
Access: MP 90.0; N on Alyeska Highway 2.2 miles to stream crossing. Before bridge, turn right on Egloff (Glacier Creek) Dr. short distance to parking/picnic area on left. Trail leads 100 yards to stream.
Fishing: Limited opportunities in summer due to turbid conditions. Try in early fall.
Pink Salmon / poor / early August / 2-4 lbs. / spoons, spinners, flies.
Chum Salmon / poor / mid-August / 6-10 lbs. / spoons, flies, bait.
Silver Salmon / fair / mid-September / 6-10 lbs. / spinners, flies, bait.
Dolly Varden / poor-fair / late July – late August / 7-15 in. / spinners, flies, bait.

5. California Creek / Glacier Creek Confluence
Access: MP 89.8; NE on East Rd. short distance and park next to highway bridge. Hike upstream along north bank of Glacier Creek about 0.25 mile to railroad trestle bridge. Confluence area is located upstream of bridge.
Fishing: Local hot spot with productive angling for mainly pink and silver salmon.
Red Salmon / poor / 4-6 lbs. (8 lbs.) / spinners, flies.
Pink Salmon / good-excellent / 2-4 lbs. (6 lbs.) / spoons, spinners.

Chum Salmon / fair / 6-10 lbs. (15 lbs.) / spoons, spinners, attractors.
Silver Salmon / fair-good / 4-10 lbs. (16 lbs.) / spinners, bait.
Dolly Varden / fair-good / 7-15 in. (4 lbs.) / spinners, flies, bait.

FISH ▽	JAN	FEB	MAR	APR	MAY	JUN	JUL	AUG	SEP	OCT	NOV	DEC
RS												
PS												
CS												
SS												
DV												

6. Glacier Creek (Lower)

Access: MP 89.8; highway crosses stream.
Fishing: Glacial drainage with limited summer opportunities. Best in fall for silver salmon when water drops and clears. Scout deep holes and runs for fish.
Pink Salmon / fair / mid-, late July / 2-4 lbs. / spoons, spinners, attractors.
Silver Salmon / fair / mid-August – late September / 4-10 lbs. / attractors, bait.
Dolly Varden / fair / early June – mid-July / 7-15 in. / attractors, bait.

7. Virgin Creek

Access: MP 89.2; highway crosses stream.
Fishing: Small muskeg stream containing sea-run char during summer months.
Dolly Varden / fair / early June – mid-July / 7-15 in. / spoons, spinners, bait.

8. Kern Creek

Access: MP 86.3; highway crosses stream. **Note:** The mouth of Kern Creek is visible at low tide only. Upstream stretches can be found on other side of railroad tracks.
Fishing: Best action is at mouth on a low tide for sea-run char; few fish upstream.
Dolly Varden / fair / early June – mid-August / 7-15 in. / spoons, spinners, bait.

9. Portage Creek (No. 2)

Access: MP 79.4; highway crosses stream.
Fishing: Glacial drainage with decent populations of salmon and char during summer and fall months. Use bait or high-visibility tackle.
Pink Salmon / poor-fair / mid-, late July / 2-4 lbs. / attractors.
Silver Salmon / fair / early, mid-September / 6-12 lbs. / attractors, bait.
Dolly Varden / fair / early June – mid-July / 7-15 in. / attractors, bait.

SEWARD HIGHWAY log continues on page 250.

Portage Glacier Road

Road begins at MP 79.2 Seward Highway (MP 0) and ends at Portage Lake (MP 5.5).

10. Willow Pond

Access: MP 1.2; N on access road by sign short distance to parking area. Trails lead 50 yards to pond.
Fishing: Pond is stocked with trout. Easily fished from shore.
Rainbow Trout / fair-good / May, September – December / 7-15 in. / spinners, flies, bait.

11. Alder Pond
Access: MP 1.5; SW on gravel road by sign, follow left fork at "Y" 0.1 mile to pond.
Fishing: Pond is stocked with trout. Easily fished from shore.
Rainbow Trout / fair-good / May, September – December / 7-15 in. / spinners, flies, bait.

12. Explorer Creek
Access A: MP 1.8; SW on gravel road short distance to three-way split, middle fork leads 0.4 mile to stream.
Access B: MP 2.4; park at paved turnoff by Explorer Pond. Trail leads 150 yards to lake outlet and stream.
Fishing: Glacial stream containing small char in early summer. Salmon spawning area.
Dolly Varden / poor-fair / early, mid-July / 7-12 in. / spinners, flies, bait.

13. Tangle Pond
Access: MP 3.3; N on gravel road by sign short distance to pond.
Fishing: Pond is stocked with trout. Easily fished from shore.
Rainbow Trout / fair-good / May, September – December / 7-16 in. / spinners, flies, bait.
Arctic Char / fair-good / May, September – January / 7-16 in. / spoons, jigs, bait.

14. Williwaw Creek / Portage Creek Confluence
Access: MP 3.6; road crosses Williwaw Creek, confluence area is located on the left.
Fishing: Salmon school at confluence in summer and fall along with a few char. Most salmon are in or near spawning condition; few bright specimens available.
Chum Salmon / poor / late July – early August / 6-10 lbs. / spoons, spinners.
Silver Salmon / poor-fair / mid-, late September / 6-10 lbs. / spoons, spinners, bait.
Dolly Varden / poor / mid-July – early September / 7-12 in. / spoons, bait.

Whittier Access Road
Whittier Access Road begins at MP 5.0 Portage Glacier Road. Follow main right of way straight through the first tunnel to tool booths and Bear Valley Staging Area. Pass through main tunnel 2.5 miles to Whittier Staging Area. All locations in and around Whittier are described in miles from the terminus of the staging area (Mile 0).

15. Barge Creek Marine
Access: Mile 0; N on gravel road (Airstrip Access Trail) immediately after staging area, 0.2 mile to end of road and beach area. Mouth of creek is next to barge, on the right.
Fishing: Salmon spawning stream. Bright specimens off mouth on high tides.
Pink Salmon / fair-good / late July – early August / 2-5 lbs. / spoons, spinners, flies.
Chum Salmon / fair / late July – early August / 6-10 lbs. / spoons, spinners, flies.
Silver Salmon / fair / late September – mid-October / 6-12 lbs. / spinners, flies, bait.
Dolly Varden / fair / mid-June – mid-August / 7-15 in. / spoons, spinners, flies.

16. Shakespeare Creek Marine

Access: Mile 0.4; road crosses stream. Access road at Mile 0.5 E to parking area and west end of Passage Canal.

Fishing: Good run of pink and stocked silver salmon; fish gather in schools near beach on tides. Try area at mouth of small clearwater stream south of Shakespeare Creek.
King Salmon / poor / 15-30 lbs. (50 lbs.) / spoons, spinners, bait.
Pink Salmon / fair-good / 2-5 lbs. (7 lbs.) / spoons, spinners, flies, bait.
Chum Salmon / poor / 6-10 lbs. (15 lbs.) / spoons, spinners, flies.
Silver Salmon / good-excellent / 6-15 lbs. (20 lbs.) / spinners, flies, bait.
Dolly Varden / fair / 7-15 in. (5 lbs.) / spoons, spinners, flies.

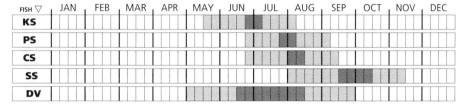

17. Passage Canal (West End)

Access: Mile 0.6-1.0; road parallels south shore of canal. Turn off at the Shakespeare Creek Marine (Mile 0.4), park, and walk on paved trail next to road to and along canal.

Fishing: Scout for schools of salmon on incoming tide. A few feeder king salmon available in spring and early summer. Small rockfish may be caught in deeper areas.
King Salmon / poor / mid-June – early July / 12-35 lbs. / spoons, spinners, bait.
Pink Salmon / fair-good / late July – early August / 2-5 lbs. / spoons, spinners, bait.
Silver Salmon / good / mid-September – mid-October / 6-15 lbs. / spoons, spinners, bait.
Dolly Varden / fair / mid-June – mid-August / 7-15 in. / spoons, spinners, flies.
Rockfish / poor / mid-June – late August / 8-20 in. / jigs, bait.

18. Whittier Creek

Access: Mile 1.3; road crosses stream. Park by side of road or in parking area south of bridge along Whittier St.

Fishing: Glacial stream with limited opportunity. Try in fall when water clears up.
Pink Salmon / poor / late July – early August / 2-5 lbs. / spoons, spinners.
Silver Salmon / fair / late September – mid-October / 6-15 lbs. / spinners, flies, bait.
Dolly Varden / poor / mid-June – mid-August / 7-15 in. / bait.

19. Whittier Harbor

Access: Mile 1.7; harbor is located N side of road. The boat ramp is a popular spot.
Fishing: Large schools of hatchery silver salmon available in fall; some pinks.
Pink Salmon / poor-fair / late July – early August / 2-5 lbs. / spoons, spinners, bait.
Silver Salmon / good / late September – mid-October / 6-15 lbs. / spoons, spinners, bait.

20. Smitty's Cove

Access: Mile 1.4; S on Whittier St. 0.5 mile to a "T," left fork 0.6 mile to end of road and cove. Private property; fee area.

Fishing: Hatchery silver salmon school up here in late summer and fall.
Pink salmon / fair-good / mid-July – early August / 2-4 lbs. / spoons, spinners, bait.
Chum salmon / poor / late July – mid-August / 6-10 lbs. / spoons, spinners, flies.
Silver salmon / good / late August – late September / 6-12 lbs. / spinners, bait.
Dolly Varden / poor / mid-June – mid-August / 7-15 in. / spoons, spinners, flies.

21. Cove Creek Marine

Access: Mile 1.4; S on Whittier St. 0.5 mile to a "T," right on Depot Rd. and immediate
left on gravel road (Blackstone Rd.) 0.2 mile up hill past old building, right on rough
road (Cove Creek Rd.) and follow right-of-way 0.6 mile to stream crossing, left on access
road after bridge short distance to parking/picnic area and cove.
Fishing: Large run of hatchery silver salmon in fall; decent return of pinks.
Pink salmon / fair-good / 2-4 lbs. (7 lbs.) / spoons, spinners, flies.
Silver salmon / good-excellent / 6-12 lbs. (20 lbs.) / spinners, flies, bait.
Dolly Varden / poor / 7-15 in. (5 lbs.) / spoons, spinners, flies.

FISH ▽	JAN	FEB	MAR	APR	MAY	JUN	JUL	AUG	SEP	OCT	NOV	DEC
PS						▓	▓					
SS								▓	▓			
DV					▓	▓	▓	▓				

SEWARD HIGHWAY log continues.

22. Ingram Creek

Access: MP 75.3; highway crosses stream.
Fishing: Clearwater stream offering mainly pinks and char; a few silvers in deep holes.
Pink Salmon / fair-good / mid-, late July / 2-4 lbs. / spoons, spinners, flies.
Silver Salmon / fair / mid-, late August / 5-10 lbs. / spinners, flies, bait.
Dolly Varden / fair / early June – mid-August / 7-15 in. / spinners, flies, bait.

23. Granite Creek

Access A: MP 63.3; highway crosses stream.
Access B: MP 62.5 - Granite Creek Campground; S on gravel road 0.5 mile to campground
and stream. Additional access by trail along stream to confluence with East Fork Sixmile
Creek.
Fishing: Salmon spawning stream with limited opportunities for resident char.
Silver Salmon / poor / late August – early September / 5-10 lbs. / spinners, flies, bait.
Dolly Varden / poor-fair / early July – early September / 7-12 in. / flies, bait.

24. East Fork Sixmile Creek

Access: MP 61.6-56.7; highway parallels stream, crossing it at MP 61.6.
Fishing: A few semi-bright chums and silvers and resident char available.
Silver Salmon / poor / late August – early September / 5-10 lbs. / spinners, flies, bait.
Dolly Varden / poor-fair / early July – early September / 7-12 in. / flies, bait.

SEWARD HIGHWAY log continues on page 252.

Hope Highway

Road begins at MP 56.1 Seward Highway (MP 0) and ends at Porcupine Creek Campground near the community of Hope (MP 17.7).

25. Canyon Creek / Sixmile Creek Confluence
Access: MP 0.2 Hope Hwy.; right on paved access road short distance to gravel road on left, 0.5 mile to parking area. Trail follows Canyon Creek 200 yards to confluence area.
Fishing: Some chums and silvers found here in late summer along with sea-run char.
Chum Salmon / fair-good / late July – early August / 6-12 lbs. / spoons, spinners, flies.
Silver Salmon / fair / mid-August – early September / 5-12 lbs. / spinners, flies, bait.
Dolly Varden / poor-fair / early July – late August / 7-12 in. / flies, bait.

26. Sixmile Creek (Middle)
Access A: MP 0.6-2.4; several pullouts E of road with trail access to creek.
Access B: MP 3.8-6.5; road parallels stream. Pullouts.
Fishing: Scout deeper holes and pools with some calmer water for salmon and char.
Chum Salmon / fair / late July – early August / 6-12 lbs. / spoons, spinners, flies.
Silver Salmon / fair / mid-August – early September / 5-12 lbs. / spinners, flies, bait.
Dolly Varden / poor-fair / early July – late August / 7-12 in. / flies, bait.

27. Sixmile Creek (Lower)
Access: MP 7.1; E on dirt road 0.3 mile to stream.
Fishing: Good number of salmon available but stream conditions can be unpredictable. Glacial water usually dictates bait or high-visibility lures. Look for calm areas.
Pink Salmon / fair-excellent / 2-4 lbs. (7 lbs.) / spoons, spinners.
Chum Salmon / fair-excellent / 6-12 lbs. (18 lbs.) / spoons, spinners, attractors.
Silver Salmon / fair-good / 5-12 lbs. (16 lbs.) / spinners, attractors, bait.
Dolly Varden / fair-good / 7-15 in. (5 lbs.) / spinners, attractors, bait.

FISH ▽	JAN	FEB	MAR	APR	MAY	JUN	JUL	AUG	SEP	OCT	NOV	DEC
PS							▨					
CS							▨					
SS								▨				
DV					▨	▨	▨	▨				

28. Resurrection Creek (Upper)
Access: MP 16.2; S on Palmer Creek Rd. 0.6 mile to a "Y," right on Resurrection Creek Rd. 3.3 miles to stream on right. Road parallels stream next 0.5 mile.
Fishing: Clearwater stream with decent opportunities for small char in summer.
Dolly Varden / poor-fair / mid-July – mid-August / 7-12 in. / flies, bait.

## CHAPTER 15

29. Resurrection Creek (Lower)

Access: MP 16.3; road crosses stream.

Fishing: A very popular spot to catch ocean bright pinks and chums. Fish the tides. Anglers hiking upstream will find deep holes and runs and sight fishing opportunities.

Pink Salmon / good-excellent / 2-4 lbs. (7 lbs.) / spoons, spinners, flies.
Chum Salmon / fair / 6-10 lbs. (15 lbs.) / spoons, spinners, flies.
Silver Salmon / fair-good / 6-10 lbs. (15 lbs.) / spinners, flies, bait.
Dolly Varden / fair / 7-15 in. (5 lbs.) / spoons, spinners, flies, bait.

FISH ▽	JAN	FEB	MAR	APR	MAY	JUN	JUL	AUG	SEP	OCT	NOV	DEC
PS							■	■				
CS							■	■				
SS								■	■			
DV						■	■	■				

SEWARD HIGHWAY log continues.

30. Lower Summit Lake

Access: MP 47.6 – 46.6; highway parallels lake.

Fishing: Mainly resident char in summer but some large trout available as well.

Rainbow Trout / fair / June, September – October / 8-18 in. / spinners, flies, bait.
Dolly Varden / fair-good / June, September – October / 7-12 in. / flies, bait.

31. Canyon Creek

Access: MP 47.3 – 46.0; highway parallels creek. Short hike E through low brush to creek.

Fishing: Summer months bring trout and small resident char into stream.

Rainbow Trout / poor / mid-June – mid-September / 7-15 in. / spinners, flies, bait.
Dolly Varden / fair / early July – mid-September / 7-12 in. / flies, bait.

32. Upper Summit Lake

Access A: MP 46.0 - Tenderfoot Creek Campground; E on dirt road 0.6 mile to campground and lake.

Access B: MP 45.8 – 44.5; highway parallels lake.

Fishing: Lake stocked with trout; fish to 8 pounds available. Resident char present.

Rainbow Trout / good / June, September – December / 8-18 in. / spinners, flies, bait.
Dolly Varden / fair-good / June, September – October / 7-12 in. / flies, bait.

Unit B: Kenai Lake Drainages

Includes all roadside waters flowing into and surrounding Kenai Lake.

UNIT REGULATIONS:

* Fishing prohibited: All flowing waters, April 15 – June 14.

* Salmon fishing prohibited: All waters, year-round.
* Only unbaited, single-hook, artificial lures: All flowing waters, year-round.

UNIT TIMING:

FISH ▽	JAN	FEB	MAR	APR	MAY	JUN	JUL	AUG	SEP	OCT	NOV	DEC
KS*												
RS*												
PS*												
CS*												
SS*												
RT												
LT												
DV												
AG												
WF												

*__*Note:__ Timing shown for salmon indicates fish in all stages of maturity.*

33. Summit Creek

Access: MP 42.6; highway crosses stream.
Fishing: A few nice-sized char are available during the fall spawning run. Scout holes.
Rainbow Trout / poor / late July – mid-September / 7-15 in. / spinners, flies.
Dolly Varden / fair / mid-August – mid-September / 8-18 in. / attractors, flies.

34. Quartz Creek (Upper)

Access A: MP 42.2 – 41.0; highway parallels stream, crossing it at MP 42.2.
Access B: MP 39.5 - Devil's Pass Trailhead; W on turnout to parking area. Trail leads about 0.5 mile to stream.
Fishing: Look for trout and char to be scattered throughout stream in late summer.
Rainbow Trout / fair / late July – mid-September / 8-16 in. / attractors, flies.
Dolly Varden / fair / early August – mid-September / 8-18 in. / attractors, flies.

35. Jerome Lake

Access: MP 38.6 – 38.3; highway parallels lake.
Fishing: Lake is stocked with trout. Resident char present. Easily fished from shore.
Rainbow Trout / good / May, September – December / 7-15 in. / spinners, flies, bait.
Dolly Varden / poor / May – June, September – January / 8-15 in. / spoons, jigs, bait.

36. Carter Lake

Access: MP 33.1 - Carter Lake Trailhead; turnout W of highway. Trail leads 1.0 mile S to lake on left.
Fishing: Lake is stocked with trout. Use canoe/float tube or cast from shore.
Rainbow Trout / good / June, September – December / 7-16 in. / spinners, flies, bait.

37. Crescent Lake

Access: MP 33.1 - Carter Lake Trailhead; turnout W of highway. Trail leads 3.0 miles S to lake inlet.

Fishing: Best place on the peninsula for hike-in grayling. Casting from shore is possible.
Dolly Varden / poor-fair / July – September / 7-15 in. / spoons, flies, bait.
Arctic Grayling / excellent / July – September / 7-14 in. / spinners, flies.

38. Moose Creek

Access A: MP 32.9; highway crosses stream.
Access B: MP 32.3; highway crosses stream. Additional access to stream mouth and Upper Trail Lake.

Fishing: Small salmon spawning stream supporting decent action for trout and char.
Rainbow Trout / poor-fair / early August – mid-September / 7-15 in. / spinners, flies.
Dolly Varden / fair / early August – mid-September / 7-18 in. / spinners, flies.

39. Upper Trail Lake

Access A: MP 32.3; N on access road short distance to Moose Creek bridge and lake inlet.
Access B: MP 30.3; NW on gravel road 0.1 mile to lake.

Fishing: Heavily silted lake with marginal angling opportunities. Use bait.
Rainbow Trout / poor-fair / August – October / 8-15 in. / spinners, bait.
Lake Trout / fair / May, August – October / 2-5 lbs. / spoons, spinners, bait.
Dolly Varden / fair / August – October / 8-15 in. / spoons, spinners, bait.

40. Lower Trail Lake

Access: MP 25.3; highway parallels lake.

Fishing: Heavily silted lake with limited angling opportunities. Use bait at outlet.
Rainbow Trout / fair / August – October / 8-15 in. / spinners, bait.
Lake Trout / fair / May, August – October / 2-5 lbs. / spoons, spinners, bait.
Dolly Varden / fair / August – October / 8-15 in. / spoons, spinners, bait.

41. Vagt Lake

Access: MP 25.3; park by bridge at S end of Trail Lake outlet. Vagt Lake Trail leads 1.5 mile NE to lake.

Fishing: Lake is stocked with trout. Some large fish present. Use canoe/float tube.
Rainbow Trout / good / May, September – December / 7-16 in. / spinners, flies, bait.

42. Trail River

Access A: MP 25.3-24.1; highway parallels river, crossing it at MP 25.3.
Access B: MP 24.1; W on gravel road 0.4 mile to river crossing, or continue 0.8 mile to campground and lower river.

Fishing: Glacial river with limited angling opportunities. Use fluorescent tackle.
Rainbow Trout / fair / early August – early October / 8-15 in. / attractors, flies.
Dolly Varden / good / early August – early October / 8-20 in. / attractors, flies.

43. Kenai Lake

Access A: MP 24.1 - Trail River Campground; W on gravel road 1.2 mile to campground. Locate trail leading along river to lake.
Access B: MP 23.5; W on #2497 road 0.2 mile to lake.
Access C: MP 23.4 - Ptarmigan Creek; SW on small gravel road along railroad tracks 0.3 mile to parking area and stream. Trail leads along creek to lake.
Access D: MP 17.0 - Primrose Creek Campground; W on gravel road 1.2 mile to campground and confluence of Primrose Creek and lake.
Fishing: Glacial lake supporting decent populations of trout and char.
Rainbow Trout / fair / July – September / 7-16 in. / spoons, flies, bait.
Lake Trout / fair / May – November / 3-5 lbs. / spoons, plugs, bait.
Dolly Varden / fair / July – September / 8-16 in. / spoons, flies, bait.

44. Ptarmigan Creek

Access A: MP 23.4; SW on small gravel road along railroad tracks 0.3 mile to parking area and stream. Trail leads along creek to Kenai Lake.
Access B: MP 23.2; highway crosses stream.
Fishing: Semi-glacial stream producing char and trout in late summer, fall.
Rainbow Trout / fair / early August – late September / 8-15 in. / attractors, flies.
Dolly Varden / fair-good / early August – late September / 8-18 in. / attractors, flies.

45. Ptarmigan Lake

Access: MP 23.2 - Ptarmigan Creek Trailhead; turnout E of highway. Trail leads 3.0 miles E to lake outlet and continues another 2.0 miles along shoreline.
Fishing: Semi-glacial lake producing char at outlet in late summer and early fall.
Dolly Varden / fair-good / August – September / 7-15 in. / spinners, flies, bait.

46. Long Lake

Access: MP 16.1; turnout E of highway. Trail W of highway leads 0.75 mile to lake.
Fishing: Lake is stocked with trout. Use canoe/float tube or cast from shore.
Rainbow Trout / good / June, September – December / 7-16 in. / spinners, flies, bait.

47. Meridian Lake

Access: MP 13.3 - Grayling Lake Trailhead; turnout W of highway. Trail leads 1.0 mile W to a "Y," right fork 0.6 mile to lake.
Fishing: Lake is stocked with trout. Use canoe/float tube or cast from shore.
Rainbow Trout / good / June, September – December / 7-16 in. / spinners, flies, bait.

48. Grayling Lake

Access: MP 13.3 - Grayling Lake Trailhead; turnout W of highway. Trail leads 1.0 mile W to a "Y," left fork 0.6 mile to lake.
Fishing: Lake contains a small population of grayling.
Arctic Grayling / poor-fair / June – September / 8-12 in. / spinners, flies.

Unit C: Resurrection Bay Drainages

Includes all roadside waters flowing into and surrounding Resurrection Bay.

UNIT REGULATIONS:

* Salmon fishing prohibited: All fresh water, year-round, except lower Resurrection River drainage.
* Ling cod fishing prohibited: All salt water, year-round.

UNIT TIMING

FISH ▽	JAN	FEB	MAR	APR	MAY	JUN	JUL	AUG	SEP	OCT	NOV	DEC
KS*												
RS*												
PS*												
CS*												
SS*												
RT												
DV												

Note: Timing shown for salmon indicates fish in all stages of maturity. Chart correlates to freshwater only.

49. Goldenfin Lake

Access: MP 11.6; turnout W of highway. Trail E of road leads 0.6 mile to lake.
Fishing: Small lake containing a population of resident char. Use canoe/float tube.
Dolly Varden / fair / June, September – October / 7-10 in. / spinners, flies, bait.

50. Troop Lake

Access: MP 10.9; turnout E of highway. Trail leads 1.0 mile E to lake.
Fishing: Lake is stocked with trout. Use canoe/float tube or cast from shore.
Rainbow Trout / good / June, September – December / 7-16 in. / spinners, flies, bait.

51. Grouse Lake

Access: MP 7.4; W on paved road short distance to lake.
Fishing: Primarily a hot spot for over-wintering sea-run char. Try outlet in spring also.
Dolly Varden / fair-good / mid-November – mid-May / 8-20 in. / jigs, flies, bait.

52. Grouse Creek

Access: MP 7.3; highway parallels stream.
Fishing: Shallow salmon spawning stream with some opportunities for sea-run char.
Dolly Varden / fair / late May, mid-September – late October / 8-20 in. / flies, bait.

53. Bear Creek

Access: MP 6.5; highway crosses stream.
Fishing: Primarily a salmon spawning stream yielding a few sea-run char.
Dolly Varden / fair / mid-August – mid-September / 8-15 in. / spoons, flies, bait.

54. Salmon Creek (Upper)

Access: MP 5.9; highway crosses stream.
Fishing: Solid opportunities for sea-run char in late summer. Salmon spawning area.
Dolly Varden / fair-good / mid-August – mid-September / 8-20 in. / flies, bait.

55. Preacher Pond

Access: MP 3.4; small turnout W of highway next to pond.
Fishing: Very small lake containing an over-wintering population of sea-run char.
Dolly Varden / fair-good / mid-November – early May / 8-20 in. / spoons, flies, bait.

SEWARD HIGHWAY log continues on page 258.

Nash Road

Road begins at MP 3.3 Seward Highway (MP 0) and ends near 4th of July Creek (MP 5.2).

56. Salmon Creek (Lower)

Access: MP 0.5; road crosses stream.
Fishing: Glacial stream with decent opportunities for salmon in late summer and fall.
Pink Salmon / good / early August / 2-4 lbs. / spinners, attractors, flies.
Chum Salmon / poor / early August / 6-12 lbs. / spinners, attractors, flies.
Silver Salmon / fair-good / early – mid-September / 6-12 lbs. / spinners, attractors, flies.
Dolly Varden / fair / mid-May, early August / 8-20 in. / spinners, attractors, flies.

57. Creek, No Name Marine

Access: MP 2.3; road crosses stream, pullout. Trail leads 100 yards to stream mouth and bay.
Fishing: Mainly a salmon spawning area with some fish available off stream mouth.
Pink Salmon / fair-good / late July – mid-August / 2-5 lbs. / spoons, spinners, flies.
Chum Salmon / fair / late July – mid-August / 6-12 lbs. / spoons, spinners, flies.
Silver Salmon / poor / early – mid-September / 5-12 lbs. / spoons, spinners, flies.
Dolly Varden / fair / early June – late July / 7-16 in. / spoons, spinners, flies, bait.

58. Fourth Of July Creek Marine

Access: MP 5.1; W on gravel road just past Fourth of July Creek crossing 0.2 mile to mouth of stream and Resurrection Bay.
Fishing: Small clearwater stream supporting angling for salmon at its mouth.
King Salmon / poor / 15-35 lbs. (50 lbs.) / spoons, spinners, bait.
Pink Salmon / fair-excellent / 2-5 lbs. (9 lbs.) / spoons, spinners, flies.
Chum Salmon / fair-good / 6-12 lbs. (18 lbs.) / spoons, spinners, flies.
Silver Salmon / fair / 6-12 lbs. (22 lbs.) / spinners, flies, bait.
Dolly Varden / fair / 8-20 in. (10 lbs.) / spoons, flies, bait.
(Chart on next page)

FISH ▽	JAN	FEB	MAR	APR	MAY	JUN	JUL	AUG	SEP	OCT	NOV	DEC
KS												
PS												
CS												
SS												
DV												

SEWARD HIGHWAY log continues.

59. Resurrection River (West Fork)

Access: MP 2.8; highway crosses stream. E on Airport Rd. short distance, immediate left after railroad tracks to small parking area.

Fishing: Semi-glacial branch of Resurrection offering salmon action in late summer and fall for mainly pinks and silvers. Scout deep areas downstream of highway bridge.

Pink Salmon / good-excellent / early August / 2-4 lbs. / spoons, spinners, flies.
Chum Salmon / fair / early August / 6-12 lbs. / spoons, spinners, flies.
Silver Salmon / fair-good / late August – mid-September / 6-12 lbs. / spinners, flies.
Dolly Varden / poor / mid-May, early August / 8-20 in. / spoons, spinners, flies.

60. Resurrection Bay (Northwest)

Note: This area includes the stretch of waterfront from the small boat harbor to the Seward Sea Life Center. Numerous access points present.

Access A: Town of Seward. From Third Ave. (Seward Hwy.), left on S. Harbor St. short distance, right on Fourth Ave. 0.1 mile, left on access road 0.1 mile to beach and harbor area on left.

Access B: Town of Seward. From Third Ave. (Seward Hwy.), left on D St. 0.1 mile, cross Fourth Ave. onto Ballaine Blvd./Railway Blvd., roads parallel bay next 0.5 mile.

Fishing: The breakwaters in front of town offer productive angling for king, pink, and silver salmon. Look for signs of fish breaching surface, indicating a possible school. Bottomfish are abundant in deeper areas, such as near the Sealife Center.

King Salmon / fair / 15-35 lbs. (50 lbs.) / spoons, spinners, bait.
Pink Salmon / fair-excellent / 2-5 lbs. (9 lbs.) / spoons, flies, bait.
Chum Salmon / poor / 6-12 lbs. (18 lbs.) / spoons, spinners.
Silver Salmon / fair-good / 6-12 lbs. (22 lbs.) / spinners, flies, bait.
Dolly Varden / fair / 8-20 in. (10 lbs.) / spoons, flies, bait.
Pacific Halibut / poor / 3-7 lbs. (85 lbs.) / jigs, bait

FISH ▽	JAN	FEB	MAR	APR	MAY	JUN	JUL	AUG	SEP	OCT	NOV	DEC
KS												
PS												
CS												
SS												
DV												
PH												

61. Seward Lagoon Creek Marine

Access: Town of Seward. From Third Ave. (Seward Hwy.), left on S. Harbor St. short distance, right on Fourth Ave. 0.1 mile, left on access road 0.2 mile to stream mouth and bay.

Fishing: Hatchery runs of king and silver salmon available along with many pinks and a few reds and chums. Snagging is a popular harvest method here.

King Salmon / good / 15-35 lbs. (50 lbs.) / spoons, spinners, bait.
Red Salmon / poor-fair / 3-6 lbs. (10 lbs.) / spinners, flies.
Pink Salmon / fair-good / 2-5 lbs. (9 lbs.) / spoons, flies, bait.
Chum Salmon / poor-fair / 6-12 lbs. (18 lbs.) / spoons, spinners.
Silver Salmon / fair-good / 6-12 lbs. (22 lbs.) / spinners, flies, bait.
Dolly Varden / fair / 8-20 in. (10 lbs.) / spoons, flies, bait.

FISH ▽	JAN	FEB	MAR	APR	MAY	JUN	JUL	AUG	SEP	OCT	NOV	DEC
KS					▨	▓	▨	▨				
RS					▨	▨	▓	▨	▨			
PS						▨	▓	▨				
CS						▨	▓	▨				
SS							▨	▓	▨	▨		
DV					▨	▓	▓	▨	▨			

Lowell Point Road

Road begins near downtown Seward at the far NW corner of Resurrection Bay (Mile 0) and ends at Lowell Point south of town (Mile 2.4).

62. Lowell Creek Marine

Access: Mile 0.3; road crosses stream.

Fishing: Hatchery runs of king and silver salmon available along with pinks and a few chums. Snagging is a popular harvest method here.

King Salmon / good / 15-35 lbs. (50 lbs.) / spoons, spinners, bait.
Pink Salmon / fair-good / 2-5 lbs. (9 lbs.) / spoons, flies, bait.
Chum Salmon / poor / 6-12 lbs. (18 lbs.) / spoons, spinners.
Silver Salmon / fair-good / 6-12 lbs. (22 lbs.) / spinners, flies, bait.
Dolly Varden / fair / 8-20 in. (10 lbs.) / spoons, flies, bait.

FISH ▽	JAN	FEB	MAR	APR	MAY	JUN	JUL	AUG	SEP	OCT	NOV	DEC
KS					▨	▓	▨					
PS						▨	▓	▨				
CS						▨	▓	▨				
SS							▨	▓	▨	▨		
DV					▨	▓	▨	▨	▨			

63. Resurrection Bay (West)

Note: This area includes the bay shoreline from Lowell Creek waterfall south to Spruce Creek.

Access: Mile 0.5 – 1.5; road parallels bay.

Fishing: Schools of salmon, primarily pinks and silvers, may be intercepted from this stretch of boulder-strewn beach. Look for fish jumping. Rockfish may be taken also.

King Salmon / poor-fair / 15-35 lbs. (50 lbs.) / spoons, spinners, bait.

Pink Salmon / fair-excellent / 2-5 lbs. (9 lbs.) / spoons, flies, bait.
Silver Salmon / fair-good / 6-12 lbs. (22 lbs.) / spinners, flies, bait.
Dolly Varden / fair-good / 8-20 in. (10 lbs.) / spoons, flies, bait.
Rockfish / fair / 8-15 in. (5 lbs.) / jigs, bait.

FISH ▽	JAN	FEB	MAR	APR	MAY	JUN	JUL	AUG	SEP	OCT	NOV	DEC
KS					▓	█	▓	▓				
PS						▓	█	█	▓			
SS							▓	█	▓	▓		
DV					▓	█	█	▓	▓			
RF					▓	▓	█	█	▓	▓		

64. Spruce Creek Marine

Access: Mile 1.5; follow beach 200 yards SE to stream mouth.
Fishing: Small schools of salmon and a few char may be found at mouth of stream.
King Salmon / poor / mid-June – early July / 15-35 lbs. / spoons, spinners, bait.
Pink Salmon / fair-good / mid-July – mid-August / 2-5 lbs. / spoons, spinners, flies.
Chum Salmon / poor / mid-July – early August / 6-12 lbs. / spoons, spinners, flies.
Silver Salmon / fair / late August – mid-September / 6-12 lbs. / spinners, flies, bait.
Dolly Varden / fair / late May – early August / 8-20 in. / spoons, spinners, flies.

65. Tonsina Creek Marine

Access: Mile 2.2; trail leads 2 miles to creek mouth. Parking is located at Mile 2.1.
Fishing: Clearwater stream with large runs of pinks and chums. Sea-run char present.
King Salmon / poor / 15-35 lbs. (50 lbs.) / spoons, spinners, bait.
Pink Salmon / fair-excellent / 2-5 lbs. (9 lbs.) / spoons, flies, bait.
Chum Salmon / fair-good / 6-12 lbs. (18 lbs.) / spoons, spinners, flies.
Silver Salmon / poor-fair / 6-12 lbs. (22 lbs.) / spinners, flies, bait.
Dolly Varden / fair / 8-20 in. (10 lbs.) / spoons, flies, bait.

FISH ▽	JAN	FEB	MAR	APR	MAY	JUN	JUL	AUG	SEP	OCT	NOV	DEC
KS					▓	█						
PS						▓	█	█	▓			
CS						▓	█	▓				
SS							▓	█	▓			
DV					▓	█	█	▓				

66. Lowell Point

Access A: Mile 2.3; right on Martins Rd. 0.3 mile to parking area and public easement to beach.
Access B: Mile 2.4; private campground with access to beach.
Fishing: Beach area is a popular surfcasting spot for pinks and silvers and sea-run char.
Pink Salmon / good-excellent / 2-5 lbs. (9 lbs.) / spoons, flies, bait.
Chum Salmon / poor / 6-12 lbs. (18 lbs.) / spoons, spinners, flies.
Silver Salmon / fair-good / 6-12 lbs. (22 lbs.) / spinners, flies, bait.
Dolly Varden / fair-good / 8-20 in. (10 lbs.) / spoons, flies, bait.

FISH ▽	JAN	FEB	MAR	APR	MAY	JUN	JUL	AUG	SEP	OCT	NOV	DEC
PS						▓	█	█	▓			
CS						▓	█	▓				
SS							▓	█	▓			
DV					▓	█	█	▓				

Other Locations

Unit A: Turnagain Arm Drainages:

Peterson Creek - MP 84.1; DV,(PS,SS) Pond, No Name - MP 83.9-82.7; DV Creek, No Name - MP 81.7; DV 20-Mile River - MP 80.7; SS,DV,(KS,RS,PS,CS) **Portage Glacier Road:** Explorer Pond - MP 2.4; DV,(RS,SS) Beaver Pond - MP 2.9; DV,(RS,SS) Williwaw Creek - MP 3.6/4.1; DV,(KS,RS,PS,CS,SS) Williwaw Ponds - MP 4.5; DV,(RS,CS,SS) Portage Lake - MP 5.5; DV,(RS,SS) **Whittier Access Road:** Placer Creek - MP 5.7; DV (RS, SS) **Seward Highway (Cont.):** Placer River - MP 78.4/77.9; SS,DV,(KS,RS,PS,CS) Lyon Creek - MP ; DV (KS, SS) Granite Creek - MP 66.5/65.4; DV,(KS,SS,RT,AG) **Hope Highway:** Bear Creek - MP 15.5; PS,DV,(CS) **Seward Highway (Cont.):** Fresno Creek - MP 48.0; DV Canyon Creek - MP 46.0-44.6; RT,DV

Unit B: Kenai Lake Drainage:

Tern Lake - MP 36.9; RT,DV,AG,(King Salmon,RS,SS) Falls Creek - MP 25.0; RT,DV,(King Salmon,RS,SS) Snow River - MP 17.7; RT,DV,AG,(RS,SS)

Unit C: Resurrection Bay Drainages:

Grouse Creek - MP 10.5-8.1; DV,(RS,PS,CS,SS) Creek, No Name - MP 4.1; DV,(RS,PS,CS,SS) Clear Creek - MP 3.8; DV,(RS,PS,CS,SS) **Nash Road:** Creek, No Name - MP 2.0; DV,(RS,PS,CS,SS) Fourth of July Creek - MP 5.1; DV,(RS,PS,CS,SS) **Seward Highway (Cont.):** Resurrection River - MP 3.0/2.8; DV,(King Salmon,RS,PS,CS,SS)

LOCATION & SPECIES APPENDIX

● - Wild/Native fish, fishable numbers.

◆ - Present in small numbers and/or only occasionally caught.

▲ - Stocked/Hatchery fish, fishable numbers.

■ - Mix of Wild and Hatchery fish, fishable numbers.

✕ - Indicated species present but currently protected by law (PROHIBITED).

#	LOCATION	KING SALMON	RED SALMON	PINK SALMON	CHUM SALMON	SILVER SALMON	LANDLOCKED SALMON	KOKANEE	STEELHEAD TROUT	RAINBOW TROUT	LAKE TROUT	ARCTIC CHAR	DOLLY VARDEN	ARCTIC GRAYLING	SHEEFISH	WHITEFISH	NORTHERN PIKE	BURBOT	PACIFIC HALIBUT	LING COD	ROCKFISH
1.	Indian Creek	✕		●	◆	●				◆			●								
2.	Bird Creek	✕	◆	●	●	■				◆			●								
3.	Penguin Creek	✕	✕	✕	✕	✕				◆			●								
4.	Glacier Creek (Upper)	✕	◆	●	●	●							●								
5.	California Creek (Mouth)	✕	●	●	●	●							●								
6.	Glacier Creek (Lower)	✕	◆	●	◆	●							●								
7.	Virgin Creek	✕	✕	✕	✕	✕							●								
8.	Kern Creek	✕	✕	✕	✕	✕							●								
9.	Portage Creek (No. 2)	✕	◆	●	◆	●							●								
	Portage Glacier Road																				
10.	Willow Pond									▲							◆				
11.	Alder Pond									▲											
12.	Explorer Creek	✕	◆	◆	◆	◆							●								
13.	Tangle Pond									▲											
14.	Williwaw Creek (Mouth)	✕	◆	◆	●	●							●								
	Whittier Access Road																				
15.	Barge Creek	◆	◆	●	●	■							●								
16.	Shakespeare Creek Marine	▲		●	◆	▲							●								
17.	Passage Canal	◆		●	◆	■							●								●
18.	Whittier Creek	▲		●	◆	▲							●								
19.	Whittier Harbor	▲		●	◆	▲							◆								

#	LOCATION	King Salmon	Red Salmon	Pink Salmon	Chum Salmon	Silver Salmon	Landlocked Salmon	Kokanee	Steelhead Trout	Rainbow Trout	Lake Trout	Arctic Char	Dolly Varden	Arctic Grayling	Sheefish	Whitefish	Northern Pike	Burbot	Pacific Halibut	Ling Cod	Rockfish
20.	Smitty's Cove	▲		●	◆	▲							◆								◆
21.	Cove Creek Marine	◆	◆	●	◆	▲							●								
	Seward Hwy. (cont.)																				
22.	Ingram Creek	×	◆	●	◆	●							●								
23.	Granite Creek	×		◆	◆	●						◆	●	◆							
24.	East Fork Sixmile Creek	×	◆	◆	◆	●						◆	●	◆							
	Hope Highway							●													
25.	Canyon Cr./6 mile (Conf)	×	◆	◆	◆	●						◆	●	◆							
26.	Sixmile Creek (Middle)	×	◆	◆	◆	●						◆	●	◆							
27.	Sixmile Creek (Lower)	×	◆	●	●	●							●	◆							
28.	Resurrection Cr. (Upper)	×		◆	◆	◆							●								
29.	Resurrection Creek	×	◆	●	●	●							●								
	Seward Hwy. (cont.)																				
30.	Lower Summit Lake										▲	◆	●								
31.	Canyon Creek										▲		●								
32.	Upper Summit Lake										▲	◆	●								
33.	Summit Creek		×			×						●	●	◆							
34.	Quartz Creek (Upper)	×	×			×						●	●	◆							
35.	Jerome Lake										▲		●								
36.	Carter Lake		×								▲										
37.	Crescent Lake													▲							
38.	Moose Creek		×			×				●			●			◆		◆			
39.	Upper Trail Lake	×	×	×		×				●	●		●			◆		◆			
41.	Lower Trail Lake	×	×	×		×				●	●		●			◆		◆			
42.	Vagt Lake									■											
43.	Trail River	×	×	×		×				●	◆		●			◆		◆			
44.	Kenai Lake	×	×	×	×	×				●	●		●			◆		◆			
45.	Ptarmigan Creek	×	×	×	×	×				●			●					◆			
46.	Ptarmigan Lake												●								
47.	Long Lake										▲										
48.	Meridian Lake										▲										
49.	Grayling Lake													▲							
51.	Goldenfin Lake												●								
52.	Troop Lake										▲										
53.	Grouse Lake	×	×	×	×	×				◆			●								
52.	Grouse Creek	×	×	×	×	×				◆			●								
53.	Bear Creek	×	×	×	×	×				◆			●								
54.	Salmon Creek	×	×	×	×	×				◆			●								
55.	Preacher Pond		×	×		×							●								
	Nash Road																				
56.	Salmon Creek	×	◆	●	●	●							●								
57.	Creek, No Name Marine	◆	◆	●	●	●							●								
58.	Fourth of July Creek	■	◆	●	●	■							●						◆	×	◆
	Seward																				
59.	Resurrection River	×	◆	●	●	●							●								
60.	Resurrection Bay (NW)	■	◆	●	●	■							●						◆	×	◆
61.	Seward Lagoon Creek	■	■	●	●	■							●						◆	×	◆
	Lowell Point Road																				
62.	Lowell Creek (Mouth)	▲	◆	●	◆	■							●						◆	×	◆
63.	Resurrection Bay (W)	■	◆	●	◆	■							●						◆	×	●
64.	Spruce Creek Marine	■	◆	●	●	■							●						◆	×	◆
65.	Tonsina Creek Marine	■	◆	●	●	■							●						◆	×	◆
66.	Lowell Point	■	◆	●	●	■							●						◆	×	◆

Steese Highway

CHAPTER

16

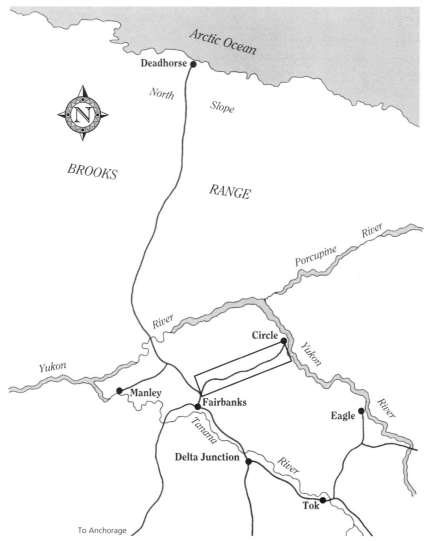

Area Covered: Fox to Circle; 151 miles.

Note: For fishing information along the Chena Hot Springs Road, see chapter 9, page 119.

Regulatory Units: (A) Chatanika River Drainage; (B) Yukon River Drainage
Number of Locations: 13

FISHING THE STEESE HIGHWAY

The Steese Highway provides good access to clearwater tributaries of Tolovana River and adjoining lakes, as well as a few streams draining into middle Yukon River. Here, as throughout most of the interior, grayling is the most prolific sport fish species available, but decent numbers of stocked rainbow trout are also taken out of small lakes and ponds along the highway. In addition, a few king, chum, and silver salmon, sheefish, whitefish, northern pike, and burbot may be encountered, particularly in the Chatanika River and Birch Creek. The salmon, it must be noted, are in or near spawning condition whenever present and not good for consumption. Angler success is fair to good in both lakes and streams.

Angling pressure is light in all locations throughout the year, with some increased effort occuring in the Chatanika River and surrounding stocked ponds.

Recommended Hot Spots: Chatanika River; roadside ponds.

Content

QUICK REFERENCE

 Road Condition   Parking Area   Camp Sites   Hiking Trails   Boat Launch   Handicap Access   Fishing Pressure

- ■ - Good to Highly developed/conditions, intense pressure
- ● - Fair to Moderately developed/conditions, moderate pressure
- ◆ - Poor to marginally developed/conditions, limited pressure
- ✕ - Prohibited

#	LOCATION	MILE POST	🚗	P	⛺	🚶	🛥	♿	🎣	PAGE
J1.	Jct.: Elliott Highway	11.0								
1.	29.5-Mile Pond	29.5	●	●				◆	◆	266
2.	31.6-Mile Pond	31.6	●	●				◆	◆	266
3.	33.5 Mile Pond	33.5	●	●				◆	◆	266
4.	34.6-Mile Pond	34.6	●	●				◆	◆	267
5.	35.8-Mile Pond	35.8	●	●				◆	◆	267
6.	36.8-Mile Pond	36.8	●	●				◆	◆	267
7.	Chatanika River	35.6-39.0	■	●	●				●	267
8.	Kokomo Creek	37.3	■	◆					◆	267
9.	Chatanika River (Upper)	56.4-60.0	●	●					◆	267
10.	Faith Creek	69.0	●	●					◆	267

Map: Unit A: Chatanika River Drainage
      Unit B: Yukon River Drainage

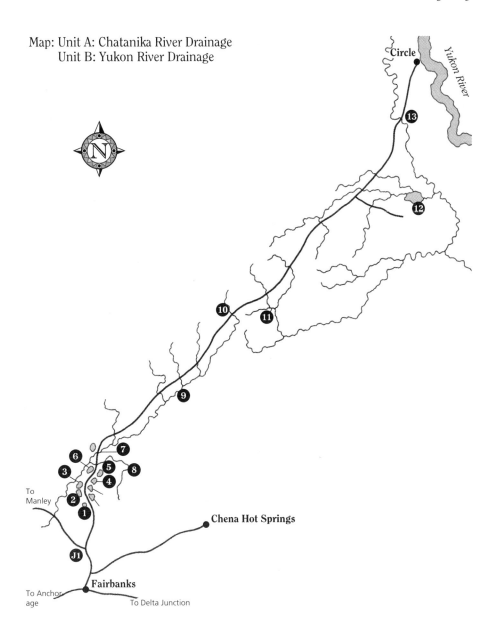

#	LOCATION	MILE POST	🚐	P	Λ	🚶🚶	🛶	♿	🎣	PAGE
11.	North Fork Birch Creek	94.0	●	●					◆	268
12.	Medicine Lake	127.8	●	●		●			◆	268
13.	Birch Creek	147.2	●	●					◆	268

STEESE HIGHWAY LOCATIONS

Unit A: Chatanika River Drainage

Includes all roadside water flowing into and surrounding Chatanika River.

UNIT REGULATIONS:

* King salmon fishing prohibited: All waters, year-round.
* Northern pike fishing prohibited: All waters, October 15 – May 31.
* Whitefish fishing prohibited: All waters, September 1 – April 30.
* Arctic grayling fishing: Catch-and-release only, April 1 – May 31 (except stocked ponds).

UNIT TIMING:

FISH ▽	JAN	FEB	MAR	APR	MAY	JUN	JUL	AUG	SEP	OCT	NOV	DEC
KS*												
CS*												
SS*												
RT												
SF												
AG												
WF												
NP												
BB												

*Note: Timing shown for salmon indicates fish in all stages of maturity.

1. 29.5-Mile Pond

Access: MP 29.5; W on gravel road short distance to pond.
Fishing: Pond is stocked with trout. Use canoe/float tube or cast from shore.
Rainbow Trout / fair-good / June, September – October / 7-15 in. / spinners, flies, bait.

2. 31.6-Mile Pond

Access: MP 31.6; N on gravel road short distance to pond.
Fishing: Pond is stocked with trout. Use canoe/float tube or cast from shore.
Rainbow Trout / fair / June, September – October / 7-15 in. / spinners, flies, bait.

3. 33.5-Mile Pond

Access: MP 33.5; N on gravel road short distance to pond.
Fishing: Pond is stocked with trout. Use canoe/float tube or cast from shore.
Rainbow Trout / fair / June, September – October / 7-15 in. / spinners, flies, bait.

4. 34.6-Mile Pond
Access: MP 34.6; S on gravel road short distance to pond.
Fishing: Pond is stocked with trout. Use canoe/float tube or cast from shore.
Rainbow Trout / good / June, September – December / 7-15 in. / spinners, flies, bait.

5. 35.8-Mile Pond
Access: MP 35.8; S on gravel road short distance to pond.
Fishing: Pond is stocked with trout. Use canoe/float tube or cast from shore.
Rainbow Trout / fair / June, September – October / 7-15 in. / spinners, flies, bait.

6. 36.6-Mile Pond
Access: MP 36.6; N on gravel road short distance to pond.
Fishing: Pond is stocked with trout. Use canoe/float tube or cast from shore.
Rainbow Trout / good / June, September – December / 7-15 in. / spinners, flies, bait.

7. Chatanika River (Middle)
Access: MP 35.6-39.0; highway parallels river, crossing it at MP 39.0. Numerous points of access.
Fishing: Decent population of grayling in summer and fall. Salmon spawning area.
Sheefish / poor / late September – early October / 4-8 lbs./ spoons, flies.
Arctic Grayling / fair-good / mid-June – mid-September / 7-14 in. / spinners, flies.
Whitefish / poor-fair / late August / 10-20 in. / attractors, flies.

8. Kokomo Creek
Access: MP 37.3; highway crosses stream.
Fishing: Clearwarer stream with opportunities for small grayling early in the season.
Arctic Grayling / poor-fair / late May – mid-June / 7-10 in. / spinners, flies.

9. Chatanika River (Upper)
Access: MP 56.4-60.0; highway parallels river. Numerous access points present.
Fishing: Grayling are abundant in summer and early fall. Salmon spawning area.
Arctic Grayling / good / mid-June – mid-September / 7-12 in. / spinners, flies.

10. Faith Creek
Access: MP 69.0; highway crosses stream.
Fishing: Stream contains a small summer popultion of grayling.
Arctic Grayling / fair / mid-June – early September / 7-12 in. / spinners, flies.

Unit B: Yukon River Drainage

Includes all roadside waters flowing into and surrounding Yukon River.

UNIT REGULATIONS:

* There are no general area-wide restrictions for waters in Unit B.

UNIT TIMING:

FISH ▽	JAN	FEB	MAR	APR	MAY	JUN	JUL	AUG	SEP	OCT	NOV	DEC
KS*							▓	▓				
CS*							▓	▓				
SS*									▓	▓		
SF									▓	▓		
AG				▓	▓	▓	▓	▓	▓			
WF									▓	▓		
NP					▓	▓	▓	▓				
BB					▓	▓	▓	▓	▓	▓		

Note: Timing shown for salmon indicates fish in all stages of maturity.

11. North Fork Birch Creek

Access: MP 94.0; S on small gravel road next to sign 0.2 mile to stream.
Fishing: Very small stream with limited opportunities for grayling in summer.
Arctic Grayling / poor-fair / mid-June – mid-August / 7-10 in. / spinners, flies.

12. Medicine Lake

Access: MP 127.8; S on Circle Hot Spring Rd. 8.3 miles to Circle Hot Springs airstrip, proceed directly across airstrip and find trail leading 2 miles to lake.
Fishing: Lake supports a healthy population of pike. Use canoe/float tube.
Northern Pike / fair-good / June – September / 2-6 lbs. / spoons, plugs, bait.

13. Birch Creek

Access A: MP 146.4; highway parallels stream.
Access B: MP 147.2; highway crosses stream.
Fishing: Worthwhile opportunities for grayling in late summer and fall. Pike possible.
Arctic Grayling / fair-good / late August – early October / 7-14 in. / spinners, flies.
Northern Pike / poor / mid-June – early September / 2-5 lbs. / spoons, plugs, bait.

Other Locations

None

LOCATION & SPECIES APPENDIX

● - Wild/Native fish, fishable numbers.
◆ - Present in small numbers and/or only occasionally caught.
▲ - Stocked/Hatchery fish, fishable numbers.
■ - Mix of Wild and Hatchery fish, fishable numbers.
✕ - Indicated species present but currently protected by law (PROHIBITED).

#	LOCATION	King Salmon	Red Salmon	Pink Salmon	Chum Salmon	Silver Salmon	Landlocked Salmon	Kokanee	Steelhead Trout	Rainbow Trout	Lake Trout	Arctic Char	Dolly Varden	Sheefish	Arctic Grayling	Whitefish	Northern Pike	Burbot	Pacific Halibut	Ling Cod	Rockfish
1.	29.5-Mile Pond									▲											
2.	31.6-Mile Pond									▲											
3.	33.5-Mile Pond									▲											
4.	34.6-Mile Pond									▲											
5.	35.8-Mile Pond									▲											
6.	36.8-Mile Pond									▲											
7.	Chatanika River	✕				●	◆								●	●	●	◆	◆		
8.	Kokomo Creek														●						
9.	Chatanika River	✕				◆	◆								◆	●	◆	◆			
10.	Faith Creek														●	◆					
11.	North Fork Birch Creek														●	◆					
12.	Medicine Lake																◆	●			
13.	Birch Creek	◆				◆	◆								◆	●	◆	●	◆		

Sterling Highway

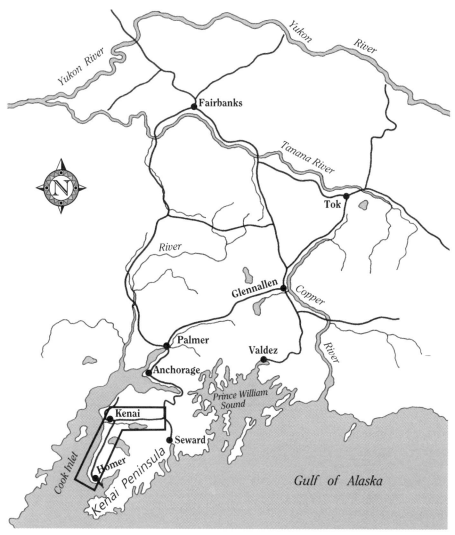

Area Covered: Tern Lake Junction - Homer Spit; 142.5 miles
Regulatory Units: (A) Kenai Lake Drainage; (B) Upper Kenai River/Skilak Lake Drainage;
(C) Lower Kenai River Drainage; (D) Central Kenai Peninsula Drainages; (E) Lower Kenai
Peninsula Drainages
Number of Locations: 82

FISHING THE STERLING HIGHWAY

The Sterling Highway parallels the famed Kenai River for many miles, crossing it and several tributary streams along the way, thus giving anglers prime opportunities to sample some of the best salmon fishing Alaska has to offer. King, red, and silver salmon are undeniably the most sought-after species and known to attain trophy, even record, size. Sterling Highway also provides excellent access to lakes on the Kenai Peninsula via Skilak Lake Road and Swanson River/Swan Lake roads among others, offering fishing for both native and stocked populations of land-locked salmon, trout, char, and grayling. Along the coast of the popular Cook Inlet, the Sterling Highway intersects several productive rivers and streams, most of them supporting good runs of salmon, trout, and char. In salt water, fishing is very productive for salmon and bottomfish, especially in Kachemak Bay. Angler success is good to excellent in both fresh and salt water.

Boaters do exceptionally well in Cook Inlet and Kachemak Bay marine waters trolling for king and silver salmon and jigging for halibut. The Kenai and Kasilof rivers are two favorite stream fisheries for king salmon and other species. Canoeists will find lesser fished locations in the Moose and Swanson river systems.

In addition to rod and reel angling, clam digging is a very popular activity along Cook Inlet's beaches between Kasilof and Anchor Point from spring to fall, and to a lesser degree also around the Homer Spit in Kachemak Bay.

Angling pressure is often very heavy in summer during the peak of salmon runs in rivers and streams between Cooper Landing and Soldotna, and in late spring and early summer between Kasilof and Homer.

Recommended Hot Spots: Kenai, Russian, Moose, Swanson, Kasilof, Ninilchik, and Anchor rivers; Quartz, Crooked, and Deep creeks; Rainbow, Lower Russian, Hidden, Longmere, Roque, Johnson, Centennial, and Encelewski lakes; Swanson River Road/Swan Lake Road lakes.

Content

QUICK REFERENCE

 Road Condition   Parking Area   Camp Sites   Hiking Trails   Boat Launch   Handicap Access   Fishing Pressure

■ - Good to Highly developed/conditions, intense pressure
● - Fair to Moderately developed/conditions, moderate pressure
◆ - Poor to marginally developed/conditions, limited pressure
✕ - Prohibited

Map 1: Unit A: Kenai Lake Drainage
       Unit B: Upper Kenai River/Skilak Lake Drainages

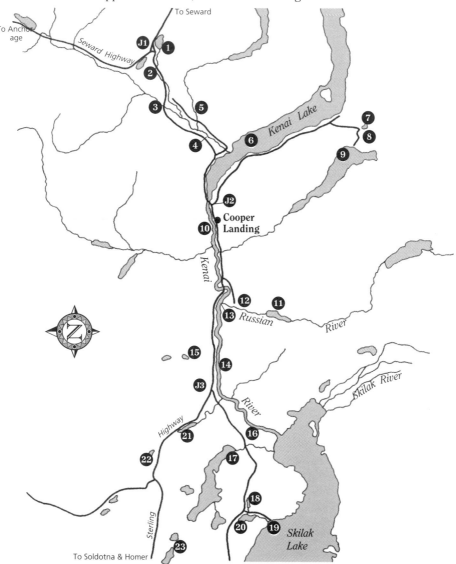

#	LOCATION	MILE POST	🚗	P	⛺	🚶	🛶	♿	⚓	PAGE
J1.	Jct.: Seward Highway	37.0								
1.	Tern Lake	37.3	●	■	◆				◆	280
2.	Daves Creek									
	Access A	37.3	●	■	◆			◆	◆	280
	Access B	37.6-40.0	■	●					◆	280
3.	Quartz Creek (Middle)	40.9	■	◆						280
4.	Quartz Creek (Lower)									
	Access A	42.0-44.0	■	●					●	280
	Access B	45.0	■	■	■				●	280
	Access C	45.0	●	●				◆	●	280
5.	Crescent Creek	45.0	●	●	◆			◆	◆	280
6.	Kenai Lake									
	Access A	45.0-47.7	■	■			■	■	●	280
	Access B	45.0	■	■	■				◆	280
J2.	Jct.: Snug Harbor Road	47.9								
	Snug Harbor Road	Milepost								
J2.	Jct.: Sterling Hwy.	0								
7.	Cleaver Lake	8.7	●	●	◆	●			◆	281
8.	Rainbow Lake	8.7	●	●	◆	●			◆	282
9.	Cooper Lake	8.7	●	●	◆		●	◆	◆	282
	Sterling Highway (cont.)	Milepost								
10.	Kenai River (Upper)	47.7-55.0	■	■	■		■	◆	●	282
11.	Lower Russian Lake	52.7	■	■	◆	■		◆		282
12.	Russian River (Lower)	52.7	■	■	■	■			■	283
13.	Russian River (Mouth)									
	Access A	52.7	■	■	■	■			■	283
	Access B	54.9	■	■	●		●	■	■	283
14.	Kenai River (Upper)	55.0-58.0	■	●	■	●	●	◆	■	284
15.	Lower Fuller Lake	57.1	■	●	◆	●			◆	284
J3.	Jct.: Skilak Lake Road (E)	58.0								
	Skilak Lake Road	Milepost								
J3.	Jct.: Sterling Hwy.	0								
16.	Kenai River (Upper)									
	Access A	0.1	■	●	●	●			●	284
	Access B	0.7	●	●			●		●	284
	Access C	2.4	●	●			●		●	284
17.	Hidden Lake	3.6	■	■	■		●	◆	●	285
18.	Upper Ohmer Lake	7.7	●	◆				◆	◆	285
19.	Skilak Lake									
	Access A	8.5	●	■	■		●	●	◆	285
	Access B	13.8	●	■	■		●	●	◆	285
20.	Lower Ohmer Lake	8.6	●	●	●			◆	◆	286
	Sterling Highway (cont.)	Milepost								
21.	Jean Lake	59.9/60.5	■	●	●			◆	◆	286
22.	Upper Jean Lake	62.0	■	◆		◆			◆	286
23.	Kelly Lake	68.4	●	●	●		●	◆	◆	287
24.	Peterson Lake	68.4	●	●	●		●	◆	◆	287
25.	Egumen Lake	70.8	■	●	◆	●			◆	287
26.	Watson Lake	71.3	●	●	●		●	◆	◆	287
27.	East Fork Moose River	71.4	■	●	◆			◆	◆	287
J4.	Jct.: Skilak Lake Road (W)	75.2								
28.	Kenai River (Middle)									287

Map 2: Unit C: Lower Kenai River Drainage

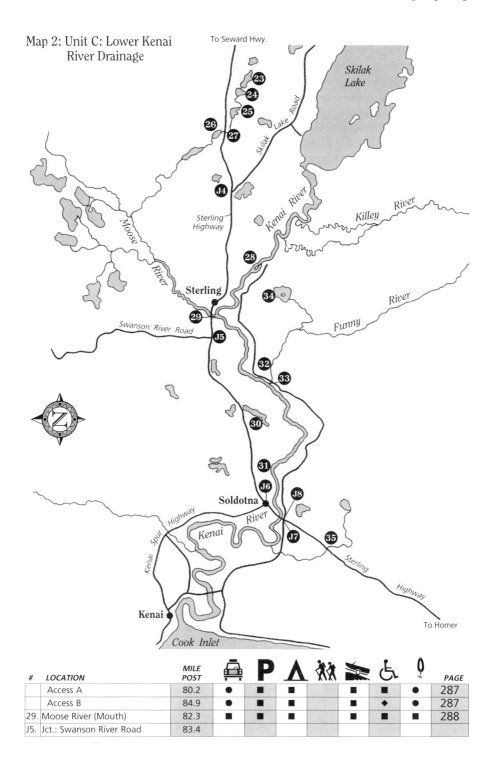

#	LOCATION	MILE POST		P	▲	👣	⛵	♿	⚓	PAGE
	Access A	80.2	●	■	■		■	■	●	287
	Access B	84.9	●	■	■		■	◆	●	287
29.	Moose River (Mouth)	82.3	■	■	■		■	■	■	288
J5.	Jct.: Swanson River Road	83.4								

#	LOCATION	MILE POST	🚗	P	Λ	🥾	🛶	♿	🎣	PAGE
30.	Longmere Lake	88.9	●	●					●	288
J6.	Jct.: Kenai Spur Highway	94.1								
31.	Kenai River (Lower)									
	Access A	94.1	●	■	■		■	◆	■	289
	Access B	94.4	●	■		■		◆	■	289
	Access C	95.9	■	■	×				■	289
	Access D	96.1	■	■	■		■	■	■	289
	Access E	96.1	■	■	×	■			■	289
J7.	Jct.: Kalifornsky Beach Rd.	96.1								
J8.	Jct.: Funny River Road	96.1								
32.	Funny River (Lower)	96.1	●	●					◆	289
33.	Funny River (Mouth)	96.1	●	●	●				●	290
34.	Aurora Lake	96.1	●	●				◆	◆	290
35.	Slikok Creek	99.4	■	◆					◆	290
	Swanson River Road									
J5.	Jct.: Sterling Hwy.	0								
36.	Mosquito Lake	7.9	●	●	◆	●			◆	291
37.	Silver Lake	9.1	●	●	◆	●			◆	291
38.	Finger Lake	9.8	●	●		●			◆	291
39.	Forest Lake	10.7	●	●	◆	●			◆	291
40.	Weed Lake	13.1	●	●	◆	●			◆	291
41.	Dabbler Lake	13.3	●	●	◆	●			◆	292
42.	Skookum Lake	13.3	●	●	◆	●			◆	292
43.	Drake Lake	13.3	●	●	◆	●			◆	292
44.	Breeze Lake	14.0	●	●	◆	●			◆	292
45.	Dolly Varden Lake	14.1	●	●	●			◆	◆	292
46.	Rainbow Lake	14.8	●	●	●			◆	◆	292
J9.	Jct.: Swan Lake Rd.	17.2								
47.	Swanson River (Upper)	17.7	●	■	●		●	●	●	292
	Swan Lake Road									
J9.	Jct.: Swanson River Rd.	0								
48.	Fish Lake	3.0	●	●				◆	◆	293
49.	Ice Lake	4.0	●	●	◆	●			◆	293
50.	Canoe Lake	4.0	●	●	◆			◆	◆	293
51.	Waterfowl Lake	4.0	●	●					◆	293
52.	Swan Lake Canoe System Lakes	4.0	●	●					◆	293
53.	Sucker Lake	4.7	●	●	◆				◆	294
54.	Little Merganser Lake	6.2	●	●	◆				◆	294
55.	Campfire Lake	7.0	●	●		●			◆	294
56.	Nest Lake	8.3	●	◆		●			◆	294
57.	Paddle Lake	12.2	●	●	◆	●			◆	294
58.	Odd Lake	12.2	●	●	◆	●			◆	294
59.	Pad Lake	12.2	●	●	◆	●			◆	294
60.	Swanson R. Canoe Route Lakes	12.2	●	●	◆	●			◆	295
	Sterling Highway (cont.)									
61.	Coal Creek									
	Access A	106.0	■	◆					◆	295
	Access B	108.8	■	◆					◆	295
62.	Roque Lake	106.9	■	◆					◆	296
63.	Kasilof River (Middle)	109.4	■	■	◆		●		◆	296
64.	Crooked Creek (Middle)									
	Access A	110.9	■	■	◆				●	296
	Access B	111.4	●					◆	●	296
J10.	Jct.: Johnson Lake Road	110.5								

Map 3: Unit D: Central Kenai Peninsula Drainages

#	LOCATION	MILE POST	🚍	**P**	Λ	🚶	🛶	♿	⚓	PAGE
65.	Johnson Lake	110.5	●	●	■		●	◆	●	296
66.	Centennial Lake	110.5	●	●					◆	296
67.	Kasilof River (Upper)	110.5	●	■	●		●	◆	◆	296
J11.	Jct.: Cohoe Loop Road	111.4								
68.	Quintin Lake	111.4	●	●					◆	297

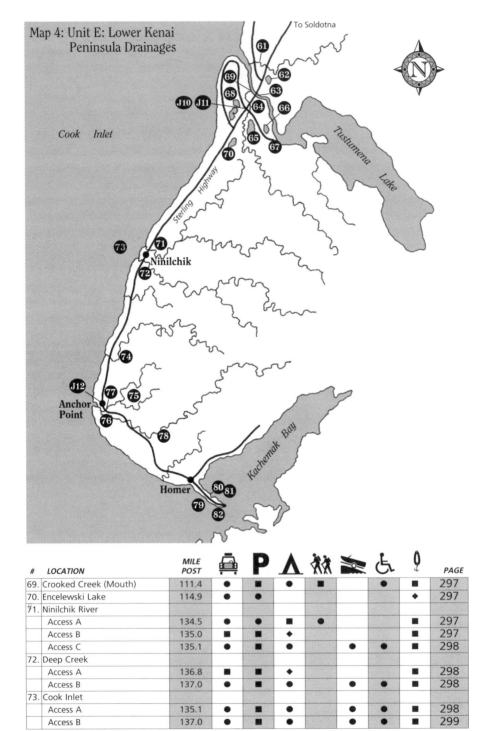

Map 4: Unit E: Lower Kenai
Peninsula Drainages

To Soldotna

Cook Inlet

Tustumena Lake

Sterling Highway

Ninilchik

Anchor
Point

Kachemak Bay

Homer

#	LOCATION	MILE POST	🚗	**P**	⛰	🚶	🛥	♿	𝒬	PAGE
69.	Crooked Creek (Mouth)	111.4	●	■	●	■		●	■	297
70.	Encelewski Lake	114.9	●	●					◆	297
71.	Ninilchik River									
	Access A	134.5	●	●	■	●			■	297
	Access B	135.0	■	■	◆				■	297
	Access C	135.1	●	■	●		●	●	■	298
72.	Deep Creek									
	Access A	136.8	■	■	◆				■	298
	Access B	137.0	●	■	●		●	●	■	298
73.	Cook Inlet									
	Access A	135.1	●	■	●		●	●	■	298
	Access B	137.0	●	■	●		●	◆	■	299

#	LOCATION	MILE POST	🚗	P	⛺	🚶	🛥	♿	⚓	PAGE
73.	Cook Inlet (cont.)									
	Access C	152.7	●	■	●		●	●	●	299
	Access D	156.7	●	■	●		●	●	■	299
74.	Stariski Creek	150.8	■	●	◆				◆	299
J12	Jct.: North Fork Rd.	156.7								
75.	North Fork Anchor River									
	Access A	156.7	■	●					◆	299
	Access B	156.7	●	●					◆	299
	Access C	156.7	●	●					◆	299
	Access D	156.7	●	●					◆	299
76.	Anchor River	156.9	■	■	■		●	●	■	300
77.	North Fork Anchor River									
	Access A	156.9	■	●	◆				◆	300
	Access B	157.0	■	◆					◆	300
78.	Anchor River (Upper)									
	Access A	159.9-163.9	■	●	●				◆	300
	Access B	164.3	●	●					◆	300
79.	Homer Spit (Ocean Side)	175.4	■	●	●			●	◆	300
80.	Dudiak Lagoon	178.1	■	■	●			■	■	301
81.	Homer Spit (Bay Side)	178.2	●	●	●				◆	301
82.	Homer Spit (East End)	179.5	■	■	●		■	■	●	301

STERLING HIGHWAY LOCATIONS

Unit A: Kenai Lake Drainage

Includes all roadside waters flowing into and surrounding Kenai Lake.

UNIT REGULATIONS:

* Fishing prohibited: All flowing waters, April 15 – June 14.
* Salmon fishing prohibited: All flowing waters, year-round.
* Rainbow trout fishing prohibited: All waters, April 15 – June 14 (except stocked lakes).
* Only unbaited, single-hook, artificial lures: All flowing waters, year-round.

Note: *Consult sport fishing regulations closely for Kenai Lake's tributaries.*

UNIT TIMING

FISH ▽	JAN	FEB	MAR	APR	MAY	JUN	JUL	AUG	SEP	OCT	NOV	DEC
KS*												
RS*												
PS*												
CS*												
SS*												
RT												
LT												
DV												
AG												
WF												

***Note:** Timing shown for salmon indicates fish in all stages of maturity.*

1. Tern Lake
Access: MP 37.3; S on gravel road 0.1 mile to lake outlet and parking area.
Fishing: Lake is very shallow with few deep spots. Limited opportunities for char.
Rainbow Trout / poor / August – September / 7-15 in. / spinners, flies, bait.
Dolly Varden / poor-fair / August – September / 7-15 in. / spinners, flies, bait.
Arctic Grayling / poor / June – September / 7-12 in. / spinners, flies.

2. Daves Creek
Access A: MP 37.3; S on gravel road 0.1 mile to stream crossing and outlet of Tern Lake.
Access B: MP 37.6 – 40.0; highway parallels stream, crossing it at MP 39.5 and 39.7.
Fishing: Some nice char available in late summer and fall. Salmon spawning area.
Rainbow Trout / fair / early August – late September / 7-15 in. / spinners, flies.
Dolly Varden / fair-good / mid-August – early October / 8-18 in. / spinners, flies.
Arctic Grayling / poor-fair / early July – mid-September / 7-14 in. / spinners, flies.

3. Quartz Creek (Middle)
Access: MP 40.9; highway crosses stream.
Fishing: Sight fishing possible in late summer. Salmon spawning area.
Rainbow Trout / fair / early August – late September / 8-18 in. / attractors, flies.
Dolly Varden / fair / early August – late September / 8-20 in. / attractors, flies.
Arctic Grayling / poor / early July – mid-September / 7-12 in. / spinners, flies.

4. Quartz Creek (Lower)
Access A: MP 42.0 – 44.0; highway parallels stream.
Access B: MP 45.0; S on Quartz Creek Rd. 0.6 mile to Quartz Creek Campground on right. Trails lead to stream.
Access C: MP 45.0; S on Quartz Creek Rd. 0.7 mile to stream crossing.
Fishing: One of the premier fly-fishing streams on the peninsula, especially productive for large char in late summer and fall. Fish to 10 pounds present. Salmon spawning area.
Rainbow Trout / fair / late July – early October / 8-18 in. / spinners, flies.
Dolly Varden / fair-good / late July – late September / 10-20 in. / attractors, flies.
Arctic Grayling / poor-fair / early July – late September / 7-14 in. / spinners, flies.
Whitefish / poor / mid-July – early October / 10-15 in. / attractors, flies.

5. Cresent Creek
Access: MP 45.0; S on Quartz Creek Rd. 2.6 miles to stream crossing. Crescent Creek Campground turn-off at mile 2.7 with trails leading to and along stream to Quartz Creek confluence.
Fishing: Small and shallow clearwater stream with limited opportunities for char.
Dolly Varden / fair / mid-August – mid-September / 8-18 in. / attractors, flies.

6. Kenai Lake
Access A: MP 45.0 – 47.7; highway parallels lake, pullouts present.
Access B: MP 45.0; SW on Quartz Creek Rd. 0.6 mile to Quartz Creek Campground on right. From campground a trail leads downstream along Quartz Creek to lake.

Fishing: Very large and deep glacial lake that can be difficult to fish. Focus efforts near outlet or the mouths of clearwater streams. Try evenings. Salmon spawning area.
Rainbow Trout / fair / July – October / 8-20 in. / spoons, spinners, bait.
Lake Trout / fair -good / October – November / 2-5 lbs. / spoons, bait.
Dolly Varden / fair / July – November / 8-20 in. / spoons, spinners, bait.

Unit B: Upper Kenai River/Skilak Lake Drainages

Includes all roadside waters flowing into and surrounding the upper and section of Kenai River, including Skilak Lake.

UNIT REGULATIONS:

* King salmon fishing prohibited: All waters, year-round.
* Rainbow trout fishing prohibited: All flowing waters, April 15 – June 14.
* Only unbaited, single-hook, artificial lures: All flowing waters, year-round.
Note: *Consult sport fishing regulations closely for Kenai and Russian rivers.*

UNIT TIMING:

FISH ▽	JAN	FEB	MAR	APR	MAY	JUN	JUL	AUG	SEP	OCT	NOV	DEC
KS*												
RS												
PS												
CS												
SS												
KO												
RT												
LT												
DV												
AG												
WF												

*Note: *Timing shown for king salmon indicates fish in all stages of maturity.*

STERLING HIGHWAY log continues on page 282.

Snug Harbor Road

Road begins at MP 47.9 Sterling Highway (Mile 0) and ends at trailhead near Cooper Lake (Mile 12).

7. Cleaver Lake

Access: MP 8.7; follow sign to the right at "Y," 2.3 miles to parking area on left. Trail on left leads 200 yards to lake.
Fishing: Lake supports a small population of native trout. Use a canoe/float tube.
Rainbow Trout / fair / June, September – December / 7-15 in. / spoons, flies, bait.

8. Rainbow Lake

Access: MP 8.7; follow sign to the right at "Y," 2.3 miles to parking area on left. Trail on left leads 0.25 mile to lake.
Fishing: Lake is stocked with trout. Use a canoe/float tube.
Rainbow Trout / good / June, September – December / 7-16 in. / spoons, flies, bait.

9. Cooper Lake

Access: MP 8.7; follow sign to the right at "Y" 3.5 miles, left on dirt road short distance to lake.
Fishing: Fairly large lake containing a decent population of char.
Rainbow Trout / fair / June, September – October / 7-18 in. / spinners, flies, bait.
Dolly Varden / fair-good / June, September – October / 7-15 in. / spinners, flies, bait.

STERLING HIGHWAY log continues.

10. Kenai River (Upper)

Note: Includes that portion of the river from the outlet of Kenai Lake downstream to the confluence with Russian River.

Access: MP 47.7 – 55.0; highway parallels river, crossing it at MP 47.7 and 53.0. Pullouts present.
Fishing: Large glacial river that is productive for trout, char, and salmon. Can be fished from shore as well as drift boat. Popular spot in late summer and fall. River remains ice-free in winter with opportunities for resident species. Major salmon spawning area.
Red Salmon / fair-good / 4-10 lbs. (16 lbs.) / flies.
Pink Salmon / poor / 2-5 lbs. (10 lbs.) / spoons, spinners, flies.
Silver Salmon / Early Run: fair-good / 5-12 lbs. (18 lbs.) / spoons, spinners, flies.
    Late Run: good-excellent / 6-15 lbs. (22 lbs.) / spoons, spinners, flies.
Rainbow Trout / good / 8-20 in. (22 lbs.) / spinners, attractors, flies.
Dolly Varden / good / 10-20 in. (15 lbs.) / spinners, attractors, flies.
Whitefish / fair / 10-15 in. (17 in.) / attrctors, flies.

FISH ▽	JAN	FEB	MAR	APR	MAY	JUN	JUL	AUG	SEP	OCT	NOV	DEC
RS												
PS												
SS												
RT												
DV												
WF												

11. Lower Russian Lake

Access: MP 52.7; S on paved road 1.0 mile to parking area on left. Russian Lakes Trail leads 2.0 miles to a "Y," right fork proceeds 0.6 mile to Russian River and lake outlet, left fork proceeds 0.8 mile to lake.
Fishing: Clearwater lake with opportunities for trout and char. Use a canoe/float tube.
Rainbow Trout / good / June, September – December / 7-18 in. / spinners, flies.
Dolly Varden / fair / June, September – January / 7-15 in. / spoons, spinners, flies.

12. Russian River (Lower)

Access: MP 52.7 - Russian River Campground; S on paved road 1.4 to 2.0 miles to parking and camping areas. Several trails lead to and along river.

Fishing: One of the most popular angling hot spots in Alaska, famed for superb red salmon action and fly-fishing for trout and char. River is small, shallow, and clear and easily waded. Sight fishing possible. Major salmon spawning area in fall.

Red Salmon / Early Run: excellent / 4-7 lbs. (12 lbs.) / flies.
    Late Run: excellent / 3-10 lbs. (16 lbs.) / flies.
Silver Salmon / fair-good / 6-12 lbs. (18 lbs.) / spinners, flies.
Rainbow Trout / good / 7-20 in. (20 lbs.) / attractors, flies.
Dolly Varden / fair-good / 8-20 in. (8 lbs.) / attractors, flies.

FISH ▽	JAN	FEB	MAR	APR	MAY	JUN	JUL	AUG	SEP	OCT	NOV	DEC
RS						▓	▓	▓				
SS								▓	▓			
RT					▒	▒	▓	▓	▓			
DV						▒	▒	▓	▒			

13. Russian River / Kenai River Confluence

Note: Includes that portion of water from the mouth of Russian River downstream to ferry crossing on Kenai River.

Access A: MP 52.7 - Russian River Campground; S on paved road 1.4 to 2.0 miles. Several trails lead 0.5 to 0.25 mile along Russian River to confluence area.

Access B: MP 54.9 - Kenai-Russian River Campground; S on paved road by sign 0.1 mile. Take ferry across Kenai River to confluence area.

Fishing: Very productive spot for salmon, especially reds. Expect anglers to stand shoulder-to-shoulder at peak of runs. Also a choice location in fall targeting trout and char. Sight fishing possible. Major salmon spawning area in fall.

Red Salmon / Early Run: excellent / 4-7 lbs. (12 lbs.) / flies.
    Late Run: excellent / 3-10 lbs. (16 lbs.) / flies.
Pink Salmon / poor / 2-5 lbs. (10 lbs.) / flies.
Silver Salmon / Early Run: fair-good / 5-12 lbs. (18 lbs.) / spinners, attractors, flies.
    Late Run: good / 6-15 lbs. (22 lbs.) / spinners, attractors, flies.
Rainbow Trout / good / 8-20 in. (22 lbs.) / spinners, attractors, flies.
Dolly Varden / good / 10-20 in. (15 lbs.) / spinners, attractors, flies.
Whitefish / poor-fair / 10-15 in. (17 in.) / ttractors, flies.

FISH ▽	JAN	FEB	MAR	APR	MAY	JUN	JUL	AUG	SEP	OCT	NOV	DEC
RS					▒	▓	▓	▓	▒			
PS							▒	▓				
SS	▒	▒	▒	▒	▒	▒	▒	▓	▓	▓	▒	▒
RT			▒	▒	▓	▒	▒	▓	▓	▓	▒	
DV	▒	▒			▒	▒	▒	▓	▓	▓	▒	
WF					▒	▒	▒	▓	▓	▓	▒	

14. Kenai River (Upper)

Note: Includes that portion of the river from the Russian River confluence downstream to Jim's Landing.

Access: MP 54.9 – 58.0; highway parallels river, several pullouts and trails present.
Fishing: The best stretch of the Upper Kenai for salmon, trout, and char. Reds and silvers are abundant, rainbows may exceed 15 pounds. Very popular area for floating and hike-in shore fishing. Major salmon spawning area in fall.
Red Salmon / Early Run: good-excellent / 4-7 lbs. (12 lbs.) / flies.
    Late Run: good-excellent / 3-10 lbs. (16 lbs.) / flies.
Pink Salmon / poor / 2-5 lbs. (10 lbs.) / spoons, spinners, flies.
Silver Salmon / Early Run: fair-good / 5-12 lbs. (18 lbs.) / spoons, spinners, flies.
    Late Run: fair-good / 6-15 lbs. (22 lbs.) / spoons, spinners, flies.
Rainbow Trout / good / 8-20 in. (22 lbs.) / spinners, attractors, flies.
Dolly Varden / good / 10-20 in. (15 lbs.) / spinners, attractors, flies.
Whitefish / fair / 10-15 in. (17 in.) attractors, flies.

FISH ▽	JAN	FEB	MAR	APR	MAY	JUN	JUL	AUG	SEP	OCT	NOV	DEC
RS												
PS												
SS												
RT												
DV												
WF												

15. Lower Fuller Lake

Access: MP 57.1; parking area. Fuller Lakes Trail leads 1.5 mile N to lake.
Fishing: Lake supports a moderate population of grayling. Use a canoe/float tube.
Arctic Grayling / fair-good / June – September / 7-14 in. / spinners, flies.

STERLING HIGHWAY log continues on page 286.

Skilak Lake Road

    Road begins at MP 58.0 Sterling Highway (MP 0) and rejoins Sterling Highway at MP 75.2 (MP 19.1).

16. Kenai River (Upper)

Access A: MP 0.1 - Jim's Landing; left on access road short distance to campground and river.
Access B: MP 0.7 - Kenai River Trail (Upper); park at trailhead S of road. Trail leads 0.3 mile to river.
Access C: MP 2.4 - Kenai River Trail (Lower); park at trailhead S of road. Trail leads 0.3 mile to a "Y," take right fork 0.5 mile to river. It parallels river from this point downstream the next 2 miles.
Access D: MP 4.7 - Hidden Creek Trail; park at trailhead S of road. Trail leads 1.5 to 2.0 miles to mouth of Hidden Creek, outlet of upper Kenai River, and inlet of Skilak Lake.

Fishing: This stretch of the river is mainly a late-season float and hike-in fishery for trout and char. In addition, great opportunities abound for red and silver salmon. The canyon area, only accessed by boat, is a hot spot for lunker rainbows.

Red Salmon / Early Run: good / 4-7 lbs. (12 lbs.) / flies.

    Late Run: good-excellent / 3-10 lbs. (16 lbs.) / flies.

Pink Salmon / poor / 2-5 lbs. (10 lbs.) / spoons, spinners, flies.

Silver Salmon / Early Run: fair-good / 5-12 lbs. (18 lbs.) / spoons, spinners, flies.

    Late Run: good-excellent / 6-15 lbs. (22 lbs.) / spoons, spinners, flies.

Rainbow Trout / good / 8-20 in. (22 lbs.) / spinners, attractors, flies.

Dolly Varden / good / 10-20 in. (15 lbs.) / attractors, flies.

Whitefish / poor-fair / 10-15 in. (17 in) / attractors, flies.

FISH ▽	JAN	FEB	MAR	APR	MAY	JUN	JUL	AUG	SEP	OCT	NOV	DEC
RS												
PS												
SS												
RT												
DV												
WF												

17. Hidden Lake

Access: MP 3.6 - Hidden Lake Campground; N on paved access road 0.7 mile to lake.

Fishing: Large, deep clearwater lake containing a decent population of fish. Use boat to access productive areas. Limited shore-fishing opportunities. Popular winter fishery.

Kokanee / fair-good / May – June, August – September / 7-12 in. / spinners, flies, bait.

Rainbow Trout / fair / May – June, September – October / 7-18 in. / spinners, flies, bait.

Lake Trout / fair / May – June, September – December / 2-6 lbs. / spoons, plugs, bait.

Dolly Varden / fair / May – June, September – January / 7-16 in. / spoons, flies, bait.

18. Upper Ohmer Lake

Access: MP 7.7; S on access road 0.2 mile to lake.

Fishing: Lake supports a moderate population of native trout. Use a canoe/float tube.

Rainbow Trout / fair / May, September – December / 7-15 in. / spinners, flies, bait.

Dolly Varden / fair / May – June, September – January / 7-15 in. / spoons, flies, bait.

19. Skilak Lake

Access A: MP 8.5; S on gravel road by sign 1.9 mile to campground and lake.

Access B: MP 13.8; S on gravel road by sign 0.9 mile to campground and lake.

Fishing: Large glacial lake with limited opportunities for trout and char. Use a boat to access lake inlet or outlet or mouths of clearwater streams. Shore fishing difficult.

Pink Salmon / poor / early, mid-August / 2-5 lbs. / spoons, spinners.

Silver Salmon / fair / mid-August, late September / 6-15 lbs. / spinners, bait.

Rainbow Trout / fair / July – October / 8-20 in. / spoons, spinners, bait.

Lake Trout / fair / April – May, October – November / 2-5 lbs. / spoons, bait.

Dolly Varden / fair / July – November / 8-20 in. / spoons, spinners, bait.

20. Lower Ohmer Lake

Access: MP 8.6 - Lower Ohmer Lake Campground; S on gravel road by sign short distance to lake.

Fishing: Lake supports a moderate population of native trout. Use a canoe/float tube.
Rainbow Trout / fair / May, September – December / 7-15 in. / spinners, flies, bait.
Dolly Varden / fair / May – June, September – January / 7-15 in. / spoons, flies, bait.

STERLING HIGHWAY log continues.

21. Jean Lake

Access: MP 59.9 – 60.5; highway parallels lake, with access road at MP 60.0 heading W to Jean Lake Campground and lake.

Fishing: Lake supports moderate populations of trout and char. Use a canoe/float tube.
Rainbow Trout / good / May, September – December / 8-18 in. / spinners, flies, bait.
Dolly Varden / fair / May – June, September – January / 8-16 in. / spoons, flies, bait.

22. Upper Jean Lake

Access: MP 62.0; N on dirt road and park, hike 200 yards N to lake.

Fishing: Lake supports a moderate population of native trout. Use a canoe/float tube.
Rainbow Trout / fair / May, September – December / 8-16 in. / spoons, flies, bait.

Unit C: Lower Kenai River Drainage

Includes all roadside waters flowing into and surrounding the lower Kenai River.

UNIT REGULATIONS:

* Rainbow trout fishing prohibited: All flowing waters, April 15 – June 14.
Note: Consult sport fishing regulations closely for Kenai and Moose rivers.

UNIT TIMING:

FISH ▽	JAN	FEB	MAR	APR	MAY	JUN	JUL	AUG	SEP	OCT	NOV	DEC
KS												
RS												
PS												
CS												
SS												
LS												
RT												
DV												
AG												
WF												
NP												

23. Kelly Lake

Access: MP 68.4 - Kelly Lake Campground; S on gravel road 0.3 mile to a "Y," left fork 0.3 mile to lake.
Fishing: Lake supports a moderate population of native trout. Use a canoe/float tube.
Rainbow Trout / fair / May, September – December / 8-18 in. / spoons, flies, bait.
Northern Pike / poor / May, September – December / 2-4 lbs. / spoons, plugs, bait.

24. Peterson Lake

Access: MP 68.4 - Peterson Lake Campground; S on gravel road 0.3 mile to a "Y," right fork 0.2 mile to lake.
Fishing: Lake supports a moderate population of native trout. Use a canoe/float tube.
Rainbow Trout / fair / May, September – December / 8-18 in. / spoons, flies, bait.
Northern Pike / poor / May, September – December / 2-4 lbs. / spoons, plugs, bait.

25. Egumen Lake

Access: MP 70.8; S at pullout and park, trail leads 0.25 mile S to lake.
Fishing: Lake supports a moderate population of native trout. Use a canoe/float tube.
Rainbow Trout / fair-good / May, September – December / 8-18 in. / spoons, flies, bait.
Northern Pike / poor / May, September – December / 2-4 lbs. / spoons, plugs, bait.

26. Watson Lake

Access: MP 71.3 - Watson Lake Campground; N on gravel road 0.7 mile to lake.
Fishing: Lake supports a moderate population of native trout. Use a canoe/float tube.
Rainbow Trout / fair / May, September – December / 8-18 in. / spinners, flies, bait.
Northern Pike / poor / May, September – December / 2-4 lbs. / spoons, plugs, bait.

27. East Fork Moose River

Access: MP 71.4; highway crosses stream.
Fishing: Very small clearwater stream with limited fall opportunities for trout.
Rainbow Trout / fair / early September – mid-October / 7-16 in. / spinners, flies.

28. Kenai River (Middle)

Note: Includes that portion of the river from the outlet of Skilak Lake downstream to the confluence with Funny River.

Access A: MP 80.2 - Bing's Landing; S on Bing's Landing Rd. by sign 0.8 mile to river.
Access B: MP 84.9 - Morgan's Landing; S on Scout Lake Loop Rd. 1.6 mile to a "T," right on Lou Morgan Rd. 2.4 miles, right on gravel road 1.5 mile to river.
Fishing: Large glacial river with superb action throughout summer and fall for salmon, trout, and char. Shore fishing opportunities limited in some places. Use a boat to access best locations or if targeting kings or trophy rainbows. Major salmon spawning area.
King Salmon / Early Run: fair-good / 15-50 lbs. (100 lbs.) / plugs, attractors.
    Late Run: good / 25-60 lbs. (100 lbs.) / plugs, attractors, bait.
Red Salmon / Early Run: poor-fair / 4-7 lbs. (12 lbs.) / flies.
(continues on next page)

N0. 28 - Kenai River continued.

Late Run: excellent / 3-10 lbs. (16 lbs.) / flies.
Pink Salmon / good-excellent / 2-6 lbs. (12 lbs.) / spoons, spinners, flies.
Silver Salmon / Early Run: good / 5-12 lbs. (18 lbs.) / spoons, spinners, bait.
Late Run: good-excellent / 6-15 lbs. (22 lbs.) / spoons, spinners, bait.
Rainbow Trout / good / 8-20 in. (22 lbs.) / spinners, attractors, flies, bait.
Dolly Varden / good / 10-20 in. (15 lbs.) / spoons, attractors, flies, bait.
Whitefish / poor-fair / 10-15 in (17 in.) / attractors, flies, bait.

FISH ▽	JAN	FEB	MAR	APR	MAY	JUN	JUL	AUG	SEP	OCT	NOV	DEC
KS												
RS												
PS												
SS												
RT												
DV												
WF												

29. Moose River / Kenai River Confluence

Access: MP 82.3 - Izaak Walton Campground; highway crosses river, S on access road E of bridge short distance to confluence area.
Fishing: Popular spot for salmon in summer and fall. The slack water is ideal for connecting with pinks and silvers. For reds, try downstream of confluence.
King Salmon / Early Run: poor / 15-50 lbs. (100 lbs.) / flies.
Late Run: poor / 25-60 lbs. (100 lbs.) / flies.
Red Salmon / Early Run: fair / 4-7 lbs. (12 lbs.) / flies.
Late Run: good-excellent / 3-10 lbs. (16 lbs.) / flies.
Pink Salmon / good-excellent / 2-6 lbs. (12 lbs.) / spoons, spinners.
Silver Salmon / Early Run: good / 5-12 lbs. (18 lbs.) / spoons, spinners, bait.
Late Run: good / 6-15 lbs. (22 lbs.) / spoons, spinners, bait.
Rainbow Trout / fair / 8-20 in. (22 lbs.) / spinners, flies, bait.
Dolly Varden / fair / 1020 in. (15 lbs.) / spoons, flies, bait.

FISH ▽	JAN	FEB	MAR	APR	MAY	JUN	JUL	AUG	SEP	OCT	NOV	DEC
KS												
RS												
PS												
SS												
RT												
DV												

30. Longmere Lake

Access: MP 88.9; S on West Dr. 0.1 mile, right on Longmere Lake Rd. 0.1 mile to access site on left and lake.
Fishing: Lake is stocked with landlocked salmon and trout. Use a canoe/float tube.
Rainbow Trout / good / May, September – December / 7-20 in. / spinners, flies, bait.

31. Kenai River (Lower)

Note: Includes that portion of the river from the confluence with Funny River downstream to the upper edge of tidal influence and Eagle Rock.

Access A: MP 94.1 - Swiftwater Campground; E on East Redoubt Ave. 0.6 mile, right on Griffin Ave. 0.8 mile, right on gravel road leading to river.

Access B: MP 94.4 - Soldotna Creek Park; SE on gravel road next to State of Alaska Maintenance Station and proceed to the left 0.2 mile to parking area. Trail leads 200 yards to river and mouth of Soldotna Creek.

Access C: MP 95.9 - Kenai River Bridge; highway crosses river.

Access D: MP 96.1 - Centennial Campground; W on Kalifornsky Beach Rd. at intersection S of Kenai River Bridge in Soldotna, short distance, right on Centennial Park Dr. 0.8 mile to river.

Access E: MP 96.1 - Slikok Creek State Park; W on Kalifornsky Beach Rd. to MP 20.5, E on College Loop Rd. 1.4 mile to a "T," right on East Poppy Ln., continue to the community college parking area. Short trail leads to river and mouth of Slikok Creek.

Fishing: Glacial drainage with great opportunities for a variety of salmon species as well as trout and char. Fishing from shore and boat is equally productive but kings best from boat. This is a very popular area in mid-summer for anglers targeting reds.

King Salmon / Early Run: fair-good / 15-50 lbs. (100 lbs.) / plugs, attractors.
　　Late Run: good / 25-60 lbs. (100 lbs.) / plugs, attractors, bait.
Red Salmon / Early Run: poor-fair / 4-7 lbs. (12 lbs.) / flies.
　　Late Run: excellent / 3-10 lbs. (16 lbs.) / flies.
Pink Salmon / excellent / 2-6 lbs. (12 lbs.) / spoons, spinners, flies.
Silver Salmon / Early Run: good / 5-12 lbs. (18 lbs.) / spoons, spinners, bait.
　　Late Run: good-excellent / 6-15 lbs. (22 lbs.) / spoons, spinners, bait.
Rainbow Trout / fair-good / 8-20 in. (20 lbs.) / attractors, flies, bait.
Dolly Varden / good / 10-20 in. (5 lbs.) / spoons, attractors, flies, bait.

FISH ▽	JAN	FEB	MAR	APR	MAY	JUN	JUL	AUG	SEP	OCT	NOV	DEC
KS												
RS												
PS												
SS												
RT												
DV												

32. Funny River (Lower)

Access: MP 96.1; E on Funny River Rd. 11.3 miles to river crossing.

Fishing: Clearwater stream with limited opportunities for salmon, trout, and char.
Pink Salmon / fair / late July – early August / 2-4 lbs. / spoons, spinners.
Silver Salmon / fair / late August – early September / 5-10 lbs. / spinners, bait.
Rainbow Trout / fair / mid-July – mid-September / 8-18 in. / spinners, flies, bait.
Dolly Varden / fair / mid-July – late September / 8-16 in. / spinners, flies, bait.

33. Funny River / Kenai River Confluence

Access: MP 96.1; E on Funny River Rd. 11.5 miles to access road on left and campground. Trails lead to confluence area.

Fishing: Salmon stack up in this slackwater area during the summer and fall months. Also a productive spot for trout and char.

Pink Salmon / good / 2-6 lbs. (12 lbs.) / spoons, spinners, flies.

Silver Salmon / Early Run: good / 5-12 lbs. (18 lbs.) / spoons, spinners, bait.

　　　Late Run: good / 6-15 lbs. (22 lbs.) / spoons, spinners, bait.

Rainbow Trout / fair-good / 8-20 in. (20 lbs.) / spinners, flies, bait.

Dolly Varden / good / 8-20 in. (15 lbs.) / spoons, attractors, flies, bait.

Whitefish / poor /10-15 in. (17 in.) / attractors, flies, bait.

FISH ▽	JAN	FEB	MAR	APR	MAY	JUN	JUL	AUG	SEP	OCT	NOV	DEC
PS												
SS												
RT												
DV												
WF												

34. Aurora Lake

Access: MP 96.1; E on Funny River Rd. 13.5 miles, right on Rabbit Run Rd. 1.0 mile, left on Browns Lake Rd. 2.0 miles, right on Lake Rd. 1.0 mile, right on Aurora Ave. 0.7 mile to access site on right and lake.

Fishing: Lake is stocked with salmon. Use a canoe/float tube.

Landlocked Salmon / good-excellent / June – March / 7-12 in. / spinners, flies, jigs, bait.

35. Slikok Creek

Access: MP 99.4; highway crosses stream.

Fishing: Small clearwater stream with limited opportunities for trout and char.

Rainbow Trout / poor-fair / mid-August – mid-September / 7-14 in. / flies, bait.

Dolly Varden / fair / mid-August – late September / 7-12 in. / spinners, flies, bait.

STERLING HIGHWAY log continues on page 295.

Unit D: Central Kenai Peninsula Drainages

Includes all roadside waters along or surrounding Swanson River Road and Swan Lake Road.

UNIT REGULATIONS:

* Fishing prohibited: All flowing waters, April 15 – June 14.

* King salmon fishing prohibited: All waters, year-round.

UNIT TIMING:

FISH ▽	JAN	FEB	MAR	APR	MAY	JUN	JUL	AUG	SEP	OCT	NOV	DEC
KS												
RS												
SS												
RT												
AC												
DV												

*Note: Timing shown for King salmon indicates fish in all stages of maturity.

Swanson River Road

Road begins at MP 83.4 Sterling Highway (MP 0) and ends at Swan Lake Road Junction (MP 17.2).

36. Mosquito Lake

Access: MP 7.9; trail leads 200 yards E to lake.

Fishing: Lake contains a population of native trout. Use a canoe/float tube.

Rainbow Trout / good / May, September – December / 8-18 in. / spinners, flies, bait.

37. Silver Lake

Access: MP 9.1; trail leads 1.0 mile W to lake.

Fishing: Lake contains a population of native trout and char. Use a canoe/float tube.

Rainbow Trout / good / May, September – December / 8-18 in. / spinners, flies, bait.

Arctic Char / fair / May, September – January / 8-18 in. / spoons, jigs, bait.

38. Finger Lake

Access: MP 9.8; trail leads 2.3 miles W to lake.

Fishing: Lake contains a population of native char. Use a canoe/float tube.

Arctic Char / good / May, September – January / 8-18 in. / spoons, jigs, bait.

39. Forest Lake

Access: MP 10.7; trail leads 200 yards NW to lake.

Fishing: Lake contains a population of native trout. Use a canoe/float tube.

Rainbow Trout / good / May, September – December / 8-18 in. / spinners, flies, bait.

40. Weed Lake

Access: MP 13.1; trail leads 200 yards E to lake.

Fishing: Lake contains a population of native trout. Use a canoe/float tube.

Rainbow Trout / fair / May, September – December / 8-16 in. / spinners, flies, bait.

41. Dabbler Lake

Access: MP 13.3; trail leads 0.3 mile E to lake on left.
Fishing: Lake contains a population of native trout and char. Use a canoe/float tube.
Rainbow Trout / good / May, September – December / 8-18 in. / spinners, flies, bait.
Arctic Char / fair / May, September – January / 8-18 in. / spoons, jigs, bait.

42. Skookum Lake

Access: MP 13.3; trail leads 1.3 mile E to a "Y," right fork 0.25 mile to lake.
Fishing: Lake contains a population of native trout and char. Use a canoe/float tube.
Rainbow Trout / good / May, September – December / 8-18 in. / spinners, flies, bait.
Arctic Char / fair / May, September – January / 8-18 in. / spoons, jigs, bait.

43. Drake Lake

Access: MP 13.3; trail leads 1.3 mile E to a "Y," left fork 0.5 mile to lake.
Fishing: Lake contains a population of native trout and char. Use a canoe/float tube.
Rainbow Trout / good / May, September – December / 8-18 in. / spinners, flies, bait.
Arctic Char / fair / May, September – January / 8-18 in. / spoons, jigs, bait.

44. Breeze Lake

Access: MP 14.0; trail leads 200 yards SW to lake.
Fishing: Lake contains a population of native trout. Use a canoe/float tube.
Rainbow Trout / fair / May, September – December / 8-16 in. / spinners, flies, bait.

45. Dolly Varden Lake

Access: MP 14.1; access site to lake E of road.
Fishing: Lake contains a population of native trout and char. Use a canoe/float tube.
Rainbow Trout / excellent / May, September – December / 8-18 in. / spoons, flies, bait.
Arctic Char / good / May, September – January / 8-18 in. / spoons, jigs, bait.

46. Rainbow Lake

Access: MP 14.8; right fork at "Y" 0.8 mile, access road on right leads to lake.
Fishing: Lake contains a population of native trout and char. Use a canoe/float tube.
Rainbow Trout / good / May, September – December / 8-16 in. / spinners, flies, bait.
Dolly Varden / fair / May, September – January / 8-18 in. / spoons, jigs, bait.

47. Swanson River (Upper)

Access: MP 17.7; end of road.
Fishing: Slow-flowing tannic river with productive angling for mainly silver salmon and trout. Bank fishing area. Canoes are used to access good holes away from road.
Silver Salmon / fair-good / late August – early September / 5-12 lbs. / spinners, bait.
Rainbow Trout / good / mid-August – early October / 7-18 in. / spinners, flies, bait.
Dolly Varden / fair / mid-August – early October / 8-15 in. / spinners, flies, bait.

Swan Lake Road

Road begins at MP 17.2 Swanson River Road (MP 0) and ends at Paddle Lake and the entrance to Swanson River Canoe System (MP 12.2).

48. Fish Lake

Access: MP 3.0; pullout S of road.
Fishing: Lake contains a population of native char. Use a canoe/float tube.
Arctic Char / fair / May, September – January / 8-15 in. / spoons, jigs, bait.

49. Ice Lake

Access: MP 4.0; Swan Lake Canoe Trail System parking area S of road. Faint trail on other side of road leads 0.5 mile N to lake.
Fishing: Lake contains a population of native trout and char. Use a canoe/float tube.
Rainbow Trout / excellent / May, September – December / 8-18 in. / spoons, flies, bait.
Arctic Char / fair / May, September – January / 8-18 in. / spoons, jigs, bait.

50. Canoe Lake

Access: MP 4.0; access site S of road.
Note: Canoe Lake is the west entrance of the Swan Lake Canoe System, providing access to multiple area lakes.
Fishing: Lake contains a population of native trout and char. Use a canoe/float tube.
Rainbow Trout / fair / May, September – December / 8-18 in. / spinners, flies, bait.
Dolly Varden / fair / May, September – January / 8-15 in. / spoons, jigs, bait.

51. Waterfowl Lake

Note: Lake is accessible in winter on foot and mechanical means of transportation following the same general pattern of lake crossing and portaging as in summer.

Access: MP 4.0; access site S of road. Cross Canoe Lake 0.7 mile to SW end of lake and marked portage, 0.25 mile due W to Waterfowl Lake.
Fishing: Lake contains a population of native trout and char. Use a canoe.
Rainbow Trout / good / May, September – December / 8-20 in. / spinners, flies, bait.
Arctic Char / fair / May, September – January / 8-20 in. / spoons, jigs, bait.

52. Swan Lake Canoe System Lakes, West Entrance

Note: Locations are on the Swan Lake Canoe System. They are accessible in winter on foot and mechanical means of transportation following the same general patterns of lake crossing and portaging as in summer.

Access: MP 4.0 – Canoe Lake; S across lake to marked starting point with access to **Chain #1** (Mile 1.5), **Contact** (Mile 1.9), **Marten** (Mile 2.3), and **Spruce** (Miles 3.2) Lakes.
(continues on next page)

Fishing: Lakes contain populations of native trout and char. Use a canoe/float tube.
Rainbow Trout / good-excellent / May, September – January / 8-20 in. / spinners, flies, bait.
Arctic Char / good / May, September – January / 8-20 in. / spoons, jigs, bait.

53. Sucker Lake

Access: MP 4.7; access site S of road.
Fishing: Lake contains a population of native trout. Use a canoe/float tube.
Rainbow Trout / fair / May, September – December / 8-16 in. / spinners, flies, bait.

54. Little Merganser Lake

Access: MP 6.2; pullout S of road.
Fishing: Lake contains a population of native trout. Use a canoe/float tube.
Rainbow Trout / fair / May, September – December / 8-18 in. / spinners, flies, bait.

55. Campfire Lake

Access: MP 7.0; parking area N of road. Trail leads 0.5 mile N to lake.
Fishing: Lake contains a population of native trout. Use a canoe/float tube.
Rainbow Trout / excellent / May, September – December / 8-18 in. / spoons, flies, bait.

56. Nest Lake

Access: MP 8.3; access site N of road. Trail leads 0.5 mile N to lake.
Fishing: Lake contains a population of native trout. Use a canoe/float tube.
Rainbow Trout / excellent / May, September – December / 8-18 in. / spoons, flies, bait.

57. Paddle Lake

Access: MP 12.2; left at "Y" 0.6 mile to parking area. Trail leads 0.25 mile N to lake.
Note: Paddle Lake is the entrance to the Swanson River Canoe System, providing access to many area lakes and the upper Swanson River.

Fishing: Lake contains a population of native trout and char. Use a canoe/float tube.
Rainbow Trout / good / May, September – December / 8-18 in. / spinners, flies, bait.
Arctic Char / fair / May, September – December / 8-18 in. / spoons, jigs, bait.

58. Odd Lake

Access: MP 12.2; left at "Y" 0.6 mile to parking area. Trail leads 0.25 mile N to Paddle Lake and E 0.1 mile to lake.
Fishing: Lake contains a population of native trout. Use a canoe/float tube.
Rainbow Trout / fair-good / May, September – December / 8-16 in. / spoons, flies, bait.

59. Pad Lake

Access: MP 12.2; left at "Y" 0.6 mile to parking area. Trail leads 0.25 mile N to Paddle Lake 0.1 mile to Odd Lake, and 200 yards to lake.
Fishing: Lake contains a population of native trout. Use a canoe/float tube.
Rainbow Trout / fair-good / May, September – December / 8-16 in. / spoons, flies, bait.

60. Swanson River Canoe Route Lakes

Note: Locations are on the Swanson River Canoe System. They are accessible in winter on foot and mechanical means of transportation following the same general patterns of lake crossing and portaging as in summer.

Access: MP 12.2; left at "Y" 0.6 mile to parking area. and trailhead. Trail leads 0.25 mile N to Paddle Lake; N across lake is marked starting point with access to **Dog** (Mile 1.7), **Chum** (Mile 2.0), **Lure** (Mile 2.2), **Channel** (Mile 2.2), and **Lonely** (Mile 3.6) lakes.
Fishing: Lakes contain populations of native trout and char. Use a canoe/float tube.
Rainbow Trout / good-excellent / May, Sept. – December / 8-20 in. / spinners, flies, bait.
Arctic Char / fair-good / May, September – January / 8-20 in. / spoons, jigs, bait.

Unit E: Lower Kenai Peninsula Drainages

Includes all roadside waters flowing into and surrounding lower Cook Inlet, including salt water.

UNIT REGULATIONS:

* Rainbow/Steelhead trout fishing: Catch-and-release, year-round (except stocked lakes).
* Only unbaited, artificial lures: All flowing waters, September 1 – December 31 (except Kasilof River).
* Halibut fishing prohibited: All salt water, January 1 – 31.

Note: Consult sport fishing regulations closely regarding open seasons, species, and areas on the Kasilof, Ninilchi, and Anchor rivers, Deep Creek, and Cook Inlet salt water.

UNIT TIMING:

FISH ▽	JAN	FEB	MAR	APR	MAY	JUN	JUL	AUG	SEP	OCT	NOV	DEC
KS												
RS												
PS												
CS												
SS												
LS												
ST												
RT												
DV												
WF												

STERLING HIGHWAY log continues.

61. Coal Creek

Access A: MP 106.0; highway crosses stream.
Access B: MP 108.8; NW on Kalifornsky Beach Rd. 2.5 miles to stream crossing.
Fishing: Small stream with limited opportunities for char in late summer and fall.
Dolly Varden / fair / mid-August – mid-September / 7-10 in. / spinners, flies, bait.

62. Roque Lake

Access: MP 106.9; lake is located E of highway.
Fishing: Lake is stocked with trout. Use a float tube or cast from shore.
Rainbow Trout / good / May, September – December / 7-15 in. / spinners, flies, bait.

63. Kasilof River (Middle)

Access: MP 109.4 – Kasilof River State Recreation Site; E on gravel road short distance to access road on left leading to large parking area and river.
Fishing: Glacial drainage with opportunities available for salmon, trout, and char. Some fishing off the bank but mainly from boat. Use high-visibility tackle and bait.
King Salmon / fair / mid-June, late July / 15-35 lbs. / attractors, plugs, bait.
Red Salmon / fair-good / mid-July / 3-8 lbs. / flies.
Pink Salmon / poor-fair / late July / 2-4 lbs. / spoons, spinners.
Silver Salmon / fair / mid-, late August / 6-10 lbs. / attractors, plugs, bait.
Rainbow Trout / poor / mid-July – mid-September / 7-15 in. / attractors, flies, bait.
Dolly Varden / fair / May, mid-July – mid-September / 8-20 in. / attractors, bait.

64. Crooked Creek

Access A: MP 110.9; highway crosses stream.
Access B: MP 111.4; E on Johnson Lake Rd. short distance to stream.
Fishing: Decent opportunities for silver salmon and char. Salmon spawning area.
Pink Salmon / poor / early August / 2-4 lbs. / spoons, spinners, flies.
Silver Salmon / fair / late August – mid-September / 6-10 lbs. / spinners, flies, bait.
Rainbow Trout / poor / early August – late September / 7-16 in. / attractors, flies, bait.
Dolly Varden / good / early August – late September / 7-16 in. / attractors, flies, bait.

65. Johnson Lake

Access: MP 110.5 – Johnson Lake State Recreation Area; E on Johnson Lake Rd. 0.5 mile, left on Tustumena Lake Rd. 0.1 mile, right on gravel access road to recreation site and lake.
Fishing: Lake is stocked with trout; occasionally winterkills. Use a canoe/float tube.
Rainbow Trout / excellent / September – December / 7-15 in. / spinners, flies, bait.

66. Centennial Lake

Access: MP 110.5; E on Johnson Lake Rd. 0.5 mile, left on Tustumena Lake Rd. 3.9 miles, left on access road short distance to lake.
Fishing: Lake is stocked with landlocked salmon and trout. Use a canoe/float tube.
Landlocked Salmon / excellent / June – March / 7-12 in. / spinners, jigs, flies, bait.
Rainbow Trout / good / May, September – December / 7-15 in. / spinners, flies, bait.

67. Kasilof River (Upper)

Access: MP 110.5; E on Johnson Lake Rd. 0.5 mile, left on Tustumena Lake Rd. 5.9 miles to end of road and river.
Fishing: Glacial river with decent opportunities for salmon, trout, and char. Use high-visibility lures and bait for success. Salmon spawning area.
King Salmon / poor / late July / 15-35 lbs. / attractors, bait.

Pink Salmon / poor / late July / 2-4 lbs. / spoons, spinners, attractors.
Silver Salmon / fair / late August / 6-10 lbs. / attractors, bait.
Rainbow Trout / poor / mid-July – early October / 7-15 in. / attractors, bait.
Dolly Varden / fair-good / May, mid-July – mid-October / 8-20 in. / attractors, bait.

68. Quintin Lake

Access: MP 111.4; W on Cohoe Loop Rd. 0.6 mile, left on Thalia Dr. 0.4 mile, left on Naiad Dr. short distance to access road on right leading to lake.
Fishing: Lake is stocked with trout. Use a canoe/float tube.
Rainbow Trout / good / May, September – December / 7-16 in. / spinners, flies, bait.

69. Crooked Creek / Kasilof River Confluence

Access: MP 111.4 - Crooked Creek Campground; W on Cohoe Loop Rd. 1.7 mile, right on Rilinda Rd. 1.5 mile to large parking area. Trail leads 0.2 mile to confluence area.
Fishing: One of the most popular spots on the peninsula, offering great opportunities for stocked and wild salmon in addition to trout and char. Expect crowds. Casting off the bank is very productive in this area. Boat anglers do better on late-run kings.
King Salmon / Early Run: good / 15-35 lbs. (60 lbs.) / attractors, plugs, flies.
    Late Run: fair / 25-50 lbs. (80 lbs.) / attractors, plugs, bait.
Red Salmon / fair / 3-8 lbs. (14 lbs.) / flies.
Pink Salmon / poor-fair / 2-4 lbs. (7 lbs.) / spoons, spinners.
Silver Salmon / fair-good / 6-10 lbs. (20 lbs.) / attractors, plugs, bait.
Steelhead Trout / poor-fair / 5-10 lbs. (20 lbs.) / attractors, plugs, flies.
Rainbow Trout / poor / 7-15 in. (4 ls.) / attractors, flies, bait.
Dolly Varden / fair-good / 8-20 in. (10 lbs.) / attractors, bait.

FISH ▽	JAN	FEB	MAR	APR	MAY	JUN	JUL	AUG	SEP	OCT	NOV	DEC
KS					▓	▓	▓	▓				
RS				▓	▓	▓	▓					
PS							▓	▓				
SS							▓	▓	▓			
ST	▓	▓							▓	▓	▓	▓
RT			▓	▓	▓	▓	▓	▓	▓	▓	▓	
DV			▓	▓	▓	▓	▓	▓	▓	▓		

70. Encelewski Lake

Access: MP 114.9; W on Tolum Rd. 0.4 mile, left on Lake View Crt. 0.9 mile to Panda Ct. on right leading short distance to cul-de-sac and lake.
Fishing: Lake is stocked with trout. Use a canoe/float tube.
Rainbow Trout / good / May, September – December / 7-16 in. / spinners, flies, bait.

71. Ninilchik River

Access A: MP 134.5 - Ninilchik State Recreation Area; E on gravel road to campground. Trails lead 200 yards to river.
Access B: MP 135.0; highway crosses river.

Access C: MP 135.1; W on Beach Access Rd. S of highway bridge 1.2 mile to end of road and river mouth. Road parallels lower river.

Fishing: Clearwater stream with opportunities for salmon, trout, and char, especially famous for its superb king action. Can be waded throughout the length of the river. This is a weekend-only fishery during king salmon season. Expect crowds in May and June.

King Salmon / good-excellent / 15-30 lbs. (55 lbs.) / attractors, flies, bait.
Red Salmon / fair / 4-8 lbs. (15 lbs.) / flies.
Pink Salmon / good-excellent / 2-4 lbs. (7 lbs.) / spoons, spinners, flies.
Silver Salmon / fair-good / 6-12 lbs. (18 lbs.) / spinners, attractors, bait.
Steelhead Trout / fair / 5-10 lbs. (18 lbs.) / attractors, flies.
Rainbow Trout / poor / 7-15 in. (5 bs.) / attractors, flies, bait.
Dolly Varden / good / 7-20 in. (7 lbs.) / attractors, flies, bait.

FISH ▽	JAN	FEB	MAR	APR	MAY	JUN	JUL	AUG	SEP	OCT	NOV	DEC
KS												
RS												
PS												
SS												
ST												
RT												
DV												

72. Deep Creek

Access A: MP 136.8; highway crosses stream.

Access B: MP 137.0 - Deep Creek State Recreation Area; W on access road 1.0 mile to lower stream area and mouth.

Fishing: Clearwater stream with opportunities for salmon, trout, and char, especially noted for its king and steelhead action. Can be waded throughout the length of the river. This is a weekend-only fishery during king salmon season. Expect crowds in May, June.

King Salmon / good-excellent / 15-30 lbs. (55 lbs.) / attractors, flies, bait.
Pink Salmon / good-excellent / 2-4 lbs. (7 lbs.) / spoons, spinners, flies.
Silver Salmon / fair-good / 6-12 lbs. (18 lbs.) / spinners, attractors, bait.
Steelhead Trout / fair / 5-10 lbs. (18 lbs.) / attractors, flies.
Rainbow Trout / poor / 7-15 in. (5lbs.) / attractors, flies, bait.
Dolly Varden / good / 7-20 in. (7 lbs.) / attractors, flies, bait.

FISH ▽	JAN	FEB	MAR	APR	MAY	JUN	JUL	AUG	SEP	OCT	NOV	DEC
KS												
PS												
SS												
ST												
RT												
DV												

73. Cook Inlet

Access A: MP 135.1 - Ninilchik River; W on Beach Access Rd. 1.2 mile to Ninilchik Harbor, mouth of river, and Cook Inlet.

Access B: MP 137.0 - Deep Creek; W on access road 1.0 mile to mouth of creek and Cook Inlet.

Access C: MP 152.7 - Whiskey Gulch; W on access road 0.4 mile to beach area and Cook Inlet.

Access D: MP 156.7 - Anchor River; W on Old Sterling Hwy. in community of Anchor Point, 0.4 mile to Anchor River (Beach) Rd. just after bridge over Anchor River, right 1.5 mile to mouth of river and Cook Inlet.

Fishing: Primarily a boat fishery targeting salmon and halibut. Expect fair action at best casting from the beach; water is very shallow near shore. Try Whiskey Gulch.

King Salmon / Early Run: excellent / 15-50 lbs. (100 lbs.) / spoons, spinners, bait.
 Late Run: fair-good / 25-60 lbs. (100 lbs.) / spoons, spinners, bait.
Red Salmon / poor-fair / 4-10 lbs. (16 lbs.) / spoons, spinners.
Pink Salmon / good / 2-6 lbs. (12 lbs.) / spoons, spinners.
Silver Salmon / Early Run: good / 5-12 lbs. (18 lbs.) / spoons, spinners, bait.
 Late Run: fair-good / 6-15 lbs. (22 lbs.) / spoons, spinners, bait.
Dolly Varden / fair-good / 8-20 in. (12 lbs.) / spoons, spinners, bait.
Pacific Halibut / good-excellent / 10-50 lbs. (450 lbs.) / jigs, bait.

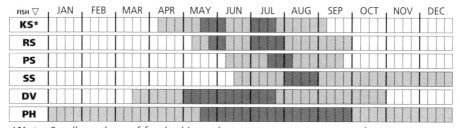

Note: Small numbers of feeder king salmon are present year-round.

74. Stariski Creek (Middle)

Access: MP 150.8; highway crosses stream.
Fishing: Small clearwater stream with decent opportunities for salmon and char.
Pink Salmon / fair / early August / 2-4 lbs. / spoons, spinners, flies.
Silver Salmon / fair / late August – mid-September / 6-10 lbs. / spinners, flies, bait.
Steelhead Trout / poor / early October – early November / 5-10 lbs. / attractors, flies.
Rainbow Trout / poor / early August – late September / 7-15 in. / spinners, flies.
Dolly Varden / fair-good / early August – early October / 7-15 in. / spinners, flies.

75. North Fork Anchor River

Note: All access points are from MP 156.7 Sterling Hwy. Indicated miles are along North Fork Road from highway junction.

Access A: Mile 0.7; stream crossing.
Access B: Mile 4.1; N on Cottenwood Ln. 0.3 mile to stream crossing.
Access C: Mile 5.0; N on Chakok Rd. 0.3 mile to stream crossing.
Access D: Mile 9.0; N on Nikolaevsk Rd. 0.4 mile to stream crossing.
Fishing: Some decent opportunities for char and a few trout in late summer and fall.
Rainbow Trout / poor-fair / early August – late September / 7-15 in. / spinners, flies.
Dolly Varden / good / early August – mid-October / 7-15 in. / spinners, flies.

76. Anchor River (Lower)

Access: MP 156.9 - Anchor River State Recreation Area; SW on Old Sterling Hwy. 0.7 mile to river crossing. Anchor River (Beach) Rd. on right just after bridge parallels river 1.5 mile, ending at river mouth and Cook Inlet.

Fishing: Clearwater river with opportunities for salmon, trout, and char, especially noted for its king and steelhead action. Can be waded throughout the length of the river. This is a weekend-only fishery during king salmon season. Expect crowds in May and June.
King Salmon / good-excellent / 15-30 lbs. (60 lbs.) / attractors, flies, bait.
Pink Salmon / good-excellent / 2-4 lbs. (7 lbs.) / spoons, spinners, flies.
Silver Salmon / good / 6-12 lbs. (18 lbs.) / attractors, flies, bait.
Steelhead Trout / fair-good / 5-12 lbs. (20 lbs.) / attractors, flies.
Rainbow Trout / poor / 7-15 in. (5 lbs.)/ attractors, flies, bait.
Dolly Varden / good-excellent / 7-20 in. (7 lbs.) / attractors, flies, bait.

FISH ▽	JAN	FEB	MAR	APR	MAY	JUN	JUL	AUG	SEP	OCT	NOV	DEC
KS												
PS												
SS												
ST												
RT												
DV												

77. North Fork Anchor River

Access A: MP 156.9; SW on Old Sterling Hwy. 0.7 mile to bridge over Anchor River. Park by bridge and hike upstream along north shore to North Fork confluence.
Access B: MP 160.0; highway crosses river.
Fishing: Decent opportunities for char in late summer and fall. Salmon spawning area.
Rainbow Trout / poor-fair / early August – late September / 7-15 in. / spinners, flies.
Dolly Varden / good / early August – mid-October / 7-15 in. / attractors, flies, bait.

78. Anchor River (Upper)

Access A: MP 159.9 – 164.3; highway parallels river, crossing it at MP 161.0.
Access B: MP 164.3; E on North Fork Rd. 2.8 miles to river crossing.
Fishing: Some trout and char available in late summer and fall. Salmon spawning area.
Steelhead Trout / fair / mid-October – early November / 5-12 lbs. / attractors, flies.
Rainbow Trout / fair / early August – mid-October / 7-18 in. / attractors, flies, bait.
Dolly Varden / good / early August – mid-October / 7-20 in. / attractors.

79. Homer Spit (Ocean Side)

Access: MP 175.4—178.5; highway parallels outer Kachemak Bay, to the west.
Fishing: Surfcasting for salmon and char. Limited opportunities; water very shallow.
Pink Salmon / fair / mid-July – late July / 2-4 lbs. / spoons, spinners, flies.
Silver Salmon / poor-fair / late July – mid-August / 6-12 lbs. / spinners, flies, bait.
Dolly Varden / fair / early May – early July / 8-20 in. / spoons, spinners, flies.
Bottomfish / poor-fair / mid-May – late August / flounder / jigs, bait.

80. Dudiak Lagoon

Note: Also known as "The Fishing Hole."

Access: MP 178.1; E on short gravel road to large parking area and lagoon.

Fishing: Artificial lagoon, a very popular spot to target hatchery runs of king and silver salmon. Bank fishing only. Best on incoming and outgoing tides. Snagging allowed by emergency order. Some char available at mouth of stream draining lagoon.

King Salmon / good-excellent / 15-35 lbs. (50 lbs.) / spinners, bait.

Pink Salmon / poor / 2-4 lbs. (6 lbs.) / spoons, spinners.

Silver Salmon / good-excellnt / 6-12 lbs. (18 lbs.) / spinners, bait.

Dolly Varden / fair / 8-20 in. (7 lbs.) / spoons, flies, bait.

FISH ▽	JAN	FEB	MAR	APR	MAY	JUN	JUL	AUG	SEP	OCT	NOV	DEC
KS					■	■						
PS							■	■				
SS								■	■			
DV				■	■	■						

81. Homer Spit (Bay Side)

Access: MP 178.2; E on gravel access road right after Dudiak Lagoon to large parking area and the shore of Kachemak Bay.

Fishing: Moderate success casting from the bank for salmon, char, and bottomfish.

King Salmon / poor-fair / late May – mid-June / 15-35 lbs. / spoons, spinners, bait.

Silver Salmon / fair / late July – mid-August / 6-12 lbs. / spoons, spinners, bait.

Dolly Varden / fair / early May – early July / 8-20 in. / spoons, spinners, flies.

Bottomfish / fair / mid-May – late August / pollock, flounder, cod / jigs, bait.

82. Homer Spit (Eastern End)

Access: MP 179.5; end of Sterling Highway (Spit Road). Small parking area left of resort has beach access.

Fishing: Surfcasting for salmon and char. Occasional catches of halibut. Fish waste discarded from processing plant in the area attracts very large numbers of bottomfish.

King Salmon / fair / 15-35 lbs. (50 lbs.) / spoons, spinners, bait.

Pink Salmon / fair-good / 2-4 lbs. (7 lbs.) / spoons, spinners, bait.

Silver Salmon / fair-good / 6-12 bs. (18 lbs.) / spoons, spinners, bait.

Dolly Varden / fair-good / 8-20 in. (7 lbs.) / spoons, flies, bait.

Bottomfish / excellent / early May – late August / pollock, flounder, cod / jigs, bait.

FISH ▽	JAN	FEB	MAR	APR	MAY	JUN	JUL	AUG	SEP	OCT	NOV	DEC
KS*				■	■	■						
PS						■	■					
SS							■	■	■			
DV			■	■	■	■	■					

Note: Small numbers of feeder king salmon are present year round.

Other Locations

Unit B: Upper Kenai River Drainages:

Cooper Creek - MP 50.5; RT,DV,(RS,PS,SS) **Skilak Lake Road:** Jean Lake Creek - MP 0.5; RT,DV,(RS,PS,SS,Arctic Grayling)   Hidden Lake Creek - MP 5.3; RT,DV,(RS,PS,SS,AG)
Sterling Highway (Cont.): Soldotna Creek - MP 92.7; *** Closed to Fishing ***

Unit C: Central Kenai Peninsula Drainages:

Swan Lake Road: Sucker Creek - MP 17.3; RT,(RS,SS,DV)

Unit E: Lower Kenai Peninsula Drainages:

Happy Valley Creek - MP 143.9; DV Creek, No Name - MP 159.7; DV,(KS,PS,SS,ST,RT)
Diamond Creek - MP 167.6; DVLOCATION & SPECIES APPENDIX

- ● - Wild/Native fish, fishable numbers.
- ◆ - Present in small numbers and/or only occasionally caught.
- ▲ - Stocked/Hatchery fish, fishable numbers.
- ■ - Mix of Wild and Hatchery fish, fishable numbers.
- × - Indicated species present but currently protected by law (PROHIBITED).

#	LOCATION	KING SALMON	RED SALMON	PINK SALMON	CHUM SALMON	SILVER SALMON	LANDLOCKED SALMON	KOKANEE	STEELHEAD TROUT	RAINBOW TROUT	LAKE TROUT	ARCTIC CHAR	DOLLY VARDEN	ARCTIC GRAYLING	SHEEFISH	WHITEFISH	NORTHERN PIKE	PACIFIC HALIBUT	BURBOT	LING COD	ROCKFISH
1.	Tern Lake		×										●			●					
2.	Daves Creek	×	×	×		×							●			●	●		◆		
3.	Quartz Creek (Middle)	×	×	×	×	×							●			●	●		◆		
4.	Quartz Creek (Lower)	×	×	×	×	×							●			●	●		●		
5.	Crescent Creek		×			×							◆			●	◆				
6.	Kenai Lake	×	×	×	×	×					●		●	●		◆	◆		◆		
	Snug Harbor Road																				
7.	Cleaver Lake												●								
8.	Rainbow Lake												▲								
9.	Cooper Lake												●			●					
	Sterling Hwy. (cont.)																				
10.	Kenai River (Upper)	×	■	●	◆	●				●		◆	●			◆	●		◆		
11.	Lower Russian Lake	×	×						×				●			●					
12.	Russian River (Lower)	×	●	◆		●							●			●	◆		◆		
13.	Russian River (Mouth)	×	■	●	◆	●				●			●			◆	●		◆		
14.	Kenai River (Upper)	×	■	●	◆	●				●		◆	●			◆	●		◆		
15.	Lower Fuller Lake													▲							
	Skilak Lake Road																				
16.	Kenai River (Upper)	×	■	●	◆	●							●	●		●	◆		●		
17.	Hidden Lake		◆			◆		●					●	●		●	◆		◆		
18.	Upper Ohmer Lake												●			●					
19.	Skilak Lake	×	◆	●	◆	●					●		●	●		●	◆		●		
20.	Lower Ohmer Lake												●			●					
	Sterling Hwy. (cont.)																				
21.	Jean Lake		◆			◆							●			●	◆		◆		
22.	Upper Jean Lake												●								
23.	Kelly Lake		◆			◆							●			◆			●		
24.	Peterson Lake		◆			◆							●			◆			●		
25.	Egumen Lake		◆			◆							●			◆			●		
26.	Watson Lake		◆			◆							●			◆			●		
27.	East Fork Moose River		×			×							●			◆			◆		
28.	Kenai River (Middle)	●	■	●	◆	●				●		◆	●	◆		◆	●		◆		
29.	Moose River (Mouth)	●	■	●	◆	●				●		◆	●	◆			◆		◆		
30.	Longmere Lake								▲					▲							
31.	Kenai River (Lower)	●	■	●	◆	●				●			●	◆		●			◆		

#	LOCATION	King Salmon	Red Salmon	Pink Salmon	Chum Salmon	Silver Salmon	Landlocked Salmon	Kokanee	Steelhead Trout	Rainbow Trout	Lake Trout	Arctic Char	Dolly Varden	Sheefish	Arctic Grayling	Whitefish	Northern Pike	Burbot	Pacific Halibut	Ling Cod	Rockfish
32.	Funny River (Lower)	×	◆	●	◆	●				●			●						◆	◆	
33.	Funny River (Mouth)	◆	◆	●	◆	●				●		◆	●						◆	◆	
34.	Aurora Lake									▲											
35.	Slikok Creek	×	×	×		×				●			●								
	Swanson River Road																				
36.	Mosquito Lake									●											
37.	Silver Lake									●		●									
38.	Finger Lake									●		●									
39.	Forest Lake									●											
40.	Weed Lake									●											
41.	Dabbler Lake									●		●									
42.	Skookum Lake									●		●									
43.	Drake Lake									●		●									
44.	Breeze Lake									●											
45.	Dolly Varden Lake									●		●									
46.	Rainbow Lake		◆							●			●								
47.	Swanson River (Upper)		◆			●				●			●								
	Swan Lake Road																				
48.	Fish Lake											●									
49.	Ice Lake									●		●									
50.	Canoe Lake		◆			◆				●			●								
51.	Waterfowl Lake									●		●									
52.	Swan L. Canoe Sys. Lakes					◆				●		●	◆								
53.	Sucker Lake		◆			◆				●			◆								
54.	Little Merganser Lake		◆			◆				●			◆								
55.	Campfire Lake									●											
56.	Nest Lake									●											
57.	Paddle Lake									●		●									
58.	Odd Lake									●		●									
59.	Pad Lake									●		●									
60.	Swanson R. Canoe Route L.									●		●									
	Sterling Hwy. (cont.)																				
61.	Coal Creek	×	◆	◆		◆							◆		●						
62.	Roque Lake									▲											
63.	Kasilof River (Middle)	■	●	●	◆	●			●	●			●						◆		—
64.	Crooked Creek (Middle)	×	◆	◆	◆	●			◆	●			●						◆		
65.	Johnson Lake									▲											
66.	Centennial Lake					▲				▲											
67.	Kasilof River (Upper)	■	◆	●	◆	●			◆	●		◆	●						◆		
68.	Quintin Lake									▲											
69.	Crooked Creek (Mouth)	■	●	●		●			●	●			●						◆		
70.	Encelewski Lake									▲								◆			
71.	Ninilchik River	■	●	●	◆	●			●	◆			●								
72.	Deep Creek	●	◆	●	◆	●			●	◆			●								
73.	Cook Inlet	■	■	●	◆	●			◆				●						●		
74.	Stariski Creek (Middle)	×	◆	●	◆	●			●	●			●								
75.	North Fork Anchor River	×	×	×	×	×			◆	●			●								
76.	Anchor River (Lower)	●	◆	●	◆	●			●	◆			●								
77.	North Fork Anchor River	×	×	×	×	×			◆	●			●								
78.	Anchor River (Upper)	×	×	×	×	×			●	●			●								
79.	Homer Spit (Ocean Side)	◆	◆	●	◆	■							●						◆		
80.	Dudiak Lagoon	▲	◆	●	◆	▲							●								
81.	Homer Spit (Bay Side)	■	◆	◆	◆	■							●						◆		
82.	Homer Spit (Eastern End)	■	◆	●	◆	■							●						◆		

Taylor Highway

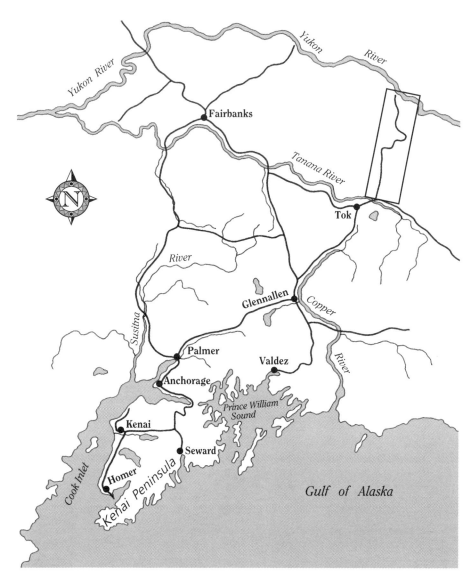

Area Covered: Tetlin Junction to Eagle; 160 miles
Regulatory Unit: Yukon River Drainage
Number of Locations: 14

FISHING THE TAYLOR HIGHWAY

The Taylor Highway provides good access to one lake and several clearwater tributaries of the large 40-Mile River. Arctic grayling, as the dominant sport fish species in the region, is available in virtually all of the waters along the road. They are encountered in greatest numbers during the late summer and fall months as fish move downstream from the headwaters of smaller rivers and streams to overwinter in the mainstem 40-Mile River. Stocked rainbow and lake trout are only available in one location - Four Mile Lake. A few sheefish, whitefish, and burbot are sometimes taken in larger watersheds. Angler success is fair to good in both lakes and streams.

Angling pressure is very light along this highway, with the little of it that occurs concentrated on Four Mile Lake and tributaries of the 40-Mile River.

Recommended Hot Spots: Four Mile Lake; West Fork Dennison River; Mosquito and Walker Forks; Taylor, O'Brien, and Alder creeks.

Content

QUICK REFERENCE

 Road Condition Parking Area Camp Sites Hiking Trails Boat Launch Handicap Access Fishing Pressure

■ - Good to Highly developed/conditions, intense pressure
● - Fair to Moderately developed/conditions, moderate pressure
◆ - Poor to marginally developed/conditions, limited pressure
× - Prohibited

#	LOCATION	MILE POST	🚗	P	⛰	🚶	⛵	♿	🎣	PAGE
J1.	Jct.: Alaska Hwy.	0								
1.	Four-Mile Lake	4.5	●	●		●			◆	308
2.	Logging Cabin Creek	43.0	●	●					◆	308
3.	West Fork Dennison River	49.2	●	◆	●				◆	308
4.	Taylor Creek	50.4	●	◆					◆	308
5.	Mosquito Fork	64.3	●	●					◆	308
6.	40-Mile River (Upper)	74.2-75.4	●	●					◆	309
7.	Walker Fork	82.0	●	●	●				◆	309
J2.	Jct.: Klondike Loop Rd.	95.7								
8.	40-Mile River (Lower)	112.5	●	●			●	●	◆	309
9.	O' Brien Creek	113.2	●	◆					◆	309
10.	Alder Creek	117.1	●	●					◆	309
11.	Columbia Creek	124.5	●	●					◆	309

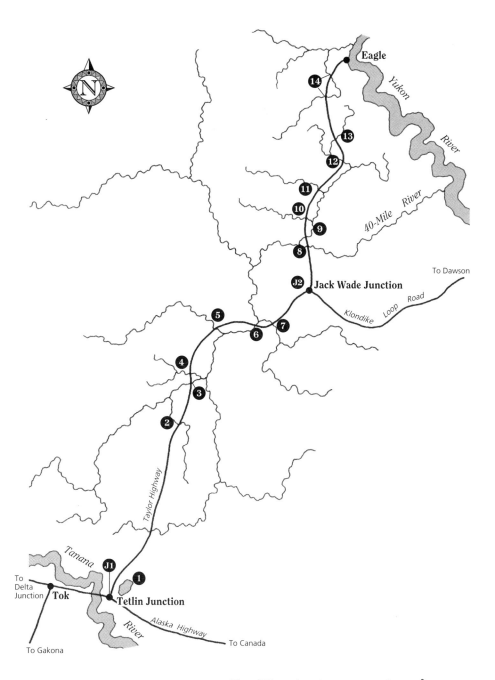

#	LOCATION	MILE POST	🚐	P	⋀	🥾	🛶	♿	📍	PAGE
12.	King Solomon Creek	133.9	●	●					◆	309
13.	N. Fork King Solomon Creek	137.8	●	◆					◆	309
14.	American Creek	151.7-155.6	●	◆					◆	309

TAYLOR HIGHWAY LOCATIONS

Unit: Yukon River Drainage

Includes all roadside waters flowing into and surrounding the Yukon River.

UNIT REGULATIONS:

* There are no general area-wide restrictions for waters in this unit.

UNIT TIMING:

FISH ▽	JAN	FEB	MAR	APR	MAY	JUN	JUL	AUG	SEP	OCT	NOV	DEC
KS*							▓	▓				
CS*							▓	▓				
RT					▓	▓			▓	▓	▓	
LT						▓	▓			▓	▓	▓
AC	▓					▓			▓	▓	▓	▓
AG					▓	▓				▓	▓	
WF									▓	▓	▓	
NP					▓	▓	▓	▓				
BB			▓							▓	▓	

Note: Timing shown for salmon indicates fish in all stages of maturity.

1. Four-Mile Lake

Access: MP 4.5; turnout E of highway. Trail leads 0.75 mile to lake.
Fishing: Lake contains a healthy population of stocked trout and char.
Rainbow Trout / good / June, September – December / 7-16 in. / spinners, flies, bait.
Lake Trout / poor / June, September – October / 2-4 lbs. / spoons, plugs, bait.
Arctic Char / fair-good / June, September – January / 7-18 in. / spoons, jigs, bait.

2. Logging Cabin Creek

Access: MP 43.0; highway crosses stream.
Fishing: Small stream supporting a spawning run of grayling early in the season.
Arctic Grayling / fair / late May – mid-June / 7-12 in. / spinners, flies.

3. West Fork Dennison River

Access: MP 49.2; highway crosses river.
Fishing: Tannic river with decent opportunities for grayling in late summer and fall.
Arctic Grayling / good / May, mid-August – mid-September / 7-14 in. / spinners, flies.

4. Taylor Creek

Access: MP 50.4; highway crosses stream.
Fishing: Productive summer and early fall fishery for grayling.
Arctic Grayling / fair-good / mid-June – mid-September / 7-14 in. / spinners, flies.

5. Mosquito Fork

Access: MP 64.3; highway crosses river.
Fishing: Grayling action is best early and late in the season. Some large fish present.
Arctic Grayling / good / May, mid-August – mid-September / 7-14 in. / spinners, flies.

6. 40-Mile River (Upper)

Access: MP 74.2-75.3; highway parallels river, crossing it at MP 75.4.
Fishing: Tannic river with early- and late-season opportunities for grayling.
Arctic Grayling / fair / May, mid-September – mid-October / 7-15 in. / spinners, flies.

7. Walker Fork

Access: MP 82.0; highway crosses river.
Fishing: Primarily a summer and early fall fishery for grayling.
Arctic Grayling / fair-good / mid-June – mid-September / 7-14 in. / spinners, flies.

8. 40-Mile River (Lower)

Access: MP 112.5; highway crosses river.
Fishing: Tannic river with early and late-season opportunities for grayling, pike, burbot.
Northern pike / fair / mid-June – mid-September / 2-4 lbs. / spoons, plugs, flies, bait.
Arctic Grayling / fair / May, mid-September – mid-October / 7-15 in. / spinners, flies.
Burbot / poor-fair / September – November / 2-5 lbs. / bait.

9. O'Brien Creek

Access: MP 113.2; highway crosses stream.
Fishing: Stream supports a decent population of grayling from late spring into fall.
Arctic Grayling / fair-good / late May – mid-September / 7-14 in. / spinners, flies.

10. Alder Creek

Access: MP 117.1; highway crosses stream.
Fishing: Productive stream for grayling during the summer and early fall months.
Arctic Grayling / fair-good / mid-June – mid-September / 7-12 in. / spinners, flies.

11. Columbia Creek

Access: MP 124.5; highway crosses stream.
Fishing: Clearwater stream offering decent summer and fall opportunities for grayling.
Arctic Grayling / fair-good / mid-June – mid-September / 7-12 in. / spinners, flies.

12. King Solomon Creek

Access: MP 133.9; highway crosses stream.
Fishing: Clearwater stream offering decent summer and fall opportunities for grayling.
Arctic Grayling / fair / mid-June – early September / 7-12 in. / spinners, flies.

13. North Fork King Solomon Creek

Access: MP 137.8; highway crosses stream.
Fishing: Small stream with limited chances for grayling during summer months.
Arctic Grayling / poor-fair / mid-June – late August / 7-10 in. / spinners, flies.

14. American Creek

Access: MP 151.7 – 155.6; highway parallels stream, crossing it at MP 151.8 and 152.5.
Fishing: Small and fairly shallow clearwater drainage with summer action for grayling.
Arctic Grayling / poor-fair / mid-June – mid-August / 7-10 in. / spinners, flies.

Other Locations
None

LOCATION & SPECIES APPENDIX

● - Wild/Native fish, fishable numbers.

♦ - Present in small numbers and/or only occasionally caught.

▲ - Stocked/Hatchery fish, fishable numbers.

■ - Mix of Wild and Hatchery fish, fishable numbers.

✕ - Indicated species present but currently protected by law (PROHIBITED).

#	LOCATION	KING SALMON	RED SALMON	PINK SALMON	CHUM SALMON	SILVER SALMON	LANDLOCKED SALMON	KOKANEE	STEELHEAD TROUT	RAINBOW TROUT	LAKE TROUT	ARCTIC CHAR	DOLLY VARDEN	ARCTIC GRAYLING	SHEEFISH	WHITEFISH	NORTHERN PIKE	BURBOT	PACIFIC HALIBUT	LING COD	ROCKFISH
1.	Four-Mile Lake									▲	●	▲									
2.	Logging Cabin Creek													●							
3.	West Fork Dennison River													●	♦						
4.	Taylor Creek													●							
5.	Mosquito Fork													●	♦						
6.	40-Mile River (Upper)	♦				♦								●	♦	♦	♦				
7.	Walker Fork													●							
8.	40-Mile River (Lower)	♦				♦							♦	●	♦	●	●				
9.	O' Brien Creek													●							
10.	Alder Creek													●							
11.	Columbia Creek													●							
12.	King Solomon Creek													●							
13.	N. Fork King Solomon Cr.													●							
14.	American Creek													●							

Tok Cutoff

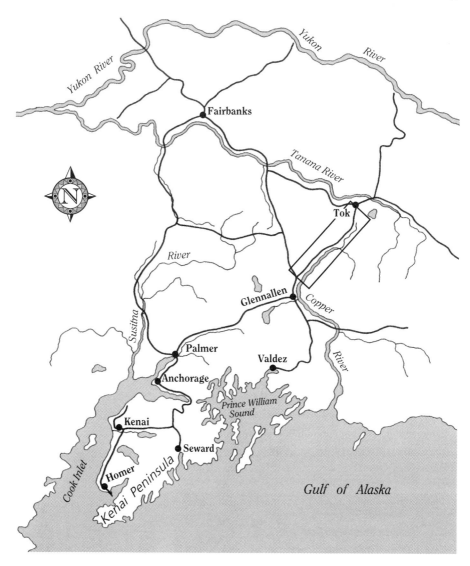

Area Covered: Gakona Junction to Tok; 125 miles
Regulatory Units: (A) Copper River Drainage; (B) Nabesna Road Drainages; (C) Tok River Drainage
Number of Locations: 24

FISHING THE TOK CUTOFF

The Tok Cutoff parallels two large rivers, Tok and Slana, and a third major system, the Copper River, providing good access to the area's lakes and streams. Grayling is by far the most abundant species both in the Copper and Tanana river drainages during the summer months, but fairly decent numbers of char, pike, and burbot are also present—especially in lakes connected to Tanana River off the Nabesna Road and in areas between Mentasta and Tok. Salmon (primarily king and red) are generally not very abundant in waters along Tok Cutoff, yet there are a few good runs occurring in the Slana River drainage. Sport fishing opportunities for salmon, however, are slim due in part to small populations area-wide, catch restrictions, and the near-spawning phase of most fish. Angler success is fair to good in both lakes and streams.

Boaters occasionally take advantage of the more remote lakes and some exploring in the Slana River system could be worth it.

Angling pressure is light in all areas along the road.

Recommended Hot Spots: Indian and Little Tok rivers; Tulsona and Jack creeks; Long, Little Twin, Big Twin, Carlson, and Mineral lakes.

Content

Pages

QUICK REFERENCE

 Road Condition   Parking Area   Camp Sites   Hiking Trails   Boat Launch   Handicap Access   Fishing Pressure

■ - Good to Highly developed/conditions, intense pressure
● - Fair to Moderately developed/conditions, moderate pressure
◆ - Poor to marginally developed/conditions, limited pressure
× - Prohibited

#	LOCATION	MILE POST	🚙	P	⛺	🚶	🛥	♿	🎣	PAGE
J1.	Jct.: Richardson Hwy.	0								
1.	Gakona River	1.9	■	●					◆	314
2.	Tulsona Creek	17.9	■	●					◆	315
3.	Sinona Creek	34.6	■	◆					◆	315
4.	Chistochina River	35.4	■	◆					◆	315
5.	Indian River	43.9		●					◆	315
J2.	Jct.: Nabesna Road	59.3								
6.	Ahtell Creek	60.8	■	●	◆				◆	315

Map: Unit A: Copper River Drainages
      Unit B: Nabesna Road Drainages
      Unit C: Tok River Drainage

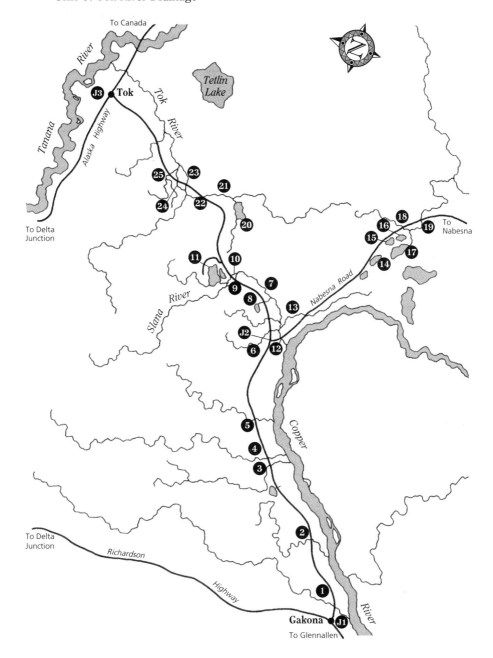

#	LOCATION	MILE POST	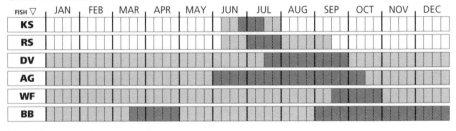 🚗	P	⛺	🚶🚶	🛶	♿	🎣	PAGE
7.	Slana River (Upper)	65.0-75.6	■	●	◆				◆	315
8.	Carlson Lake	68.0	■	●					◆	315
9.	Slana Slough	76.0	■	●					◆	315
10.	Mable Creek	76.3	■	◆					◆	315
	Nabesna Road									
J2.	Jct.: Tok Cutoff	0								
11.	Slana River (Lower)	1.5	■	●					◆	316
12.	Rufus Creek	7.1	■	◆					◆	316
13.	Long Lake	23.2	●	◆					◆	317
14.	Little Twin Lake	27.9	●	◆		●			◆	317
15.	Big Twin Lake	28.1	●	●					◆	317
16.	Jack Lake	29.0	●	◆		●			◆	317
17.	Chalk Creek	32.2	●	◆					◆	317
18.	Jack Creek	35.9	●	●					◆	317
	Tok Cutoff (cont.)									
19.	Mineral Lake	89.5	■	◆		●			◆	318
20.	Little Tok River (Upper)	91.0	■	●	◆				◆	318
21.	Little Tok River (Lower)	98.0	■	●	◆				◆	318
22.	Tok Overflow #1	103.3	■	◆				◆	◆	318
23.	Tok River (Middle)	103.8	■	●					◆	318
24.	Tok Overflow #2	104.7	■	●				◆	◆	318
J3.	Jct.: Alaska Highway	125.0								

TOK CUTOFF LOCATIONS

Unit A: Copper River Drainage

Includes all roadside waters flowing into and surrounding the Copper River.

UNIT REGULATIONS:

* There are no general area-wide restrictions for waters in Unit A.

UNIT TIMING:

FISH ▽	JAN	FEB	MAR	APR	MAY	JUN	JUL	AUG	SEP	OCT	NOV	DEC
KS												
RS												
DV												
AG												
WF												
BB												

1. Gakona River

Access: MP 1.9; highway crosses river.

Fishing: Glacial river with limited spring and fall opportunities for grayling and burbot.
Arctic Grayling / fair / May, mid-September – mid-October / 7-12 in. / spinners, flies.
Burbot / poor-fair / mid-September – late October / 2-4 lbs. / bait.

2. Tulsona Creek

Access: MP 17.9; highway crosses stream, paralleling it more or less from MP 15.0 until stream crossing. Additional access possible near bridge via paved section of Old Tok Cutoff.

Fishing: Tannic stream containing a healthy population of grayling.
Arctic Grayling / good / mid-May – mid-September / 7-12 in. / spinners, flies.

3. Sinona Creek

Access: MP 34.6; highway crosses stream.

Fishing: Clearwater stream with limited seasonal opportunities for grayling and char.
Dolly Varden / poor / mid-July – mid-September / 7-14 in. / spinners, flies, bait.
Arctic Grayling / fair / mid-June – mid-September / 7-12 in. / spinners, flies.

4. Chistochina River

Access: MP 35.4; highway crosses river.

Fishing: Glacial drainage yielding fall action for grayling as water clears.
Arctic Grayling / fair / mid-September – mid-October / 7-14 in. / spinners, flies.

5. Indian River

Access: MP 43.9; highway crosses river.

Fishing: A productive summer and early fall grayling fishery. Salmon spawning stream.
Arctic Grayling / good / mid-June – mid-September / 7-14 in. / spinners, flies.

6. Ahtell Creek

Access: MP 60.8; highway crosses stream.

Fishing: Clearwater stream supports a population of grayling in summer and fall.
Arctic Grayling / fair-good / mid-June – mid-September / 7-14 in. / spinners, flies.

7. Slana River

Access: MP 65.0-74.4; highway parallels river, crossing it at MP 74.4.

Fishing: Glacial river containing good population of grayling and whitefish. Try in fall.
Arctic Grayling / fair / mid-September – mid-October / 7-14 in. / spinners, attractors.
Whitefish / fair / mid-September – mid-October / 10-15 in. / attractors, bait.

8. Carlson Lake

Access: MP 76.3; lake is located 2.5 miles NW of highway. Follow Carlson Creek.

Fishing: Semi-remote lake that offers action for grayling in summer and fall.
Arctic Grayling / good / June – September / 7-14 in. / spinners, flies.

9. Slana Slough

Access: MP 74.6-76.0; highway parallels slough for several miles, crossing it at MP 76.0.

Fishing: Semi-glacial drainage with fall opportunities for out-migrating grayling.
Arctic Grayling / fair / mid-September – mid-October / 7-14 in. / spinners, flies.

10. Mable Creek
Access: MP 76.3; highway crosses stream.
Fishing: Slow-flowing stream with fall opportunities for out-migrating grayling.
Arctic Grayling / fair / mid-September – mid-October / 7-14 in. / spinners, flies.

Note: Tok Cutoff continues on page 318.

Unit B: Nabesna Road Drainages
Includes all roadside waters along or surrounding Nabesna Road.

UNIT REGULATIONS:
* King salmon fishing prohibited: All waters, July 20 – December 31

UNIT TIMING:

FISH ▽	JAN	FEB	MAR	APR	MAY	JUN	JUL	AUG	SEP	OCT	NOV	DEC
KS												
RS												
RT												
LT												
DV												
AG												
WF												
BB												

Nabesna Road
Road begins at MP 59.8 (MP 0) Tok Cutoff and ends in the community of Nabesna (MP 45).

11. Slana River (Lower)
Access: MP 1.5; road crosses river, better access via gravel road NE of bridge.
Fishing: Glacial river containing good population of grayling and whitefish. Try in fall.
Arctic Grayling / fair / mid-September – mid-October / 7-14 in. / spinners, attractors.
Whitefish / fair / mid-September – mid-October / 10-15 in. / attractors, bait.

12. Rufus Creek
Access: MP 7.1; road crosses stream.
Fishing: Very small spring-fed clearwater stream with summer action for grayling, char.
Dolly Varden / poor / late May – mid-June / 7-10 in. / spinners, flies, bait.
Arctic Grayling / poor-fair / mid-May – mid-June / 7-10 in. / spinners, flies.

13. Long Lake
Access: MP 23.2; lake is adjacent to right side of road.
Fishing: Large clearwater large containing healthy numbers of grayling and burbot.

Arctic Grayling / good / June – September / 7-14 in. / spinners, flies.
Burbot / fair / March – April, September – December / 2-4 lbs. / bait.

14. Little Twin Lake

Access: MP 27.9; trail leads 0.3 mile S to lake.
Fishing: Summer and fall opportunities for char and grayling, burbot in winter.
Lake Trout / fair / June, September – November / 2-4 lbs. / spoons, plugs, bait.
Arctic Grayling / good / June – September / 7-14 in. / spinners, flies.
Burbot / fair / March – April, September – December / 2-4 lbs. / bait.

15. Big Twin Lake

Access: MP 28.1; lake is adjacent to right side of road.
Fishing: Productive lake for grayling in summer and fall. Some burbot available.
Arctic Grayling / good / June – September / 7-14 in. / spinners, flies.
Burbot / fair / March – April, September – December / 2-4 lbs. / bait.

16. Jack Lake

Access: MP 29.0; old cat trail leads 1.0 mile S to lake.
Fishing: Summer and fall opportunities for char and grayling, burbot in winter.
Lake Trout / fair / June, September – November / 2-4 lbs. / spoons, plugs, bait.
Arctic Grayling / good / June – September / 7-14 in. / spinners, flies.
Burbot / fair / March – April, September – December / 2-4 lbs. / bait.

17. Chalk Creek

Access: MP 32.2; road crosses stream.
Fishing: Small clearwater stream supporting a population of grayling in summer.
Arctic Grayling / fair / mid-June – mid-August / 7-12 in. / spinners, flies.

18. Jack Creek

Access: MP 35.9; road crosses stream.
Fishing: Decent number of grayling present through summer into fall.
Arctic Grayling / fair-good / early June – mid-September / 7-14 in. / spinners, flies.

Unit C: Tok River Drainage

Includes all roadside waters flowing into and surrounding Tok River.

UNIT REGULATIONS:

* Dolly Varden Fishing: Catch-and-release only, all waters, year-round.
* Arctic grayling fishing prohibited: All waters, November 1 – May 14.
* Northern pike fishing prohibited: All waters, April – May 31.

UNIT TIMING:

FISH ▽	JAN	FEB	MAR	APR	MAY	JUN	JUL	AUG	SEP	OCT	NOV	DEC
DV												
AG												
WF												
NP												
BB												

Tok Cutoff Log Continues.

19. Mineral Lake

Access: MP 89.9; lake is located 0.5 mile SE by trail.
Fishing: One of the better lakes in the area, featuring great action for grayling and pike.
Arctic Grayling / good-excellent / June – September / 7-14 in. / spinners, flies.
Northern Pike / good / June – September / 2-6 lbs. / spoons, plugs, bait.
Burbot / fair / March – April, September – December / 2-4 lbs. / bait.

20. Little Tok River (Upper)

Access: MP 91.0; highway parallels river.
Fishing: Clearwater drainage with productive opportunities for grayling.
Arctic Grayling / good / mid-June – mid-September / 7-14 in. / spinners, flies.

21. Little Tok River (Lower)

Access: MP 98.0; highway crosses river.
Fishing: Deep, semi-glacial river with summer and fall grayling action. Some big fish.
Arctic Grayling / good / early June – late September / 8-16 in. / spinners, flies.

22. Tok Overflow #1

Access: MP 103.3; highway crosses stream.
Fishing: Clearwater drainage offering limited opportunities in summer for grayling.
Arctic Grayling / poor-fair / mid-May – mid-September / 7-12 in. / spinners, flies.

23. Tok River (Middle)

Access: MP 103.8; highway crosses river.
Fishing: Glacial river with late-season action for grayling as water begins to clear.
Arctic Grayling / fair / mid-September – mid-October / 7-15 in. / spinners, flies.

24. Tok Overflow #2

Access: MP 104.7; highway crosses stream.
Fishing: Clearwater drainage offering limited opportunities in summer for grayling.
Arctic Grayling / poor-fair / mid-May – mid-September / 7-12 in. / spinners, flies.

Other Locations

Unit A: Copper River Drainage:
Porcupine Creek - MP 64.2; Arctic Grayling

Unit B: Nabesna Road Drainages:
Rock (Kettle) Lake - MP 22.1; Arctic Grayling

Unit C: Tok River Drainage:
Clearwater Creek - MP 109.2; Arctic Grayling

LOCATION & SPECIES APPENDIX

● - Wild/Native fish, fishable numbers.
◆ - Present in small numbers and/or only occasionally caught.
▲ - Stocked/Hatchery fish, fishable numbers.
■ - Mix of Wild and Hatchery fish, fishable numbers.
✕ - Indicated species present but currently protected by law (PROHIBITED).

#	LOCATION	KING SALMON	RED SALMON	PINK SALMON	CHUM SALMON	SILVER SALMON	LANDLOCKED SALMON	KOKANEE	STEELHEAD TROUT	RAINBOW TROUT	LAKE TROUT	ARCTIC CHAR	DOLLY VARDEN	ARCTIC GRAYLING	SHEEFISH	WHITEFISH	NORTHERN PIKE	BURBOT	PACIFIC HALIBUT	LING COD	ROCKFISH
1.	Gakona River (Upper)				◆									●							
2.	Tulsona Creek													●							
3.	Sinona Creek				◆								●	●							
4.	Chistochina River				◆									●							
5.	Indian River				◆								◆	●							
6.	Ahtell Creek												◆	●							
7.	Slana River (Upper)				◆								◆	●							
8.	Carlson Lake												◆	●							
9.	Slana Slough				◆								◆	●							
10.	Mable Creek				◆								◆	●							
	Nabesna Road																				
11.	Slana River (Lower)				◆								◆	●							
12.	Rufus Creek												●	●							
13.	Long Lake													●							
14.	Little Twin Lake									●				●							
15.	Big Twin Lake													●							
16.	Jack Lake									●				●							
17.	Chalk Creek													●							
18.	Jack Creek													●							
	Tok Cutoff (cont.)																				
19.	Mineral Lake												◆	●				●			
20.	Little Tok River (Upper)												◆	●				◆			
21.	Little Tok River (Lower)												◆	●				◆			
22.	Tok Overflow #1												◆	●							
23.	Tok River (Middle)												◆	●				◆			
24.	Tok Overflow #2												◆	●							

APPENDIX . . . . *Other Resources*

. . . .

The Alaska Roadside Angler's Guide

• Created by avid fishers and long-time residents, The Alaska Roadside Angler's Guide is an awesome reference tool for people seeking the best of Alaska's roadside fishing opportunities and a perfect companion publication to The Highway Angler.

• Full-color, 230-page guidebook, complete with hundreds of photographs of fish, fishing action, and scenery.

• Top angling destinations, as well as dozens of other popular fisheries. Proven angling strategies, methods, and techniques that work best.

• Colorful area and location maps outlining trails, cabins, parking spots, campgrounds, boat launches, etc.

• Access descriptions along with complete facility information.

• All game fish species available, including tackle, biology, and timing.

• Listing of guides, lodges, tackle shops, and other local services.

• Great resource for the budget conscious angler.

• Unique color-coded run timing and species identification charts.

• Current restrictions and legal angling methods.

• Travel Planning section for easy do-it-yourself trips.

• Tons of other angling tips and advice to catch fish in Alaska's roadside waters.

Books are available at retail stores throughout Southcentral and Interior Alaska. Can be ordered at *highwayangler.com* and directly from the publisher: Fishing Alaska Publications, P.O. Box 90557, Anchorage, AK 99509, (907) 345-1177.

Autographed/personalized copies available upon request.

Publications Available From Fishing Alaska Publications:

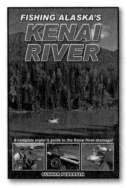

Fishing Alaska's KENAI RIVER

This publication is the definitive guide to angling Alaska's most popular sport fishery. Perhaps no other river in the world can present such profuse sport fishing opportunities along with easy access, affordable accommodations, and beautiful vistas. Anglers line the riverbanks in summer hoping to land one or more of the hundreds of thousands of red and silver salmon caught every year while both power and drift boats navigate the turquoise waters in search of trophy king salmon to 90 pounds or more and 35-inch rainbow trout.

This book focuses on the entire Kenai River drainage, the mainstem river as well as tributary streams and lakes, and all the game fish available. Hot spots within the river system are highlighted, accompanied with detailed information on access, facilities, services, species present, timing, proven methods and techniques, preferred tackle, and much, much more.

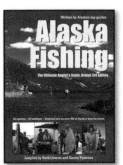

Alaska Fishing: The Ultimate Angler's Guide

The most comprehensive "insiders" guide on Alaska fishing, revised, updated, and expanded in this new deluxe, full color 3rd Edition. Written by the state's top fishing experts, this latest version now covers all 17 major Alaska sport species (fresh and salt water), all methods (fly, spin, and bait), and all six regions of the state, with details on over 300 of the most productive Alaska fishing locations.

Includes information on regional climate/conditions, run timing, visitor services, costs, trophy and record fishes, USGS map references, guides' tips, fishing regulations, trip planner, and best flies n Alaska. Beautifully illustrated, Alaska Fishing has over 500 color photos, maps, charts, diagrams, and drawings.

Books are available at retail stores throughout Southcentral and Interior Alaska. Can be ordered at *highwayangler.com* and directly from the publisher: Fishing Alaska Publications, P.O. Box 90557, Anchorage, AK 99509, (907) 345-1177.

Autographed/personalized copies available upon request.

Eklutna Tailrace *156*
Elbow Lake *136*
Elephant Lake *143*
Eliza Lake *47*
Elliott Highway *101*
Elmendorf AFB *56*
Encelewski Lake *297*
Eska Creek *130*
Eska Lake *130*
Explorer Creek *248*

F

Fairbanks Area *107, 111*
Fairbanks City *112*
Fairbanks City Drainages *111, 120*
Faith Creek *267*
Farmer Lake *166*
Fielding Lake *227*
Finger Lake *163, 291*
Fish Creek *72, 90, 166, 169, 204, 316*
Fish Lake *57, 194, 226, 293*
Fishhook-Willow Road *187*
Fishing The Road System *3*
Fishing Tips *33*
Flat Lake *170*
Flies *37-39*
Florence Lake *185*
Forest Lake *291*
Forgotten Lake *136*
Fort Greely Meadows Road *229*
Fort Greely Ridge Road *228*
Fort Richardson *58*
Fort Wainwright *113*
Four-Mile Lake *308*
Fourth Of July Creek Marine *257*
Freshwater Species *11*
Fort Hamlin Hills Creek *72*
Funny River *289*

Funny River / Kenai River Confluence *290*

G

Gakona River *314*
Galbraith Lake *76*
Gardiner Creek *47*
Gate Lake *197*
George Lake *136*
Gergie Lake *133*
Ghost Lake *229*
Gilahina River *98*
Gillespie Lake *225*
Glacier Creek *246, 247*
Glacier Lake *88*
Glenn Highway *123, 157*
Globe Creek *105*
Gold Creek *75*
Golden Lake *161*
Goldenfin Lake *256*
Goose Creek *192*
Granite Creek *130, 250*
Grayling *23*
Grayling Lake *74, 119, 255*
Green Lake *57*
Grey's Creek *189*
Grouse Creek *256*
Grouse Lake *256*
Gulkana River *85, 223, 224*
Gulkana River Drainage *85*
Gunn Creek *226*
Gwen Lake *58*

H

Haggard Creek *224*
Hammond River *74*
Happy Valley Creek *77*
Harding Lake *234*
Hatcher Pass Road *187*
Hess Creek *72*
Hidden Lake *47, 118, 285*
Hillberg Lake *57*

Homer Spit (Bay Side) *300*
Homer Spit (East End) *301*
Homer Spit (Ocean Side) *300*
Homestead Lake *169*
Honeybee Lake *183*
Honolulu Creek *200*
Hook-Up / Fighting Skills *36*
Hope Highway *251*
Horizon Lake *76*
Horseshoe Creek *199*
Horseshoe Lake *169, 202*
Hot Springs Slough *106*
How To Use This Book *3*
Humpback Salmon *14-15*
Hutlinana Creek *105*

I

Ice Lake *293*
Ida Lake *130*
Indian Creek *246*
Indian River *315*
Ingram Creek *250*
Introduction *1*
Irene Lake *158*
Island Lake *46, 76, 144*
Isom Creek *72*

J

"J" Lake *229*
Jack Creek *317*
Jack Lake *317*
Jack River *201*
Jan Lake *48*
Jean Lake *286*
Jerome Lake *253*
Jerry Lake *90*
Jewel Lake *64*
Jigs *37-39*
Jim Creek *156*
Jim Lake *157*
Jim River *73, 74*
Joe Lake *90*